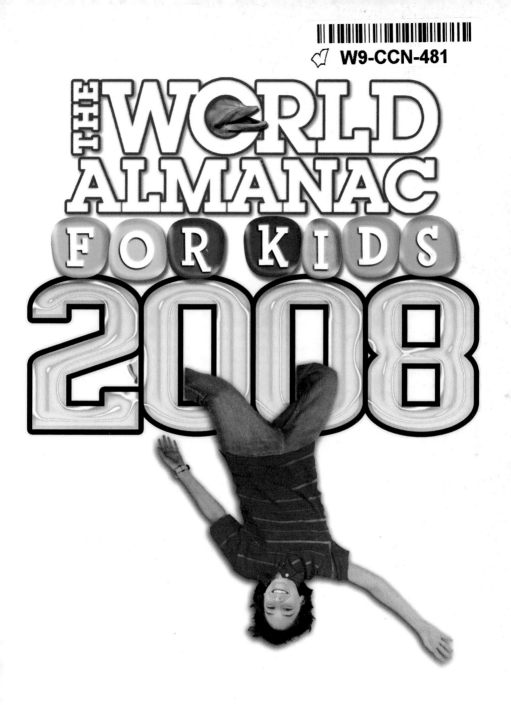

THE WORLD ALMANAC FOR KIDS 2008

WORLD ALMANAC BOOKS
A Division of World Almanac Education Group, Inc.
A WRC Media Company

EDITOR: C. Alan Joyce

CONSULTANTS: Margaret Altoff, Supervisor of Social Studies K-12, School District 11, Colorado Springs, Colorado; Richard Hogen, Director of Preschool/Elementary Division, National Science Teachers Association

CONTRIBUTORS: Jennifer Dunham, Lisette Johnson, Zoë Kashner, Emily Keyes, Ken Park, Maria Brock Schulman, Aram Schvey, Evan Schwartz

KID ADVISORS: Max Bartell, Old Westbury, New York; Camille Boushey, Yakima, Washington; Leonard and Andrea Chen, Kent, Washington; Abigail Cline, Fort Lauderdale, Florida; Vanessa Cole, Killeen, Texas; Sariah Dilka, Castle Rock, Colorado; Kevin Finn, Arlington, Virginia; Natasha Hallam, Tye, Texas; Elyse Stephens, Emmaus, Pennsylvania; Cheney Ravitz, Takoma Park, Maryland; Carly Lee and Jordanna Roman, Larchmont, New York; Tony Sanchez, Phoenix, Arizona; Breanna Simpson, Philadelphia, Pennsylvania

DESIGN: BILL SMITH STUDIO

Creative Director: Brian Kobberger **Project Director:** David Borkman
Design: Geron Hoy, Michael Gibson, Jason Roumas, Ron Leighton, Mie Tsuchida
Production: Eric Murray, Dan Colish, Martha Grossman, Mie Tsuchida

WORLD ALMANAC BOOKS

Managing Editor: Lisa Lazzara; **Editors:** Sarah Janssen, Vincent G. Spadafora; **Associate Editors:** M. L. Liu, Andy Steinitz; **Desktop Production Associate:** Sean Westmoreland

WORLD ALMANAC EDUCATION GROUP
President/Publisher: Peter M. Esposito
Business Manager: Babette Romaine
Associate Publisher/Photo Research: Edward A. Thomas
Vice President – Sales and Marketing: Lola A. Valenciano
Sales & Marketing Coordinator: Sheena Scott

WRC MEDIA INC.
Interim President: Michael D. Helfand
Chief Financial Officer: Robert S. Yingling

CONTENTS

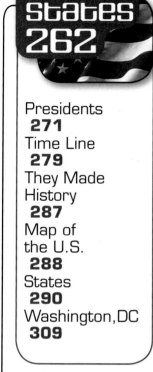

PLAIN JANE
America Ferrera proves there's more to beauty than what meets the eye as the title character in *Ugly Betty*.

MOST VALUABLE PARTNERS
NFL legend Emmitt Smith sambaed to victory with former *Dancing With the Stars* champ Cheryl Burke.

TWO PAWS UP
The Dog Whisperer, Cesar Millan, brings "exercise, discipline, and affection" to a new class of canines—and their owners.

THAT'S SO ZOEY
Jamie Lynn Spears continues to conquer her formerly boys-only boarding school in the new season of *Zoey 101*.

HIT PARADE
Cowell & Co. return for a sixth season of the musical cheers (and jeers) that *American Idol* fans love.

MOVIES

DOH! IT'S ABOUT TIME
The Simpsons make their long-awaited leap from TV to the big screen.

FRIENDS FOREVER

In *Bridge to Terabithia*, Josh Hutcherson and AnnaSophia Robb create an imaginary kingdom together.

OLDE FASHIONED FAVORITES

Shrek, Puss-in-Boots, and Donkey are joined by new character Artie (voiced by Justin Timberlake) in the search for a new ruler for the land of Far, Far Away in *Shrek the Third*.

MOVIES

YO HO HO!

Chow-Yun Fat joins Geoffrey Rush and Johnny Depp as they venture "off the map" in *Pirates of the Caribbean: At World's End*.

BY THE BOOK

Daniel Radcliffe and Emma Watson have their work cut out for them during their fifth year at Hogwarts, in *Harry Potter and the Order of*

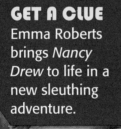

GET A CLUE
Emma Roberts brings *Nancy Drew* to life in a new sleuthing adventure.

MUSIC

DOUBLE IDENTITY

Miley Cyrus (*Hannah Montana*) and Ashley Tisdale (*The Suite Life of Zack & Cody*) perform on MTV's *Total Request Live* in June 2006. Miley planned to release her first album in June 2007.

STILL EVOLVING

Ciara's second album, *Ciara: The Evolution*, debuted at number one in 2006.

ALL-AMERICAN REJECTS?

Nick, Tyson, Mike, and Chris took a break from touring in 2007, but still found time to record a new song for the Disney film *Meet the Robinsons*.

SIMPLY DREAMY

Anika Noni Rose (left), pop superstar Beyoncé (middle), and former *American Idol* contestant Jennifer Hudson (right) brought the Broadway musical *Dreamgirls* (which won 6 Tony awards in 1982) to life on the silver screen.

SPORTS

SUPER HISTORY

Chicago Bears coach Lovie Smith (left) and Indianapolis Colts coach Tony Dungy (right) were the first black coaches to ever lead teams in a Super Bowl, during Super Bowl XLI.

MANNING GETS HIS RING

Super Bowl MVP quarterback Peyton Manning led the Indianapolis Colts to a 29-17 win over the Chicago Bears in Super Bowl XLI.

GRAND SLAMMING AWAY

Swiss tennis star Roger Federer is the only active tennis player with 10 career Grand Slam singles championships. He won three Grand Slam tournaments in 2006, and the 2007 Australian Open.

TIGER HUNTS FOR A RECORD

Tiger Woods, seen here at the Buick Invitational, has won 12 career "majors," second only to Jack Nicklaus's record of 18 wins.

SPORTS

BECKS GETS PAID

The L.A. Galaxy signed English midfielder David Beckham to a 5-year, $250-million contract to come play in the U.S.

MOST VALUABLE PHILLIE

Phillies' first base star Ryan Howard blasted 58 home runs and drove in 149 RBIs in 2006 and was named the National League MVP. He hopes to lead his team to victory in the ultra-competitive NL East.

WWE CHAMP

John Cena, who claimed the WWE title for the third time in September 2006, hoists his belt at a press conference in Italy.

SIPPING FROM THE CUP

Kristine Lilly helped the U.S. Women's National Soccer team to a 2006 CONCACAF Gold Cup. Next stop: China, in September 2007, to compete in the Women's World Cup.

NEWS

LONGEST-LIVING PRESIDENT PASSES

Former president Gerald Ford died December 26, 2006 at the age of 93. Ford, who became the 38th president after Richard Nixon resigned in 1974, gave Nixon a controversial pardon for any crimes he may have committed while serving as president.

COURAGEOUS HEARTS

President George W. Bush visits Purple Heart recipient Army Spc. Sue Downes at Walter Reed Army Medical Center in December 2006.

LADY SPEAKER

In January 2007, Congresswoman Nancy Pelosi became the first female Speaker of the House of Representatives.

U.S. POPULATION ESTIMATE

CENSUSBUREAUUSCENSUSBUR

The U.S. Census Bureau:
Chronicling the Growth of the Nation
The Growth of American Cities: 1900–2000

Cities With Population
Over 100,000

MAJOR MILESTONE
The U.S. population reached an estimated 300 million on October 17, 2006.

SUBWAY SUPERMAN
New York City construction worker Wesley Autrey, shown here with daughters Syshe and Shuqui, dove in front of a subway train to save a stranger's life in January 2007.

ANIMALS

How many whiskers does a cat have? ➡ page 26

Furry or scaly, creepy or crawly, schoolbus-sized or microscopic—animals fascinate people of all stripes. Here are some facts about the Animal Kingdom.

WEIRD ANIMAL FACTS

Homing pigeons are pigeons that have been bred for speed and the ability to fly long distances. They are trained to fly back to their home, sometimes over hundreds of miles, after being released from another location. They can fly between 30 and 50 miles per hour. Homing pigeons were used during both World Wars to carry messages when other forms of communication couldn't be used.

A pigeon named G.I. Joe is credited with saving the lives of many British soldiers in 1943. These soldiers had taken over an Italian city that U.S. forces planned to bomb. After radio communication failed between the soldiers and home base, G.I. Joe was released with a message to cancel the bombing. He flew back to home base with the message, and the bombing was canceled. For his actions, a British organization awarded G.I. Joe the Dickin Medal for gallantry. He was the only animal from the U.S., out of more than 50 animals in all, who received this medal for heroic service in World War II.

One of the most venomous animals in the world is a kind of **box jellyfish**, *Chironex fleckeri,* also known as a sea wasp. Sea wasps live in the waters off northern Australia. Their box-shaped bodies, or "bells," can grow 15 inches across. But their stinging tentacles can measure 10 to 15 feet long. Venom from a sea wasp sting can kill a human in minutes. Sea turtles, though, can eat sea wasps without being stung. Sea wasps feed on fish and shrimp.

🏠 ●WAforKids.com ↪

Go to **www.WAforKids.com** and type **028** into the code box for these activities:
- Take a fun quiz to find out "Which Bug Is Most Like You."
- Are you species smart? Show what you know about animals with the chapter quiz.
- Get facts about Gila monsters, snakes, sharks, pandas, and more!

LIFE ON EARTH

This time line shows how life developed on Earth. The earliest life forms are at the bottom of the chart. The most recent are at the top of the chart.

	Years Ago	Animal Life on Earth
Cenozoic	10,000 to present	Human civilization develops.
Cenozoic	1.8 million to 10,000	Large mammals like mammoths, saber-toothed cats, and giant ground sloths develop. Modern human beings evolve. This era ends with an ice age.
Cenozoic	65 to 1.8 million	Ancestors of modern-day horses, zebras, rhinos, sheep, goats, camels, pigs, cows, deer, giraffes, camels, elephants, cats, dogs, and primates begin to develop.
Mesozoic	144 to 65 million	In the Cretaceous period, new dinosaurs appear. Many insect groups, modern mammal and bird groups also develop. A global extinction of most dinosaurs occurs at the end of this period.
Mesozoic	206 to 144 million	The Jurassic is dominated by giant dinosaurs. In the late Jurassic, birds evolve.
Mesozoic	248 to 206 million	In the Triassic period, marine life develops again. Reptiles also move into the water. Reptiles begin to dominate the land areas. Dinosaurs and mammals develop.
Paleozoic	290 to 248 million	A mass extinction wipes out 95% of all marine life.
Paleozoic	354 to 290 million	Reptiles develop. Much of the land is covered by swamps.
Paleozoic	417 to 354 million	The first trees and forests appear. The first land-living vertebrates, amphibians, and wingless insects appear. Many new sea creatures also appear.
Paleozoic	443 to 417 million	Coral reefs form. Other animals, such as the first known freshwater fish, develop. Relatives of spiders and centipedes develop.
Paleozoic	542 to 443 million	Animals with shells (called trilobites) and some mollusks form. Primitive fish and corals develop. Evidence of the first primitive land plants.
Precambrian	3.8 billion to 542 million	First evidence of life on Earth. All life is in water. Early single-celled bacteria and achaea appear, followed by multi-celled organisms, including early animals.
Precambrian	4.6 billion	Formation of the Earth.

ANIMAL KINGDOM

The world has so many animals that scientists looked for a way to organize them into groups. A Swedish scientist named Carolus Linnaeus (1707-1778) worked out a system for classifying both animals and plants. We still use it today.

The Animal Kingdom is separated into two large groups—animals with backbones, called **vertebrates**, and animals without backbones, called **invertebrates**.

These large groups are divided into smaller groups called **phyla**. And phyla are divided into even smaller groups called **classes**. The animals in each group are classified together when their bodies are similar in certain ways.

Vertebrates
Animals with Backbones

FISH	Swordfish, tuna, salmon, trout, halibut, goldfish
AMPHIBIANS	Frogs, toads, mud puppies
REPTILES	Turtles, alligators, crocodiles, lizards
BIRDS	Sparrows, owls, turkeys, hawks
MAMMALS	Kangaroos, opossums, dogs, cats, bears, seals, rats, squirrels, rabbits, chipmunks, porcupines, horses, pigs, cows, deer, bats, whales, dolphins, monkeys, apes, humans

Invertebrates
Animals without Backbones

PROTOZOA	The simplest form of animals
COELENTERATES	Jellyfish, hydra, sea anemones, coral
MOLLUSKS	Clams, snails, squid, oysters
ANNELIDS	Earthworms
ARTHROPODS	
Crustaceans	Lobsters, crayfish
Centipedes and Millipedes	
Arachnids	Spiders, scorpions
Insects	Butterflies, grasshoppers, bees, termites, cockroaches
ECHINODERMS	Starfish, sea urchins, sea cucumbers

Homework Help

How can you remember the animal classifications from most general to most specific? Try this sentence:

King **P**hilip **C**ame **O**ver **F**rom **G**reat **S**pain.
K = Kingdom; **P** = Phylum; **C** = Class; **O** = Order; **F** = Family; **G** = Genus; **S** = Species

WHAT IS BIODIVERSITY?

The Earth is shared by millions of species of living things. The wide variety of life on Earth, as shown by the many species, is called "biodiversity" (bio means "life" and diversity means "variety"). Human beings of all colors, races, and nationalities make up just one species, *Homo sapiens*.

Species, Species Everywhere

Here is just a sampling of how diverse life on Earth is. The numbers are only estimates, and more species are being discovered all the time!

ARTHROPODS (1.1 million species)
insects: 750,000 species
moths & butterflies: 165,000 species
flies: about 122,000 species
cockroaches: about 4,000 species
crustaceans: 44,000 species
spiders: 35,000 species

FISH (24,500 species)
bony fish: 23,000 species
skates & rays: 450 species
sharks: 350 species
seahorses: 32 species

BIRDS (9,000 species)
perching birds: 5,200-5,500 species
parrots: 353 species
pigeons: 309 species
raptors (eagles, hawks, etc.): 307 species
penguins: 17 species
ostrich: 1 species

MAMMALS (9,000 species)
rodents: 1,700 species
bats: 1,000 species
monkeys: 242 species
whales & dolphins: 83 species
cats: 38 species
apes: 21 species
pigs: 14 species
bears: 8 species

REPTILES (8,000 species)
lizards: 4,500 species
snakes: 2,900 species
tortoises & turtles: about 294 species
crocodiles & alligators: 23 species

AMPHIBIANS (5,000 species)
frogs & toads: 4,500 species
newts & salamanders: 470 species

PLANTS (260,000 species)
flowering plants: 250,000 species
bamboo: about 1,000 species
evergreens: 550 species

Biodiversity Q&A

What percentage of all known living species are invertebrates (without backbones)?
About 95%. Although they all lack backbones, invertebrates can differ greatly in form, size, and habitat. They range from giant clams in the ocean to microscopic worms that live in other animals.

True or false? Snakes aren't found naturally in the wild in Ireland. True. According to legend, St. Patrick banished snakes from Ireland. More likely, ancient snakes never migrated to the Emerald Isle, which doesn't have much biodiversity. Snakes are also not found in the wild in Iceland, Greenland, and Antarctica. Not only is the ground fozen year-round in these places, they're completely surrounded by water, like Ireland.

Why is biodiversity important? Forms of life are interlinked. If one species of plant or animal becomes extinct it affects other life forms. Studies have shown that biomes, or environments, with wider varieties of life forms can better survive difficult conditions, such as drought.

BIGGEST, SMALLEST, FASTEST

IN THE WORLD

WORLD'S BIGGEST ANIMALS

Marine mammal: Blue whale (100 feet long, 200 tons)

Heaviest land mammal: African bush elephant (12 feet high, 4-7 tons)
Tallest land mammal: Giraffe (18 feet tall)

Reptile: Saltwater crocodile (20-23 feet long, 1,150 pounds)

Heaviest snake: Green anaconda (16-30 feet, 550 pounds)
Longest snake: Reticulated python (26-32 feet long)

Fish: Whale shark (40-60 feet long, 10-20 tons)

Bird: Ostrich (9 feet tall, 345 pounds)

Insect: Stick insect (15 inches long)

WORLD'S SMALLEST ANIMALS

Mammal: Bumblebee bat (1.1-1.3 inches)

Fish: *Paedocypris progenetica* or stout infantfish (0.31-0.33 inches)

Bird: Bee hummingbird (1-2 inches)

Snake: Thread snake and brahminy blind snake (4.25 inches)

Lizard: Jaragua sphaero and Virgin Islands dwarf sphaero (0.63 inches)

Insect: Fairyfly (0.01 inches)

WORLD'S FASTEST ANIMALS

Marine mammal: Killer whale and Dall's porpoise (35 miles per hour)

Land mammal: Cheetah (70 miles per hour)

Fish: Sailfish (68 miles per hour, leaping)

Bird: Peregrine falcon (200 miles per hour)

Insect: Dragonfly (35 miles per hour)

Snake: Black mamba (14 miles per hour)

HOW FAST DO ANIMALS RUN?

This table shows how fast some animals can go on land. A snail can take more than 30 hours just to go 1 mile. But humans at their fastest are still slower than many animals. The human record for fastest speed for a recognized race distance is held by Michael Johnson, who won the 1996 Olympic 200-meter dash in 19.32 seconds, for an average speed of about 23.16 miles per hour.

MILES PER HOUR	
Cheetah	70
Pronghorn antelope	60
Elk	45
Ostrich	40
Rabbit	35
Giraffe	32
Grizzly bear	30
Elephant	25
Wild turkey	15
Crocodile	10
Tiger beetle	5.5
Snail	0.03

HOW LONG DO ANIMALS LIVE?

Most animals do not live as long as humans do. A monkey that's 14 years old is thought to be old, while a person at that age is still considered young. The average life spans of some animals in the wild are shown here. An average 10-year-old boy in the U.S. can expect to live to be about 75.

Galapagos tortoise	100+ years
Box turtle	100 years
Blue whale	80 years
Alligator	50 years
Chimpanzee	50 years
Macaw	50 years
African elephant	35 years
Bottlenose dolphin	30 years
Gorilla	30 years
Horse	20 years
Periodical cicada	17 years
Tiger	16 years
Lion	15 years
Lobster	15 years
Cat (domestic)	15 years
Cow	15 years
Tarantula	15 years
Dog (domestic)	13 years
Camel (bactrian)	12 years
Moose	12 years
Pig	10 years
Squirrel	10 years
Deer (white-tailed)	8 years
Goat	8 years
Kangaroo	7 years
Chipmunk	6 years
Beaver	5 years
Rabbit (domestic)	5 years
Guinea pig	4 years
Mouse	3 years
Opossum	1 year
Worker bee	6 weeks
Adult housefly	1-3 weeks

ANIMAL WORDS

Animal	Male	Female	Young
bear	boar	sow	cub
cat	tom	queen	kitten
cattle, elephant, moose, whale	bull	cow	calf
deer	buck, stag	doe	fawn
donkey	jack	jenny	foal
ferret	hob	jill	kit
fox	reynard	vixen	kit, cub, pup
goat	buck, billy	nanny, doe	kid
goose	gander	goose	gosling
gorilla	male	female	infant
hawk	tiercel	hen	eyas
horse	stallion	mare	foal, filly (female), colt (male)
kangaroo	buck	doe	joey
lion	lion	lioness	cub
pig	boar	sow	piglet
rabbit	buck	doe	kit, bunny
swan	cob	pen	cygnet
turkey	gobbler, tom	hen	chick, poult

WHAT ARE GROUPS OF ANIMALS CALLED?

Here are some (often odd) names for animal groups:

BEARS: *sleuth* of bears	**KITTENS**: *kindle* or *kendle* of kittens
CATS: *clowder* of cats	**LEOPARDS**: *leap* of leopards
CATTLE: *drove* of cattle	**MONKEYS**: *troop* of monkeys
CROCODILES: *bask* of crocodiles	**MULES**: *span* of mules
CROWS: *murder* of crows	**NIGHTINGALES**: *watch* of nightingales
FISH: *school* or *shoal* of fish	**OWLS**: *parliament* of owls
FLIES: *swarm* or *cloud* of flies	**OYSTERS**: *bed* of oysters
FOXES: *skulk* of foxes	**PEACOCKS**: *muster* of peacocks
GIRAFFES: *tower* of giraffes	**RAVENS**: *unkindness* of ravens
HARES: *down* of hares	**SHARKS**: *shiver* of sharks
HAWKS: *cast* of hawks	**SQUIRRELS**: *dray* or *scurry* of squirrels
HYENAS: *cackle* of hyenas	**TURTLES**: *bale* of turtles
JELLYFISH: *smack* of jellyfish	**WHALES**: *pod* of whales

PETS AT THE TOP

Here are some of the most popular pets in the United States and the approximate number of each pet in 2005:

1. Freshwater fish	139,000,000	5. Birds	16,600,000
2. Cats	90,500,000	6. Reptiles	11,000,000
3. Dogs	73,900,000	7. Saltwater fish	9,600,000
4. Small animals	18,200,000		

Source: American Pet Products Manufacturers Association's 2005/2006 National Pet Owners Survey

PETS Q&A

How many whiskers do cats usually have? **24, or 12 whiskers on each side of a cat's face. These 12 whiskers are arranged in four rows of three each.**

True or false? Dogs and cats are color-blind. **False. Despite the myth, dogs and cats can see in color, though not all the colors humans can see. For example, dogs can see blues but not greens.**

What breed of dog was the second most popular in the U.S. in 2006? **The Yorkshire terrier. According to the American Kennel Club, it is the first time in nearly 70 years that a small dog has ranked so high on its annual list of most popular dogs. The "Yorkie" overtook many larger breeds, including the golden retriever and German shepherd, in its climb to number two, right after the first-place Labrador retriever.**

ENDANGERED SPECIES

When a species becomes extinct, it reduces the variety of life on Earth. In the world today, 7,725 known species of animals (and even more plant species) are threatened with extinction, according to the World Conservation Union. Humans have been able to save some endangered animals and are working to save more.

Some Endangered Animals

Polar Bears Polar bears live on the Arctic ice in the U.S., Canada, Greenland, Norway, and Russia. Temperatures there can drop as low as -50°F, but a 4-inch layer of fat under the bears' coats helps keep them warm. They are among the world's largest land predators. They may weigh 400-1,400 pounds. Polar bears travel great distances to hunt for seals and walruses. But global warming is causing their Arctic ice home to shrink. An estimated 20,000 to 25,000 polar bears remain in the wild. The species is classified as vulnerable, just below endangered status, by the World Conservation Union.

Ivory-Billed Woodpecker As early as the 1800s, the numbers of ivory-billed woodpeckers began to drop. Their habitat—old, swampy forests in the southeastern U.S. and Cuba—was being cut down. They were hunted for their bills (which are made of bone, not ivory). The last reliable sighting of one in the U.S. was in 1944, and they were among the first animals to be listed by the U.S. as endangered. They were believed to be extinct until one was "rediscovered" in 2004. The sighting has yet to be confirmed so scientists are trying to find more proof that they're still around. Averaging 18-20 inches long, they are the largest woodpecker in the U.S. and the third largest in the world. They feed mostly on beetle larvae.

FACTORS THAT CAN MAKE A SPECIES ENDANGERED:

HABITAT DESTRUCTION. As human populations grow, they need places to live and work. People build houses and factories in areas where plants and animals live. Filling in wetlands and clearing forests (**deforestation**) are examples of this threat.

OVERHARVESTING. People may catch a kind of fish or hunt an animal until its numbers are too low to reproduce fast enough. Bison, or buffalo, once roamed the entire Great Plains until they were almost hunted into extinction in the 19th century. They are now protected by law, and their numbers are increasing.

ALIEN SPECIES are plants and animals that have been moved by humans into areas where they are not naturally found. They may have no natural enemies there and can push out native species. Red fire ants and zebra mussels are examples of alien species in the U.S.

POLLUTION in the air, water, and land can harm plants and animals. It can poison them or make it hard for them to grow or reproduce. Factories are not the only source of pollution. Oil, salt, and other substances dumped on roads can wash into streams, rivers, and lakes. Acid rain damages and kills trees, especially in the mountains where trees are often surrounded by acidic clouds and fog.

All About >> FLAMINGOS

Flamingos are found in many parts of the world. They live in large, salty, shallow lakes and lagoons. They can stand 3 to 5 feet tall.

Flamingos feed by wading through water on their long legs and stirring up the mud at the bottom. They take the muddy liquid into their bills, which they hold upside down in the water. Comb-like structures in their bills filter out the water and mud, leaving behind food such as algae, fish, and brine shrimp.

Flamingos are born grey. The feathers of both male and female flamingos do not turn pinkish-red until after a year or two. They are also born with a straight bill that curves with age.

Certain pigments in the food they eat give flamingos their special color. In zoos, a pigment is sometimes added to flamingos' feed so their pinkish hue does not fade.

No one knows for sure why flamingos sometimes stand on one leg. They might do it to stay warm or to dry out their other leg. Flamingos are very social animals. In Africa, more than a million flamingos might gather in one place during breeding season.

All About >> PENGUINS

Penguins in the wild are found only in the Southern Hemisphere. Some can be found on the continent of Antarctica; Galapagos penguins live as far north as the equator.

Penguins vary in size. The little, or fairy, penguins are the smallest of the 17 species of penguins. They only stand about 1 foot high and weigh 2 pounds. Emperor penguins (like the ones in the movie *March of the Penguins*) are the largest penguins. They can grow to almost 4 feet high and weigh up to 90 pounds.

Penguins cannot fly, but they are excellent swimmers. They can swim up to about 10 miles per hour over short distances. Emperor penguins can dive as deep as 1,500 feet and stay underwater for as long as 18 minutes without having to surface for air. Some penguin species may spend up to 75% of their lives in the water. A layer of fat under waterproof feathers helps penguins stay warm. They feed on fish, squid, and shrimp-like animals called krill. They are hunted by seals and killer whales.

All About >> MOTHS

Moths and butterflies belong to the order *Lepidoptera*. Most moths are nocturnal, though a few are more active during the day, like butterflies. They are also usually less brightly colored than butterflies.

Moths are called larvae, or caterpillars, after they hatch out of an egg. In the pupa stage, the larvae encase themselves in a cocoon. They emerge from the cocoon as adults with wings.

Moths eat plants, fruit, and even fabrics such as wool. They can be destructive when they feed. Gypsy moths, which are native to Europe and Asia, were introduced to the U.S. in the 1860s. Their caterpillars have devastated North American forests, killing off many of the trees whose leaves they eat. Some moths, however, are useful to humans. The cocoons spun by silkworms, which are actually caterpillars of certain moth species, are used to produce silk.

Atlas moths are the largest *Lepidoptera* in the world. The surface of their wings can measure 65 square inches. White witch moths have the longest wingspans, at up to 12 inches. The smallest moths may have a wingspan of only 0.1 inches.

Moths "taste" with their feet. By stepping on a plant, they can tell whether or not they should lay their eggs there.

All About >> GIANT SQUIDS

A giant squid was filmed for the first time in December 2006. In 2004, the same team of Japanese scientists had taken the first-ever photos of a live giant squid in the wild.

Not much is known about these creatures because of where they live: about 650 to 3,000 feet below the surface of all the world's oceans. Most of what people know about giant squids has been learned by studying dead or dying ones captured in nets or washed ashore.

Giant squids can range from 20 to 60 feet long and weigh up to half a ton or more. They have eight arms and two feeding tentacles, which they use to capture fish and other prey. Despite their immense size, they are sometimes eaten by sperm whales. That's a lot of calamari!

Scientists used to believe that giant squids were the world's largest invertebrates and had the biggest eyes of any known animal. But now they think the colossal squid might grow to be even heavier. An intact colossal squid was caught by fishermen near Antarctica in February 2007.

GET BUGGED

What's a really heavy insect? The African goliath beetle only gets to be about 4 to 5 inches long compared to the stick insect, which can grow up to 15 inches long. But the goliath can weigh nearly a quarter of a pound.

What characteristics do all insects share? Insects do not have backbones. They have three pairs of walking legs. (Spiders, which have eight legs, are arachnids, not insects.) Also, insects' bodies can be divided into a head, thorax, and abdomen. Another thing they lack is lungs. Instead, insects breathe through tubes that open directly onto the surface of their bodies.

True or false? Malaria, a disease transmitted through mosquito bites, kills more than one million people each year. True. You could say the mosquito is one of the most dangerous creatures in the world. Malaria can be prevented and cured, but over one million people still die from it each year. Most of the victims are younger children in Africa, where people often lack the resources to prevent the spread of the disease.

How fast can a cockroach move? 4 miles per hour. Cockroaches are one of the fastest insects on land. At their top speed, over short distances, they run only on their two hind legs. That's because those legs are longer than their front legs.

ANT COLONY

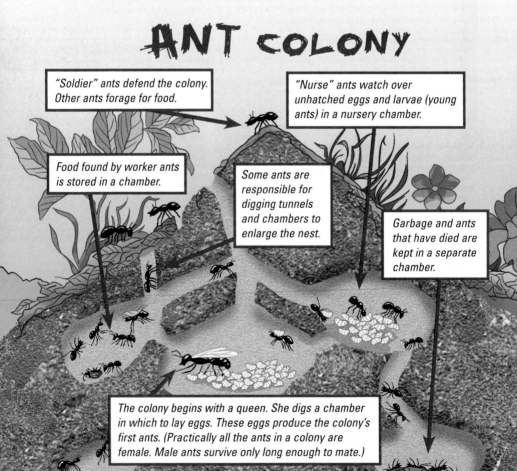

"Soldier" ants defend the colony. Other ants forage for food.

"Nurse" ants watch over unhatched eggs and larvae (young ants) in a nursery chamber.

Food found by worker ants is stored in a chamber.

Some ants are responsible for digging tunnels and chambers to enlarge the nest.

Garbage and ants that have died are kept in a separate chamber.

The colony begins with a queen. She digs a chamber in which to lay eggs. These eggs produce the colony's first ants. (Practically all the ants in a colony are female. Male ants survive only long enough to mate.)

ON THE JOB:
ANIMAL BEHAVIOR COUNSELOR

Katherine Miller, Senior Behavior Counselor at the American Society for the Prevention of Cruelty to Animals (ASPCA), New York, NY

What do you do as a behavior counselor?
I evaluate dogs and cats coming to our shelter. I get to know them. Then when potential adopters come to the ASPCA, I can recommend an animal based on what they're looking for. I see myself as sort of a matchmaker. I also do counseling after an adoption if an owner has questions about an animal.

How do you evaluate an animal?
If an animal has been in someone's home, we'll start by asking that person questions. After the animal is taken in, we do several tests. (This is for dogs now.) Pets are rather possessive of their food. We give them a bowl of food, and we use a plastic hand to try to take it away, to see if they'll bite the hand. We find out if they're friendly with kids. We bring out a toddler doll and judge the dogs' reaction when they see the doll for the first time.

What kind of behavior work do you do with animals?
It can be as simple as teaching a dog not to jump up on people. Also, animals sometimes come in as strays or as victims of cruelty. A caring, warm environment is new to them, so it takes time for them to get used to it. Most dogs respond very well to our training. We see progress over weeks and months. Some dogs have been here nine months. We don't have time limits for how long they can stay at the shelter.

What kind of training do you have?
I have a Ph.D. in animal behavior. Then I studied with an animal behaviorist at the ASPCA. Other people that I work with have gone through a school for dog trainers. But the best training is a lot of hands-on experience working alongside someone who has been trained already. You learn about animal body language, what to expect from each animal, and how to resolve problems.

And it's important to know what's normal for a breed so you can counsel people on what types of dogs are best for them. For example, working breeds have behaviors that are different from toy breeds, which were bred to sit in your lap.

What's the most difficult part of your job?
When a decision has to be made to euthanize [kill] an animal. Occasionally, we feel a dog or cat would be dangerous as a pet. So the behavior staff, the medical staff, and shelter staff will meet to discuss that. That decision is never made lightly because these animals weren't born that way. It's because of what people did to them that they can't be in a home with people.

What advice do you have for kids interested in working with animals?
Volunteer at a shelter to walk dogs or socialize with the cats. Assist on a farm or volunteer at a zoo. The best way to find what you'll be happiest doing is to have experience with a variety of animals and a variety of settings. **WEB SITE** *www.aspca.org*

ART

What color complements red? ➡️ page 34

ART Q&A

IS ARTISTIC TALENT SOMETHING YOU ARE BORN WITH OR SOMETHING YOU CAN LEARN?

Learning to draw is a skill like writing or playing a sport. Some people are naturally more talented, but anyone can learn to draw. Even people with severe physical disabilities can make masterpieces.

WHEN I SEE A PAINTING IN A MUSEUM, WHAT MIGHT I SAY ABOUT IT?

Look at the painting without thinking too hard about it. How does it make you feel? Happy, sad, confused, silly? Study the painting and try to discover the colors, shapes, and textures that create those feelings in you.

Look at the information card next to the work of art. Usually, it will tell you who painted it, when it was made, and what media (materials) were used. You can compare it to other works of art by the same artist, from the same time, or in the same medium.

HOW OLD IS ART?

Art goes back to our earliest records of human life. See the cave paintings on the next page for an example.

WHAT IS ART?

The answer is up for debate. People who study this question are studying aesthetics (ess-THET-ics), which is a kind of philosophy. Usually art is something that an artist interprets for an audience. Art reveals something that you can see, that then makes you think and feel.

DIFFERENT KINDS OF ART

Throughout history, artists have painted pictures of nature (called landscapes), pictures of people (called portraits), and pictures of flowers in vases, food, and other objects (known as still lifes). Today many artists create pictures that do not look like anything in the real world. These are examples of abstract art.

▶ Photography, too, is a form of art. Photos record both the commonplace and the exotic and help us look at events in new ways.

▶ Sculpture is a three-dimensional form made from clay, stone, metal, or other material. Sculptures can be large, like the Statue of Liberty, or small. Some are realistic. Others have no form you can recognize.

▶ Contemporary artists today often use computers and video screens to create art. Some video art uses 20 or 30 video screens that show different colors or images to create one big work of art.

ART ALL-STARS

Check out these famous works of art.

Lascaux (13,000-15,000 B.C.)

Lascaux is a cave in France. It contains some of the earliest known cave art. The cave was discovered in 1940 by four teenagers. The images found on the cave walls consist of handprints and animals such as bison, deer, horses, and cattle. It is believed that the paintings may have been part of a ritual to help make a successful hunt.

VINCENT VAN GOGH (1853-1890)
Sunflowers (1888)

Van Gogh was a Dutch-born painter who lived in France for many years. He is the most famous painter of the Expressionist movement. Expressionism stresses the emotion and inner vision of the artist, instead of depicting the subject matter as it appears. This is done through distorted lines and shapes and the use of intense color. *Sunflowers* shows a wild, vibrantly colored bouquet in a vase.

MARY CASSATT (1844-1926)
The Maternal Kiss (1897)

Cassatt was born in America, but lived and worked in France as an Impressionist painter. Characteristics of Impressionist painting include visible brushstrokes, open composition, ordinary subject matter, and unusual visual angles. It is painted in lively, yet soft colors. Cassatt's painting technique is both relaxed and realistic at the same time.

AUGUSTE RODIN (1840-1917)
The Thinker (1902)

Rodin modeled his sculptures in clay and often casted them in bronze. *The Thinker* is a sculpture of a seated man with his head propped on his fist. He appears deep in thought. *The Thinker* is believed to based on the Italian poet Dante. It has become a symbol for philosophy and intellectual activity. As a result of its fame, the sculpture has been used as the basis for a joke many times. This began in Rodin's lifetime.

COLOR WHEEL

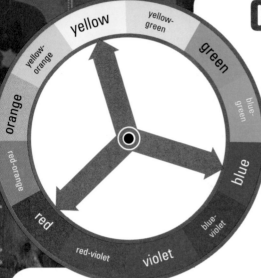

This color wheel shows how colors are related to each other.

Primary colors The most basic colors are **RED**, **YELLOW**, and **BLUE**. They're called primary because you can't get them by mixing any other colors. In fact, the other colors are made by mixing red, blue, or yellow. Arrows on this wheel show the primary colors.

Secondary colors **ORANGE**, **GREEN**, and **VIOLET** are the secondary colors. They are made by mixing two primary colors. You make orange by mixing yellow and red, or green by mixing yellow and blue. On the color wheel, **GREEN** appears between **BLUE** and **YELLOW**.

Tertiary colors When you mix a primary and a secondary color, you get a tertiary, or intermediate, color. **BLUE-GREEN** and **YELLOW-GREEN** are intermediate colors.

More Color Terms

VALUES The lightness or darkness of a color is its value.
Tints are light values made by mixing a color with white. **PINK** is a tint of **RED**.
Shades are dark values made by mixing a color with black. **MAROON** is a shade of **RED**.

COMPLEMENTARY COLORS

are contrasting colors that please the eye when used together. These colors appear opposite each other on the wheel and don't have any colors in common. **RED** is a complement to **GREEN**, which is made by mixing **YELLOW** and **BLUE**.

ANALOGOUS COLORS

The colors next to each other on the wheel are from the same "family." **BLUE**, **BLUE-GREEN**, and **GREEN** all have **BLUE** in them and are analogous colors.

COOL COLORS

are mostly **GREEN**, **BLUE**, and **PURPLE**. They make you think of cool things like water and can even make you feel cooler.

WARM COLORS

are mostly **RED**, **ORANGE**, and **YELLOW**. They suggest heat and can actually make you feel warmer.

ART: PASS-AROUND PICTURE
PROJECT

This artistic game was invented by a group called the Surrealists in 1925 and is often called Exquisite Corpse. Three artists take turns drawing on a sheet of paper, folding it to conceal their work, and then passing it to the next player for a further contribution.

Materials: *Paper and crayons, colored pencils, or markers*

Step 1: Fold the paper into thirds.

Fold a blank sheet of paper into thirds, as shown at right, then unfold it.

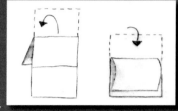

Step 2: Set up the order of artists.

Find two friends and assign numbers to yourselves: 1, 2, and 3. Artist #1 will draw in the top section of the paper, Artist #2 will draw in the middle section, and Artist #3 will draw in the bottom section. Each artist will draw different parts of a body:

Top section (Artist #1) - Head, neck, and shoulders

Middle section (Artist #2) - Body and arms

Bottom section (Artist #3) - Legs and feet

You can draw any kind of creature you want, as long as you draw your assigned body parts. It can be real or unreal, plant, human, monster, or animal.

Step 3: Pass around the drawing.

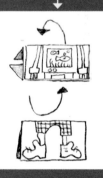

Each artist should sit with his or her back to the other artists while drawing. Artist #1 begins by drawing the creature's head, neck, and shoulders in the top section of the paper. Then Artist #1 folds the top section back so that only the middle and bottom sections are visible, and passes the paper to Artist #2. After Artist #2 draws in the middle section of the paper, he or she folds the middle section back so that only the bottom section is visible, then passes the paper to Artist #3. Artist #3 finishes the picture by drawing the creature's legs and feet in the bottom section.

Step 4: Color in the drawing.

Unfold the paper and look at your drawing. Pass your paper from artist to artist and color the section that you have drawn with colored pencils, crayons, or marker. Hang your art on the wall and enjoy!

BIRTHDAYS

What American playwright was born on the 4th of July? ➡ page 38

Wolfgang Amadeus Mozart

Cesar Chavez

JANUARY
Birthstone: Garnet

1 J.D. Salinger, author, 1919
2 Kate Bosworth, actress, 1983
3 Eli Manning, football player, 1981
4 Isaac Newton, physicist/ mathematician, 1643
5 Alvin Ailey, choreographer, 1931
6 Early Wynn, baseball player, 1920
7 Liam Aiken, actor, 1990
8 Stephen Hawking, physicist, 1942
9 Dave Matthews, musician, 1967
10 Jake Delhomme, football player, 1975
11 Amanda Peet, actress, 1972
12 Christiane Amanpour, journalist, 1958
13 Orlando Bloom, actor, 1977
14 Dave Grohl, musician, 1969
15 Rev. Martin Luther King Jr., civil rights leader, 1929
16 Sade, singer, 1959
17 Jim Carrey, actor, 1962
18 Mark Messier, hockey player, 1961
19 Katey Sagal, actress, 1957
20 Buzz Aldrin, astronaut, 1930
21 Geena Davis, actress, 1956
22 Sir Francis Bacon, philosopher, 1561
23 John Hancock, revolutionary leader, 1737
24 Mischa Barton, actress, 1986
25 Alicia Keys, singer, 1981
26 Wayne Gretsky, hockey player, 1961
27 Wolfgang Amadeus Mozart, composer, 1756
28 Elijah Wood, actor, 1981
29 Heather Graham, actress, 1970
30 Christian Bale, actor, 1974
31 Justin Timberlake, singer, 1981

FEBRUARY
Birthstone: Amethyst

1 Langston Hughes, poet, 1902
2 Bob Marley, singer, 1945
3 Elizabeth Blackwell, first woman physician, 1821
4 Rosa Parks, civil rights activist, 1913
5 Sara Evans, singer, 1971
6 Ronald Reagan, 40th president, 1911
7 Frederick Douglass, abolitionist, 1817
8 Ted Koppel, journalist, 1940
9 Travis Tritt, singer, 1963
10 Emma Roberts, actress, 1991
11 Jennifer Aniston, actress, 1969
12 Charles Darwin, scientist, 1809
13 Grant Wood, artist, 1891
14 Drew Bledsoe, football player, 1972
15 Matt Groening, cartoonist, 1954
16 Jerome Bettis, football player, 1972
17 Chaim Potok, novelist, 1929
18 Molly Ringwald, actress, 1968
19 Haylie Duff, singer/actress, 1985
20 Ansel Adams, photographer, 1902
21 Jennifer Love Hewitt, actress, 1979
22 Edna St. Vincent Millay, poet, 1892
23 Dakota Fanning, actress, 1994
24 Steve Jobs, computer innovator, 1955
25 Sean Astin, actor, 1971
26 Marshall Faulk, football player, 1973
27 Josh Groban, singer, 1981
28 Lemony Snicket (Daniel Handler), author, 1970
29 Ja Rule, rapper, 1976

Dakota Fanning

MARCH
Birthstone: Aquamarine

1 Frederic Chopin, composer, 1810
2 Dr. Seuss, author, 1904
3 Jessica Biel, actress, 1982
4 Landon Donovan, soccer player, 1982
5 Jake Lloyd, actor, 1989
6 D.L. Hughley, actor/comedian, 1964
7 Laura Prepon, actress, 1980
8 Marcia Newby, gymnast, 1988
9 Bow Wow, actor/rapper, 1987
10 Carrie Underwood, singer, 1983
11 Benji and Joel Madden, musicians, 1979
12 Edward Albee, playwright, 1928
13 Percival Lowell, astronomer, 1855
14 Albert Einstein, physicist/ Nobel laureate, 1879
15 Ruth Bader Ginsburg, U.S. Supreme Court justice, 1933
16 Lauren Graham, actress, 1967
17 Mia Hamm, soccer player, 1972
18 Queen Latifah, rapper, actress, 1970
19 Jason LaRue, baseball player, 1974
20 Spike Lee, filmmaker, 1957
21 Matthew Broderick, actor, 1962
22 Reese Witherspoon, actress, 1976
23 Jason Kidd, basketball player, 1973
24 Peyton Manning, football player, 1976
25 Sheryl Swoopes, basketball player, 1971
26 Keira Knightley, actress, 1985
27 Mariah Carey, singer, 1970
28 Vince Vaughn, actor, 1970
29 Sam Walton, Wal-Mart founder, 1918
30 Vincent Van Gogh, artist, 1853
31 Cesar Chavez, labor leader, 1927

APRIL
Birthstone: Diamond

1 Phil Niekro, baseball player, 1939
2 Hans Christian Andersen, author, 1805
3 Amanda Bynes, actress, 1986
4 Heath Ledger, actor, 1979
5 Booker T. Washington, educator, 1856
6 Zach Braff, actor, 1975
7 Jackie Chan, actor, 1954
8 Kirsten Storms, actress, 1984
9 Jesse McCartney, actor/singer, 1987
10 John Madden, sportscaster, 1936
11 Jason Varitek, baseball player, 1972
12 Beverly Cleary, author, 1916
13 Thomas Jefferson, 3rd president, 1743
14 Vivien Cardone, actress, 1993
15 Emma Watson, actress, 1990
16 Kareem Abdul-Jabbar, basketball player, 1947
17 Jennifer Garner, actress, 1972
18 Alia Shawkat, actress, 1989
19 Kate Hudson, actress, 1979
20 Tito Puente, musician, 1923
21 Queen Elizabeth II, British monarch, 1926
22 Robert J. Oppenheimer, physicist, 1904
23 Andruw Jones, baseball player, 1977
24 Kelly Clarkson, singer, 1982
25 Jason Lee, actor, 1970
26 Kane, WWE wrestler, 1967
27 Samuel Morse, inventor, 1791
28 Harper Lee, author, 1926
29 Uma Thurman, actress, 1970
30 Kirsten Dunst, actress, 1982

Dwayne "The Rock" Johnson

MAY
Birthstone: Emerald

1 Tim McGraw, musician, 1967
2 Dwayne "The Rock" Johnson, actor/wrestler, 1972
3 Sugar Ray Robinson, boxer, 1921
4 Dawn Staley, basketball player, 1970
5 Brian Williams, journalist, 1959
6 Martin Brodeur, hockey player, 1972
7 Johannes Brahms, composer, 1833
8 Enrique Iglesias, singer, 1975
9 Rosario Dawson, actress, 1979
10 Bono, musician/activist, 1960
11 Salvador Dali, artist, 1904
12 Tony Hawk, skateboarder, 1968
13 Stevie Wonder, singer, 1950
14 Amber Tamblyn, actress, 1983
15 L. Frank Baum, author, 1856
16 Janet Jackson, singer, 1966
17 Sugar Ray Leonard, boxer, 1956
18 Tina Fey, actress/comedian, 1970
19 Malcolm X, militant civil rights activist, 1925
20 Stan Mikita, hockey player, 1940
21 John Muir, naturalist, 1838
22 Sir Arthur Conan Doyle, author, 1859
23 Margaret Wise Brown, author, 1910
24 Tracy McGrady, basketball player, 1979
25 Mike Myers, actor, 1963
26 Sally Ride, astronaut, 1951
27 André 3000, musician, 1975
28 Jim Thorpe, Olympic champion, 1888
29 Andre Agassi, tennis champion, 1970
30 Manny Ramirez, baseball player, 1972
31 Walt Whitman, poet, 1819

JUNE
Birthstone: Pearl

1 Justine Henin-Hardenne, tennis player, 1982
2 Freddy Adu, soccer player, 1989
3 Carl Everett, baseball player, 1971
4 Angelina Jolie, actress, 1975
5 Richard Scarry, author/illustrator, 1919
6 Cynthia Rylant, author, 1954
7 Anna Kournikova, tennis player, 1981
8 Kanye West, musician, 1977
9 Natalie Portman, actress, 1981
10 Maurice Sendak, author/illustrator, 1928
11 Diana Taurasi, basketball player, 1982
12 Anne Frank, diary writer, 1929
13 William Butler Yeats, poet, 1865
14 Harriet Beecher Stowe, author, 1811
15 Neil Patrick Harris, actor, 1973
16 Kerry Wood, baseball player, 1977
17 Venus Williams, tennis player, 1980
18 Sir Paul McCartney, musician, 1942
19 Paula Abdul, singer/TV personality, 1962
20 Nicole Kidman, actress, 1967
21 Prince William of Great Britain, 1982
22 Donald Faison, actor, 1974
23 Clarence Thomas, U.S. Supreme Court justice, 1948
24 Solange Knowles, singer/actress, 1986
25 Carlos Delgado, baseball player, 1972
26 Babe Didrikson Zaharias, Olympic champion, 1914
27 Tobey Maguire, actor, 1975
28 John Elway, football player, 1960
29 Theo Fleury, hockey player, 1968
30 Michael Phelps, Olympic champion, 1985

Booker T. Washington

Carlos Delgado

JULY
Birthstone: Ruby

1 Missy Elliott, rapper, 1971
2 Lindsay Lohan, actress, 1986
3 Tom Cruise, actor, 1962
4 Neil Simon, playwright, 1927
5 P.T. Barnum, showman/circus founder, 1810
6 George W. Bush, 43rd president, 1946
7 Michelle Kwan, figure skater, 1980
8 John D. Rockefeller, industrialist, 1839
9 Tom Hanks, actor, 1956
10 Jessica Simpson, singer, 1980
11 E.B. White, author, 1899
12 Topher Grace, actor, 1978
13 Harrison Ford, actor, 1942
14 Matthew Fox, actor, 1966
15 Rembrandt van Rijn, artist, 1606
16 Will Farrell, actor, 1967
17 Donald Sutherland, actor, 1935
18 Kristin Bell, actress, 1980
19 Edgar Degas, artist, 1834
20 Sir Edmund Hillary, Everest climber, 1919
21 Josh Hartnett, actor, 1978
22 Keyshawn Johnson, football player, 1972
23 Daniel Radcliffe, actor, 1989
24 Jennifer Lopez, actress/singer, 1969
25 Ray Billingsley, cartoonist, 1957
26 Kate Beckinsale, actress, 1973
27 Alex Rodriguez, baseball player, 1975
28 Beatrix Potter, author, 1866
29 Allison Mack, actress, 1982
30 Jaime Pressley, actress, 1977
31 J.K. Rowling, author, 1965

Missy Elliott

AUGUST
Birthstone: Peridot

1 Francis Scott Key, composer/lawyer, 1779
2 Isabel Allende, writer, 1942
3 Tom Brady, football player, 1977
4 Jeff Gordon, racecar driver, 1971
5 Neil Armstrong, astronaut, 1930
6 Andy Warhol, artist, 1928
7 Charlize Theron, actress, 1975
8 Roger Federer, tennis player, 1981
9 Eric Bana, actor, 1968
10 Antonio Banderas, actor, 1960
11 Stephen Wozniak, computer pioneer, 1950
12 Ann M. Martin, author, 1955
13 Alfred Hitchcock, filmmaker, 1899
14 Halle Berry, actress, 1966
15 Ben Affleck, actor, 1972
16 Steve Carell, actor, 1963
17 Robert De Niro, actor, 1943
18 Meriwether Lewis, explorer, 1774
19 Bill Clinton, 42nd president, 1946
20 Fred Durst, musician, 1970
21 Stephen Hillenburg, SpongeBob creator, 1961
22 Bill Parcells, football coach, 1941
23 Julian Casablancas, singer, 1978
24 Rupert Grint, actor, 1988
25 Marvin Harrison, football player, 1972
26 Branford Marsalis, musician, 1960
27 Alexa Vega, actress, 1988
28 Jack Black, actor, 1969
29 LeAnn Rimes, country singer, 1982
30 Andy Roddick, tennis player, 1982
31 Chris Tucker, actor, 1972

Francis Scott Key

Adam Sandler

SEPTEMBER
Birthstone: Sapphire

1 Conway Twitty, country singer, 1933
2 Keanu Reeves, actor, 1964
3 Shaun White, Olympic snowboarder, 1986
4 Beyoncé Knowles, singer/actress, 1981
5 Michael Keaton, actor, 1951
6 Mark Chesnutt, singer, 1963
7 Shannon Elizabeth, actress, 1973
8 Latrell Sprewell, basketball player, 1970
9 Adam Sandler, actor, 1966
10 Bill O'Reilly, TV personality, 1949
11 Ludacris, rapper, 1977
12 Benjamin McKenzie, actor, 1978
13 Roald Dahl, author, 1916
14 Nas, rapper, 1973
15 Prince Harry of Great Britain, 1984
16 Alexis Bledel, actress, 1981
17 Rasheed Wallace, basketball player, 1974
18 Lance Armstrong, cyclist, 1971
19 Ryan Dusick, musician, 1977
20 Red Auerbach, basketball coach, 1917
21 Hiram Revels, first black U.S. senator, 1822
22 Tom Felton, actor, 1987
23 Ray Charles, musician, 1930
24 Paul Hamm, gymnast, 1982
25 Will Smith, actor/rapper, 1968
26 Serena Williams, tennis player, 1981
27 Avril Lavigne, singer, 1984
28 Hilary Duff, actress/singer, 1987
29 Enrico Fermi, physicist/Nobel laureate, 1901
30 Elie Wiesel, author, 1928

OCTOBER
Birthstone: Opal

1 William Boeing, founder of Boeing Company, 1881
2 Mohandas Gandhi, activist, 1869
3 Ashlee Simpson, singer, 1984
4 Rachael Leigh Cook, actress, 1979
5 Parminder Nagra, actress, 1975
6 Elisabeth Shue, actress, 1963
7 Rachel McAdams, actress, 1976
8 R. L. Stine, author, 1943
9 Brandon Routh, actor, 1979
10 Dale Earnhardt Jr., racecar driver, 1974
11 Michelle Trachtenberg, actress, 1985
12 Hugh Jackman, actor, 1968
13 Ashanti, singer, 1980
14 Usher, singer, 1978
15 Elena Dementieva, tennis player, 1981
16 John Mayer, musician, 1977
17 Mae Jemison, astronaut, 1956
18 Wynton Marsalis, musician, 1961
19 Ty Pennington, TV personality, 1965
20 Snoop Dogg, rapper/actor, 1971
21 Dizzy Gillespie, trumpet player, 1917
22 Ichiro Suzuki, baseball player, 1973
23 Tiffeny Milbrett, soccer player, 1972
24 Kevin Kline, actor, 1947
25 Ciara, singer, 1985
26 Jon Heder, actor, 1977
27 Teddy Roosevelt, 26th president, 1858
28 Bill Gates, computer pioneer, 1955
29 Winona Ryder, actress, 1971
30 John Adams, 2nd president of the United States, 1735
31 Juliette Gordon Low, Girl Scouts' founder, 1860

Condoleezza Rice

NOVEMBER
Birthstone: Topaz

1 Bo Bice, singer, 1975
2 Nelly, rapper, 1974
3 Walker Evans, photographer, 1903
4 Laura Bush, First Lady, 1946
5 Johnny Damon, baseball player, 1973
6 John Philip Sousa, composer, 1854
7 Marie Curie, scientist/Nobel laureate, 1867
8 Parker Posey, actress, 1968
9 Nick Lachey, singer, 1973
10 Brittany Murphy, actress, 1977
11 Leonardo DiCaprio, actor, 1974
12 Ryan Gosling, actor, 1980
13 Rachel Bilson, actress, 1981
14 Condoleezza Rice, 1954
15 Zena Grey, actress, 1988
16 Marg Helgenberger, actress, 1958
17 Reggie Wayne, football player, 1978
18 Owen Wilson, actor, 1968
19 Larry Johnson, football player, 1979
20 John R. Bolton, former U.N. ambassador, 1948
21 Jena Malone, actress, 1984
22 Jamie Lee Curtis, actress, 1958
23 Billy the Kid (William Bonney), outlaw, 1859
24 Katherine Heigl, actress, 1978
25 Jenna and Barbara Bush, Pres. Bush's daughters, 1981
26 Charles Schulz, cartoonist, 1912
27 Bill Nye, "The Science Guy," 1955
28 Jon Stewart, TV host, 1962
29 Louisa May Alcott, author, 1832
30 Mark Twain, author, 1835

DECEMBER
Birthstone: Turquoise

1 Richard Pryor, actor, 1940
2 Lucy Liu, actress, 1967
3 Brendan Fraser, actor, 1967
4 Tyra Banks, model/TV personality, 1973
5 Cliff Floyd, baseball player, 1972
6 Otto Graham, football player/coach, 1921
7 Aaron Carter, actor/singer, 1987
8 AnnaSophia Robb, actress, 1993
9 Felicity Huffman, actress, 1962
10 Raven, actress, 1985
11 Mos Def, actor/rapper, 1973
12 Edvard Munch, artist, 1863
13 Jamie Foxx, actor, 1967
14 Craig Biggio, baseball player, 1965
15 Adam Brody, actor, 1979
16 Ludwig van Beethoven, composer, 1770
17 Sean Patrick Thomas, actor, 1970
18 Brad Pitt, actor, 1963
19 Jake Gyllenhaal, actor, 1980
20 Rich Gannon, football player, 1965
21 Ray Romano, actor/comedian, 1957
22 Diane Sawyer, journalist, 1945
23 Alge Crumpler, football player, 1977
24 Ryan Seacrest, DJ/TV personality, 1974
25 Clara Barton, American Red Cross founder, 1821
26 Marcelo Rios, tennis player, 1975
27 Carson Palmer, football player, 1979
28 Denzel Washington, actor, 1954
29 Jude Law, actor, 1972
30 LeBron James, basketball player, 1984
31 Val Kilmer, actor, 1959

Clara Barton

John Mayer

Talkin' 'Bout Your Generation

Do you ever feel like your parents don't really get your slang or the clothes and music you like? Ever feel like you don't really get the stuff they like either? Maybe it's because you're from different generations.

A generation usually spans about 20 years. Not everyone agrees on which years each generation covers, but the labels can be helpful in describing the shared experiences and popular culture of a group of the population.

Generation Y (born about 1980-2000)

- Also known as "Millennials," "Echo Boomers," or "the Internet Generation"
- About 27.8% of the U.S. population, or around 82 million people in 2005
- First generation to grow up fluent in—and some say too reliant on—digital technology
- Seen as confident and cooperative, eager to "fix" the world by solving its problems

Generation X (born about 1965-79)

- About 20.6% of the U.S. population, or around 61 million people in 2005
- Born during the so-called "Baby Bust," a drop in birthrates after the Baby Boom
- A generation with many "latchkey kids" due to the growing number of divorces and families with two working parents
- Seen as unmotivated and intimidated by world problems that they didn't create
- Independent-minded and obsessed with pop culture

Baby Boomers (born about 1946-64)

- About 27.9% of the population, or around 83 million people in 2005
- The "Baby Boom" began right after World War II, as millions of soldiers returned home
- Baby boomers witnessed the civil rights and women's rights movements, as well as the Vietnam War
- Seen as idealistic and spoiled, used to getting what they want, and denying they are aging.

MOST POPULAR NAMES

Boys (born 1970-79)	Girls (born 1970-79)	Boys (born 1990-99)	Girls (born 1990-99)
1. Michael	1. Jennifer	1. Michael	1. Jessica
2. Christopher	2. Amy	2. Christopher	2. Ashley
3. Jason	3. Melissa	3. Matthew	3. Emily
4. David	4. Michelle	4. Joshua	4. Samantha
5. James	5. Kimberly	5. Jacob	5. Sarah

⌂ ●WAforKids.com ↱

Go to **www.WAforKids.com** and type 040 into the code box. Then you can:
- Enter your birth date, and find a whole list of famous people that share it.
- Follow links to great sites that will help you create your own family tree.
- Follow links to the "Name Wizard," a site that will chart a name's popularity over the last century.

GENEALOGY TRACING YOUR FAMILY TREE

Genealogy is the study of one's family, tracing back through generations of relatives. The first place to start in your family genealogy is with yourself. Write down the answers to the following questions:

- What is your full name (include middle name)?
- When and where were you born (town, city, state, country)?

Next, write down the name, birth date, and place of birth for each of your parents (ask them or the adult who takes care of you). Then, interview your grandparents and other relatives. Get their birthdates and places of birth as well. If any of these people have died, record their date of death. You might also ask about interesting events in their lives.

Now, you have the beginnings of a family tree. Fill out as much of this chart as you can.

PARENT
Name _____
Birth _____
Death _____

ME
Your
Name _____
Birth _____

PARENT
Name _____
Birth _____
Death _____

GRANDPARENT
Name _____
Birth _____
Death _____

GRANDPARENT
Name _____
Birth _____
Death _____

GRANDPARENT
Name _____
Birth _____
Death _____

GRANDPARENT
Name _____
Birth _____
Death _____

When you find out more about a relative, you may get access to photographs and photocopies of important documents. Documents might include birth certificates, marriage licenses, or immigration papers.

To find out where you can get official copies of "vital records" such as birth, death, and marriage certificates for a particular state, check the website of the U.S. National Center for Health Statistics (www.cdc.gov/nchs). Baptism, marriage, and burial records can often be found at family churches. Also, many libraries have U.S. Census records for 1790-1930. Make sure to keep copies of the documents you find.

Additional Sources

A good book for children to read is *Climbing Your Family Tree: Online and Off-Line Genealogy for Kids*, by Ira Wolfman. (*www.workman.com/familytree*)

The Church of Jesus Christ of Latter Day Saints (the Mormons) has Family History Centers throughout the world. There you can access their databases and programs, and possibly find members of your family.

▲ Old family photos are a great way to explore your family history.

BOOKS

How many different languages have the *Harry Potter* books been translated into? ➡ page 46

BOOK AWARDS, 2007

Newbery Medal
For the author of the best children's book
2007 winner: *The Higher Power of Lucky,* by Susan Patron

Winner of the 2007 Newbery Medal

the higher power of lucky

Caldecott Medal
For the artist of the best children's picture book
2007 winner: *Flotsam,* by David Wiesner

Michael L. Printz Award
For excellence in literature written for young adults
2007 winner: *American Born Chinese,* by Gene Luen Yang

Coretta Scott King Award
For artists and authors whose works encourage expression of the African American experience

2007 winners:
Author Award: **Copper Sun,** by Sharon Draper ⟶
Illustrator Award: **Moses: When Harriet Tubman Led Her People to Freedom**, illustrated by Kadir Nelson (written by Carole Boston Weatherford)

SHARON DRAPER
COPPER SUN

NEW BOOK **SPOTLIGHT**

Fantasy fans around the world are saddened by the end of the Harry Potter series. However, there are many other fantasy series for fans to dive into. Try the Septimus Heap series by Angie Sage, which includes *Book 1: Magyk, Book 2: Flyte,* and the brand-new (in March 2007) *Book 3: Physik.*

🏠 ●WAforKids.com ↱

Go to **www.WAforKids.com** and type **042** into the code box for more facts and fun:

• Are you a book-a-holic? Take the chapter quiz to find out.

• Learn all about comic books, and solve a Record-Breaking Books puzzle.

• Get more homework help on book awards and the history of books!

Famous Authors FOR KIDS

Author	Try the Book
Brian Jacques (1939-) was such a good writer at age 10 that one of his teachers believed an adult had really written one of his stories. He has held many jobs in his life—including sailor, firefighter, boxer, and truck-driver.	*Redwall*
 **J.K. Rowling** (1965-) is the author of the world-famous Harry Potter series. Her friends call her "Joanne," but she used "J.K." on her books so that boys wouldn't be turned off by a story written by a woman. In 2006, *Forbes* magazine ranked her the second-wealthiest female celebrity in the world (after talk-show host Oprah Winfrey).	*Harry Potter and the Sorcerer's Stone* (the first book in the Harry Potter series)
Judy Blume (1938-) grew up in Elizabeth, New Jersey. Some of her books deal with controversial issues, such as racism and divorce. As a result, her books have been banned from some schools and libraries. However, in 2000 the U.S. Library of Congress honored her with a Living Legend award.	*Superfudge*
 **Beverly Cleary** (1916-) wrote her first book, *Henry Huggins,* in 1950. She had been a librarian and knew that kids wanted to read books about other young people. Her beloved characters include bratty Ramona; always-embarrassed Beezus; and Ribsy, the dog that constantly gets into trouble. She has written more than 30 books for kids. The University of California, Berkeley, named a residence hall after her.	*Beezus and Ramona*
R.L. (Robert Lawrence) Stine (1943-) grew up in Columbus, Ohio. He began to write jokes and stories on a typewriter when he was 9. He published several books of jokes under the name "Jovial Bob Stine." He is best known for his *Goosebumps* series of horror fiction books for children.	*Night of the Living Dummy*
Roald Dahl (1916-1990) is the author of the famous *Charlie and the Chocolate Factory,* which was made into a movie in 2005. Dahl enlisted in the British Royal Air Force during World War II and flew a plane over Africa. He wrote 18 books for children and had five children of his own.	*The B.F.G.*

BOOKS TO READ

There are two major types of literature: fiction and nonfiction. A fiction book includes people, places, and events that are often inspired by reality, but are mainly from an author's imagination. Nonfiction is about real things that actually happened and should be totally accurate. Nonfiction may be about how something works or the history of an event or a person's life.

Within these two groups there are smaller subgroups called genres (ZHAN-ruz).

Fiction

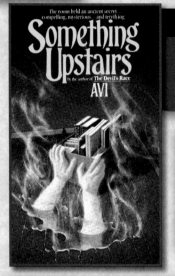

Mysteries and Thrillers

These adventure stories will keep you up late, as you follow a main character who must uncover a secret.

Try These *Something Upstairs*, **by Avi;** *Troubling a Star*, **by Madeleine L'Engle**

Fantasy and Science Fiction

This genre is one of the most popular for teen readers. You've heard of the Harry Potter books, but there are thousands of books for kids and teens in this genre.

Try These *The Neverending Story*, **by Michael Ende;** *The Princess Bride*, **by William Goldman**

Realistic Fiction

Do you like stories that might have happened to you? Realistic fiction is about real-life situations that teens and kids deal with every day.

Try These *Walk Two Moons*, **by Sharon Creech;** *Shiloh*, **by Phyllis Reynolds Naylor**

Historical Fiction

If you think history is just about facts, this is the genre for you. Authors take exciting historical events and put the most interesting fictional characters right in the middle of them.

Try These *Little House in the Big Woods*, **by Laura Ingalls Wilder;** *Roll of Thunder, Hear My Cry*, **by Mildred D. Taylor**

Myths and Legends

These made-up stories go way back. Some are from nineteenth-century America, others are from ancient Greece and Africa.

Try These *D'Aulaires' Book of Greek Myths*, by Ingri D'Aulaire and Edgar Parin D'Aulaire; *Italian Folk Tales*, by Italo Calvino, translated by George Martin

Graphic Novels, Comics, and Manga

Check out these adventure series that use drawings and text to tell complicated adventure stories.

Try These *Queen Bee*, by Chynna Clugston; *Iron West*, by Doug TenNapel

Nonfiction

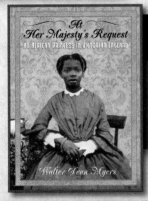

Biographies, Autobiographies, and Memoirs

Do you like reading all about the details of a real person's life? This genre is for you.

Try These *At Her Majesty's Request: An African Princess in Victorian England*, by Walter Dean Myers; *Cleopatra: Goddess of Egypt, Enemy of Rome*, by Polly Schoyer Brooks

History

Books in this genre can be about an event, an era, a country, or even a war.

Try These *Slavery Time When I Was Chillun*, by Belinda Hurmence; *Remember World War II: Kids Who Survived Tell Their Stories*, by Dorinda Makanaonalani Nicholson

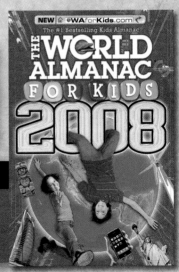

Reference

Books that supply facts and practical information on one topic or many, including almanacs, atlases, dictionaries, and encyclopedias.

Try This *The World Almanac for Kids*

ALL ABOUT
HARRY POTTER

HARRY POTTER by the Numbers

$3,516,611,015	Total worldwide ticket sales for the first four Harry Potter movies, as of Feb. 13, 2007.
$1,000,000,000	Estimated net worth of author J.K. Rowling.
325,000,000	Estimated total copies of Harry Potter books sold worldwide as of May 2007.
885,943	Total number of words in the first six Harry Potter novels.
287,000	Estimated copies of *Harry Potter and the Half-Blood Prince* sold per hour on the first day of its release in the U.S. This made it the fastest-selling book in history.
64	Estimated number of languages Harry Potter has been translated into, including Ancient Greek and Urdu!

QUIZ: How Well Do You Know HARRY POTTER?

1. How old will Harry Potter be on July 31, 2007?
2. What is Harry's best subject at Hogwarts?
3. Where do the Dursleys tell everyone Harry goes to school?
4. What is Harry's wand made of?
5. What is Harry's middle name?
6. What home is Harry now the owner of?
7. Who was Harry's date to the Yule Ball?

ANSWERS ON PAGES 334-337.
FOR MORE PUZZLES GO TO
WWW.WAFORKIDS.COM

BOOK SUMMARIES:
HARRY POTTER RETROSPECTIVE

1. *Harry Potter and the Sorcerer's Stone* (1997, 320 pages) Originally published as *Harry Potter and the Philosopher's Stone*, this first book in the series introduced the world to Harry Potter, an orphan who is told he's a famous wizard!

2. *Harry Potter and the Chamber of Secrets* (1998, 352 pages) Students at Hogwarts are being attacked, and rumors suggest that the mysterious Chamber of Secrets has been opened, releasing a fearsome monster!

3. *Harry Potter and the Prisoner of Azkaban* (1999; 448 pages) The notorious Sirius Black escapes from Azkaban Prison and comes to Hogwarts looking for Harry.

4. *Harry Potter and the Goblet of Fire* (2000, 734 pages) Harry is selected to compete in the magical Triwizard Tournament, even though he never entered the competition!

5. *Harry Potter and the Order of the Phoenix* (2003, 870 pages) After Lord Voldemort returns to power, Dumbledore revives the Order of the Phoenix to fight him.

6. *Harry Potter and the Half-Blood Prince* (2005, 652 pages) Harry discovers a mysterious potions book written by someone called the "Half-Blood Prince."

PREVIEW:

7. *Harry Potter and the Deathly Hallows* (2007) Harry must destroy all the horcruxes before finally fighting Lord Voldemort, fulfilling Professor Trelawney's prophecy that one of them will kill the other.

All About >> THE MOVIES

What's it really like to go to Hogwarts? The stars of the Harry Potter movies know. Daniel Radcliffe, who plays Harry, says that filming the movies really is like going to school. Beginning a new film is like coming back from summer vacation. Of course, the stars of Harry Potter get to do a lot of cool stuff that other kids don't get to do, like play Quidditch, fight dragons, and talk to ghosts. Even eating slugs can be a lot of fun, according to Rupert Grint (Ron Weasley) who had to cough up the slimy creatures while filming *Chamber of Secrets*. The special effects wizards on the set made fake slug slime that tasted like chocolate, orange, and lemon.

That's why so many kids want to be part of the Potter magic. In 2006, more than 15,000 girls tried out for the part of Luna Lovegood. The part eventually went to 14-year-old Evanna Lynch, who makes her film debut as Harry's slightly-loony friend in *Harry Potter and the Order of the Phoenix*, which opens July 13, 2007.

BUILDINGS

What structure is on the Cambodian flag? → page 51

TALLEST BUILDINGS IN THE WORLD

Here are the world's tallest buildings, with the year each was completed. Heights listed here don't include antennas or other outside structures.

Taipei 101
Taipei, Taiwan (2004)
Height: 101 stories, 1,667 feet

Petronas Towers 1 & 2
Kuala Lumpur, Malaysia (1998)
Height: each building is 88 stories, 1,483 feet

◀ Sears Tower
Chicago, Illinois (1974)
Height: 110 stories, 1,451 feet

Jin Mao Tower
Shanghai, China (1999)
Height: 88 stories, 1,381 feet

Two International Finance Centre
Hong Kong, China (2003)
Height: 88 stories, 1,362 feet

CITIC Plaza
Guangzhou, China (1996)
Height: 80 stories, 1,283 feet

The Tallest TOWERS

The world's **tallest free-standing structure** is the 1,815-foot **CN Tower** in Toronto, Canada (built 1973-75). It is not exactly a building since it does not have stories. "Free-standing" means it supports its own weight and is not attached to anything. Brave visitors can walk across the glass floor at the 1,122-foot level!

The world's **tallest structure** is the **KVLY-TV tower** in Fargo, North Dakota. It's 2,063 feet tall (including the 113-foot antenna) and made of steel. The tower is anchored and supported by more than 7.5 miles of steel wires.

WORLD'S TALLEST WHEN BUILT

Great Pyramid of Giza, Egypt
Built c. 2250 B.C. Height: 480 feet.

Cologne Cathedral, Germany
Built 1248-1880. Height: 515 feet.

Washington Monument, Washington D.C.
Built 1848-84. Height: 555 feet.

Eiffel Tower, Paris, France
Built 1887-89. Height: 984 feet.

Chrysler Building, New York, NY
Built 1930. Height: 1,046 feet.

Empire State Building, New York, NY
Built 1931. Height: 1,250 feet. ▶

Ostankino Tower, Moscow, Russia
Built 1963-67. Height: 1,771 feet.

A Short History of Tall Buildings

For most of history, people built tall structures to honor gods, kings, and other powerful leaders, not for living. Building tall required lots of wealth and workers. But the biggest challenge was gravity. Each part of a wall had to support everything above it. Building higher required thicker walls at the base. Too many windows would weaken the building. The Great Pyramid required an area equal to 10 football fields and more than 2 million massive stone blocks. The Washington Monument, the last entirely stone structure to reach a record height, has walls 15 feet thick at its base.

By the 1880s, three **key factors in the evolution of tall buildings** were in place:

1. A NEED FOR SPACE Crowded cities had less space for building, and land got expensive. To create more space, buildings had to go up instead of out.

2. BETTER STEEL PRODUCTION Mass-producing steel meant more of it was available for construction. Long vertical **columns** and horizontal girders could be joined to form a strong cube-like grid that was lighter than a similar one made of stone or brick. Weight was also directed down the columns to a solid **foundation**, usually underground, instead of to walls.

3. THE ELEVATOR Tall buildings need elevators! The first elevator, powered by steam, was installed in a New York store in 1857. Electric elevators came along in 1880.

As buildings got taller, a new problem sprang up—**wind**. Too much movement could damage buildings or make the people inside uncomfortable. Some tall buildings, like New York's Citicorp Center, actually have a counter-weight near the top. A computer controls a 400-ton weight, moving it back and forth to lessen the building's sway.

In California and Japan, **earthquakes** are a big problem and special techniques are needed to make tall buildings safer from quakes.

The final height of the Dubai Tower in the United Arab Emirates is being kept secret, but builders predict it will surpass the 1,815-foot CN Tower as the world's tallest free-standing structure when finished in 2009. The tower is Y-shaped to "confuse the wind" and keep it from bending. Extra concrete walls add support on the first 100 floors where people will live. Offices will be on the higher floors. Special balconies will let people go outside 152 floors up.

IT'S NOT ALL ABOUT... TALL!

When it comes to buildings, the tall ones grab people's attention. But many other buildings are interesting and fun to look at. Here are a few really cool buildings.

EL TEMPLE DE LA SAGRADA FAMILIA, Barcelona, Spain

Architect Antonio Gaudí proved he had no shortage of imagination when he designed the "Temple of the Holy Family." Work began in 1883, and it is still in progress. This very detailed project has so many carvings and towers yet to be built that it may be many years before it's ever finished.

THE GLASS HOUSE, New Canaan, Connecticut

When architect Philip Johnson designed his own home in 1949, he created something beautiful and unique. What makes this house special is the structure: it is a steel frame with outside walls made of clear glass. This makes the house totally see-through. (Johnson did enclose the bathroom in brick!) In an interview, Johnson said, "It's the only house in the world where you can watch the sun set and the moon rise at the same time."

LA GRAND ARCHE DE LA DÉFENSE, Paris, France

The missing middle makes this 360-foot-tall cube hard to forget. Finished in 1989, this government office building was designed as a modern version of the city's famous military memorial, L'Arc de Triomphe. You could fit another famous Paris landmark, the Cathedral of Notre-Dame (198.5 feet tall), underneath the arch!

WALT DISNEY CONCERT HALL, Los Angeles, California

This addition to the Music Center of Los Angeles County, designed by the architect Frank O. Gehry, opened in October 2003 as the new home of the Los Angeles Philharmonic. On the outside it looks like a ship with its sail at full mast, and the auditorium with its curved wood ceiling looks like the hull of the ship. Not only does the curvy design look great, it also improves the acoustics, or the quality of the sound.

HISTORICAL WONDERS

PARTHENON
Athens, Greece; 447-436 B.C.

The temple to Greek goddess Athena in the Acropolis is considered a perfect example of symmetry, or balance. It's an example of the Greek style known as the Doric order. It looks beat up because an explosion knocked out the roof and several pillars in 1687 and Britain's Lord Elgin removed the outside statues in the 1800s.

ANGKOR WAT
Angkor, Cambodia; c. 1150 A.D.

This massive temple complex covers 400 acres and is surrounded by a big moat. The towers are shaped like lotus flowers. Every surface along its winding corridors is carved with Hindu tales. It's a source of pride for Cambodians, who have placed it on their flag.

CATHEDRAL NOTRE-DAME DE PARIS
Paris, France; 1163-1351

"Gothic" might stir up images of ghouls. However gothic architecture was meant to be uplifting, not scary. Instead of using thicker walls to build taller, the cathedral used pointed arches and rib-like supports called flying buttresses on the outside that lean into the walls to prop them up. Those buttresses also allow more space for bigger windows, usually stained glass, including large round "rose" windows. The scary monstrous statues along the rooftop are not Gothic. They're water spouts added in the 1800s.

FORBIDDEN CITY
Beijing, China; 1406-1420

This was the exclusive home for emperors of the Ming and Qing dynasties for 492 years. The palace grounds are the world's largest (178 acres). It was "forbidden" because people could not enter without the emperor's permission. The palace itself contains thousands of wooden chambers and great halls that cover 37 acres. Every roof is yellow, the color of Chinese royalty.

BRIDGES

There are four main bridge designs: beam, arch, truss, and suspension or cable-stayed.

BEAM

The beam bridge is the most basic kind. A log across a stream is a simple style of beam bridge. Highway bridges are often beam bridges. The span of a beam bridge, or the length of the bridge without any support under it, needs to be fairly short. Long beam bridges need many supporting poles, called piers.

ARCH

You can easily recognize an arch bridge, because it has arches holding it up from the bottom. The columns that support the arches are called abutments. Arch bridges were invented by the ancient Greeks.

TRUSS

The truss bridge uses mainly steel beams, connected in triangles to increase strength and span greater distances.

SUSPENSION

On suspension bridges, the roadway hangs from smaller cables attached to a pair of huge cables running over two massive towers. The ends of the giant cables are anchored firmly into solid rock or huge concrete blocks at each end of the bridge. The weight of the roadway is transferred through the cables to the anchors. On a cable-stayed bridge, the cables are attached directly from the towers (pylons) to the deck.

FAMOUS SHAPES PUZZLE

Can you match the names of the famous structures to their silhouettes?

1. Flatiron Building
2. The Great Sphinx
3. The Pyramids of Giza
4. Stonehenge
5. Space Needle

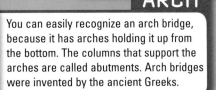

ANSWERS ON PAGES 334-337. FOR MORE PUZZLES GO TO WWW.WAFORKIDS.COM

PARTS OF A SUSPENSION BRIDGE

Anchorage Main cables are attached here, adding strength and stability

Deck Surface of the bridge

Main cable Primary load-bearing cables, secured by anchorages

Pier Supports for pylons

Pylon Tower supports that hold up cables and decks

Suspender cable Vertical cables that hold up the deck

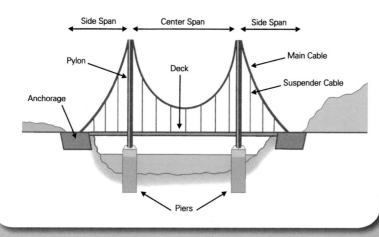

DAM FACTS

Dams are built to control the flow of rivers. They can provide water for drinking or farming, prevent flooding, and create electricity. The first dams were embankment dams built thousands of years ago out of walls of rocks and dirt to prevent flooding or to make lakes called reservoirs for irrigation. Embankment dams are still made but require a lot of land. To save space, most dams are now made of concrete. They sometimes use the same properties as bridges, like abutments, to help hold back water. "Hydroelectric" dams are used to generate electricity by channeling the force of rivers and waterfalls into tunnels in the dam to move enormous turbines (wheel-shaped engines).

CAMPING

At which camp can you learn break dancing basics? ➡ page 55

CAMP IS FOR EVERYONE

RESIDENT CAMP: Usually for kids age 7 or older. Campers stay overnight, usually in cabins, tents, or tepees. Stays can last a few days, a week, or more.

DAY CAMP: For kids as young as 4. Many of the same activities as a resident camp, but everyone goes home at the end of the day.

SPECIALTY CAMP: Helps kids learn a special skill, like horseback riding, water skiing, or dancing, to name just a few.

SPECIAL NEEDS CAMP: Each year, more than a million kids with special needs go to summer camp.

did you know?

The Boy Scouts of America was founded in 1910. Many former scouts have gone on to great things. Of the 312 pilots and scientists selected as astronauts for NASA since 1959, 180 were scouts or have been active in scouting. Other famous names that made it all the way to the top rank of Eagle Scout include: President Gerald Ford; Dr. Robert M. Gates, the current U.S. Secretary of Defense; and record-setting pilot Stephen Fossett.

THE AMERICAN CAMP ASSOCIATION®

The American Camp Association is a resource for parents and kids to help them find the right camp to fit any need and budget. For more information, visit

WEB SITE *www.CAMPParents.org*

4 FUN CAMPS

Would you like to do something a little different next summer? Try one of these unusual camps.

Hip-Hop Camp

Do you think you've got what it takes to flow? Put aside the old campfire songs and bust a rhyme at Progressive Arts Alliance's "RHAPSODY Hip-Hop Summer Arts Camp" in Cleveland, Ohio. You can also learn the basics of break dancing, hip-hop art, and DJ-ing.

WEB SITE *www.paalive.org*

Really Rough It

Do you think you have what it takes to be a pioneer? Show what you can do at this day camp on the Hickory Ridge Homestead, in North Carolina. Here, kids can take part in activities like tinsmithing, candle making, and hearth cooking led by people in period costumes. **WEB SITE** *www.horninthewest.com/museum.htm*

RoboCamp

Robots are the center of attention for campers at RoboCamp, hosted by Carnegie Mellon University in Pittsburgh, Pennsylvania. This five-day program lets kids work in teams to learn programming, and to design and build their own robots. Camp ends with a graduation ceremony at the National Robotics Engineering Center.

WEB SITE *www.rec.ri.cmu.edu/education*

Future Inventors

At Camp Invention, you may meet the next Steve Jobs (he's the founder of Apple, home of Mac computers and iPods). A typical day involves solving puzzles to learn how to fix a rocket ship, crossing a river of hot lava, or capturing sea creatures for observation. There are branches of this camp in 47 states. Look for one in yours.

WEB SITE *www.invent.org/camp_invention*

CRIME

INFAMOUS CRIMINALS

John Wilkes Booth

(1838-65) First presidential assassin. Booth was a famous actor but also a strong supporter of slavery and the South in the Civil War. On the night of April 14, 1865—five days after the South formally surrendered—President Abraham Lincoln attended a play at Ford's Theatre in Washington, DC. During the play *Our American Cousin,* Booth entered Lincoln's box seat and fired a single, fatal shot into the back of Lincoln's head. Booth shouted, "*Sic semper tyrannis*!" (Virginia's state motto, which means "Thus always to tyrants") and "The South is avenged!" He then jumped 12 feet from the box onto the stage, breaking one of his legs in the process, and escaped. He spent several days on the run before soldiers found him hiding in a barn in Virginia. When Booth refused to surrender, the soldiers set fire to the barn and shot him.

Charles Ponzi (1882-1949)

Con artist who invented a type of fraud that became known as a "Ponzi scheme." In 1919, in Boston, Ponzi told people he could give them a quick 50% return on their money. (For example, if someone gave Ponzi $50, he claimed he would invest it for 90 days and give them back $75.) When people received a huge return, they usually re-invested their money and told their friends they could easily make some money in this way. Most banks at the time only paid a 5% return on savings accounts, so people were eager to participate in Ponzi's scheme. In reality, Ponzi used money from new investors to pay earlier ones and kept some of the money for himself. He accumulated several million dollars over the course of a few months. After a local newspaper investigated Ponzi, he was arrested for fraud and sent to prison.

Al Capone

(1899-1947) Notorious gangster. Born in Brooklyn, New York, Capone

was known as "Scarface" because of a knife cut on his left cheek. He dropped out of school in the sixth grade and joined a gang. In 1925, Capone took over as leader of a Chicago criminal organization dealing in illegal liquor and gambling. This was during the era of Prohibition (1920-33), when most alcohol in the U.S. was illegal. Some of his men murdered seven members of a rival Chicago gang on February 14, 1929, in a crime dubbed the "St. Valentine's Day Massacre." Capone was never convicted of murder or other violent crimes, but in 1931 he was found guilty of not paying income taxes. He spent seven years in prison, some of that on Alcatraz Island, in San Francisco Bay.

LEGAL PROCESS

In the U.S., the federal and state governments have their own courts. The **federal courts**, or U.S. courts, hear cases such as those involving disputes between states. **State courts** hear other types of cases. Most of the legal work in this country occurs at the state level.

Different states organize their court systems differently. Below is a description of how a typical criminal case might proceed after a judge has determined there was sufficient reason to arrest a suspect (the person accused of a crime).

1 Grand jury. Citizens with no connection to the case review evidence and decide if there is enough to indict, or charge, the defendant with a crime.

2 Arraignment. A judge tells the defendant what crimes he or she has been charged with by the grand jury. The defendant can plead guilty, not guilty, or no contest. (No contest means the person will not fight the charges but does not admit to being guilty.)

3 Trial. A prosecutor presents evidence of the defendant's guilt. A defense attorney represents the defendant's best interests. Witnesses may testify about what they know. A jury listens to all the evidence and arguments. The judge makes sure everyone follows the rules.

4 Deliberations. Jury members discuss the evidence and try to agree on a verdict, or decision about the defendant's guilt. They must agree that the defendant is guilty "beyond a reasonable doubt." If they cannot agree, the defendant may receive a trial before a new jury.

5 Conviction and sentencing. If the defendant is found guilty, the judge sentences the person, or says how he or she will be punished.

6 Appeal. The defendant may appeal a guilty verdict to an appellate court, which may agree or disagree with the original verdict. It may send the case back to the lower court for a new trial.

DISASTERS

What is the "Ring of Fire?" ➡ page 61

Hurricanes

Hurricanes—called typhoons or cyclones in the Pacific—are Earth's biggest storms. When conditions are right, they form over the ocean from collections of storms and clouds known as tropical disturbances. Strong winds create a wall of clouds and rain that swirl in a circle around a calm center called the **eye.**

Hurricane Categories:

1: 74-95 mph
2: 96-110 mph
3: 111-130 mph
4: 131-155 mph
5: over 155 mph

The eye develops as **warm, moist air** is forced upward in the storm by **denser, cooler air.** From the outer edge of the storm to the inner eye, the pressure drops and wind speeds rise sharply, creating swirling **convection currents** around the eye. If wind speeds reach 39 mph, the storm is named. If wind speeds top 74 mph, the storm is called a **hurricane.**

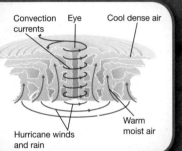

Convection currents
Eye
Cool dense air
Warm moist air
Hurricane winds and rain

Hurricanes can be up to 300 miles wide. On land, the storm can snap trees and tear buildings apart. Strong winds blowing toward shore can create a rise in the ocean water called a **storm surge**. It can combine with heavy rains to cause flooding and massive damage.

For the Atlantic Ocean, Caribbean Sea, and Gulf of Mexico, hurricane season runs from June 1 to November 30. Most hurricanes happen in August, September, and October, when the oceans are warmest.

Notable U.S. Hurricanes

Date	Location	What Happened?	Deaths
Sept. 8, 1900	Galveston, TX	Category 4 storm flooded the island with 15-foot waves.	8,000+
Sept. 19, 1938	NY, CT, RI, MA	"The Long Island Express," with storm surges rising 10-25 feet, caused $306 million in damages.	600+
Aug. 24-26, 1992	FL, LA	Hurricane Andrew swept across the Gulf of Mexico, leaving 250,000 homeless.	65
Aug. 25-29, 2005	LA, MS, AL, GA, FL	Hurricane Katrina, with 175 mph winds and a 25-foot high storm surge, caused about $125 billion in damage.	1,833

Hurricane Names

The U.S. began using women's names for hurricanes in 1953 and added men's names in 1978. When all letters (except Q, U, X, Y, and Z) are used in one season, any additional storms are named with Greek letters. Six Greek letters were needed to name 2005 storms.

2007 names: Andrea, Barry, Chantal, Dean, Erin, Felix, Gabrielle, Humberto, Ingrid, Jerry, Karen, Lorenzo, Melissa, Noel, Olga, Pablo, Rebecca, Sebastien, Tanya, Van, and Wendy

Tornadoes

Tornadoes are rapidly spinning columns of air. They form when winds change direction, speed up, and spin around in or near a thunderstorm. They can also spin off from hurricanes.

Tornadoes can happen any time that the weather is right, but they are more common between March and July. They can happen in any state, but strong tornadoes touch down most often in the U.S. southeast or central plains.

According to the National Oceanic and Atmospheric Administration's (NOAA), an average of 1,200 tornadoes occur in the U.S. each year. They cause an average of 60 deaths and 1,500 injuries each year and over $400 million in damage.

Tornadoes are measured by how much damage they cause. In February 2007, the U.S. began using the Enhanced Fujita (EF) Scale (at left) to measure tornadoes. The EF-Scale provides an estimate of a tornado's wind speed based on the amount of damage. If a tornado doesn't hit anything, it may be hard to classify it.

Wind speeds are difficult to measure directly, because measuring instruments can be destroyed in more violent winds. The highest wind speed ever recorded—318 mph—was taken in May 1999 in an Oklahoma tornado.

Tornado Categories:

WEAK

EF0: 65-85 mph

EF1: 86-110 mph

STRONG

EF2: 111-135 mph

EF3: 136-165 mph

VIOLENT

EF4: 166-200 mph

EF5: over 200 mph

U.S. Tornado Records (since record keeping began in 1950)

YEAR: The 1,819 tornadoes reported in 2004 topped the previous record of 1,424 in 1998.

MONTH: In May 2003, there were a total of 516 tornadoes, easily passing the old record of 399 set in June 1992.

TWO-DAY PERIOD: On April 3 and 4, 1974, 147 tornadoes touched down in 13 states.

WEB SITE For more information on storms and weather, go to the NOAA Education page: *www.education.noaa.gov/cweather.html*

59

EARTHQUAKES

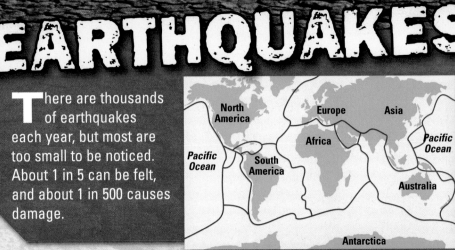

There are thousands of earthquakes each year, but most are too small to be noticed. About 1 in 5 can be felt, and about 1 in 500 causes damage.

WHAT CAUSES EARTHQUAKES?

To understand earthquakes, imagine the Earth as an egg with a cracked shell. The cracked outer layer (the eggshell) is called the **lithosphere,** and it is divided into huge pieces called **plates** (see map above). Underneath the lithosphere is a softer layer called the **asthenosphere**. The plates are constantly gliding over this softer layer, moving away, toward, or past one another. Earthquakes result when plates collide.

The cracks in the lithosphere are called **faults**. Many quakes occur along these fault lines.

MAJOR EARTHQUAKES

The earthquakes listed here are among the largest and most destructive recorded in the past 50 years. (See also "Tsunamis," page 61.)

Year	Location	Magnitude	Deaths (estimated)
1960	near Chile	9.5	5,000
1970	Northern Peru	7.8	66,000
1976	Tangshan, China	8.0	255,000
1988	Soviet Armenia	7.0	55,000
1989	United States (San Francisco area)	7.1	62
1990	Western Iran	7.7	40,000+
1994	United States (Los Angeles area)	6.8	61
1995	Kobe, Japan	6.9	5,502
1998	Northeastern Afghanistan	6.9	4,700+
1999	Western Turkey	7.4	17,200+
2001	Western India	7.9	30,000+
2003	Southeastern Iran	6.5	41,000+
2005	Pakistan and India	7.6	80,000+

VOLCANOES

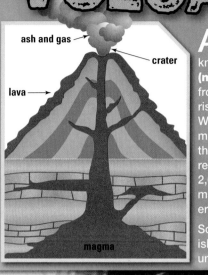

ash and gas

crater

lava

magma

A volcano is a mountain or hill **(cone)** with an opening on top known as a **crater**. Hot melted rock **(magma)**, gases, and other material from inside the Earth mix together and rise up through cracks and weak spots. When enough pressure builds up, the magma can escape, erupting through the crater. Magma is called lava when it reaches the air. Lava may be hotter than 2,000°F. The cone of a volcano is often made of layers of lava and ash that have erupted, then cooled.

Some islands, like the Hawaiian islands, are really the tops of undersea volcanoes.

Where is the Ring of Fire?

The hundreds of active volcanoes near the edges of the Pacific Ocean make up what is called the **Ring of Fire**. They mark the boundary between the plates under the Pacific Ocean and the plates under the surrounding continents. (Earth's plates are explained on page 60, with the help of a map.) The Ring of Fire runs from Alaska, along the west coast of South and North America, to the southern tip of Chile. The ring also runs down the east coast of Asia, starting in the far north. It continues down past Australia.

Some Famous Volcanic Eruptions

Year	Volcano (place)	Deaths (estimated)
79	Mount Vesuvius (Italy)	16,000
1586	Kelut (Indonesia)	10,000
1792	Mount Unzen (Japan)	14,500
1815	Tambora (Indonesia)	10,000
1883	Krakatau, or Krakatoa (Indonesia)	36,000
1902	Mount Pelée (Martinique)	28,000
1980	Mount St. Helens (U.S.)	57
1982	El Chichón (Mexico)	1,880
1985	Nevado del Ruiz (Colombia)	23,000
1986	Lake Nyos (Cameroon)	1,700
1991	Mount Pinatubo (Philippines)	800

TSUNAMIS

Tsunami (pronounced *tsoo-NAH-mee*) comes from two Japanese words: "tsu" (harbor) and "nami" (wave). These huge waves are sometimes called tidal waves, but they have nothing to do with the tides.

The strongest tsunamis happen when a big part of the sea floor lifts along a fault (see page 60), pushing up a huge volume of water. The resulting waves are long and low, and might not even be noticed in deep

water. They move at speeds of up to 500 miles per hour. As they near shore, they slow down and the great energy forces the water upward into big waves.

On December 26, 2004, a magnitude-9.3 earthquake off the Indonesian island of Sumatra triggered a tsunami in the Indian Ocean. The tsunami hit 12 countries. An estimated 226,000 people were killed, and 1.6 million were left homeless.

MAJOR DISASTERS

Here are a few famous disasters of different kinds.

Hindenburg *disaster*

Aircraft Disasters

Date	Location	What Happened?	Deaths
May 6, 1937	Lakehurst, NJ	German zeppelin (blimp) *Hindenburg* caught fire as it prepared to land.	36
Aug. 12, 1985	Japan	Boeing 747 jet collided with Mt. Osutaka. Japan's worst single-aircraft disaster in history.	520
March 27, 1977	Tenerife, Canary Islands	Two Boeing 747s collide on the runway of Los Rodeos airport.	582
Sept. 11, 2001	New York, NY; Arlington, VA; Shanksville, PA	Two hijacked planes crashed into the World Trade Center, one into the Pentagon, one went down in a PA field.	Nearly 3,000

Explosions and Fires

Date	Location	What Happened?	Deaths
June 15, 1904	New York City	*General Slocum,* wooden ship carrying church members up the East River, caught fire.	1021
March 25, 1911	New York City	Triangle Shirtwaist Factory caught fire. Workers were trapped inside.	146
Nov. 28, 1942	Boston, MA	Fire swept through the Coconut Grove nightclub; patrons panicked. Deadliest nightclub fire in U.S. history.	146
Dec. 3, 1984	Bhopal, India	A pesticide factory explosion spread toxic gas; worst industrial accident in history.	15,000

Rail Disasters

Date	Location	What Happened?	Deaths
Jan. 16, 1944	León Prov., Spain	Train crashed in the Torro Tunnel.	500
March 2, 1944	Salerno, Italy	Passengers suffocated when train stalled in tunnel.	521
Feb. 6, 1951	Woodbridge, NJ	Commuter train fell through a temporary overpass.	84
June 6, 1981	Bihar, India	Train plunged off of a bridge into the river; India's deadliest rail disaster ever.	800+

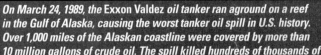

did you know? On March 24, 1989, the **Exxon Valdez** *oil tanker ran aground on a reef in the Gulf of Alaska, causing the worst tanker oil spill in U.S. history. Over 1,000 miles of the Alaskan coastline were covered by more than 10 million gallons of crude oil. The spill killed hundreds of thousands of birds and fish, and thousands of sea otters. About $3 billion has been spent on clean-up so far, but the spill's damage continues to affect the environment.*

Lusitania *disaster*

Ship Disasters

Date	Location	What Happened?	Deaths
April 14, 1912	near Newfoundland	Luxury liner *Titanic* collided with iceberg.	1,503
May 7, 1915	Atlantic Ocean, near Ireland	British steamer *Lusitania* torpedoed and sunk by German submarine.	1,198
Jan. 30, 1945	Baltic Sea	Liner *Wilhelm Gustloff* carrying German refugees and soldiers sunk by Soviet sub. Highest death toll for a single ship.	6,000-7,000
Aug. 12, 2000	Barents Sea	Explosions sank Russian submarine *Kursk*; multiple rescue attempts failed.	118
Sept. 26, 2002	Atlantic Ocean near The Gambia	Senegalese ferry capsized.	1,863
Feb. 3, 2006	Red Sea	Egyptian ferry returning from Saudi Arabia sank after fire broke out onboard.	1,000+

Other Disasters

Date	Location	What Happened?	Deaths
Aug. 1931	China	Vast flooding on the Huang He River. Highest known death toll from a flood.	3,700,000
1984	Africa (chiefly Ethiopia)	Several years of severe drought caused one of the worst modern famines.	800,000+
April 1986	Chernobyl, USSR (now Ukraine)	Explosions at a nuclear power plant leaked radioactive material. 135,000 people were exposed to harmful levels of radiation.	31+
Summer 2003	Europe	A severe summer heat wave swept across Europe. More than 14,000 died in France alone.	35,000
Feb. 2006	The Philippines	Landslide on Leyte Island buries a village.	1,000

did you know?

One of the worst snowstorms in U.S. history happened March 11-14, 1888, just a week before the first day of spring. Much of the northeastern U.S. was buried in up to four feet of snow, with towering snowdrifts up to 30 feet high! At least 400 people died in the "Great White Hurricane," many of them in New York City. People were stranded by blocked streets, huge drifts, and powerless streetcars. There was no way to bring food or supplies into the city.

ENVIRONMENT

What is a non-renewable energy source? ➡ page 73

HOME SWEET BIOME

A "biome" is a large natural area that is home to certain types of plants. The animals, climate, soil, and even the amount of water in the region also help distinguish a biome. There are more than 30 kinds of biomes in the world. But the following types cover most of Earth's surface.

Forests

Forests cover about one-third of Earth's land surface. Pines, hemlocks, firs, and spruces grow in the cool **evergreen forests** farthest from the equator. These trees are called **conifers** because they produce cones.

Temperate forests have warm, rainy summers and cold, snowy winters. Here **deciduous trees** (which lose their leaves in the fall and grow new ones in the spring) join the evergreens. Temperate forests are home to maple, oak, beech, and poplar trees, and to wildflowers and shrubs. These forests are found in the eastern United States, southeastern Canada, northern Europe and Asia, and southern Australia.

Still closer to the equator are the **tropical rain forests**, home to the greatest variety of plants on Earth. About 60 to 100 inches of rain fall each year. Tropical trees stay green all year. They grow close together, shading the ground. There are several layers of trees. The top, **emergent layer** has trees that can reach 200 feet in height. The **canopy**, which gets lots of sun, comes next, followed by the **understory**. The **forest floor**, covered with roots, gets little sun. Many plants cannot grow there.

Tropical rain forests are found mainly in Central America, South America, Asia, and Africa. They once covered more than 8 million square miles. Today, because of

destruction by humans, fewer than 3.4 million square miles of rain forest remain. More than half the plant and animal species in the world live there. Foods such as bananas and pineapples first grew there. Many kinds of plants from rain forests are used to make medicines.

When rain forests are burned, carbon dioxide is released into the air. This adds to the **greenhouse effect** (see page 70). As forests are destroyed, the precious soil is easily washed away by the heavy rains.

Emergent Layer

Canopy

Understory

Forest Floor

Tundra & Alpine Region

In the northernmost regions of North America, Europe, and Asia surrounding the Arctic Ocean are plains called the **tundra**. The temperature rarely rises above 45°F, and it is too cold for trees to grow there. Water in the ground freezes the soil solid (permafrost) so plant and tree roots can't dig down. Most tundra plants are mosses and lichens without roots. In some areas, the soil thaws for about two months each year. This may allow wildflowers or small shrubs to grow. This kind of climate and plant life also exists along the edges of Antarctica and in the **alpine** regions, on top of the world's highest mountains (such as the Himalayas, Alps, Andes, and Rockies), where small plants also grow.

What Is the Tree Line? On mountains in the north (such as the Rockies) and in the far south (such as the Andes), there is an altitude above which trees will not grow. This is the **tree line** or **timberline**. Above the tree line, you can see low shrubs and small plants.

Deserts

The driest areas of the world are the **deserts**. Hot or cold (Antarctica has desert), they receive less than 10 inches of rain in a year. Many contain an amazing number of plants that store water in thick bodies or roots deep underground. Rain can spur fields of wildflowers to spontaneously bloom. Shrubby sagebrush and spiny cacti are native to dry regions of North and South America. Prickly pear, barrel, and saguaro cacti can be found in the southwestern United States. African and Asian deserts contain shrubs called euphorbias. Date palms grow in desert oases of the Middle East and North Africa.

Red Rock Canyon, Nevada

Prairie in Indiana

Grasslands

Areas that are too dry to have green forests, but not dry enough to be deserts, are called **grasslands**. The most common plants found there are grasses. Cooler grasslands are found in the Great Plains of the United States and Canada, in the steppes of Europe and Asia, and in the pampas of Argentina. The drier grasslands are used for grazing cattle and sheep. In the **prairies**, there is a little more rain. Wheat, rye, oats, and barley are grown there. The warmer grasslands, called **savannas**, are found in central and southern Africa, Venezuela, southern Brazil, and Australia. Most savannas have moist summers and cool, dry winters.

Oceans

Covering two-thirds of the earth, the **ocean** is by far the largest biome. Within the ocean are smaller biomes that include **coastal areas**, **tidal zones**, and **coral reefs**. Reefs are found in relatively shallow warm waters. Like tropical rain forests, reefs are home to thousands of species of plant and animal life. Australia's Great Barrier Reef is the largest in the world.

The Great Barrier Reef, Australia

WATER, WATER *EVERYWHERE*

Earth is the water planet. More than two-thirds of its surface is covered with water, and every living thing on it needs water to live. Scientists looking for life on other planets start by looking for water. Water is not only part of our daily life (drinking, cooking, cleaning, bathing); it makes up 75% of our brains and 60% of our whole bodies! Humans can survive for about a month without food, but only for about a week without water. People also use water to cool machines in factories, to produce power, and to irrigate farmland.

HOW MUCH IS THERE TO DRINK?

Seawater makes up 97% of the world's water. Another 2% of the water is frozen in ice caps, icebergs, glaciers, and sea ice. Half of the 1% left is too far underground to be reached. That leaves only 0.5% of freshwater for all the people, plants, and animals on Earth. This supply is renewable only by rainfall.

WHERE DOES DRINKING WATER COME FROM?

Most smaller cities and towns get their freshwater from **groundwater**—melted snow and rain that seeps deep into the ground and is drawn out from wells. Larger cities usually rely on lakes or reservoirs for their water. Some areas of the world with little fresh water have turned to a process called desalination (removing salt from seawater) as a solution. But this process is slow and expensive.

THE HYDROLOGICAL CYCLE: Water's Endless Journey

Water is special. It's the only thing on Earth that exists naturally in **all three physical states**: solid (ice), liquid, and gas (water vapor). It never boils naturally (except around volcanoes), but it evaporates (turns into a gas) easily into the air. These unique properties send water on a cycle of repeating events.

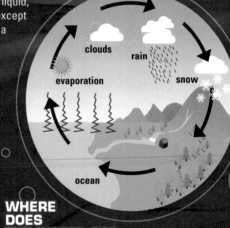

HOW DOES WATER GET INTO THE AIR?

Heat from the sun causes surface water in oceans, lakes, swamps, and rivers to turn into water vapor. This is called **evaporation**. Plants release water vapor into the air as part of the process called **transpiration**. Animals also release a little bit when they breathe.

HOW DOES WATER COME OUT OF THE AIR?

Warm air holds more water vapor than cold air. As the air rises into the atmosphere, it cools and the water vapor **condenses**—changes back into tiny water droplets. These droplets form clouds. As the drops get bigger, gravity pulls them down as **precipitation** (rain, snow, sleet, fog, and dew are all types of precipitation).

WHERE DOES THE WATER GO?

Depending on where the precipitation lands, it can: **1.** evaporate back into the atmosphere, **2.** run off into streams and rivers, **3.** be absorbed by plants, **4.** soak down into the soil as groundwater, or **5.** fall as snow on a glacier and be trapped as ice for thousands of years.

1970s:
DISCO DAYS

Women: Girls were "staying alive" in "hot pants," polyester pantsuits, bell-bottoms, and platform shoes.
Men: "Mr. Disco" wore polyester bell-bottoms, brightly colored shirts, and gold chains on the dance floor.

1990s:
ANYTHING GOES

Women: Dr. Martens big black boots, hooded sweatshirts, and layered T-shirts for the neo-hippie chick.
Men: "Grungy" guys kept themselves warm in lumberjack flannels and their money secure with trucker chain wallets. The "hip-hoppers," on the other hand, warmed up in puffy athletic jackets and sneakers.

2000s:
HIP-HOP STYLE

Women: Girls hang out in low-rise jeans, tight T-shirts with bare midriffs, and bell-bottoms. Peasant tops and chunky necklaces are also trendy.

Men: Guys keep a beat in baggy jeans, gold chains, and athletic gear.

did you know?

Denim fabric is "mad" popular in America. But at first, it was actually a French product, produced in a town called Nimes. It was popularized in America when Levi Strauss patented the first pair of blue jeans in 1873.

Fashion
AROUND THE WORLD

TOGAS

A toga is a robe that is draped and wrapped around one's body. The toga was worn by government officials in ancient Rome until about 100 A.D. Only men wore togas. Women wore a dress-like outfit called a stola. During winter, some Romans wore leggings to stay warm. There were many different styles of togas, but most were made from white wool. When Emperors passed laws requiring togas to be worn, they became a symbol of Roman citizenship. If a person was banished from the Roman Empire, he had to leave his toga behind.

KILTS

Although both Ireland and England also claim the kilt, it originated in Scotland as early as the 10th century. Traditionally worn by men, the multi-colored pattern on a kilt can identify the clan, or family, of the wearer. The original kilt was called a *feileadh mhor* (philamore), or "big wrap." Held at the waist by a leather belt, the usually woolen wrap was worn around the waist and over one shoulder, leaving the other arm free to carry a sword.

WIGS

People were wearing wigs as long ago as 3500 B.C. In ancient Egypt, people wore wigs made from vegetable matter and human hair to protect their heads from the sun. Wigs were common in Greek and Chinese theater, and were worn in ancient Roman, Assyrian, and Phoenician cultures. In Europe during the 16th and 17th centuries, wigs were associated with royalty or high fashion. Today, people wear wigs for fashion, convenience, or religious observance.

did you know?

What Not to Wear *A sumptuary law is a law that applies to personal habits, including dress. Laws passed in Rome in 216 B.C. limited women to wearing no more than half an ounce of gold. Later, laws were passed that forbade men to wear silk. Around 1300 A.D. these kinds of laws were made in Europe. In Florence, people were not allowed to wear anything red or made from silk. In England, only knights were allowed to wear fur and only the royal family could wear purple. During the 16th century, French and English rulers often made these laws for religious or moral reasons. Sumptuary laws passed in colonial America in 1651 forbade colonists to wear gold, silk, lace, silver, or hats made from beaver fur.*

KIMONOS

Robes were first worn in Japan around 300 A.D. It was popular during the Heian period, around 800, for Japanese women to wear many layers of robes. Royalty wore up to 16 layers! The original Japanese word for clothing, *kimono*, stuck with the fashion. During the 15th century, warriors wore kimonos to represent their leader. Today they are worn for traditional festivals and special events, including weddings. A bridal kimono is called a *shiro-muku*.

VEILS

The tradition of covering one's face or head with a veil was practiced more than 5,000 years ago in the ancient kingdom of Sumeria, the modern-day Middle East. Veils were worn to protect the face from desert wind. But some veils revealed the origin, tribe, or even skills of a person. In this tradition, men of the northern African Tuareg tribe wear veils today as a status symbol, even as they eat and drink!

As early as the 1st century, some Hindu women wore veils to show modesty, as many Muslim women all over the world do today. A *hijab* is the most popular form of headscarf worn by Muslim women, and is not particular to a certain color or country. The *chador* is a long black shawl that covers the entire body and head. It is typically worn in Iran. The *burqa* is a robe that covers the entire body and face, and is worn mostly in Afghanistan.

The veil has made many appearances in Western history as well. In medieval Europe, women wore chest-length veils called wimples. Today veils are worn in Western cultures for weddings, mourning, and religious ceremonies.

MATCHING GAME

TRADITIONAL CLOTHING	COUNTRY OF ORIGIN
Lederhosen (short pants with suspenders)	Uganda
Pien-fu (2-piece robe)	Chile
Kikoi (sarong-type skirt)	China
Chamanto (knee-length poncho)	Germany
Kamiks (watertight boots)	Morocco
Kaftan (belted shirt-dress)	Arctic Inuit people

ANSWERS ON PAGES 334-337. FOR MORE PUZZLES GO TO WWW.WAFORKIDS.COM

TIMELESS TOYS

One of the most popular toys in history, the **Barbie Doll** was "born" in 1959. Created by Mattel, Inc., founders Ruth and Elliot Handler, the doll was named after their daughter Barbie. Ken, named after their son, appeared in 1961.

PLAY-DOH® compound was introduced in 1956. Made from a combination of salt, water, flour, and other secret ingredients, it was only available in off-white when it first came out. Today, it comes in 50 colors. Since it was invented, more than 700 million pounds of the stuff has been made.

Lincoln Logs were invented in 1916, by John Wright, son of architect Frank Lloyd Wright. He got the idea while watching his father design an earthquake-proof building in Japan. More than 100 million Lincoln Log sets have been sold since then.

Edwin Binney and C. Harold their first box of **Crayola c** 1903. There were 8 colors— 120 today. The Crayola facto Pennsylvania, now turns out billion crayons each year.

Plastic **LEGO** bricks were i Denmark by Ole Kirk Christi The company, whose name Danish words "LEg GOdt" (p since made more than 206 b Imagine if you had to clean your room.

Other Classic Toys

• Teddy Bear	• 1902
• Yo-Yo	• 1929
• Silly Putty®	• 1949
• Etch A Sketch®	• 1960

WAforKids.com

Go to **www.WAforKids.com** for these activities:

- Puzzle out dozens of World Almanac for Kids games, both online and to-print pages.
- Take quizzes on fun topics like weird food around the world, sports, a

Samorost 2

VIDEO GAME TIME LINE

1962	Spacewar, played on an early microcomputer, is the first fully interactive video game.
1974	Atari's Pong, one of the first home video games, has "paddles" to hit a white dot back and forth on-screen.
1980	Pac-Man, Space Invaders, and Asteroids (first to let high scorers enter initials) invade arcades.
1985	Nintendo Entertainment System comes to the U.S. Super Mario Bros. is a huge hit!
1987	Legend of Zelda game released.
1989	Nintendo's handheld video game system, Game Boy, debuts.
1996	Nintendo 64 is released.
2000	Sony's PlayStation 2 arrives.
2001	Microsoft's Xbox and Nintendo's GameCube hit the shelves.
2005	Sony's PSP, a new handheld video game system, goes on sale.
2006	Nintendo Wii, which features a wand-like controller, is released.

WEB CONNECT:
⑩ CAN'T MISS INTERNET GAMES

There are tons of great games that can be played on the internet. And most are free. Here are 10 that every kid should check out.

Battleships A computerized version of the board game Battleship. (www.miniclip.com/games/battleships/en/)

Bookworm Deluxe Find words in a jumble, but watch out for flaming blocks that can set fire to your library. (www.popcap.com/gamepopup.php?theGame=bookworm)

Hypervelocity Racer Drive a race car and avoid potholes and other race cars. (www.surfnetkids.com/games/hypervelocity_racing.htm)

Matchsticks You may have played this one in real life. Remove sticks to create shapes. (www.surfnetkids.com/games/matchsticks.htm)

Papa Louie Deliver pizzas while battling pizza monsters. (www.miniclip.com/games/papa-louie/en/)

Planetary Rescue Squad Use physics to deliver supplies to space explorers. (pbskids.org/dragonflytv/games/game_planetary.html)

Samorost All you have to do is click on the objects in the correct order to solve each puzzle. (www.samorost.net/samorost1)

3 Puck Chuck Sort of like a pool table with air hockey pucks instead of balls. (pbskids.org/zoom/games/3puckchuck/)

Viking Quest Construct a Viking boat, hire a crew, and raid England. (www.bbc.co.uk/history/ancient/vikings/launch_gms_viking_quest.shtml)

Whizzball A puzzle game where you have to get a marble to hit its target. You can also build puzzles for others to try. (kids.discovery.com/games/whizzball/whizzball.html)

TAKE A "CHANCE":
UNDERSTANDING PROBABILITY

Probability can be a fun subject, and it may be a little more fun and easier to learn about if you think of it in terms of the dice you play games with.

A single die has six different faces, numbered 1 through 6. Each has an equal chance of coming up. So the chance, or **probability,** of rolling any one of the numbers with one die is one in six. We write this as the ratio or fraction 1/6 because there are six possible **outcomes.**

What if you roll two dice? There are 36 possible outcomes, because each die can come out one of six ways: 6 x 6 = 36. The lowest possible outcome would be 2 (a 1 on each die). The highest possible outcome would be 12 (a 6 on each die).

With two dice, some totals are more likely to come up than others. Pretend one die is red and the other is blue. The only way to roll a total of 2 (called "snake eyes") is for the red die to come up as a 1 and the blue die to come up as a 1. So the probability of shaking 2 is 1 in 36 (1/36). But there are two ways to shake a 3. The red die could have a 1 and the blue die could have a 2, or the red die could be a 2 and the blue die could be a 1. So the probability of shaking a 3 is 2 in 36 (2/36, which equals 1/18).

The total that has the highest probability of coming up is 7. The red die can be any of the numbers from 1 to 6, and the blue die can be the number that makes seven when added to the number on the red die (1 and 6, 2 and 5, 3 and 4, 4 and 3, 5 and 2, 6 and 1). Because there are six possible combinations to total 7, the chances of rolling a 7 are 6 in 36 (6/36, which equals 1/6, or one out of six).

Look below for your chances of shaking each total with two dice.

2	*1 in 36*
3	*2 in 36*
4	*3 in 36*
5	*4 in 36*
6	*5 in 36*
7	*6 in 36*
8	*5 in 36*
9	*4 in 36*
10	*3 in 36*
11	*2 in 36*
12	*1 in 36*

WHAT ARE THE CHANCES?

With dice, as described above, there are only a limited number of options for an end result. With humans, things are a little more complicated. For example, how likely is it that a high school athlete will turn pro? First, you take the number of high school kids who play sports (about 8,548,100). Then, you take the number of new job openings for professional athletes each year (about 3,500). Divide the first number by the second number, and then you have your chances—one out of 2,442. Here are some other chances:

• Two people in a group of 23 have the same birthday, 1 in 2

• Your friend's favorite ice cream flavor is vanilla, 1 in 3

• You'll catch a baseball at a Major League Baseball game: 1 in 563

• A person will be struck by lightning in their lifetime, 1 in 5,000

• A person auditioning will win American Idol, 1 in 100,000

• You'll be dealt a royal flush in poker: 1 in 649,739

• A person in the U.S. will be killed while riding in a streetcar, 1 in 1,874,034

• You'll become president of the U.S., 1 in 15,000,000

• A meteor will land on your house: 1 in 182,000,000,000,000

HOW TO PLAY:
A FEW FUN PRACTICAL JOKES

GUMMY GROSS-OUT

Chew a piece of gum, and then spit it into your hand. Then, walk over to two or more friends who are talking to each other. Put your hand wherever a litterer might stick gum—under a table or chair, or even on the side of a garbage can. Keep your gum clean inside your hand. Pull your hand back, and look excited to have "found" a piece of gum. Pop it in your mouth and smile! The key is to look like you have no idea anyone is watching. If someone sees you and looks grossed out, try to look embarrassed to complete the joke.

SHORT SHEETING

This is a classic prank. It's perfect for playing on a sibling, during a sleepover party, or on a bunkmate at camp. Tuck one end of the top sheet under the top of the mattress. Then, fold the sheet in half, pull up the blanket over the sheet, and pull the top layer of the sheet over the blanket. When your sibling or friend tries to get into bed, he or she will be confused about why the sheet is only half as long as it should be, and it's impossible to get inside the covers. Ideally, make sure the lights are off before the person crawls in bed.

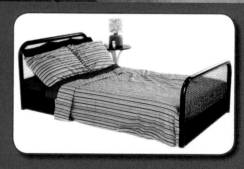

MADE YOU LOOK!

This one usually only works once with each person. Go up to a friend or family member and strike up a normal conversation. Keep looking over the person's shoulder when he or she talks to you. Even get up on your tip-toes to peer behind the person. Make worried expressions with your face. When the person finally turns around and looks, say the classic words—"Made you look!"

IT TASTED GOOD AT FIRST

Tired of your brother or sister asking you to bring them snacks while he or she watches TV? Next time, have an adult help you slice up an onion into very small pieces. Discretely slip the onion into your sibling's favorite snack. (For example, if it's a cupcake, push the onion into the frosting and hide it.) Because your sibling won't be expecting it, he or she won't know what hit them, and the facial expressions as he or she tries to figure out the unknown taste will be hilarious.

GEOGRAPHY

Who was the first woman to reach the North Pole by dogsled?

➡ page 87

SIZING UP THE EARTH

The word "geography" comes from the Greek word *geographia*, meaning "writing about the Earth." It was first used by the Greek scholar Eratosthenes, who was head of the great library of Alexandria in Egypt. Around 230 B.C., when many people believed the world was flat, he did a remarkable thing. He calculated the circumference of the Earth. His figure of about 25,000 miles was close to the modern measurement of 24,901 miles!

Actually, the Earth is not perfectly round. It's flatter at the poles and bulges out a little at the middle. This bulge around the equator is due to centrifugal force from the Earth's rotation. ("Centrifugal" means "moving away from the center." Think of how a merry-go-round pushes you to the outside as it spins.) The Earth's diameter is 7,926 miles at the equator, but only 7,900 miles from North Pole to South Pole. The total surface area of the Earth is 196,940,000 square miles.

GEOGRAPHY 1 2 3

Longest Rivers
1. Nile (Egypt and Sudan)—4,160 miles
2. Amazon (Brazil and Peru)—4,000 miles
3. Chang (China)—3,964 miles (formerly called the Yangtze)

Tallest Mountains
1. Mount Everest (Tibet and Nepal)—29,035 feet
2. K2 (Kashmir)—28,250 feet
3. Kanchenjunga (India and Nepal)—28,208 feet

Biggest Islands
1. Greenland (Atlantic Ocean)—840,000 square miles
2. New Guinea (Pacific Ocean)—306,000 square miles
3. Borneo (Pacific Ocean)—280,100 square miles

Biggest Desert Regions
1. Sahara Desert (North Africa)—3.5 million square miles
2. Australian Deserts—1.3 million square miles
3. Arabian Peninsula—1 million square miles

Biggest Lakes
1. Caspian Sea (Europe and Asia)—143,244 square miles
2. Superior (U.S. and Canada)—31,700 square miles
3. Victoria (Kenya, Tanzania, Uganda)—26,828 square miles

Highest Waterfalls
1. Angel Falls (Venezuela)—3,212 feet
2. Tugela Falls (South Africa)—2,800 feet
3. Monge Falls (Norway)—2,540 feet

READING A MAP

▶ **DIRECTION** Maps usually have a compass rose that shows you which way is north. On most maps, like this one, it's straight up. The compass rose on this map is in the upper left corner.

▶ **DISTANCE** Of course the distances on a map are much shorter than the distances in the real world. The scale shows you how to estimate the real distance. This map's scale is in the lower left corner.

▶ **PICTURES** Maps usually have little pictures or symbols to represent real things like roads, towns, airports, or other points of interest. The map legend (or key) tells what they mean.

▶ **FINDING PLACES** Rather than use latitude and longitude to locate features, many maps, like this one, use a grid system with numbers on one side and letters on another. An index, listing place names in alphabetical order, gives a letter and a number for each. The letter and number tell you in which square to look for a place on the map's grid. For example, Landisville can be found at A-1 on this map.

▶ **Using the map** People use maps to help them travel from one place to another. What if you lived in Mountville and wanted to go to the GeoNova office? First, locate the two places on the map. Mountville is in A-3, and GeoNova is in D-1. Next, look at the roads that connect them and decide on the best route. (There could be several different ways to go.) One way is to travel east on Route 462, take a left onto Route 741, turn right onto Route 722, and then turn left onto highway 501.

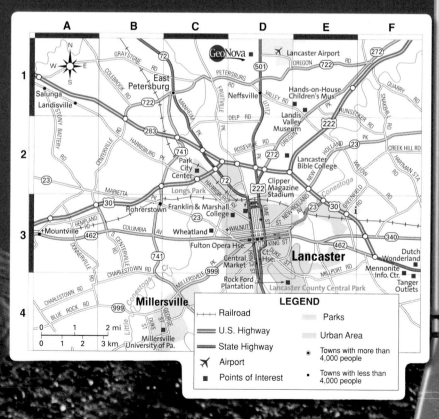

Early Exploration

AROUND 1000	**Leif Ericson**, from Iceland, explored "Vinland," which may have been the coasts of northeast Canada and New England.
1271-95	**Marco Polo** (Italian) traveled through Central Asia, India, China, and Indonesia.
1488	**Bartolomeu Dias** (Portuguese) explored the Cape of Good Hope in southern Africa.
1492-1504	**Christopher Columbus** (Italian) sailed four times from Spain to America and started colonies there.
1497-98	**Vasco da Gama** (Portuguese) sailed farther than Dias, around the Cape of Good Hope to East Africa and India.
1513	**Juan Ponce de León** (Spanish) explored and named Florida.
1513	**Vasco Núñez de Balboa** (Spanish) explored Panama and reached the Pacific Ocean.
1519-21	**Ferdinand Magellan** (Portuguese) sailed from Spain around the tip of South America and across the Pacific Ocean to the Philippines, where he died. His expedition continued around the world.
1519-36	**Hernando Cortés** (Spanish) conquered Mexico, traveling as far west as Baja California.
1527-42	**Alvar Núñez Cabeza de Vaca** (Spanish) explored the southwestern United States, Brazil, and Paraguay.
1532-35	**Francisco Pizarro** (Spanish) explored the west coast of South America and conquered Peru.
1534-36	**Jacques Cartier** (French) sailed up the St. Lawrence River to the site of present-day Montreal.
1539-42	**Hernando de Soto** (Spanish) explored the southeastern United States and the lower Mississippi Valley.
1603-13	**Samuel de Champlain** (French) traced the course of the St. Lawrence River and explored the northeastern United States.
1609-10	**Henry Hudson** (English), sailing from Holland, explored the Hudson River, Hudson Bay, and Hudson Strait.
1682	**Robert Cavelier, sieur de La Salle** (French), traced the Mississippi River to its mouth in the Gulf of Mexico.
1768-78	**James Cook** (English) charted the world's major bodies of water and explored Hawaii and Antarctica.
1804-06	**Meriwether Lewis and William Clark** (American) traveled from St. Louis along the Missouri and Columbia rivers to the Pacific Ocean and back.
1849-59	**David Livingstone** (Scottish) explored Southern Africa, including the Zambezi River and Victoria Falls.

SOME FAMOUS EXPLORERS

These explorers, and many others, risked their lives on trips to explore faraway and often unknown places. Some sought fame. Some sought fortune. Some just sought challenge. All of them increased people's knowledge of the world.

MARCO POLO (1254?-1324),
Italian traveler who journeyed by land all the way to China and back. He worked for the Chinese emperor Kublai Khan and even governed a Chinese city. For a long time his writings were the only knowledge people in Europe had about the Far East.

CHRISTOPHER COLUMBUS (1451-1506),
Italian navigator who sailed for Spain. He had hoped to find a fast route to Asia by going west from Europe. Instead he became the first European (other than the Vikings) to reach America, landing in the Bahamas in October 1492.

FERDINAND MAGELLAN (1480-1521),
Portuguese navigator and explorer who set sail from Spain in 1519, seeking a western route to the Spice Islands of Indonesia. He became the first European to cross the Pacific Ocean, but was killed by natives in the Philippines. However, because he passed the easternmost point he had reached on an earlier voyage, he is recognized as the first person to circumnavigate the Earth.

MERIWETHER LEWIS (1774-1809) and WILLIAM CLARK (1770-1838),
American soldiers and explorers. In 1804-06 they led an expedition 8,000 miles across the wilderness of the American West and back, gaining detailed knowledge of the huge Louisiana Territory that the United States had bought from France.

MATTHEW HENSON (1866-1955),
the first famous African American explorer. Hired as an assistant to explorer Robert Peary (1856-1920), he traveled on seven expeditions to Greenland and the Arctic region. In April 1909, Peary and Henson became the first to reach, or nearly reach, the North Pole. (Recent research suggests they may have fallen short by about 30 to 60 miles.)

JACQUES COUSTEAU (1910-1997),
French undersea explorer and environmentalist. He helped invent the Aqualung, allowing divers to stay deep underwater for hours, and made award-winning films of what he found there.

ANN BANCROFT (1955-),
American educator and explorer. In 1986, she became the first woman to reach the North Pole by dogsled, and in 1992-93 was leader of the first all-woman expedition to reach the South Pole on skis.

Ann Bancroft and her partner Liv Arnesen

BENEDICT ALLEN (1960-),
British explorer. He has published nine books about his journeys, often alone and on foot, through some of the most remote and extreme environments on Earth. While studying the Niowra people of New Guinea, he participated in a secret ceremony that left many scars on his body.

 WEB SITE For a site about explorers with lots of useful links, try **www.kidinfo.com/American_History/Explorers.html**

LOOKING AT OUR WORLD

THINKING GLOBAL

Shaped like a ball or sphere, a globe is a model of our planet. Like Earth, it's not perfectly round. It is an oblate spheroid (called a "geoid") that bulges a little in the middle.

In 1569, Gerardus Mercator found a way to project the Earth's curved surface onto a flat map. One problem with a Mercator map (like the one on page 89) is that land closer to the poles appears bigger than it is. Australia looks smaller than Greenland on this type of map, but in reality it's not.

North Pole

North America

40 degrees north latitude

20 degrees north latitude

Africa

South America

Equator

20 degrees south latitude

40 degrees south latitude

South Pole

LATITUDE AND LONGITUDE

Imaginary lines that run east and west around Earth, parallel to the equator, are called **parallels**. They tell you the **latitude** of a place, or how far it is from the equator. The equator is at 0 degrees latitude. As you go farther north or south, the latitude increases. The North Pole is at 90 degrees **north latitude**. The South Pole is at 90 degrees **south latitude**.

Imaginary lines that run north and south around the globe, from one pole to the other, are called **meridians**. They tell you the degree of **longitude**, or how far east or west a place is from the prime meridian (0 degrees).

Which Hemispheres Do You Live In?

Draw an imaginary line around the middle of Earth. This is the **equator**. It splits Earth into two halves called **hemispheres**. The part north of the equator, including North America, is the **northern hemisphere**. The part south of the equator is the **southern hemisphere**.

An imaginary line called the **Greenwich meridian** or **prime meridian** divides Earth into east and west. It runs north and south around the globe, passing through the city of Greenwich in England. North and South America are in the **western hemisphere**. Africa, Asia, and most of Europe are in the **eastern hemisphere**.

THE TROPICS OF CANCER AND CAPRICORN

If you find the equator on a globe or map, you'll often see two dotted lines running parallel to it, one above and one below (see pages 145 and 154–155). The top one marks the Tropic of Cancer, an imaginary line marking the latitude (about 23°27' North) where the sun is directly overhead on June 21 or 22, the beginning of summer in the northern hemisphere.

Below the equator is the Tropic of Capricorn (about 23°27' South). This line marks the sun's path directly overhead at noon on December 21 or 22, the beginning of summer in the southern hemisphere. The area between these dotted lines is the tropics, where it is consistently hot because the sun's rays shine more directly than they do farther north or south.

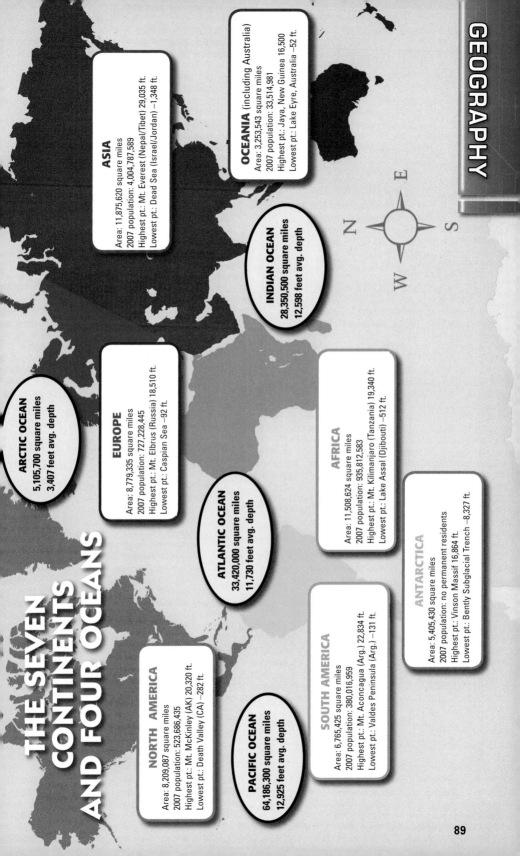

THE SEVEN CONTINENTS AND FOUR OCEANS

ASIA
Area: 11,875,620 square miles
2007 population: 4,004,787,589
Highest pt.: Mt. Everest (Nepal/Tibet) 29,035 ft.
Lowest pt.: Dead Sea (Israel/Jordan) –1,348 ft.

OCEANIA (including Australia)
Area: 3,253,543 square miles
2007 population: 33,514,981
Highest pt.: Jaya, New Guinea 16,500
Lowest pt.: Lake Eyre, Australia –52 ft.

INDIAN OCEAN
28,350,500 square miles
12,598 feet avg. depth

ARCTIC OCEAN
5,105,700 square miles
3,407 feet avg. depth

EUROPE
Area: 8,779,335 square miles
2007 population: 727,228,445
Highest pt.: Mt. Elbrus (Russia) 18,510 ft.
Lowest pt.: Caspian Sea –92 ft.

AFRICA
Area: 11,508,624 square miles
2007 population: 935,812,583
Highest pt.: Mt. Kilimanjaro (Tanzania) 19,340 ft.
Lowest pt.: Lake Assal (Djibouti) –512 ft.

ATLANTIC OCEAN
33,420,000 square miles
11,730 feet avg. depth

ANTARCTICA
Area: 5,405,430 square miles
2007 population: no permanent residents
Highest pt.: Vinson Massif 16,864 ft.
Lowest pt.: Bently Subglacial Trench –8,327 ft.

NORTH AMERICA
Area: 8,209,087 square miles
2007 population: 523,686,435
Highest pt.: Mt. McKinley (AK) 20,320 ft.
Lowest pt.: Death Valley (CA) –282 ft.

PACIFIC OCEAN
64,186,300 square miles
12,925 feet avg. depth

SOUTH AMERICA
Area: 6,765,425 square miles
2007 population: 380,016,959
Highest pt.: Mt. Aconcagua (Arg.) 22,834 ft.
Lowest pt.: Valdes Peninsula (Arg.) –131 ft.

N E W S

89

WHAT'S INSIDE THE EARTH?

Starting at the Earth's surface and going down you find the lithosphere, the mantle, and then the core.

The lithosphere, the rocky crust of the Earth, extends for about 60 miles.

The dense, heavy inner part of the Earth is divided into a thick shell, the mantle, surrounding an innermost sphere, the core. The mantle extends from the base of the crust to a depth of about 1,800 miles and is mostly solid.

Then there is the Earth's core. It has two parts: an inner sphere of scorchingly hot, solid iron almost as large as the moon and an outer region of molten iron. The inner core is much hotter than the outer core. The intense pressure near the center of Earth squeezes the iron in the inner core into a solid ball nearly as hot as the surface of the Sun. Scientists believe the core formed billions of years ago during the planet's fiery birth. Iron and other heavy elements sank into the planet's hot interior while the planet was still molten. As this metallic soup cooled over millions of years, crystals of iron hardened at the center.

In 1996, after nearly 30 years of research, it was found that, like the Earth itself, the inner core spins on an axis from west to east, but at its own rate, outpacing the Earth by about one degree per year.

lithosphere

mantle — about 1,800 miles

outer core — about 1,300 miles

core — about 1,500 miles

Homework Help

There are three types of rock:

1 IGNEOUS rocks form from underground magma (melted rock) that cools and becomes solid. Granite is an igneous rock made from quartz, feldspar, and mica.

2 SEDIMENTARY rocks form on low-lying land or the bottom of seas. Layers of small particles harden into rock such as limestone or shale over millions of years.

3 METAMORPHIC rocks are igneous or sedimentary rocks that have been changed by chemistry, heat, or pressure (or all three). Marble is a metamorphic rock formed from limestone.

CONTINENTAL DRIFT

The Earth didn't always look the way it does now. It was only in the early 20th century that a geologist named Alfred Lothar Wegener came up with the theory of continental drift. Wegener got the idea by looking at the matching rock formations on the west coast of Africa and the east coast of South America. He named the enormous first continent Pangaea. The continents are still moving, athough most move no faster than your fingernails grow.

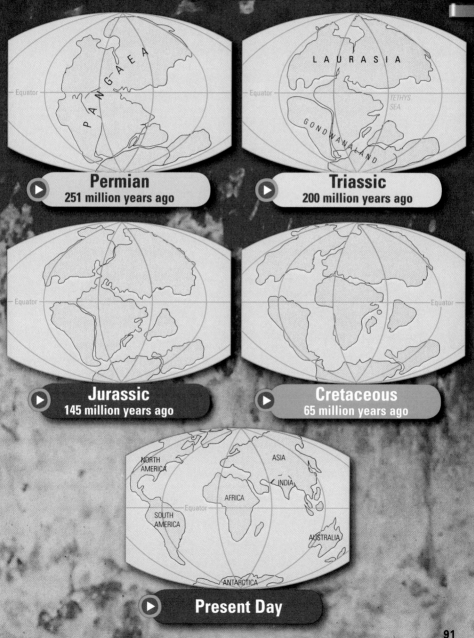

Permian
251 million years ago

Triassic
200 million years ago

Jurassic
145 million years ago

Cretaceous
65 million years ago

Present Day

91

HEALTH

How many minutes should you exercise every day? ➡ page 95

KIDS' HEALTH ISSUES

ALLERGIES

Our immune systems protect us from harmful substances. Certain people's immune systems, however, try to fight off even harmless substances. Common **allergens**—the substances people are allergic to—include pollen and peanuts. If a person inhales, eats, or touches an allergen, he or she might have an allergic reaction. The person might look as if he or she has a cold or have trouble breathing. In severe cases, a person can die from an allergic reaction.

Some people are born more likely to have an allergy. They can control it by taking medication or staying away from whatever they're allergic to. Sometimes kids outgrow their allergies.

Carly Roman has severe allergies. She had to drink a medicated shake as her only food for 8 weeks.

ASTHMA

Asthma is a condition that makes breathing difficult. Allergens, polluted air, vigorous exercise, or stress can trigger an asthma attack. When someone has an attack, his or her airways narrow and can't carry as much air to the lungs.

An asthma attack might last up to a few hours. After one attack, another might not occur until hours, days, or years later. Asthma can't be cured, but people can take medication to prevent it and to treat it. They can also avoid things that trigger an attack. About 9% of American kids, or 6.5 million, had asthma in 2005.

OBESITY

When people eat more calories than they burn off through exercise, their bodies store that extra energy as fat. In 2003-04, 17% of all kids in the U.S., or more than 12 million, were overweight.

Someone is considered overweight if his or her **body mass index (BMI)** is above a certain number. If a person's BMI is even higher, he or she is considered obese. To calculate your BMI, visit **WEB SITE** *apps.nccd.cdc.gov/dnpabmi.*

DIABETES

The body usually produces a hormone called **insulin**, which helps it absorb sugar for energy. People with type 1 diabetes produce little or no insulin. No one is sure why some people have it.

People who are overweight or obese may develop type 2 diabetes, which is more common in the U.S. People with type 2 diabetes don't respond to insulin the way they should. As a result, they're more likely to suffer a heart attack or stroke. People with type 2 diabetes must watch what they eat, lose weight, and be more active. If that doesn't help, people can inject insulin to manage their diabetes.

It's estimated that only about 0.22% of American youths under 20 have diabetes. But one in six overweight youths are at risk of developing diabetes.

NEW FOOD PYRAMID

To stay healthy, it is important to eat the right foods and to exercise. In 2005, the U.S. government designed a new food pyramid to help people track what they should eat. The pyramid recommends different amounts of food depending on age, gender, and activity level. The colored parts of the pyramid stand for different foods. The width of each part shows you about how much of that food you should be eating. The figure on the steps reminds you to be physically active.

GRAINS
Make half of the grains you eat whole, such as whole-grain bread, cereal, brown rice, and pasta.

VEGETABLES
Try more dark green and orange vegetables.

FRUITS
Choose from fresh, frozen, canned, or dried fruit.

OILS
Not a food group but essential for good health. Fish and nuts have oil. Corn and canola oils are good, too.

MILK
Get your calcium from low-fat or fat-free milk products.

MEAT & BEANS
Eat lean meats. Don't forget to try fish, beans, peas, and nuts.

MyPyramid.gov STEPS TO A HEALTHIER YOU

To figure out what you should be eating, based on your age, gender, and activity level, use the calculator online: **WEB SITE** *www.mypyramid.gov*

For example, an active girl between the ages of 9 and 13 should eat between 1,800 and 2,200 calories daily, including:

Fruits	1.5-2 cups	Meat & Beans	5-6 ounces
Vegetables	2.5-3 cups	Milk	3 cups
Grains	6-7 ounces	Oils	5-6 teaspoons

YOUR BODY
Know What Goes Into It
NUTRITION FACTS: KNOWING HOW TO READ THE LABEL

Every food product approved by the Food and Drug Administration (FDA), whether it's a can of soup or a bag of potato chips, has a label that describes the nutrients derived from that product. For instance, the chips label on this page shows the total calories, fat, cholesterol, sodium, carbohydrate, protein, and vitamin content per serving.

A serving size is always defined (here, it is about 12 chips or 28 grams). This label shows that there are 9 servings per container. Don't be fooled by the calorie count of 140–these are calories per serving and not per container. If you ate the entire chips bag, you would have eaten 1,260 calories!

Nutrition Facts

Serving Size 1 oz. (28g/About 12 chips)
Servings Per Container About 9

Amount Per Serving		
Calories 140	Calories from Fat 60	
		% Daily Value*
Total Fat 7g		**11%**
Saturated Fat 1g		**5%**
Trans Fat 0g		
Cholesterol 0mg		**0%**
Sodium 170mg		**7%**
Total Carbohydrate 18g		**6%**
Dietary Fiber 1g		**4%**
Sugars less than 1g		
Protein 2g		

Vitamin A 0%	•	Vitamin C 0%	
Calcium 2%	•	Iron 2%	
Vitamin E 4%	•	Thiamin 2%	
Riboflavin 2%	•	Vitamin B6 4%	
Phosphorus 6%	•	Magnesium 4%	

* Percent Daily Values are based on a 2,000 calorie diet. Your daily values may be higher or lower depending on your calorie needs:

	Calories:	2,000	2,500
Total Fat	Less than	65g	80g
Sat Fat	Less than	20g	25g
Cholesterol	Less than	300mg	300mg
Sodium	Less than	2,400mg	2,400mg
Total Carbohydrate		300g	375g
Dietary Fiber		25g	30g

Calories per gram:
Fat 9 • Carbohydrate 4 • Protein 4

Why You Need To Eat:

Fats are needed to help kids grow and to stay healthy. Fats contain nine calories per gram—the highest calorie count of any type of food. So you should limit (but not avoid) intake of fatty foods. Choose unsaturated fats, like the fat in nuts, over saturated fats and trans fats, like the fat in doughnuts.

Carbohydrates are a major source of energy for the body. Simple carbohydrates are found in white sugar, fruit, and milk. Complex carbohydrates, also called starches, are found in bread, pasta, and rice.

Cholesterol is a soft, fat-like substance produced by your body. It's also present in animal products such as meat, cheese, and eggs but not in plant products. Cholesterol helps with cell membrane and hormone production, but there are two main types. Bad cholesterol, or LDL, gets stuck easily in blood vessels, which can lead to a heart attack or stroke. Good cholesterol, or HDL, helps break down bad cholesterol.

Proteins help your body grow and make your immune system stronger. Lean meats and tofu are good options.

Vitamins and Minerals are good for all parts of your body. For example, vitamin A, found in carrots, promotes good vision; calcium, found in milk, helps build bones; and vitamin C, found in fruits, helps heal cuts.

SOME LOW-FAT FOODS

Bananas
Oatmeal
Plain popcorn
Apples
Sunflower seeds
Lentils

SOME FATTY FOODS

Ice cream
Cheeseburgers
Buttered popcorn
Chocolate candy
Potato chips

HAVE FUN GETTING FIT

Why Work Out?

In 2003-04, more than 12 million children in America, or 17% of kids, were considered overweight. Overweight kids run the risk of developing serious health problems including diabetes, asthma, and high blood pressure.

Exercise is a great way to prevent obesity and improve health. Children are urged to get at least 60 minutes of moderately intense exercise every day. Exercise can help reduce the risk of developing diseases like cancer or diabetes and also help build healthy bones, muscles, and joints.

HOW TO WORK OUT

Begin with a five-minute warm-up! Warm-up exercises heat the body up, so that muscles become soft, limber, and ready for more intense activity. Warm-up exercises include jumping jacks, walking, and stretching.

After warming up, do an activity that you like, such as running or playing basketball with your friends. This increases your heart rate.

After working out, cool down for 5 to 10 minutes. Cooling down is like a reverse warm-up. It lets your heart rate slow gradually. Walking is an example of a cool-down activity. Afterward, do some stretching. This helps your muscles remove waste, such as lactic acid, that your muscles make while exercising. Also remember to drink plenty of water during and after your exercise.

Building up strength through your workouts can be very beneficial. This doesn't mean you should lift the heaviest weights possible! It's better to do more lifts using light weights (1/2 lb or 1 lb) than fewer lifts with very heavy weights. Give your body time to recover between strength workouts.

Energy drinks may claim to boost your energy while supplying nutrients. The occasional energy drink won't hurt you, but keep in mind that one can contain as much caffeine as a cup of coffee. Caffeine can dehydrate you and keep you from getting enough sleep. Energy drinks also contain lots of sugar and calories.

ACTIVITY

	CALORIES PER MINUTE
Racquetball	10
Jogging (6 miles per hour)	8
Martial arts	8
Playing basketball	7
Playing soccer	6
Bicycling (10-12 miles per hour)	5
Raking the lawn	4
Skating or rollerblading (easy pace)	4
Swimming (25 yards per minute)	3
Walking (3 miles per hour)	3
Yoga	3
Playing catch	2

If you're interested in running, try **WEB SITE** *www.kidsrunning.com*
There you'll find advice, activities, stories, poems, and more—all about running.

BODY BASICS:

Your body is made up of many parts. Even though we are all individuals, our bodies share similar structures. These structures make up different systems in the body.

CIRCULATORY SYSTEM In the circulatory system, the **heart** pumps **blood**. Blood travels through tubes, called **arteries**, to all parts of the body. Blood carries oxygen and food that the body needs to stay alive. **Veins** carry blood back to the heart.

DIGESTIVE SYSTEM The digestive system moves food through the **esophagus**, **stomach**, and **intestines**. As food passes through, some of it is broken down into tiny particles called **nutrients**. Nutrients enter the bloodstream and are carried to all parts of the body. The digestive system changes whatever food isn't used into waste that is eliminated from the body.

ENDOCRINE SYSTEM

The endocrine system includes **glands**. There are two kinds of glands. **Exocrine** glands produce liquids such as sweat and saliva. **Endocrine** glands produce chemicals called **hormones**. Hormones control body functions like growth.

- Brain
- Trachea (windpipe)
- Esophagus
- Lungs
- Heart
- Liver
- Stomach
- Small intestine
- Large intestine

NERVOUS SYSTEM The nervous system enables us to think, feel, move, hear, and see. It includes the **brain**, the **spinal cord**, and **nerves** throughout the body. Nerves in the spinal cord carry signals between the brain and the rest of the body. The brain has three major parts. The **cerebrum** controls thinking, speech, and vision. The **cerebellum** is responsible for physical coordination. The **brain stem** controls the respiratory, circulatory, and digestive systems.

RESPIRATORY SYSTEM The respiratory system allows us to breathe. Air enters the body through the nose and mouth. It goes through the **windpipe**, or **trachea**, to two tubes called **bronchi**, which carry air to the **lungs**. Oxygen from the air is absorbed by tiny blood vessels in the lungs. The blood then carries oxygen to the heart, from where it is sent to the body's cells.

DO

MUSCULAR SYSTEM Muscles are made up of elastic fibers. There are three types of muscle: **skeletal**, **smooth**, and **cardiac**. Skeletal muscles help the body move—they are the large muscles we can see. Smooth muscles are found in our digestive system, blood vessels, and air passages. Cardiac muscle is found only in the heart. Smooth and cardiac muscles are **involuntary** muscles—they work without us having to think about them.

REPRODUCTIVE SYSTEM Through the reproductive system, adult human beings are able to create new human beings. Reproduction begins when a man's **sperm** cell fertilizes a woman's **egg** cell.

URINARY SYSTEM This system, which includes the **kidneys**, cleans waste from the blood and regulates the amount of water in the body.

IMMUNE SYSTEM The immune system protects your body from diseases by fighting against certain outside substances, or **antigens**. This happens in different ways. For example, white blood cells called **B lymphocytes** learn to fight viruses and bacteria by producing **antibodies** to attack them. Sometimes, as with **allergies**, the immune system makes a mistake and creates antibodies to fight a substance that's really harmless.

BRAIN DIAGRAM

The typical human brain only weighs about three pounds. But it's like the control center of the body, responsible for making sure everything functions properly. Different parts of the brain do different things.

Right hemisphere of cerebrum

- Controls left side of body
- Location of things relative to other things
- Recognizes faces
- Music
- Emotions

Left hemisphere of cerebrum

- Controls right side of body
- Ability to understand language and speech
- Ability to reason
- Numbers

Cerebrum

Cerebellum

Controls coordination, balance

Brain stem

Regulates vital activities like breathing and heart rate

THE FIVE SENSES

Your senses gather information about the world around you. The five senses are **hearing**, **sight**, **smell**, **taste**, and **touch**. You need senses to find food, resist heat or cold, and avoid situations that might be harmful. Your ears, eyes, nose, tongue, and skin sense changes in the environment. Nerve receptors send signals about these changes to the brain, where the information is processed.

HEARING

1

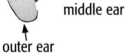

eardrum

inner ear

middle ear

outer ear

auditory nerve

The human ear is divided into three parts—the outer, middle, and inner. The **outer ear** is mainly the flap we can see on the outside. Its shape funnels sound waves into the **middle ear**, where the eardrum is located. The **eardrum** vibrates when sound waves hit it, causing three tiny bones behind it to vibrate as well. These vibrations are picked up in the **inner ear** by tiny filaments of the **auditory nerve**. This nerve changes the vibrations into nerve impulses and carries them to the brain.

did you know?

Our eyes contain two types of cells. Rods detect shape and movement and work better in low light. They are located at the edge of the retina. Cones detect color and detail and are densest in the center of the retina. At night, you can see stars more easily out of the corner of your eyes because your rods pick up the stars' dim light.

SIGHT

2

The **lens** of the eye is the first stop for light waves, which tell you the shapes and colors of things around you. The lens focuses light waves onto the **retina**, located on the back wall of the eye. The retina has light-sensitive nerve cells. These cells translate the light waves into patterns of nerve impulses that travel along the **optic nerve** to your brain, where an image is produced. So in reality, all the eye does is collect light. It is the brain that actually forms the image.

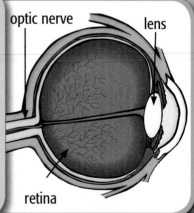

optic nerve

lens

retina

SMELL

3

In our noses are nerve cells called **olfactory receptors**. Tiny mucus-covered hairs from these receptors detect chemicals in the air. These chemicals make what we call odor, or scent. This information then travels along the **olfactory nerves** to the brain. Nerves from the olfactory receptors connect with the **limbic system**, the part of the brain that deals with emotions. That's why we tend to like or dislike a smell right away. The smell can leave a strong impression on our memory, and very often a smell triggers a particular memory.

TASTE

4

Taste buds are the primary receptors for taste. They are located on the surface and sides of the tongue, on the roof of the mouth, and at the back of the throat. These buds can detect four qualities—**sweet** (like sugar), **sour** (like lemons), **salty** (like chips), and **bitter** (like coffee). Taste signals come together with smell signals in the same part of your brain. That's why you need both senses to get a food's full flavor. If you've ever had a stuffed up nose, you may have noticed that you can only taste the four things that a tongue can pick up and nothing else.

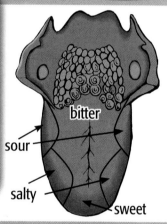

bitter
sour
salty
sweet

TOUCH

5

Your sense of touch allows you to feel temperature, pain, and pressure. These environmental factors are all sensed by nerve fibers located in the **epidermis**, the outer layer of skin, and the **dermis**, the second layer of skin, throughout the body. As with all the other senses, nerves send information to the brain through the nervous system.

HOLIDAYS

When is Be Late For Something Day? ➡ page 101

HOLIDAYS IN THE UNITED STATES

There are no official holidays for the whole U.S. But there are federal holidays, when workers for the federal government get the day off. Many offices, and most banks and schools, in the 50 states are closed on these days.

There are also other holidays that may not be an occasion for a day off from school but are enthusiastically celebrated. Holidays marked with a ▶ are federal holidays.

▶ **NEW YEAR'S DAY** The U.S. and most other countries celebrate the beginning of the new year on January 1.

▶ **MARTIN LUTHER KING JR. DAY** Observed on the third Monday in January, this holiday marks the birth (January 15, 1929) of the civil rights leader Rev. Dr. Martin Luther King Jr. In 2008, it will be celebrated on January 21.

VALENTINE'S DAY February 14 is a day for sending cards or gifts to people you love.

▶ **PRESIDENTS' DAY** On the third Monday in February (February 18, 2008), most states celebrate the births of both George Washington (born February 22, 1732) and Abraham Lincoln (born February 12, 1809).

MOTHER'S DAY Mothers are honored on the second Sunday in May (May 11, 2008).

▶ **MEMORIAL DAY/DECORATION DAY** The last Monday in May (May 26, 2008) is set aside to remember those who died serving in the military.

FATHER'S DAY Fathers are honored on the third Sunday in June (June 15, 2008).

▶ **FOURTH OF JULY/INDEPENDENCE DAY** July 4 is the anniversary of the 1776 signing of the Declaration of Independence.

▶ **LABOR DAY** Labor Day, the first Monday in September, honors American workers. It falls on September 3 in 2007 and September 1 in 2008.

▶ **COLUMBUS DAY** Celebrated on the second Monday in October, Columbus Day is the anniversary of October 12, 1492, the day Christopher Columbus was thought to have arrived in the Americas. It falls on October 8 in 2007 and October 13 in 2008.

HALLOWEEN In ancient Britain, Druids wore grotesque costumes to scare away evil spirits. Today while "trick-or-treating" on October 31, children ask for candy and gather money for UNICEF.

▶ **ELECTION DAY** The first Tuesday after the first Monday in November (November 6 in 2007 and November 4 in 2008), Election Day is a mandatory holiday in some states.

▶ **VETERANS DAY** Veterans Day, November 11, honors veterans of wars. It marks the anniversary of the armistice (agreement) that ended World War I.

▶ **THANKSGIVING** Thanksgiving was first observed by the Pilgrims in 1621 as a day for thanks and feasting. In 1863, Abraham Lincoln revived the tradition. It comes on the fourth Thursday in November—November 22 in 2007 and November 27 in 2008.

HANUKKAH This eight-day Jewish festival of lights begins on the evening of December 4 in 2007 and December 21 in 2008.

▶ **CHRISTMAS** Christmas is both a religious and a legal holiday celebrated on December 25.

KWANZAA This seven-day African-American festival begins on December 26. It celebrates seven virtues, such as self-determination.

ODD HOLIDAYS

You can ring in the New Year by observing **Belly Laugh Day** on January 24 or **Bubble Wrap® Appreciation Day** on January 22. Here are a few other odd "days" you've probably never heard of:

July 2007

- 2: I Forgot Day
- 15: National Ice Cream Day (a.k.a. Sundae Sunday)
- 24: National Drive-Thru Day
- 27: Walk on Stilts Day

August 2007

- 4: National Mustard Day
- 6: National Fresh Breath Day
- 8: National Underwear Day
- 25: Kiss-And-Make-Up Day

September 2007

- 5: Be Late For Something Day
- 15: International Eat an Apple Day
- 19: Talk Like a Pirate Day
- 24: National Punctuation Day

October 2007

- 1: World Vegetarian Day
- 10: International Top Spinning Day
- 15: National Grouch Day
- 31: National Knock-Knock Day

November 2007

- 4: Use Your Common Sense Day
- 15: I Love to Write Day
- 21: World Television Day
- 23: Buy Nothing Day

December 2007

- 9: National Day of the Horse
- 21: Underdog Day
- 26: National Whiners' Day
- 31: Make Up Your Mind Day

January 2008

- 8: Joygerm Day
- 16: Appreciate a Dragon Day
- 21: Squirrel Appreciation Day
- 23: National Handwriting Day

February 2008

- 1: Bubble Gum Day
- 2: National Wear Red Day
- 26: Spay Day USA
- 28: National Chili Day

March 2008

- 4: March Forth: Do Something Day
- 14: International Ask a Question Day
- 18: Awkward Moments Day
- 22: International Goof-Off Day

April 2008

- 10: National Siblings Day
- 11: Barbershop Quartet Day
- 17: National High Five Day
- 25: National Hairball Awareness Day

May 2008

- 1: Save the Rhino Day
- 4: International Respect for Chickens Day
- 16: International Sea Monkey Day
- 18: Visit Your Relatives Day

June 2008

- 1: Pen Pal Day
- 2: National Bubba Day
- 13: Blame Someone Else Day
- 28: National Handshake Day

CALENDAR BASICS

Holidays and calendars go hand in hand. Using a calendar, you can see what day of the week it is and watch out for the next special day. Calendars divide time into days, weeks, months, and years. According to our calendar, also known as the Gregorian calendar, a year is the time it takes for one revolution of Earth around the Sun: 365¼ days. To make things easier, we just add an extra day, February 29, in "leap years," which happen every 4 years.

THE NAMES OF THE MONTHS

January	named for the Roman god Janus, guardian of gates (often shown with two faces, looking backward and forward)
February	named for Februalia, a Roman time of sacrifice
March	named for Mars, the Roman god of war (the end of winter meant fighting could begin again)
April	"aperire," Latin for "to open," as in flower buds
May	named for Maia, the goddess of plant growth
June	"Junius," the Latin word for the goddess Juno
July	named after the Roman ruler Julius Caesar
August	named for Augustus, the first Roman emperor
September	"septem," the Latin word for seven (the Roman year began in March)
October	"octo," the Latin word for eight
November	"novem," the Latin word for nine
December	"decem," the Latin word for ten

Other Calendars

The **Gregorian calendar** is used by the U.S. and much of the rest of the world. But some nations and religions use other calendars. Many other calendars are called lunar calendars, which means they are based on the length of the moon's revolution around the Earth (which averages 29½ days) rather than the Earth's movement around the Sun. Even so, each lunar calendar is unique and reflects the culture to which it belongs.

Islamic Calendar The Islamic calendar is used by Muslim people around the world. Twelve lunar months, each beginning with the new moon, make up the year. The year is 354 days long (355 days in leap years). Year 1 of the Islamic calendar began in the Gregorian year 622, on the day after the flight of Muhammad from Mecca to Medina. Muharram 1 (New Year's Day) in Islamic year 1429 is estimated to fall on January 9, 2008.

Jewish Calendar The Jewish calendar has months of 29 and 30 days, and its years are either 12 or 13 months long. It is a lunar-solar calendar, which means its months are lunar, but its years adjust to the movement of the Earth around the Sun. It is the official calendar in Israel and is used as a religious calendar by Jewish people worldwide. Year 1 of the Jewish calendar year is the estimated date of creation as described in the Old Testament. Rosh Hashanah (New Year) in the year 5768 begins at sundown on September 12, 2007, on the Gregorian calendar.

Chinese Calendar The Chinese calendar is a lunar-solar calendar, similar to the Jewish calendar. But it has several important differences. The Chinese calendar runs on a 60-year cycle. Within the cycle, years are given one of twelve animal designations. For instance, if you were born between February 10, 1994, and January 29, 1995, you were born in the Year of the Dog.

HOW WE CELEBRATE

Every American family has different holiday traditions. Some may open presents on Christmas morning, others on Christmas Eve. Some may have lots of friends over for Passover Seder, while others may invite only family. Find out about a few of the ways holidays are celebrated in other cultures and countries.

Diwali

Hindus around the world celebrate Diwali, or the "Festival of Lights," in October or November. This five-day festival symbolizes the victory of good over evil. People light lamps (called deeps) inside and out, and watch huge fireworks displays. On the third day, relatives and friends visit each other for meals. Celebrations last well into the night. Some people gamble for hours—a tradition that has its origins in dice games played by Hindu gods.

Christmas

Traditions vary a great deal from country to country. For instance, in Southern Hemisphere nations, the holiday falls in the middle of the summer (so much for a "White Christmas!"). In fact, Bondi Beach in Sydney, Australia, hosts an annual turkey barbecue on Christmas, complete with a surfing Santa.

Ramadan

Ramadan is the ninth month of the Islamic calendar. It is believed that during Ramadan, Allah revealed the first verses of the Koran (the Islamic holy book) to Muhammad. During Ramadan, Muslims fast between sunrise and sunset. Usually children don't begin to fast until they are around the age of 12. In the evening, people visit mosques and recite prayers from the Koran, and also shop and watch television. Ramadan ends with the festival of Eid al-Fitr, when people eat large meals, visit friends and family, and give treats to children.

HOMEWORK HELP

What's the difference between "its" and "it's"? ➡ page 105

If you need to study for an exam or write a research paper, there are helpful hints in this chapter.

In other chapters, you can find lots of information on topics you may write about or study in school. **Facts About Nations,** pages 156-179, and **Facts About U.S. States,** pages 292-309, are good places to look. For math tips and formulas, look up the chapter on **Numbers**. For good books to read, and write about, see the **Books** chapter. Plus, there are many other study and learning tips throughout the book. Look for the **"Homework Help" icon!**

THOSE TRICKY TESTS

GETTING READY

Being prepared for a test can relieve some of your jitters and can make test taking a lot easier! Here are some tips to help you get ready.

▶ Take good notes in class and keep up with assignments, so you don't have to learn material at the last minute! Just writing down the notes helps you remember the information.

▶ Make a study schedule and stick to it! Don't watch TV or listen to distracting music while studying.

▶ Start reviewing early if you can—don't wait until the night before the test.

▶ Go over the headings, summaries, and questions in each chapter to review key points. Read your notes and highlight the most important topics.

▶ Take study breaks so you can concentrate and stay alert.

▶ Get a good night's sleep and eat a good breakfast before the test.

THE BIG EVENT

Follow these suggestions for smooth sailing during test time:

▶ Take a deep breath and relax! That will help calm your nerves.

▶ If you are allowed, skim through the entire exam so you know what to expect and how long it may take.

▶ As you start each part of the exam, read directions carefully.

▶ Read each question carefully before answering. For a multiple choice question, check every possible answer before you decide on one. The best answer could be the last one.

▶ Don't spend too much time on any one question. Skip hard questions and go back to them at the end.

▶ Keep track of time so you can pace yourself. Use any time left at the end to go back and review your answers. Make sure you've written the answer you meant to select.

GRAMMAR:
IT'S EASIER THAN YOU THINK

Here are a few rules to remember to help your writing.

Use a comma to show a pause—especially both before and after a group of words. This is called using paired commas. You should also use a comma after introductory words and phrases like "next" and "after a while."

▶ **RIGHT:** *My favorite aunt, Emily Jones, is an expert when it comes to using commas. The rules for good writing, I am afraid, are often hard to remember. After a while, I figured out the answer to the problem.*

Never let a sentence run on into another sentence without a period in between.

WRONG: *My teacher drives to school every day, she lives 12 miles away.*

▶ **RIGHT:** *My teacher drives to school every day. She lives 12 miles away.*

When a phrase at the beginning of a sentence has a verb form ending in -ing, make sure it does not refer to the wrong thing.

WRONG: *Walking into the cafeteria, my milk spilled onto the floor.*

▶ **RIGHT:** *Walking into the cafeteria, I spilled my milk onto the floor.* [Think about it... your milk wasn't walking into the cafeteria.]

Use the "subjective" form of personal pronouns (I, we, he, she, they) when something is the subject of a sentence. Use the "objective" [me, us, him, her, them] when it is the object of the sentence or of a preposition (like with or by).

WRONG: *Michael and me played basketball.* [You should use I, since it's the subject.]

WRONG: *Can you play with Ashley and I?* [You should use me since it's the object of the preposition with.]

Hint: Don't use myself in sentences like those two above. Never use myself when you could use me, or I, instead.

It's a Common Mistake. Unlike nearly all other possessive words, its does not use an apostrophe to show possession.

WRONG: *Every game has it's rules.*

▶ **RIGHT:** *Every game has its rules.*

Use an apostrophe for it's only when you mean it is, as in the heading above. If you keep on the lookout, you might find this mistake before long in something an adult has written.

IF NOTHING ELSE, REMEMBER THIS:

After you finish a writing assignment, look it over carefully. Be sure to read what is really on the paper and not what you think you wrote. Don't be surprised if you find some obvious mistakes—like a capital letter you forgot to use or a simple word that you misspelled. Even book editors have to check and re-check their work.

DIFFERENT TYPES OF NON-FICTION WRITING

There are four main types of paragraphs or essays you might be asked to write in school: **expository, narrative, descriptive, and persuasive.**

Expository

An expository paragraph "exposes" information about a subject. It is sometimes called an information paragraph because it gives information about a person, place, thing, or idea. Almost all of the writing in *The World Almanac for Kids* is expository. And most of the writing you do for school will be expository. Here are some expository writing suggestions:

- Write a summary of a book you have read.
- Compare and contrast Presidents George Washington and Abraham Lincoln.

transitional phrases help the paragraph hold together

Penguins

state the topic right away

details support the topic

Penguins star in the movies *March of the Penguins* and *Happy Feet*, but they're just as interesting when they aren't in the spotlight. Penguins are birds, but they are pretty different from most of the birds we see every day. For one thing, penguins can't fly, but their wings act as flippers when they swim in the ocean. Also, even though most birds breed in the spring, the Emperor penguin breeds in the winter. When warmer weather comes, the chicks are old enough to catch their own fish to eat. In conclusion, penguins may be birds, but some of their most interesting qualities aren't bird-like at all.

Narrative

A narrative paragraph tells a story about an event. You can find narrative writing in a newspaper report on a local event. Here are some narrative writing suggestions:

- Write an essay about a carnival or fair that you remember.
- Write a report about the last sports event you watched or attended.

use nouns, verbs, and adjectives to keep the action exciting

The Near-Death of Sally the Salamander

say what the event was right away

try to build suspense by telling the story with the most interesting details you can

Once, I almost killed a very cute salamander by accident. When I was nine, my brother and I were planting flowers by the creek near our house. I accidentally chopped off a salamander's leg with a shovel. Luckily, salamanders have the ability to regenerate parts of their bodies. I rescued the critter and named it Sally. I made Sally a home from an old hamster cage. I found bugs for her to eat. She was very quiet and never bothered me, but I could tell that she was restless. When her leg had re-grown, I took her back to the creek. Every time I go there now, I look for her to make sure she's in perfect health. But I'm afraid that all the salamanders look the same!

Descriptive

A descriptive paragraph describes a person, place, thing, or idea. It uses sensory detail to give the reader a better idea of what the topic is really like. This is the kind of writing you will see in books about travel, food, art, and celebrities. Here are some descriptive writing suggestions:

- Describe a job you might want to have as an adult, and why you'd be good for it.
- What is your favorite view (such as from your home or a park)? Why do you like it?

use your five senses to help the reader imagine what the thing is like

Thanksgiving: My Favorite Holiday

Thanksgiving is my favorite holiday because it satisfies all my senses: taste, smell, sight, sound and touch. I enjoy the feel of the hugs I get from my cousins, who I only see once a year. We love watching the Macy's Thanksgiving parade on television in the morning, and seeing the hundreds of colorful and elaborate floats. We also hear the fun songs of Broadway actors and popular singers. We love watching the football game, and throwing the ball ourselves outside. The food is my favorite part, though. When the electric knife starts to whir, my nose and mouth fill with the smell and taste of moist turkey, fluffy potatoes, cheesy vegetables, syrupy cranberries, and crunchy pecan pie.

name the thing you are describing right away

use many different details to paint a scene

Persuasive

A persuasive paragraph tries to convince the reader of the writer's point of view. It uses facts, statistics, details, and logic to make an argument. Here are some persuasive writing suggestions:

- Why do you need a cell phone?
- Should kids be allowed to vote for president? Why or why not?

connecting words help your ideas work together

My Vote for Our Next Field Trip: The Museum of Natural History

Our class should take a trip to the Museum of Natural History. The most important reason is that seeing artifacts from around the world is a lot more interesting than reading about them in a book. At the museum, there are life-size models, hands-on activities, and sometimes even movies to watch. In addition, if we took a trip to the museum, we would be motivated to prepare for it by learning about the things we will see. Another reason to go is that more than half of our class has never been to the museum. Many of those same students are the ones who find history class boring. This trip could change their minds.

state your opinion in the topic sentence

provide specific reasons for your point of view

HOW TO WRITE A
RESEARCH PAPER

Doing Research

To start any research paper or project, the first thing to do is research.

▶ **Encyclopedias are a good place to start.** They can give you a good overview of the subject.

▶ **The electronic catalog** of your school or town library will probably be your main source for finding books and articles about your subject. A librarian can help show you how this works.

▶ You can also use **the Internet** as a research tool (see opposite page).

▶ As you read each source, **write down the facts and ideas** that you may need. Include the title and author for each source and the page numbers for where you found the particular information. You might try using 3 x 5 index cards.

Writing It Down

The next step is to organize your facts. **Develop a rough outline** of your ideas in the order in which they'll appear. Then, write a draft of your paper. It should contain three main parts:

INTRODUCTION The introduction, or first paragraph, explains your topic and your point of view on it. It should draw readers into the paper and let them know what to expect.

BODY The body of the paper develops your ideas. Use specific facts, examples, and details to make your points clear and convincing. Use separate paragraphs for each new idea and use words and phrases that link one paragraph to the next so your ideas flow smoothly.

CONCLUSION Summarize your main points in the final paragraph, or conclusion.

Showing Your Sources

You may need to do a **bibliography** at the end of your paper. This is a list of all the sources you used to prepare the report.

FOR A BOOK: Author. *Title.* City Published: Publisher, Year.
>> Kwek, Karen. *Welcome to Chile.* Milwaukee, Wisc.: Gareth Stevens, 2004.

FOR A MAGAZINE ARTICLE: Author. "Article Title." *Magazine Title*, Date of Issue, Pages.
>> Swift, E.M. "One Big Headache." *Sports Illustrated*, Feb. 12, 2007, 22-23.

FOR ONLINE (INTERNET): Author(s). Name of Page [online]. Date of Posting/Revision. [cited year day month]. <URL>.
>> The World Almanac for Kids. Animals. [cited 2007 March 4]. <http://www.worldalmanacforkids.com/explore/animals.html>.

Hint: Avoid using the exact same wording as your source. If you do use an exact quote, refer to your source and use quotation marks.

RESEARCH ON THE INTERNET

Using Library Resources

Your school or public library is a great place to start. It probably has a list (catalog) of its books and periodicals (newspapers and magazines) available from computers at the library, or even from home over the Internet through your library's web site. You can search using **keywords** (words that describe your subject) in three basic ways: by **author**, by **title**, or by **subject**.

For example, doing a subject search for "Benjamin Franklin" will give you a list of books and articles about him, along with their locations in the library.

Your library may also subscribe to online reference databases that companies like The World Almanac create especially for research. These are accessible over the Internet and could contain almanacs, encyclopedias, other reference books, or collections of articles. You can access these databases from the library, and maybe even from home from your library's web site.

When you write your report, don't copy directly from books, articles, or the Internet—that's **plagiarism**, a form of cheating. Keep track of all your **sources**— the books, articles, and web sites you use—and list them in a **bibliography**. (See page 108 for some examples.)

Why shouldn't I just search the Internet?

The library's list may look just like other information on the Internet. But these sources usually have been checked by experts. This is not true of all the information on the Internet. It could come from almost anybody, and may not be trustworthy.

When can I use the Internet?

The Internet is still a great way to look things up. You can find addresses or recipes, listen to music, or find things to do. You can look up information on hobbies or musical instruments, or read a magazine or newspaper online.

If you search the Internet on your own, make sure the web site you find is reliable. A U.S. government site or a site produced by a well-known organization or publication is usually your best bet.

Using a Search Engine

The best way to find web sites is to use a search engine. Here are some helpful ones:

Yahooligans (www.yahooligans.com)
Kidsclick (www.kidsclick.org)
Lycos Zone (lycoszone.lycos.com)
Ask Jeeves Kids (www.ajkids.com)

Start by typing one or two search terms—words that describe your topic. The search engine scans the Internet and gives you a list of sites that contain them. The results appear in a certain order, or **rank**. Search engines use different ways of measuring which web sites are likely to be the most helpful. One way is by counting how many times your search terms appear on each site. The site that's listed first may not have what you want. Explore as many of the sites as possible.

You might have to narrow your search by using more keywords. Or try using **directories** to help find what you need.

●WAforKids.com   Go to *www.WAforKids.com* for more Homework Help.

109

INVENTIONS

Which country's inventors gave us both dynamite and the cell phone? ➡ page 111

Many important inventions and discoveries came before history was written. These include the wheel, pottery, many tools, and the ability to make fire. More recent inventions help us to travel faster, communicate better, and live longer.

FAMOUS AMERICAN INVENTORS

BENJAMIN FRANKLIN (1706-1790) American founding father whose famous kite experiment proved that lightning is a form of electricity. Besides being an accomplished statesman and philosopher, Franklin invented the lightning rod, a radiator stove, an odometer to record mileage traveled by his carriage, and bifocal glasses.

ALEXANDER GRAHAM BELL (1847-1922) Scottish American professor who invented the telephone. An expert in deaf education, Bell also founded the American Association to Promote the Teaching of Speech to the Deaf. In Boston in 1876, Bell spoke the first words transmitted over a distance. He said to his assistant, Thomas Watson, "Mr. Watson, come here; I want you."

THOMAS EDISON (1847-1931) American inventor who held more than 1,000 patents for such famous innovations as the electric light bulb, a motion picture viewer, and a phonograph. Founder of the world's first large central electric-power station in New York City, Edison is considered one of the most important inventors in history.

GEORGE WASHINGTON CARVER (1864-1943) African-American educator and inventor who created hundreds of new products (such as cheese, milk, flour, and soap) from peanuts and other legumes. This made the peanut one of the country's leading cash crops, and helped to revitalize farming in the American South. Carver, whose parents were slaves, went on to advise many world leaders, including Presidents Calvin Coolidge and Franklin D. Roosevelt.

NIKOLA TESLA (1856-1943) Serbian-born electrical engineer who invented the first practical system for generating and transmitting alternating current (AC) power. He also created the Tesla coil, which is used in modern electronic equipment, and demonstrated the first wireless radio-controlled boat in 1898 at New York City's Madison Square Garden.

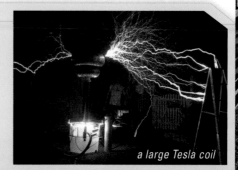

a large Tesla coil

Invention TIME LINE

YEAR	INVENTION	INVENTOR (COUNTRY)
105	paper	Ts'ai Lun (China)
1250	magnifying glass	Roger Bacon (England)
1447	movable type	Johann Gutenberg (Germany)
1590	2-lens microscope	Zacharias Janssen (Netherlands)
1608	telescope	Hans Lippershey (Netherlands)
1714	mercury thermometer	Gabriel D. Fahrenheit (Germany)
1752	lightning rod	Benjamin Franklin (U.S.)
1785	parachute	Jean Pierre Blanchard (France) ▶
1800	electric battery	Alessandro Volta (Italy)
1829	steam locomotive	George Stephenson (England)
1834	refrigeration	Jacob Perkins (England)
1837	telegraph	Samuel F. B. Morse (U.S.)
1842	anesthesia (ether)	Crawford W. Long (U.S.)
1846	sewing machine	Elias Howe (U.S.)
1866	dynamite	Alfred Nobel (Sweden)
1867	typewriter	Christopher Sholes, Carlos Glidden, & Samuel W. Soulé (U.S.)
1870	telephone*	Antonio Meucci (Italy), Alexander G. Bell (U.S.)
1879	practical light bulb	Thomas A. Edison (U.S.)
1886	automobile (gasoline)	Karl Benz (Germany) ▶
1891	escalator	Jesse W. Reno (U.S.)
1891	submarine (modern)	John Holland (U.S.)
1893	moving picture viewer	Thomas A. Edison (U.S.)
1895	diesel engine	Rudolf Diesel (Germany)
1895	X-ray	Wilhelm Roentgen (Germany)
1898	tape recorder	Valdemar Poulsen (Denmark)
1902	air conditioning	Willis Haviland Carrier (U.S.)
1913	modern radio receiver	Reginald A. Fessenden (U.S.)
1922	insulin	Sir Frederick G. Banting (Canada)
1923	television**	Vladimir K. Zworykin** (U.S.)
1926	rocket engine	Robert H. Goddard (U.S.)
1929	penicillin	Alexander Fleming (Scotland)
1939	jet airplane	Hans van Ohain (Germany)
1942	electronic computer	John V. Atanasoff & Clifford Berry (U.S.)
1948	Velcro®	Georges de Mestral (Switzerland)
1957	laser***	Gordon Gould (U.S.)
1973	CAT scanner	Godfrey N. Hounsfield (England)
1975	personal computer	E. Roberts, W. Yates, & J. Bybee (U.S.)
1977	space shuttle	NASA (U.S.)
1978	artificial heart	Robert K. Jarvik (U.S.)
1979	cellular telephone	Ericsson Company (Sweden)
1994	digital camera	Apple Computer, Kodak (U.S.)
1995	DVD (digital video disk)	Matsushita (Japan)
2001	Segway® Personal Transporter (PT)	Dean Kamen (U.S.) ▶

* Meucci developed a version of the telephone (early 1870s); Bell received a patent for another version.
** Others who helped invent the television include Philo T. Farnsworth (1926) and John Baird (1928).
*** First working laser built in 1960 by Theodore Maiman.

did you know?

In 1862, Swedish inventor Alfred Nobel opened a nitroglycerin factory; it blew up in 1864. He experimented with ways to make explosives safer to handle and invented dynamite in 1866. This made him extremely wealthy, and in his will he said that most of his fortune should be used to establish the Nobel Prizes. They are awarded each year to people who have "contributed most . . . to the benefit of mankind" in six different fields, including Peace.

LANGUAGE

Do you hear with your *ojos* or your *orejas*? ➡ page 115

TOP LANGUAGES

Mandarin, the principal language of China, has the most native speakers of any language. Spanish ranks second as the most common native, or first, language in the world.*

LANGUAGE	KEY PLACES WHERE SPOKEN	NATIVE SPEAKERS
Mandarin	China, Taiwan	873,014,298
Spanish	South America, Spain	322,299,171
English	U.S., Canada, Britain, Australia	309,352,280
Hindi	India	180,764,791
Portuguese	Portugal, Brazil	177,457,180
Bengali	Bangladesh, India	171,070,202
Russian	Russia	145,031,551
Japanese	Japan	122,433,899

*Estimates as of 2004.

	LANGUAGE USED AT HOME	SPEAKERS OVER 5 YEARS OLD
1	Speak only English	215,423,557
2	Spanish, Spanish Creole	28,101,052
3	Chinese	2,022,143
4	French	1,643,838
5	German	1,382,613
6	Tagalog (Philippines)	1,224,241
7	Vietnamese	1,009,627
8	Italian	1,008,370
9	Korean	894,063
10	Russian	706,242
11	Polish	667,414
12	Arabic	614,582
13	Portuguese	564,630
14	Japanese	477,997
15	French Creole	453,368
16	Greek	365,436
17	Hindi	317,057
18	Persian	312,085
19	Urdu	262,900
20	Gujarathi (from India & parts of Africa)	235,988

Which LANGUAGES Are SPOKEN in the UNITED STATES?

Most Americans speak English at home. But since the beginning of American history, immigrants have come to the U.S. from all over the world. Many have brought other languages with them.

"¡Hola!" That's how more than 28 million Spanish-speaking Americans say "hi" at home.

The table at the right lists the most frequently spoken languages in the U.S., as of the 2000 census.

LANGUAGE EXPRESS

Ciao! (Italian)
Hello! (English)
Konnichi wa! (Japanese)

Surprise your friends and family with words from other languages.

English	Italian	French	German	Chinese
January	gennaio	janvier	Januar	yi-yue
February	febbraio	février	Februar	er-yue
March	marzo	mars	Marz	san-yue
April	aprile	avril	April	si-yue
May	maggio	mai	Mai	wu-yue
June	giugno	juin	Juni	liu-yue
July	luglio	juillet	Juli	qi-yue
August	agosto	août	August	ba-yue
September	settembre	septembre	September	jiu-yue
October	ottobre	octobre	Oktober	shi-yue
November	novembre	novembre	November	shi-yi-yue
December	dicembre	decembre	Dezember	shi-er-yue
blue	azzurro	bleu	blau	lan
red	rosso	rouge	rot	hong
green	verde	vert	grün	lu
yellow	giallo	jaune	gelb	huang
black	nero	noir	schwarz	hei
white	bianco	blanc	weiss	bai
happy birthday!	buon compleanno!	joyeux anniversaire!	Glückwunsch zum Geburtstag!	sheng-ri kuai le!
hello!	ciao!	bonjour!	hallo!	ni hao!
good-bye!	arrivederci!	au revoir!	auf Wiedersehen!	zai-jian!
fish	pesci	poisson	Fisch	yu
bird	uccello	oiseau	Vogel	niao
horse	cavallo	cheval	Pferd	ma
one	uno	un	eins	yi
two	due	deux	zwei	er
three	tre	trois	drei	san
four	quattro	quatre	vier	si
five	cinque	cinq	fünf	wu

⌂ ●WAforKids.com ↱

Go to www.WAforKids.com and type 120 into the code box for these activities:
- Take a fun quiz about "Weird Words and Phrases" and show what you know about quotes with a "Who Said It?" quiz.
- Are you a wonderful wordsmith? Find out with a chapter quiz.
- Get even more facts about figures of speech, what it's like to be a writer, and what your name means.

¡SAY IT EN ESPAÑOL!

Spanish is the most commonly spoken language in the U.S. after English. More than 28 million people speak Spanish at home. That's almost 10 percent of all people in the U.S.

Pronouncing **Spanish** Words

In Spanish, the vowels only make one type of sound. The sound each vowel makes in Spanish is the same sound it makes in the English words at right.

Also, if you see the letters J, G, or X followed by a vowel, pronounce them like the English "H." So, "Frijoles" sounds like "Free-hole-ace." "Ejecutivo" sounds like "Eh-he-coo-tee-vo." "Región" sounds like "Ray-hee-own."

Try your pronunciation on the words and phrases on this page.

A	w**a**ter
E	b**e**t
I	f**ee**t (like you are saying the letter *e*)
O	sl**ow**
U	t**u**be

Sister Languages

There are some words that sound alike in both Spanish and English. These are called cognates. See if you can guess how each kid listed at right answered the question: **What do you want to be when you grow up?**

Julio	Yo quiero ser *músico*.
Maria	Un dia, yo quisiera ser *autora*.
Juan	Yo quiero ser *banquero*.
Olivia	Un dia, yo quisiera ser *doctora*.
Jose	Yo quiero ser *presidente*.

Answers: Julio—musician; Maria—author; Juan—banker; Olivia—doctor; Jose—president.

Basic Spanish Phrases

Hello	Hola
Goodbye	Adiós
How are you?	¿Cómo estás?
Please	Por favor
Thank you	Gracias
It's nice to meet you.	Mucho gusto en conocerte.

Food

Next time you're having dinner, ask your brother to pass the *arroz*.

Salad **Ensalada**

Juice **Jugo**

Beans **Frijoles**

Rice **Arroz**

Chicken **Pollo**

Your Body
Es Su Cuerpo

Use your *boca* to say these parts of the body (*cuerpo*). Use your *cabeza* to remember how to say them!

| Head | Cabeza |

Face	Cara
Eyes	Ojos
Mouth	Boca

Ears	Orejas
Neck	Cuello
Hair	Cabello

| Arm | Brazo |
| Belly | Barriga |

| Hand | Mano |

Leg	Pierna
Knee	Rodilla
Foot	Pie

Numbers

1	uno	6	seis
2	dos	7	siete
3	tres	8	ocho
4	cuatro	9	nueve
5	cinco	10	diez

Joke en Español

Teacher ¿Como se escribe "nariz" en inglés? (How do you write "nose" in English?)

Student No sé. (I don't know.)

Teacher ¡Correcto! (Correct!)

115

THE ENGLISH LANGUAGE

Facts About English

▶ According to the *Oxford English Dictionary*, the English language contains between 250,000 and 750,000 words. (The number depends on whether you count different meanings of the same word as separate words and on how many obscure technical terms you count.)

▶ The most frequently used letters of the alphabet are E, T, A, and O, in that order.

▶ Here are the 30 most common English words: the, of, and, a, to, in, is, that, it, was, he, for, as, on, with, his, be, at, you, I, are, this, by, from, had, have, they, not, or, one. Try to make a sentence with just these words. Here's an example: "I had to be with it for that is not the one they have."

New Words

English is always changing as new words are born and old ones die out. Many new words come from the fields of electronics and computers, from the media, or from slang.

hoodie: a hooded sweatshirt, usually with a zipper down the front

qigong: pronounced chee-gong, this is a Chinese philosophy of exercise, now increasingly popular around the world. *Qi*, or *chi*, is the Chinese term for "vital life energy."

ringtone: a sound or song that is programmed in or downloaded to ring from a cell phone.

In Other Words: SIMILES

Similes are comparisons of two dissimilar things that use "as" or "like." Here are some to wrap your brain around:

graceful as a swan—"smooth and elegant." Swans are admired for their long necks and the way they quietly glide through the water. Ballerinas are often compared to swans, with their extended, smooth movements on the stage.

quiet as a mouse—"almost too quiet to hear." Mice are quiet and shy, and good at hiding. Even their squeaks are practically too soft to hear.

strong as an ox—"stronger than most people." Oxen are cattle that are trained to pull very heavy loads.

GETTING TO THE ROOT

Many English words and parts of words can be traced back to Latin or Greek. If you know the meaning of a word's parts, you can probably guess what it means. A root (also called a stem) is the part of the word that gives its basic meaning but can't be used by itself. Roots need other word parts to complete them: either a prefix at the beginning, or a suffix at the end, or sometimes both. The following tables give some examples of Greek and Latin roots, prefixes, and suffixes.

LATIN

root	basic meaning	example
-alt-	high	altitude
-dict-	to say	dictate
-port-	to carry	transport
-scrib-/-script-	to write	prescription
-vert-	turn	invert

prefix	basic meaning	example
de-	away, off	defrost
in-/im-	not	invisible
non-	not	nontoxic
pre-	before	prevent
re-	again, back	rewrite
trans-	across, through	trans-Atlantic

suffix	basic meaning	example
-ation	(makes verbs into nouns)	invitation
-fy/-ify	make or cause to become	horrify
-ly	like, to the extent of	highly
-ment	(makes verbs into nouns)	government
-ty/-ity	state of	purity

GREEK

root	basic meaning	example
-anthrop-	human	anthropology
-biblio-	book	bible
-bio-	life	biology
-dem-	people	democracy
-phon-	sound	telephone
-psych-	soul	psychology

prefix	basic meaning	example
anti-/ant-	against	antisocial
auto-	self	autopilot
biblio-/bibl-	book	bibliography
micro-	small	microscope
tele-	far off	television

suffix	basic meaning	example
-graph	write, draw, describe, record	photograph
-ism	act, state, theory of	realism
-ist	one who believes in, practices	capitalist
-logue/-log	speech, to speak	dialogue
-scope	see	telescope

JOKES AND RIDDLES

1. Who is President if the Vice President dies?

2. A farmer combined four bales of hay with two bales of hay. How many bales does he have?

3. What keeps the beat for your head?

4. Why is Communist Karl Marx buried in London's Highgate Cemetery?

5. What do you lose when you stand up?

6. What's the last thing you take off before you go to bed?

7. Why was the chef arrested?

8. Why is the letter E like London?

9. What happens to a white hat when you throw it in the Red Sea?

10. Why do birds fly south for the winter?

11. Think of words ending in "gry." Two are "angry" and "hungry." There are three words in "the English language." What is the third word? *HINT:* Everyone uses it every day and if you've listened closely, I've already said the answer.

12. Why is an island like the letter T?

13. Two mothers and their two daughters went shopping. They each bought something, but came home with only three new things. Why?

14. What does everyone do at the same time, all day long, every day?

15. What can you put in a wooden box so that it's lighter?

16. How far can a deer run into the woods?

17. You can keep it only after giving it to someone else. What is it?

18. What's black and white and read all over?

19. What has wheels and flies but never leaves the ground?

20. How could a cowboy ride into town on Friday, stay three days, and then ride out on Friday?

21. What comes once in a minute, twice in a moment, but never in a billion years?

22. What are the next three letters in this pattern? O, T, T, F, F, S, S, _ , _, _

23. What can you hold without using your limbs?

24. What's white when it's dirty?

25. "Railroad crossing look for the cars." Can you spell that without any R's?

26. How many birth days does the average person have?

27. Some months have 31 days, some months only have 30. How many have 28 days?

28. Name three consecutive days without saying Sunday, Tuesday, or Friday.

29. A herder had 11 sheep. All but 9 died. How many were left?

30 Why can't a man living in Cincinnati be buried south of the Ohio River?

31 Is it legal in Texas for a man to marry his widow's sister?

32 What goes up when the rain comes down?

33 What's a snake's favorite school subject?

34 How do you keep a rhinoceros from charging?

35 What time is it when an elephant sits on a fence?

36 When is a car not a car?

37 What has arms but can't hug?

38 You're the driver of a bus. You stop on a corner and pick up 6 people. At the second stop, 4 people get on and 3 people get off. When you stop again, 5 people get on and 2 people get off. At the last stop, 5 people get on and 1 person gets off. How old is the bus driver?

39 You live in a one-story purple house. Everything in the house is purple. The walls are purple, the refrigerator is purple, the plates are purple, etc. What color are the stairs?

40 A plane flying from New York to Canada unfortunately crashes into a mountain right at the border. Do you bury the survivors in the U.S. or Canada?

WORD-CONNECT

Antonyms are words that have the opposite meaning. For example, "big" and "small" are antonyms. The answers to this crossword puzzle are all antonyms of the clues given below. Can you fill in all the blanks?

ACROSS
1 Vertebrate (hint: see p. 117, Latin prefixes)
6 Worst
7 Dangerous
9 Old
10 Poor
12 City
14 Beginning
15 Clean

DOWN
2 Mean
3 Full
4 Never
5 Cry
8 Hard
11 Open
13 No

ANSWERS ON PAGES 334-337. FOR MORE PUZZLES GO TO
WWW.WAFORKIDS.COM

MAGIC

Which magician caught a bullet in his mouth? ➡ see below

HARRY HOUDINI

(1874-1926)

Harry Houdini was born in Budapest, Hungary, and came to the U.S. at the age of four with the name Ehrich Weiss. His father was a rabbi. One of Ehrich's jobs as a youth was as a locksmith's apprentice.

As a young man, Houdini performed card tricks and other sleight-of-hand illusions, but moved on to more fantastic escapes that appeared to risk his life. By the time he was 25, Houdini was a celebrity in the U.S. and Europe.

Houdini's most famous escapes are still talked about today. He jumped into San Francisco Bay with a 75-pound ball and chain around his ankles while wearing handcuffs, and swam back to the surface unharmed. He escaped from a real prison cell. He even escaped from straitjackets while suspended from tall buildings upside down.

CRISS ANGEL

(1967-)

Born Christopher N. Sarantakos, Criss Angel blends elements of traditional magic with performance art. In 2002, in a nod to Houdini, he submerged himself in a 220-gallon tank, chained and shackled, for 24 hours—and escaped unharmed. In another tribute to Houdini, Angel escaped from a straitjacket while being suspended upside down 10 stories above the ground. He has also been lit on fire, caught a bullet in his mouth, and been suspended from a flying helicopter via fishhooks embedded in his skin. His show on the A&E channel, *Criss Angel Mindfreak,* has been airing since 2005.

JACKS TRAVEL IN PACKS!

In this card trick, the magician (that's you!) creates an illusion that three jacks magically move from one pile of cards to another.

STEP 1: Deal all four jacks face-up, one at a time, left to right. Below each of the four jacks, deal cards face-down, left-to-right until there are three face-down cards under each jack. The face-down cards are random cards from the deck; it does not matter what they are. Tell the audience, "You probably know that animals travel in groups. You've heard of a flock of seagulls? Or a leap of leopards? It might surprise you to know that jacks travel in packs. In fact, jacks will even fly through the air to stay together. Don't believe me? Just watch!"

Turn each jack face down and put it at the bottom of the three-card pile below it. You should now have four piles of four face-down cards. The jack should be the bottom card in each pile. Take each pile, beginning with the far left one and place it on top of the next pile, so that you now have all of the cards (face-down) in your hand. Tell the audience, "I'm going to deal out the cards in rows of four."

STEP 2: Deal the top four cards left to right. Pause. Lift up the next card on the deck (the fifth card overall), and use it to point to the fourth card you just dealt. Say, "Every fourth card is a jack, so the jacks will all end up in the fourth pile." Then, **PUT THE CARD YOU USED TO POINT AT THE BOTTOM OF THE DECK IN YOUR HAND.** Slip it under the deck casually so the audience doesn't notice. Now, continue to deal the rest of the cards from the top of the deck, left to right, making four face-down piles of cards. You will now have only one jack at the bottom of the far-right pile, and three jacks on top of the third pile. But of course, the audience doesn't know this!

STEP 3: Slide out the bottom-most card from the fourth pile and show it to the audience (it will be a jack). Tell the audience, "As I told you, this row has the jacks in it. But remember, jacks travel in packs! If I move one jack, all his buddies will move too. Just watch!"

Now, move the bottom-most card in the third pile to the bottom of the fourth pile (where the jack was), and put the jack, face-down, on the bottom of the third pile. Tell the audience, "I just moved one jack to this third pile, but all of the other jacks moved through the air to be with their friend. Just look!"

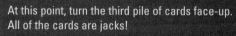

At this point, turn the third pile of cards face-up. All of the cards are jacks!

MILITARY

What medal is the highest honor for U.S. soldiers? ➡ page 125

American Revolution

Why? The British king sought to control American trade and tax the 13 colonies without their consent. The colonies wanted independence.

Who? British and American loyalists vs. American revolutionaries with French support

When? 1775-1783

Result? The colonies gained independence.

did you know? Paul Revere never completed his "midnight ride." The British captured him after he left Lexington. Another messenger, Samuel Prescott, finished the trip to warn people in Concord.

War of 1812

Why? Britain interfered with American commerce and forced American sailors to join the British navy.

Who? Britain vs. United States

U.S.S. Constitution

When? 1812-1814

Result? There was no clear winner. The U.S. unsuccessfully invaded Canada, a British colony. The British burned Washington, D.C., and the White House but were defeated in other battles.

Mexican War

Why? The U.S. annexed Texas. It also sought control of California, a Mexican province.

Who? Mexico vs. United States

When? 1846-1848

Result? Mexico ceded land in Texas, California, and New Mexico. The U.S. paid Mexico millions of dollars in return.

Civil War

Why? The Southern states seceded from the U.S. The U.S. fought to keep them.

Who? Confederacy vs. Union

When? 1861-1865

Result? The United States remained a unified country. Slavery was abolished.

did you know? More people died in the Civil War from infectious diseases like typhoid fever and diarrhea spread by poor hygiene and crowded living than from actual fighting.

Spanish-American War

Why? The Americans supported Cuban independence from Spain.

Who? United States vs. Spain

When? 1898

The Charge of San Juan Hill

Result? Spain handed the Philippines, Guam, and Puerto Rico over to the U.S. Cuba became independent.

World War I

Why? Colonial and military competition between European powers.

Who? Allies (including the U.S., Britain, France, Russia, Italy, and Japan) vs. Central Powers (including Germany, Austria-Hungary, and Turkey)

I WANT YOU FOR U.S. ARMY
NEAREST RECRUITING STATION

When? 1914-1918 (The U.S. entered in 1917)

Result? The Allies defeated the Central Powers. An estimated 8 million soldiers and close to 10 million civilians were killed.

did you know?

On Christmas day in 1914, some British and German soldiers met peacefully in the "No Man's Land" between their trenches. They shook hands, shared stories and gifts, and buried their dead.

World War II

Why? The Axis sought world domination.

Who? Axis (including Germany, Italy, and Japan) vs. Allies (including the U.S., Britain, France, and the Soviet Union). The U.S. did not enter the war until Japan attacked Pearl Harbor in 1941.

When? 1939-1945 (U.S. dropped atomic bombs on Hiroshima and Nagasaki.)

Result? The Allies defeated the Axis. The Holocaust (the Nazi effort to wipe out the Jews and other minorities) was stopped. The U.S. helped rebuild Western Europe and Japan. The Soviet Union set up Communist governments in Eastern Europe.

Yalta summit in 1945 with Winston Churchill, Franklin Roosevelt and Josef Stalin

did you know?

The Allied invasion of Nazi-occupied France on June 6, 1944, known as D-Day, was the biggest invasion in world history. More than 150,000 American, British, and Canadian soldiers stormed the beaches of Normandy.

Korean War

Why? North Korea invaded South Korea. In many ways, the conflict was part of the Cold War between the Communist and non-Communist nations.

Who? North Korea with support from China and the Soviet Union vs. South Korea backed by the United States and its allies

When? 1950-1953

Result? The war ended with a cease-fire agreement. North Korean forces retreated north of the 38th parallel. Korea remains divided.

USS Missouri at Chongjin, Korea

Vietnam War

Why? Communists (Viet Cong) backed by North Vietnam attempted to overthrow South Vietnam's government.

Who? North Vietnam with support from the Soviet Union and China vs. South Vietnam with support from the U.S. and its allies

When? 1959-1975

Result? The U.S. withdrew its troops in 1973. In 1975, South Vietnam surrendered. Vietnam became a unified Communist country

Persian Gulf War

Why? Iraq invaded and annexed Kuwait. It refused to withdraw despite United Nations demands.

Who? Iraq vs. U.S.-led coalition

When? 1991

Result? The coalition drove out Iraqi forces from Kuwait.

A-10A Thunderbolt II ground attack plane flying during Desert Storm, 1991

Where Are We Now?

Afghanistan War

Why? The U.S. demanded that Afghanistan's Taliban regime turn over Osama bin Laden, the man who planned the 9/11 terrorist attacks. The Taliban claimed not to know bin Laden's whereabouts.

Who? Taliban regime vs. Afghani Northern Alliance fighters, supported by the U.S. and its allies

When? 2001-

Result? The Taliban regime was defeated, but U.S. troops are still fighting Taliban resisters and hunting for bin Laden.

did you know?

Small handheld or gun-mounted cameras, powered by two AA batteries and weighing less than a pound, allow U.S. soldiers to see in total darkness or through smoke or fog.

Iraq War

Why? The U.S. accused Iraq of hiding weapons of mass destruction (WMDs) and supporting terrorists.

Who? Iraq vs. United States, Great Britain, and their allies

When? 2003-

Result? Saddam Hussein's government was toppled. Hussein was captured, put on trial, and hanged. No WMDs were found. Attacks from different groups on U.S. troops and Iraqi civilians have been ongoing.

TOP ⑩ NATIONS WITH LARGEST ARMED FORCES

1.	China	2,255,000		6.	South Korea	688,000
2.	United States	1,474,000		7.	Pakistan	619,000
3.	India	1,325,000		8.	Turkey	515,000
4.	North Korea	1,106,000		9.	Vietnam	484,000
5.	Russia	1,037,000		10.	Egypt	469,000

Source: International Institute for Strategic Studies, 2005-06. Figures are for active troops.

MEDALS

The **MEDAL OF HONOR** is the nation's highest medal for any branch of the military. It's awarded by the President and Congress to a person who risks his or her life by going "above and beyond the call of duty" in battle. The five-pointed star is worn around the neck. It's been awarded about 3,450 times since 1863.

The **PURPLE HEART** is given to any soldier who is wounded or killed in battle. It is the oldest American decoration for military merit, first awarded by General George Washington in 1782. Washington's face has been on the medal since 1932.

HEROIC ACTION

MICHAEL NOVOSEL, the son of Croatian immigrants, had already flown B-29 bombers in the Pacific during World War II and transport planes in the Korean War when he returned to the army in 1964 to go to Vietnam. He was 41. After being told he was too old and too high a rank, he accepted a lower rank and became a Medical Evacuation pilot. These "Dustoff" pilots, as they were called, had a dangerous job flying helicopters into the middle of battle zones to rescue injured soldiers. In two tours, or periods of duty (1966-67, 1969-70), he flew 2,543 missions and rescued 5,589 wounded soldiers. He earned the Medal of Honor for his work and bravery. He retired in 1985 after 42 years of active service and more than 12,400 flying hours.

AUDIE MURPHY was the most decorated U.S. Soldier in World War II. The Texas farm boy ran away from home at 15, was orphaned at 17, and joined the army shortly after turning 18. For his 27 months of fighting in Europe, he earned every medal for valor that the Army offered. He was wounded three times, and received three Purple Hearts. He received the Medal of Honor for single handedly resisting a German attack that included 6 tanks by using a machine gun attached to a burning tank destroyer. He also received 3 medals from France and one from Belgium, for a total of 33 in all. He returned to America as a hero and later acted in Western movies.

money

What does the pyramid on the dollar bill mean? ➡ page 128

▶ Where Does the U.S. Government Get Money?

Excise taxes (taxes on tobacco and gasoline, for example): **3%**

Estate and gift taxes: **1%**

Other sources: **3%**

Income taxes on businesses: **15%**

Income taxes on individuals: **43%**

Insurance, hospital, and retirement taxes: **35%**

▶ Where Does the U.S. Government Spend Money?

Social Security and income security (incl. public assistance and unemployment): **34%**

Education, training, employment, and social services: **4%**

Interest on the public debt: **9%**

Health (including Medicare): **22%**

Defense (military): **20%**

Other, including agriculture, commerce, environment, international affairs, justice, space and technology, and transportation: **11%**

HOW MUCH MONEY IS IN CIRCULATION?

At the end of September 2006, the total amount of money in circulation in the United States came to **$790,556,011,806**. About $36.6 billion was in coins, the rest in paper money.

Paper Money

Coins

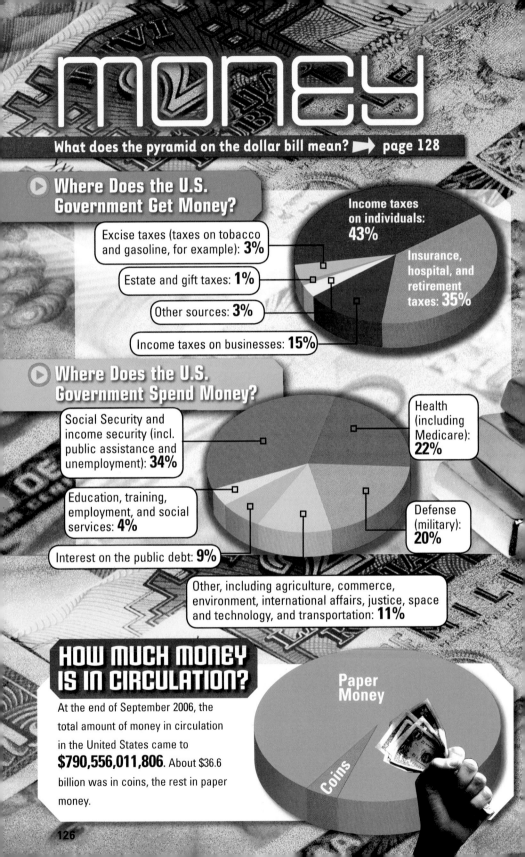

MAKING MONEY

What Is the U.S. Mint?

The U.S. Mint, founded in 1792, is part of the Treasury Department. The Mint makes all U.S. coins and safeguards the nation's $100 million in gold and silver bullion (uncoined bars of metal). Reserves of these precious metals are held at West Point, New York, and Fort Knox, Kentucky. The Mint turns out coins at four production facilities (Denver, Philadelphia, San Francisco, and West Point). For more information, visit the U.S. Mint's website at **WEB SITE** *www.usmint.gov*

What Coins Does the Mint Make?

Branches of the U.S. Mint in Denver and Philadelphia currently make coins for circulation, or everyday use. In 2006, these two facilities made 14.8 billion coins, including 7.9 billion pennies, 1.4 billion nickels, 2.7 billion dimes, and 2.8 million quarters. A tiny "D" or "P" near the year, called a mint mark, tells you which one made the coin. A Lincoln cent or "penny" with no mint mark was probably made at the Philadelphia Mint, which has by tradition never marked pennies. The U.S. Mint also makes commemorative coins in honor of events, like the Olympics, or people, like Benjamin Franklin.

Where is Paper Money Made?

The Bureau of Engraving and Printing (BEP), established in 1862, designs and prints all U.S. paper money. This agency, which is also part of the Treasury Department, prints postage stamps and other official certificates as well. The BEP's production facilities in Washington, D.C., and Ft. Worth, Texas, made 8.2 billion bills in 2006. About 95% of them are used to replace worn-out money. Even though bills are made of a special paper that is 75% cotton and 25% linen, they wear out pretty fast if they are used a lot. The $1 bill only lasts an average of 22 months, while the $50 bill lasts for about 5 years and the $100 bill lasts for about 8.5 years. For more information visit the BEP's website: **WEB SITE** *www.moneyfactory.com*

NEW U.S. Coins

For the next ten years (2007-16), four new dollar coin designs will be minted each year. They will be similar in shape and color to the Sacagawea dollar but images of past presidents will be on the front. The coins will be issued in the order that the presidents served with their years of service underneath. The Statue of Liberty will be on the back. The phrases "E Pluribus Unum," "In God We Trust," and the mint mark will be on the side. Look for George Washington, John Adams, Thomas Jefferson, and James Madison coins in 2007.

New U.S. State Quarters are still being minted, too. In 2007, Montana, Washington, Idaho, Wyoming, and Utah were put into circulation. Oklahoma, New Mexico, Arizona, Alaska, and Hawaii are due in the program's final year, 2008.

JOHN ADAMS
2nd PRESIDENT 1797-18

The U.S. $1 Bill: AN OWNER'S MANUAL

Everybody knows that George Washington is on the U.S. one-dollar bill, but did you ever wonder what all that other stuff is?

Plate position
Shows where on the 32-note plate this bill was printed.

The Treasury Department seal: The balancing scales represent justice. The pointed stripe across the middle has 13 stars for the original 13 colonies. The key represents authority.

Plate serial number
Shows which printing plate was used for the face of the bill.

Serial number
Each bill has its own.

Federal Reserve District Number
Shows which district issued the bill.

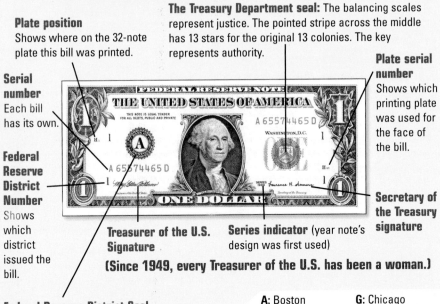

Treasurer of the U.S. Signature

Series indicator (year note's design was first used)

Secretary of the Treasury signature

(Since 1949, every Treasurer of the U.S. has been a woman.)

Federal Reserve District Seal
The name of the Federal Reserve Bank that issued the bill is printed in the seal. The letter tells you quickly where the bill is from. Here are the letter codes for the 12 Federal Reserve Districts:

A: Boston
B: New York
C: Philadelphia
D: Cleveland
E: Richmond
F: Atlanta
G: Chicago
H: St. Louis
I: Minneapolis
J: Kansas City
K: Dallas
L: San Francisco

Front of the Great Seal of the United States: The bald eagle is the national bird. The shield has 13 stripes for the 13 original colonies. The eagle holds 13 arrows (symbol of war) and an olive branch (symbol of peace). Above the eagle is the motto "E Pluribus Unum," Latin for "out of many, one," and a constellation of 13 stars.

Plate serial number
Shows which plate was used for the back.

Back of the Great Seal of the United States:
The pyramid symbolizes something that lasts for ages. It is unfinished because the U.S. is always growing. The eye, known as the "Eye of Providence," probably comes from an ancient Egyptian symbol. The pyramid has 13 levels; at its base are the Roman numerals for 1776, the year of American independence. "Annuit Coeptis" is Latin for "God has favored our undertaking." "Novus Ordo Seclorum" is Latin for "a new order of the ages." Both phrases are from the works of the Roman poet Virgil.

Toussaint Gaskins: Investment Advisor

Investment Advisors help people manage their money. They help plan people's savings for future events like college or retirement. That includes investing in (buying) mutual funds, bonds, or stocks that look like they will do well over the short term or long term. It can take years or decades for the money to be available once invested, so investing with timing goals in mind is important.

What are you currently working on?

My homework! I'm preparing for a meeting with the person who controls the money for the entire state of Maryland—The State Comptroller. He controls how all of the money is spent by the state government, similar to the way your parents control how money is spent in your household.

What is your workday like?

In the morning, I'll watch financial TV shows, like CNBC, and read newspapers. I meet with my clients either in person or on the phone. I'll probably speak with 10 to 20 everyday. In a work week, I'll spend at least 25 hours in the office and 15 hours outside. I usually give one presentation a week. I also go out to eat with clients in nice restaurants or play golf when the weather is warm. I'm always introducing myself to new people.

How many clients do you have?

I usually advise 200-300 people at a time. I advise individuals, small businesses, and people in government. I help people budget and invest money so they get the most in return. That could mean helping a family pay for college or helping the state of Maryland spend tax money better. I like sharing what I know with other people. I've handled $100,000,000 for a client and I have personally made over $30,000 in a day. I really believe that I can help to make someone's life better.

How did you get interested in being a financial advisor?

I was always comfortable in front of people. As a kid I acted in church and school plays and played team sports like basketball. In college I read the *Wall Street Journal*, which reports how businesses and world events affect each other. It was new and different. I really liked to help people solve their problems, and I wanted to understand how to make money work for me instead of me having to work for it all of the time.

What can kids do to become a financial advisor?

Learn to love to read and to be a great listener, understand math, and don't be afraid to speak in front of people. Always be prepared and have confidence in yourself. Graduate from college and know how finance, accounting, economics, and marketing work.

The biggest mistakes a financial advisor can make are not listening to all of the concerns of the client and not asking enough questions. When I receive a "Thank You" note or phone call from a satisfied client, that's when I know they're happy with my performance.

Most importantly, dream great dreams. Believe in yourself. Try your best to reach your goals.

MOVIES & TV

What book is *The Wizard of Oz* movie based on? ➡ page 132

MOVIE & TV FACTS

What a Bounty! *Pirates of the Caribbean: Dead Man's Chest* holds the record for highest one-day box office sales in the U.S. It also set a record for highest opening-day sales. The movie made $55.8 million when it opened in theaters on July 7, 2006.

Giving Credit *The Lord of the Rings: The Return of the King* (2003) has one of the longest closing credits of any movie. Hundreds of people, including a horse makeup artist, are listed in the credits, which last for nearly 10 minutes.

Turn That Off! Kids age 2-11 watched an average of 23 hours of TV a week in 2006. Among people of all ages, however, teens age 12-17 watched the least amount of TV— an average of 22 hours a week.

A Good Run Before *The Simpsons*, *The Flintstones* held the record for TV's longest running prime-time animated series. The cartoon, about two Stone Age families, lasted six seasons, from 1960 to 1966. *The Simpsons*, which has been on air since 1989, is currently in its 18th season.

The Simpsons ▶

ALL-TIME TOP ANIMATED MOVIES*			ALL-TIME TOP MOVIES*		
1	*Shrek 2* (2004)	$436.7	1	*Titanic* (1997)	$600.8
2	*Finding Nemo* (2003)	339.7	2	*Star Wars: Episode IV— A New Hope* (1977)	461.0
3	*The Lion King* (1994)	328.5	3	*Shrek 2* (2004)	436.7
4	*Shrek* (2001)	267.7	4	*E.T. the Extra-Terrestrial* (1982)	435.0
5	*The Incredibles* (2004)	261.4	5	*Star Wars: Episode I— The Phantom Menace* (1999)	431.1
6	*Monsters, Inc.* (2001)	255.9	6	*Pirates of the Caribbean: Dead Man's Chest* (2006)	423.3
7	*Toy Story 2* (1999)	245.9	7	*Spider-Man* (2002)	403.7
8	*Cars* (2006)	244.1	8	*Star Wars: Episode III— Revenge of the Sith* (2005)	380.3
9	*Aladdin* (1992)	217.4	9	*The Lord of the Rings: The Return of the King* (2003)	377.0
10	*Ice Age: The Meltdown* (2006)	195.3	10	*Spider-Man 2* (2004)	373.4

Source: *Variety*
*Through February 8, 2007. Gross in millions of dollars based on box office sales in the U.S. and Canada.

TOP TV SHOWS IN 2006-07

AGES 6-11

NETWORK
1. *American Idol*
2. *Are You Smarter Than a Fifth Grader?*
3. *Extreme Makeover: Home Edition*
4. *Survivor*
5. *Dancing With the Stars*

CABLE
1. *Class of 3000*
2. *Courage the Cowardly Dog*
   The Grim Adventures of Billy & Mandy
   Camp Lazlo
3. *Pokémon: Battle Frontier*
   Naruto

▲ *Survivor*

AGES 12-17

NETWORK
1. *American Idol*
2. *Are You Smarter Than a Fifth Grader?*
3. *Family Guy*
4. *House*
5. *The Simpsons*

CABLE
1. *Cory in the House*
2. *WWE Raw*
3. *Monday Night Football*
   The Suite Life of Zack & Cody
4. *Zoey 101*
   Hannah Montana

HITTING THEATERS IN 2007...

▶ Kick off summer with *Surf's Up*. The movie follows a young penguin (voiced by Shia LaBeouf) on his way to his first major surfing competition (June).

▶ In *Nancy Drew*, a teenager tries to solve the murder of a Hollywood actress. Emma Roberts stars as the young detective. Based on the Nancy Drew books (June).

▶ Remy wants to be more than just a sewer-dwelling rat in *Ratatouille*. He wants to be a chef, despite his family's disapproval (June).

▶ The Simpsons family will make their first big screen appearance in *The Simpsons Movie* (July).

▶ A boy learns he is the last of a group of immortals dedicated to the fight between Light and Dark in *The Dark Is Rising*. Based on the book series by Susan Cooper (September).

▶ After the grocery store has closed for the night, the mascots of different products come alive in *Foodfight!* (November).

▶ A princess is banished by an evil queen from their animated world to present-day, real-life New York City in *Enchanted*. Stars include Amy Adams, James Marsden, and Susan Sarandon (November).

...AND IN 2008

▶ Three siblings discover a magical world of faeries after moving into the rundown Spiderwick estate. *The Spiderwick Chronicles* comes out in February.

▶ Based on the Dr. Seuss book, *Horton Hears a Who* is about an elephant who hears voices coming from a speck of dust—except no one believes him. The movie will come out in March.

▶ *Madagascar 2* will hit screens in November. ▼

131

BOOKS TO FILM

Movie: *The Wizard of Oz* (1939)
Book: *The Wonderful Wizard of Oz* by L. Frank Baum (1900)

The making of the classic film *The Wizard of Oz* was delayed by script problems. No one knew exactly how to make L. Frank Baum's magical story come to life on screen. Another problem was that 16-year-old Judy Garland was much older than the Dorothy Gale character that Baum had written about. When filming first began, Garland was dressed in a blond wig and childish make-up to make her look younger, but that idea was quickly scrapped.

Readers of *The Wonderful Wizard of Oz* could easily spot where changes were made to adapt the movie for the big screen. In Baum's story, Dorothy's slippers were silver, but ruby slippers looked more dramatic in Technicolor! Baum's book was also pretty violent for a children's book—the Wizard sends Dorothy to kill the Wicked Witch, not just to get her broomstick. The Tin Man (Tin Woodsman, in the book) uses his ax on forest creatures. In the end, the filmmakers didn't think that moviegoers would buy all of Baum's fantasy, and they changed the story so Dorothy would wake up at the end as if it were all a dream.

Movies: *Willy Wonka and the Chocolate Factory* (1971); *Charlie and the Chocolate Factory* (2005)
Book: *Charlie and the Chocolate Factory* by Roald Dahl (1964)

Charlie and the Chocolate Factory was first adapted to the big screen in 1971. Dahl himself wrote the original screenplay, but it was heavily changed. By the time the movie came out, much of Dahl's original story had been altered, and he was rumored to have hated the film. During Veruca Salt's downfall in the book, she is judged a "bad nut" by nut-selecting squirrels; in the first film version, she is judged a bad egg by the golden egg machine.

Fortunately, in the Hollywood movie business, there's usually a second chance! The screenwriter for the 2005 remake *Charlie and the Chocolate Factory* had never seen the original film before he began writing. He wrote a script working solely from Dahl's novel. The squirrel scene was reinstated. But other changes were made. For instance, in the book, Willy Wonka never mentions his father, but in the movie, his candy-hating dentist father becomes a big part of the story. There's much debate among Charlie fans over which movie follows the book more closely—and whether that's important.

Movies: *The Princess Diaries (2001); The Princess Diaries 2: Royal Engagement* (2004)
Book: *The Princess Diaries, Volume 1* by Meg Cabot (2000)

In both the book and the movie, Mia Thermopolis is an awkward high schooler being raised by a single mother. She learns her father is a prince and that she will inherit Genovia's throne from him.

The movie is set in San Francisco, the book in New York City. In the movie, Mia is 15 going on 16. (Anne Hathaway reportedly earned the role of klutzy Mia after falling off her chair while auditioning for the movie.) In the book, Mia is only 14. In the movie Mia is also more fond of her grandmother, Clarisse Renaldo, who helps Mia learn how to act like a princess.

The Princess Diaries 2, a sequel to the first movie, is not based on any of Meg Cabot's books. Cabot has published seven volumes so far out of a total 10 volumes planned for this series.

Movie: *The Chronicles of Narnia: The Lion, the Witch, and the Wardrobe* (2005)
Book: *The Chronicles of Narnia: The Lion, the Witch, and the Wardrobe* by C.S. Lewis (1950)

The Chronicles of Narnia is a series of seven books. *The Lion, the Witch, and the Wardrobe* is the first book in the series. (A movie version of *Prince Caspian*, the next book in the series, is expected to come out in May 2008.)

Both the book and movie follow four siblings who enter the land of Narnia through a magical wardrobe. There are some differences, however. In the book, the White Witch is much more fearful of Aslan than she is in the film. The movie and book also reflect different attitudes toward women. In the book, Father Christmas tells Susan and Lucy he doesn't want them to participate in battle, because battles are ugly when women fight. In the movie, however, he merely says wars are ugly.

movies & tv match-ups

Match these duos with the movie or TV show in which they belong.

DUOS	MOVIE OR TV SHOW
Mac & Blooregard	*Unfabulous*
Katara & Sokka	*Pirates of the Caribbean*
Will & Elizabeth	*Howl's Moving Castle*
Peter & Mary Jane	*Spider-Man*
Susan & Reed	*Foster's Home for Imaginary Friends*
Sophie & Calcifer	*Zoey 101*
Addie & Geena	*Fantastic Four*
Quinn & Lola	*Avatar: The Last Airbender*

ANSWERS ON PAGES 334–337. FOR MORE PUZZLES GO TO WWW.WAFORKIDS.COM

MUSEUMS

Which museum is especially for bad art? ➡ page 135

Museums collect things of great interest, such as works of art or everyday objects from different times in the past, and show them off to visitors. Some museums teach you all about science and technology.

The American Museum of Natural History, in New York City, dates back to

1869, and is the biggest natural science museum in the world. It has huge dinosaur skeletons, lifelike scenes of animals in different environments, and exhibits that show humans as they lived tens of thousands of years ago. The museum's **Rose Center for Earth and Space** (pictured at right) contains interactive exhibits about astronomy and astrophysics, as well as the world's most advanced star projector. Inside the Hayden Planetarium, the projector takes you on a journey through a virtual re-creation of the Milky Way Galaxy.
WEB SITE www.amnh.org

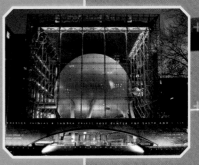

Exploratorium, **in San Francisco, California**, is a place to learn about everything from frogs to earthquakes to space weather. Grope through darkness in the Tactile Dome, where the sense of touch is your only guide. There are "hands-on" exhibits in all areas of science, with plenty of things to look at, pick up, and tinker with. **WEB SITE** www.exploratorium.com

The Smithsonian Institution, in Washington, DC, is

not just one museum, but 18 museums, most of them located along the Mall in Washington. It's the biggest museum complex in the world, holding about 142 million objects, from First Ladies' dresses to the first airplane flown by the Wright Brothers. **WEB SITE** www.si.edu

MUSEUMS OF ALL KINDS

The Andy Warhol Museum in **Pittsburgh, Pennsylvania**, showcases the art of Andy Warhol (1928-1987), who is famous for his portraits of celebrities and familiar objects like Campbell's soup cans. Some of Warhol's "installations" are also on display here, including *Silver Clouds*, a room filled with reflective, helium-filled balloons. **WEB SITE** *www.warhol.org*

Jamestown Settlement in **Williamsburg, Virginia**. This "living museum" includes re-creations of an Indian village, a fort, and the first permanent English settlement in America. Museum staff wear costumes and show what life was like for colonists 400 years ago. **WEB SITE** *www.historyisfun.org*

The International UFO Museum and Research Center in **Roswell, New Mexico**, is dedicated to research into UFOs, or "unidentified flying objects" from outer space. Some say that a UFO crashed in the nearby desert back in 1947. **WEB SITE** *www.iufomrc.com*

The Museum of Bad Art (MOBA) in **Dedham, Massachusetts**, is housed in the basement of a community theater, just outside the men's room. MOBA is dedicated to preserving "art too bad to be ignored," including a sculpture entitled *The Haircut*, which invites viewers to leave clippings of their own hair! **WEB SITE** *www.museumofbadart.org*

National Museum of Health and Medicine in **Washington, DC**. Founded during the Civil War as the Army Medical Museum, it holds specimens for research in military medicine and surgery. One of the most popular exhibits has artifacts from President Lincoln's assassination, including the bullet. **WEB SITE** *nmhm.washingtondc.museum*

did you know?

The American Museum of Natural History in New York City was the inspiration for the 2006 blockbuster film Night at the Museum. The exhibits don't really come to life after dark, but you can spend a night at the museum. Several times a year, it offers a special sleepover program for children ages 8 to 12, who are allowed to explore the museum with flashlights and sleep beneath a 94-foot-long blue whale.

MUSIC & DANCE

What musical instrument is played without being touched? ➡ page 138

TOP ALBUMS OF 2006

1. *Some Hearts*............................Carrie Underwood ➤
2. *High School Musical Soundtrack* ....High School Musical
3. *All the Right Reasons*...............Nickelback
4. *Me and My Gang* ....Rascal Flatts
5. *The Breakthrough* ....Mary J. Blige
6. *Curtain Call: The Hits** ....Eminem
7. *Back to Bedlam*...........................James Blunt
8. *The Road and the Radio*.............Kenny Chesney
9. *The Legend of Johnny Cash* ......Johnny Cash
10. *Breakaway*.................................Kelly Clarkson

This album contains explicit lyrics.
Edited version, which may be suitable for kids, is available.
Source: The Billboard 200, Billboard Magazine

All About >> THE ORIGINS OF HIP HOP

Hip Hop music was born in the 1970s, primarily in African American neighborhoods in New York City including the South Bronx. In many soul and funk songs (by artists such as James Brown and Sly and the Family Stone), there were long musical sections without lyrics, known as "breaks." Some creative DJs began playing only the breaks of songs, back to back. Dancers invented a unique style of dancing, known as break dancing, to go along with this "new" music. Other performers, known as MCs, created rhythmic, rhyming lyrics to accompany the breaks. These were the first rappers. As time went on, rap groups such as the Furious Five and the Cold Crush Four grew in popularity. In 1979, a group called the Sugar Hill Gang released "The Rapper's Delight," which became the first rap recording to hit the "pop" charts. Since then, hip hop has become a part of American pop culture, drawing on jazz, rock n' roll, soul, and funk music influences.

MAKING SENSE of the WORLD

Unlike folklore or fables, myths were once thought to be true. The Greeks and Romans explained many things in nature by referring to the gods. (So did other ancient peoples, such as the Egyptians and the Norse.) To the Greeks a rough sea meant that POSEIDON was angry. Lightning was the work of ZEUS, ruler of the sky. The sun went across the sky because APOLLO drove the chariot of the sun.

Head of Zeus

One of the most famous nature stories is about PERSEPHONE, or Proserpina, the daughter of Zeus and DEMETER. HADES fell in love with her and kidnapped her to the Underworld, where people went after death. Demeter was so sad and angry that she ignored the Earth's crops, causing them to die. Zeus demanded Persephone's return. Hades agreed but fed Persephone some pomegranate seeds, knowing that anyone who ate in the Underworld had to stay there. When Zeus learned of this, he decided Persephone would spend a third of every year in the Underworld and the rest on Earth. When Persephone is on Earth, Demeter is happy. Flowers bloom and crops grow. But when Persephone is with Hades, Demeter mourns and plants wither and die. This is how the Greeks explained the seasons.

A famous place in ancient Greece was the PARTHENON. It still exists in ruins atop the Acropolis above Athens. When it was built in the fifth century BC, it housed an enormous statue of Athena, the guardian goddess of Athens. Made of gold and ivory, she was estimated to have weighed 2,500 pounds.

Greek & Roman Heroes

Besides stories about the gods, Greek and Roman mythology has many stories about heroes with superhuman qualities. They were somewhere between ordinary humans and gods.

- ODYSSEUS, the king of Ithaca, was a hero of the Trojan War in the *Iliad*. It was his idea to build a huge wooden horse, hide Greek soldiers inside, and smuggle them into the city of Troy to capture it. The *Odyssey* is the story of his long and magical trip home after the war.

Odysseus

- ACHILLES was the greatest warrior of the Greeks, and fought and died in the **Trojan War**. He was shot by an arrow in the heel, the only weak part of his body. The tendon that connects the human calf and heel is called the Achilles tendon.

- AENEAS's story follows his journey from his home in Troy, to Carthage in north Africa, and then to Rome. He settled there, and became the forefather of the Romans.

But the most popular hero was Herakles, or **Hercules**. The most famous of his deeds were his 12 labors. They included killing the **Hydra**, a many-headed monster, and capturing the three-headed dog **Cerberus**, who guarded the gates of the Underworld. Hercules was so great a hero that the gods granted him immortality. When his body lay on his funeral pyre, Athena came and carried him off to Mount Olympus in her chariot.

NATIONS

In what country can you find the tallest building in the world?
➡ page 176

GOVERNMENTS

Among the world's 194 independent nations there are various kinds of governments.

Totalitarianism In **totalitarian** countries the rulers have strong power, and the people have little freedom. North Korea currently has a totalitarian government.

Monarchy A country with a king or queen can be called a **monarchy**. Monarchies are almost always hereditary, meaning the throne is passed down in one family.

Democracy The word **democracy** comes from the Greek words *demos* ("people") and *kratos* ("rule"). In a democracy, the people rule. In most modern democracies, there are too many people to agree on everyday decisions. So people make decisions through the leaders they choose. These democracies are called **representative** democracies. If people are unhappy with their leaders, they can vote them out of office. Winston Churchill, a former British prime minister, probably had that in mind when he said, "Democracy is the worst form of government except all those other forms that have been tried from time to time."

UN SECRETARY-GENERAL BAN KI-MOON of South Korea became the eighth secretary-general of the United Nations January 1, 2007, succeeding Kofi Annan. So what does the secretary-general do?

The secretary-general heads the Secretariat, which has a staff of thousands from all different countries. The Secretariat oversees the UN's day-to-day operation. The secretary-general makes sure that programs and policies the UN has agreed on, such as peacekeeping operations, are running smoothly. He also functions as a diplomat. He tries to resolve disputes between countries. In addition, the secretary-general is an advocate for those who are less fortunate. He learns what social and economic problems exist around the world and prepares reports on them. As a leader, the secretary-general upholds the UN's commitment to world peace.

The secretary-general is appointed by the General Assembly on the Security Council's recommendation. The term of office is five years, which can be renewed.

Before becoming secretary-general, Ban served in the South Korean government. (Ban is his family name, Ki-moon is his personal name.) He can speak Korean, English, and French

A COMMUNITY OF NATIONS

The **United Nations (UN)** was started in 1945 after World War II. The first members were 51 nations, 50 of which met in San Francisco, California. They signed an agreement known as the UN Charter. The UN now has 192 members, including Montenegro, which joined in 2006. Only two independent nations—Taiwan and Vatican City—are not members.

HOW THE UN IS ORGANIZED

➤ **GENERAL ASSEMBLY** **What It Does:** Discusses world problems, admits new members, appoints the secretary-general, decides the UN budget. **Members:** All UN members; each country has one vote.

➤ **SECURITY COUNCIL** **What It Does:** Handles questions of peace and security. **Members:** Five permanent members (China, France, UK, Russia, U.S.) who must all vote the same way before certain proposals can pass; ten elected by the General Assembly to two-year terms. In early 2007, the ten were Republic of the Congo, Ghana, Peru, Qatar, and Slovakia (terms ending Dec. 31, 2007) and Belgium, Indonesia, Italy, Panama, and South Africa (terms ending Dec. 31, 2008).

➤ **ECONOMIC AND SOCIAL COUNCIL** **What It Does:** Deals with issues related to economic development, population, education, health, and human rights. **Members:** 54 member countries elected to three-year terms.

➤ **INTERNATIONAL COURT OF JUSTICE (WORLD COURT)** located in The Hague, Netherlands. **What It Does:** UN court for disputes between countries. **Members:** 15 judges, each from a different country, elected to nine-year terms.

➤ **SECRETARIAT** **What It Does:** Carries out the UN's day-to-day operations. **Members:** UN staff, headed by the secretary-general.

For more information, e-mail inquiries@un.org ***or write to:*** Public Inquiries Unit, Dept. of Public Information, United Nations, Room GA-57, New York, NY 10017

WEB SITE www.un.org

UN Peacekeepers

The Security Council sets up UN peacekeeping missions to try to stop people from fighting while countries or groups try to work out their differences. There were 15 peacekeeping missions operating around the globe in February 2007, such as one in the Sudan and another in Lebanon. UN peacekeepers usually wear blue helmets or berets with white UN letters.

●WAforKids.com

Go to **www.WAforKids.com** and type **143** into the code box for more facts and fun:

- Quiz yourself (or your parents!) on flags from around the globe
- Download crossword puzzles filled with fun facts about other countries
- Get even more homework help on every nation of the world

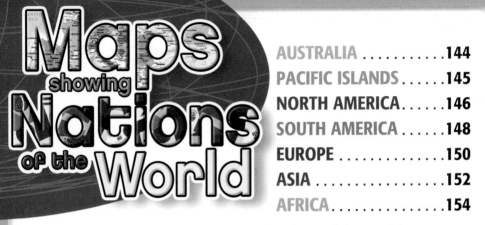

Maps showing Nations of the World

Maps showing the continents and nations of the world appear on pages 144-155. Flags of the nations appear on pages 156-179. A map of the United States appears on pages 288-289.

AUSTRALIA

⊛ National Capital

★ State Capital

• Other City

1:40,886,000

0   250   500 mi

0   250   500 km

Two-Point Equidistant Projection

© GeoNova

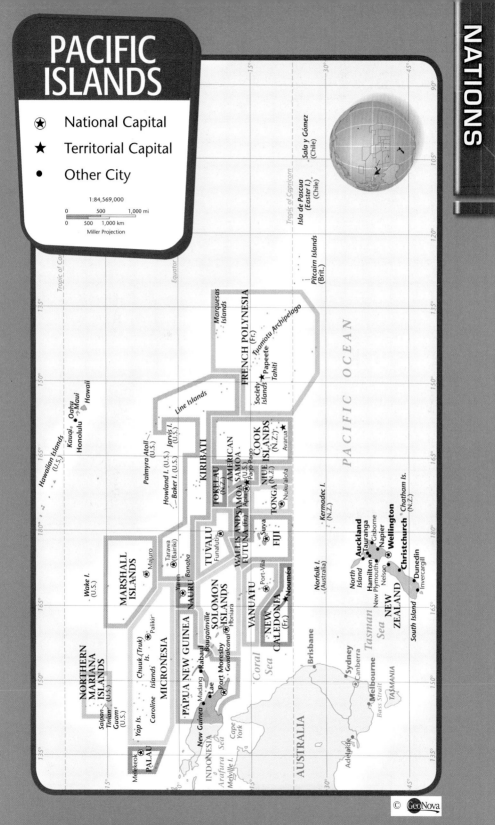

PACIFIC ISLANDS

★ National Capital
★ Territorial Capital
• Other City

1:84,569,000

| 0 | 500 | 1,000 mi |
| 0 | 500 | 1,000 km |

Miller Projection

Sala y Gómez (Chile)

Isla de Pascua (Easter I.) (Chile)

Pitcairn Islands (Brit.)

Tropic of Capricorn

Tropic of Cancer

Equator

PACIFIC OCEAN

Marquesas Islands

FRENCH POLYNESIA (Fr.)

Tuamotu Archipelago

Society Islands ★ Papeete
Tahiti

COOK ISLANDS (N.Z.) ★ Avarua

Line Islands

Hawaiian Islands (U.S.)

Kauai Oahu Maui
Honolulu Hawaii

Palmyra Atoll (U.S.)

Howland I. (U.S.)
Baker I. (U.S.)

Jarvis I. (U.S.)

KIRIBATI

AMERICAN SAMOA (U.S.)
Pago Pago

SAMOA
Apia

TOKELAU (N.Z.)

NIUE (N.Z.)

TONGA ★ Nukualofa

Kermadec I. (N.Z.)

Chatham Is. (N.Z.)

Wake I. (U.S.)

MARSHALL ISLANDS
Majuro

Tarawa (Bairiki)
Banaba

NAURU ★ Yaren

TUVALU
Funafuti

WALLIS AND FUTUNA (Fr.)

FIJI
Suva

VANUATU
Port-Vila

NEW CALEDONIA (Fr.) ★ Nouméa

Norfolk I. (Australia)

North Island

New Plymouth
Hamilton

Auckland
Tauranga
Gisborne
Napier
Nelson ★ Wellington

Christchurch

South Island

Dunedin
Invercargill

NEW ZEALAND

Tasman Sea

NORTHERN MARIANA ISLANDS (U.S.)

Saipan
Tinian (U.S.)
Guam (U.S.)

Chuuk (Truk)
Caroline Islands ● Palikir

MICRONESIA

Yap Is.

PALAU
Melekeok

New Guinea

PAPUA NEW GUINEA
Port Moresby

Madang
Lae

Rabaul
Bougainville

SOLOMON ISLANDS
Honiara

Guadalcanal

Coral Sea

Brisbane

AUSTRALIA

Sydney
Canberra

Melbourne

TASMANIA

Bass Strait

Adelaide

Cape York

Arafura Sea

Melville I.

INDONESIA

© GeoNova

145

SWEDEN

NORWAY

GREAT BRITAIN

ICELAND

Spitsbergen

Greenland Sea

Denmark Strait

Cape Farewell

Arctic Circle

Tasiilaq

Nuuk

Nord

Cape Morris Jessup

GREENLAND (KALAALLIT NUNAAT) (Den.)

Knud Rasmussen Land

Oqaanaaq (Thule)

Gise Fiord

Baffin Bay

Davis Strait

Labrador Sea

Hebron

NEWFOUNDLAND AND LABRADOR

St. Anthony

Happy Valley Goose Bay

Schefferville

Labrador City

Sept-Îles

Island of Newfoundland

Corner Brook

St. John's

St. Pierre & Miquelon (Fr.)

Sydney

Anticosti I.

NEW P.E.I.

BRUNS.

QUEBEC

St. Lawrence

Chicoutimi

Chibougamau

Mooseonee

CANADIAN SHIELD

ONTARIO

James Bay

Belcher Is.

Hudson Strait

Ungava Peninsula

Povungnituk

Iqaluit

Pangnirtung

Repulse Bay

Southampton I.

Hudson Bay

Churchill

York Factory

Winnipeg

North Pole

Arctic Ocean

Alert

Ellesmere I.

Queen Elizabeth Islands

Resolute

Arctic Bay

Pond Inlet

Baffin Island

Cambridge Bay

Victoria I.

Holman

Banks I.

Sachs Harbour

Kugluktuk

Déline

Great Bear L.

NUNAVUT

NORTHWEST TERRITORIES

Yellowknife

Ft. Smith

Uranium City

Flin Flon

La Ronge

Prince Albert

MANITOBA

SASK.

Thompson

Saskatoon

Regina

GREAT

ROCKY

Winnipeg

CANADA

Beaufort Sea

Inuvik

Fort McPherson

Mackenzie

Great Slave L.

Ft. Simpson

Hay River

Peace River

Fort McMurray

La Loche

Edmonton

ALBERTA

Athabasca

Saskatchewan

Calgary

Point Barrow

Barrow

BROOKS RANGE

Fort Yukon

Yukon

ALASKA

Kotzebue

Point Hope

Nome

Bethel

Fairbanks

Dawson

Mayo

Carmacks

YUKON

Whitehorse

Watson Lake

BRITISH COLUMBIA

Williams Lake

Prince George

Jasper

Fraser

RANGE

COAST MOUNTAINS

Skagway

Juneau

Sitka

Ketchikan

Prince Rupert

Kitimat

Queen Charlotte Is.

Vancouver I.

Victoria

Vancouver

Seattle

Mt. McKinley 6,194 m. (20,320 ft.)

ALASKA RANGE

Anchorage

Valdez

Kenai

Seward

Kodiak

Yakutat

Mt. Logan 5,959 m. (19,551 ft.)

Gulf of Alaska

Bering Sea

Bering Strait

RUSSIA

Arctic Circle

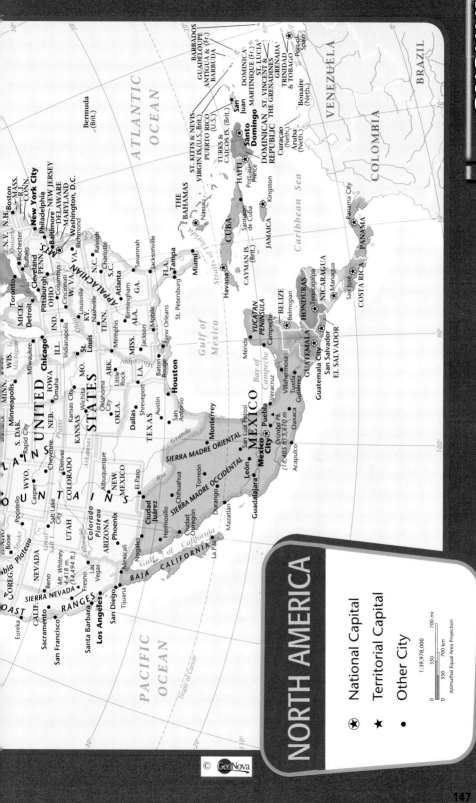

ATLANTIC OCEAN

PACIFIC OCEAN

Caribbean Sea

Gulf of Mexico

Gulf of California

Bay of Campeche

Straits of Florida

NORTH AMERICA

⊛ National Capital

★ Territorial Capital

• Other City

1:39,978,000

0   350   700 mi
0   350 700 km
Azimuthal Equal Area Projection

© GeoNova

147

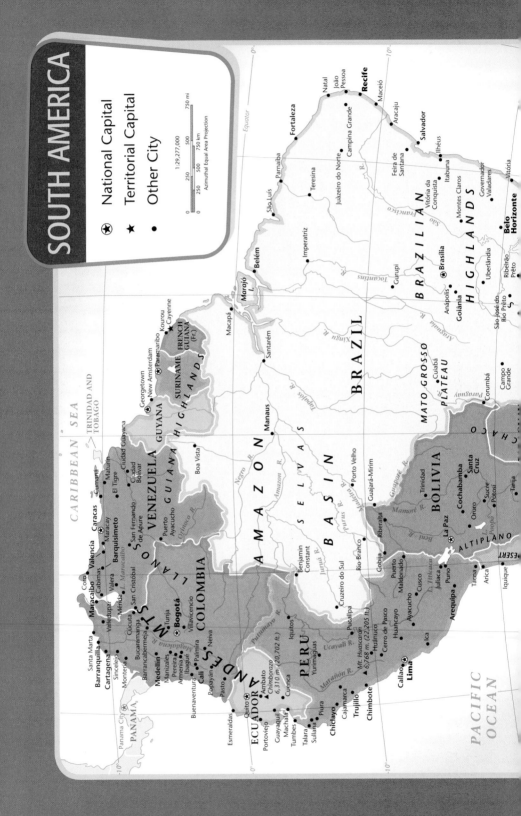

SOUTH AMERICA

⊛ National Capital

★ Territorial Capital

• Other City

1:29,277,000

0   250   500   750 km
0   250   500   750 mi

Azimuthal Equal Area Projection

CARIBBEAN SEA

PACIFIC OCEAN

TRINIDAD AND TOBAGO

PANAMA

Panama City

Colombia

Santa Marta
Barranquilla
Cartagena
Sincelejo
Montería
Coro
Maracaibo
Cabimas
Valencia
Valencia
Valera
Mérida
San Cristóbal
Cúcuta
Bucaramanga
Barrancabermeja
Valledupar

Venezuela

Maracay
Caracas
Cumaná
El Tigre
Maturín
Ciudad Guayana
Ciudad Bolívar
San Fernando de Apure
Puerto Ayacucho

Georgetown
Guyana
New Amsterdam
Paramaribo
Suriname
Cayenne
Kourou
FRENCH GUIANA (Fr.)

GUIANA HIGHLANDS

Boa Vista

Macapá

Marajó I.

Belém

São Luís

Parnaíba
Teresina
Imperatriz

Fortaleza

Natal
João Pessoa
Recife
Maceió
Aracaju

Campina Grande
Juazeiro do Norte
Feira de Santana
Salvador
Ilhéus
Itabuna

AMAZON

Manaus

Santarém

SELVAS

BASIN

Porto Velho

Guajará-Mirim

BRAZIL

MATO GROSSO PLATEAU

Cuiabá

Campo Grande

Corumbá

BRAZILIAN HIGHLANDS

Gurupi
São José do Rio Preto
Uberlândia
Uberaba
Anápolis
Brasília
Goiânia
Montes Claros
Governador Valadares
Vitória
Belo Horizonte
Ribeirão Prêto

Benjamin Constant

Cruzeiro do Sul

Rio Branco

Cobija
Puerto Maldonado
Riberalta
Trinidad

Bolivia

Santa Cruz
Cochabamba
La Paz
Oruro
Sucre
Potosí

ALTIPLANO

CHACO

Tarija

Colombia

Medellín
Manizales
Pereira
Armenia
Ibagué
Bogotá
Tunja
Villavicencio
Neiva
Cali
Palmira
Popayán
Pasto
Buenaventura

Esmeraldas

Ecuador

Quito
Ambato
Chimborazo 6,310 m. (20,702 ft.)
Portoviejo
Guayaquil
Machala
Cuenca
Tumbes
Talara
Sullana
Piura

Peru

Chiclayo
Cajamarca
Trujillo
Chimbote
Callao
Lima
Cerro de Pasco
Huánuco
Pucallpa
Iquitos
Yurimaguas
Mt. Huascarán 6,768 m. (22,205 ft.)
Huancayo
Ica
Ayacucho
Cusco
Juliaca
Puno
Arequipa
Tacna
Arica
Iquique

DESERT

ANDES MTS.

LLANOS

L. Maracaibo

L. Titicaca

L. Poopó

Orinoco R.
Negro R.
Amazon R.
Xingu R.
Tapajós R.
Madeira R.
Purus R.
Juruá R.
Ucayali R.
Marañón R.
Putumayo R.
Guaporé R.
Mamoré R.
Beni R.
Pilcomayo R.
Paraguay R.
São Francisco R.
Tocantins R.
Araguaia R.
Magdalena R.

Equator

0°

10°

10°

0°

10°

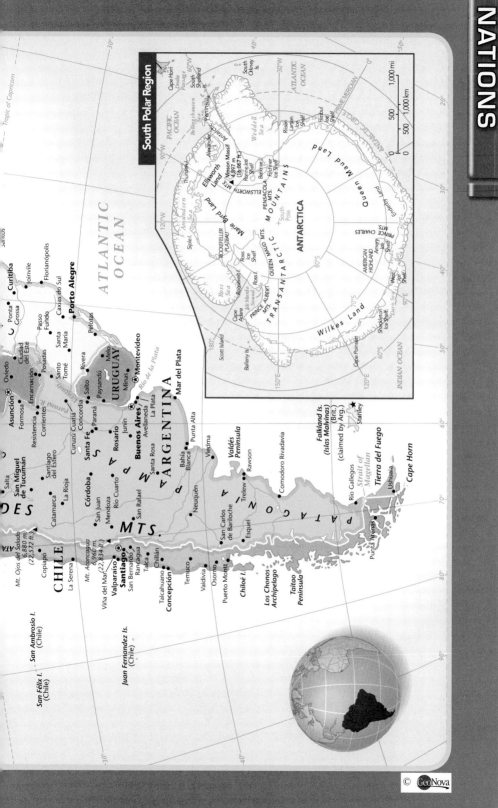

South Polar Region

ATLANTIC OCEAN

PACIFIC OCEAN

Cape Horn
South Orkney Is.
South Shetland Is.

Weddell Sea

Ronne Ice Shelf
Filchner Ice Shelf

ATLANTIC OCEAN

Queen Maud Land

Antarctic Peninsula

Bellingshausen Sea

Alexander I.

Thurston I.

Ellsworth Land
Vinson Massif 4,897 m (16,067 ft.)

Marie Byrd Land

ELLSWORTH MTS.

PENSACOLA MTS.

ROOSEVELT PLATEAU

Ross Ice Shelf

Amundsen Sea

Spiel.

MOUNTAINS

ANTARCTICA

+ South Pole

QUEEN MAUD MTS.

Enderby Land

PRINCE CHARLES MTS.

AMERICAN HIGHLAND

Amery Ice Shelf

West Ice Shelf

TRANSANTARCTIC

Ross Sea

McMurdo Ross I.
Cape Adare

PRINCE ALBERT MTS.

Wilkes Land

Shackleton Ice Shelf

Cape Poinsett

Ballery Is.

Scott Island

INDIAN OCEAN

ANTARCTIC CIRCLE

PRIME MERIDIAN

1,000 mi
1,000 km
500

ATLANTIC OCEAN

Curitiba
Joinville
Ponta Grossa
Florianópolis
Caxias do Sul
Passo Fundo
Santa Maria
Pelotas
Porto Alegre

Oviedo
Asunción
Formosa
Encarnación
Resistencia
Posadas
Ciudad del Este
Santo Tomé
Corrientes
Santa Fe
Curuzú Cuatiá
Concordia
Paraná
Rivera
Salto
Paysandú
Rosario
Junín
URUGUAY
Minas
Melo
Montevideo
Mar del Plata
Rio de la Plata
Buenos Aires
Avellaneda
La Plata
Santa Rosa
Punta Alta
Bahía Blanca
Viedma
Valdés Peninsula
Rawson
Trelew
Comodoro Rivadavia

Salta
San Miguel de Tucumán
Santiago del Estero
Catamarca
La Rioja
Córdoba
San Juan
Río Cuarto
Mendoza
San Rafael
Neuquén
San Carlos de Bariloche
Esquel
ARGENTINA
PATAGONIA
Mt. Ojos del Salado (22,572 ft.) 6,880 m
Copiapó
La Serena
CHILE
Mt. Aconcagua 6,960 m (22,834 ft.)
Viña del Mar
Valparaíso
Santiago
San Bernardo
Rancagua
Talca
Chillán
Talcahuano
Concepción
Temuco
Valdivia
Osorno
Puerto Montt
Chiloé I.
Los Chonos Archipelago
Taitao Peninsula
San Ambrosio I. (Chile)
San Félix I. (Chile)
Juan Fernández Is. (Chile)

Falkland Is. (Islas Malvinas) (Brit.) (claimed by Arg.)
Stanley

Tierra del Fuego
Río Gallegos
Punta Arenas
Strait of Magellan
Ushuaia
Cape Horn

MTS.

Tropic of Capricorn

© GeoNova

149

EUROPE

⊛ National Capital

• Other City

1:22,107,000

| 0 | 250 | 500 mi |

| 0 | 250 | 500 km |

Azimuthal Equal Area Projection

Arctic Circle

Reykjavík ⊛ Akureyri

ICELAND

Norwegian   *Sea*

Tromsø

Bodø   Kiru

Faroe Is.
(Den.)

Trondheim

Shetland Is.
(Brit.)

Sundsvall

NORWAY

SWEDEN

Bergen

Orkney
Is.

Stavanger

Oslo ⊛

Uppsala

Stockholm

Linköping

Gotland

Hebrides

Aberdeen

Skagerrak

Göteborg

Öland

Glasgow

Edinburgh

Kattegat

Baltic

Belfast

UNITED KINGDOM

Newcastle

(GREAT BRITAIN)

Jutland

Århus

Copenhagen ⊛ Helsingborg

Dublin ⊛

Irish
Sea

Liverpool

Leeds

DENMARK

Odense

Malmö

IRELAND

Cork

Manchester   Sheffield

North

Gdańsk

Birmingham

Sea

Szczecin

Cardiff   Bristol

NETHERLANDS

Hamburg

Land's End

Portsmouth

Amsterdam ⊛

Bremen

Hannover

Berlin ⊛

English Channel

London

Rotterdam

Poznań

Channel Is.
(Brit.)

Brussels ⊛

Antwerp

Essen

GERMANY

Łódź

Le Havre

Lille

Cologne

Leipzig

Dresden

Wrocła

Brest

Rouen

BELGIUM

Liège

Bonn

Frankfurt

Prague ⊛

Katowice

LUXEMBOURG

Paris ⊛

Luxembourg

Mannheim

CZECH REP.

Ostrava

Nantes

Loire

Strasbourg

Stuttgart

Brno

SLOVAK

Dijon

Munich

Linz

Vienna ⊛ Bratislava

FRANCE

Bern ⊛

Zurich

LIECHTENSTEIN

ATLANTIC

Geneva

SWITZERLAND

AUSTRIA

Graz

Budape

OCEAN

Lyon

Mt. Blanc
4807 m
(15,771 ft)

Milan

Ljubljana

SLOVENIA

HUNGA

Bay
of
Biscay

Bordeaux

Verona

Venice

SLOVENIA

Pécs

Cape Finisterre

Vigo

Gijón

Toulouse

Turin

Genoa

Bologna

CROATIA

Zagreb

Porto

Bilbao

Marseille

Nice

Florence

SAN
MARINO

BOSNIA &
HERZEGOVIN

Valladolid

Toulon

MONACO

Sarajevo

Ligurian Sea

Split

PORTUGAL

IBERIAN

Zaragoza

Pico de Aneto
3404 m
(11,168 ft)

ANDORRA

Elba

MONTENEG

Lisbon ⊛

Badajoz

Tagus

Madrid ⊛

Corsica
(Fr.)

VATICAN
CITY

⊛ **Rome**

Dubrovnik

Podgoric

PENINSULA

Barcelona

ITALY

Cape
St. Vincent

Córdoba

SPAIN

Valencia

Balearic Sea

Majorca

Bari

Sevilla

Alicante

Palma

Minorca

Naples

Salerno

Cádiz

Granada

Balearic Is.
(Sp.)

Sardinia
(It.)

Co

Strait of
Gibraltar

Málaga

GIBRALTAR
(Brit.)

Cagliari

Tyrrhenian
Sea

Ioni
Sea

Mediterr

Palermo

⊛ Algiers

a n

Rabat ⊛

Tunis

Catania

Mt. Etna
3323 m
(10,902 ft)

Casablanca

Sicily

MOROCCO

M O U N T A I N S

ALGERIA

TUNISIA

Valletta

⊛ **MALTA**

A T L A S

Sea

North
Cape
mmerfest

*Barents
Sea*

Nar'yan-Mar

Pechora

PLAND
Murmansk
KOLA
PENINSULA
Apatity

Pechora

Arctic Circle

Ob

Irtysh

FINLAND

Oulu

Belomorsk

White Sea

Divina

Arkhangel'sk

Ukhta

Serov

R   U   S   S   I   A

Berezniki

Petropavl

Syktyvkar

Yekaterinburg

Kotlas

Perm'

Chelyabinsk

U

R

A

L

Tampere
Lahti

*Lake
Onega*

Petrozavodsk

Kirov

Izhevsk

Ufa

Qostanay

Helsinki

*Lake
Ladoga*

Vologda

Naberezhnyye
Chelny

Kama

Magnitogorsk

St.
Petersburg

Cherepovets

M

O

U

N

T

A

I

N

S

Tallinn

Velikiy
Novgorod

Yaroslavl'

Kazan

ESTONIA

Tartu

Ivanovo

Nizhniy
Novgorod

Pskov

EUROPEAN

Tver'

Ul'yanovsk

Tol'yatti

Orenburg

Orsk

LATVIA

Moscow

Saransk

Samara

Aktobe

a

Daugavpils

Ryazan'

Penza

Oral

HUANIA

Vitsyebsk

Smolensk

Tula

Volga

KAZAKHSTAN

nas

Vilnius

Mahilyow

Lipetsk

Tambov

Ural

ad

Minsk

Bryansk

Saratov

Atyraū

*Aral
Sea*

Hrodna

BELARUS

Homyel'

Kursk

Voronezh

ERN

Brest

saw

Volgograd

UZBEKISTAN

ND

Kyiv

Kharkiv

Astrakhan

L'viv

UKRAINE

Dnieper

Luhans'k

Donets'k

Caspian

THIAN

Chernivtsi

Dnipropetrovs'k

Don

Aktaū

ce

MOLDOVA

Kryvyy Rih

Zaporizhzhia

Rostov na Donu

brecen

Iaşi

Chişinău

Mykolaiv

Mariupol'

*Sea of
Azov*

Stavropol'

Groznyy

Makhachkala

TURKMENISTAN

Sea

Odesa

CRIMEA

Krasnodar

Türkmenbashy

ROMANIA

Sevastopol'

Simferopol'

C A U C A S U S

GEORGIA

Baku

işoara

Ploieşti

Black   Sea

Tbilisi

AZERBAIJAN

Bucharest

Constanţa

ARMENIA

de

Danube

Varna

Trabzon

Yerevan

BULGARIA

Burgas

Sofia

kopje

Plovdiv

Tabriz

Tehran

NIA

İstanbul

IRAN

Thessaloniki

Ankara

TURKEY

Larisa

Aegean

İzmir

ECE

Adana

Athens

ONNESE

Cyclades

Baghdad

Tigris

Rhodes

Nicosia

SYRIA

Euphrates

IRAQ

Sea of Crete

CYPRUS

LEBANON

Beirut

Crete

Iraklion

Damascus

*Persian
Gu*

ATLANTIC OCEAN

IRELAND

PORTUGAL

UNITED
KINGDOM

SPAIN

NORWAY

Barents
Sea

MOROCCO

FRANCE

BEL. NETH. DEN.

SWEDEN

GERMANY

SWITZ.

FINLAND

E U R O P E

Murmansk

ALGERIA

ITALY

CZECH
AUS. REP.

ESTONIA

Arkhangel'sk

POLAND LITH. LAT.

St. Petersburg

TUNISIA

HUNG.

BELARUS

Moscow

R U S S

SERB.

ROM. MOL.

URAL MOUNTAINS

LIBYA

GREECE

BUL.

UKRAINE

Izmir

İstanbul

Yekaterinburg

Chelyabinsk

Ankara

Black
Sea

Volgograd

Irtysh

Magnitogorsk

Tor

TURKEY

GEORGIA

Astrakhan'

Omsk

Novosibirsk

CYPRUS

Nicosia

Tbilisi

Caspian
Sea

KAZAKHSTAN

Astana

Novoku

CHAD

LEBANON

ARMENIA

Aral

Karaganda

Pavloda

Beirut

Yerevan

AZERBAIJAN

Sea

Semey

Tel Aviv

SYRIA

Tabriz

Baku

Lake
Balkhash

Jerusalem

Damascus

TURKMENISTAN

UZBEKISTAN

Almaty

ISRAEL

Amman

IRAQ

Tehran

Ashgabat

Tashkent

Bishkek

Ür

EGYPT

JORDAN

Baghdad

Dushanbe

KYRGYZSTAN

Sinai

Al-Basrah

Mashhad

Kashi

AFRICA

SAUDI

Kuwait City

Esfahan

TAJIKISTAN

Takla Mak
Desert

ARABIA

KUWAIT

IRAN

AFGHANISTAN

SUDAN

Jeddah

Manama

Shiraz

Kabul

Islamabad

XIZAN

Mecca

Riyadh

Kerman

Kandahar

Srinagar

(TIBE

BAHRAIN

Lahore

Amritsar

QATAR

Doha

Abu Dhabi

PAKISTAN

Delhi

NEPAL

UNITED ARAB
EMIRATES

Muscat

Sukkur

New Delhi

Kathmandu

ERITREA

Karachi

Hyderabad

Jaipur

Lucknov

OMAN

Sanaa

Kanpur

Gang

Red Sea

Ahmadabad

I N D I A

Ko
(Calc

ETHIOPIA

DJI.

YEMEN

Nagpur

Gulf of Aden

Aden

Socotra
(Yemen)

Arabian
Sea

Mumbai

Hyderabad

SOMALIA

Equator

Bengalooru
(Bangalore)

Chennai
(Madras)

ishu

Laccadive
Islands
(India)

Madurai

Kochi

SRI LANK

Colombo

Male

INDIAN

OCEA

MALDIVES

ASIA

⊛ National Capital

★ Territorial Capital

• Other City

1:51,084,000

0   500   1,000 mi

0   500   1,000 km

Two-Point Equidistant Projection

Nile

Tropic of Cancer

Mediterranean Sea

Ka
Se

152

North Pole
ARCTIC
OCEAN
180°
160°
140°
120°
80°
70°
60°
50°
40°

Chukchi
Sea
Bering
Sea
ALASKA
170°

East
Siberian
Sea
Anadyr

Laptev
Sea

Lena

KAMCHATKA
PENINSULA
Magadan
180°

Petropavlovsk-
Kamchatskiy

Sea of
Okhotsk
170°

Yakutsk

SIBERIA

Sakhalin
Kuril
Islands
(Russia)
30°

Komsomolsk
na Amure
Khabarovsk

noyarsk Bratsk
Blagoveshchensk
Sapporo
160°

Lake
Baikal
Chita

Irkutsk Ulan-Ude
Harbin
Vladivostok
Sea of
Japan
(East Sea)
JAPAN
Sendai

Ulaanbaatar
Changchun
Shenyang
Tokyo
Yokohama
Kyoto

MONGOLIA
Pyongyang
N. KOREA
Kobe Osaka
20°

ALTAY
GOBI DESERT
Beijing
Dalian
Seoul
Hiroshima

MTS.
Hohhot
Tianjin
S. KOREA

JIANG
Jinan
Qingdao
Nagasaki

Taiyuan
Yellow
Sea

Lanzhou
Zhengzhou
East
China
Sea
150°

CHINA
Xi'an
Nanjing
Shanghai

rest
n.
5 ft.)
Chengdu
Wuhan
Wenzhou
Okinawa (Japan)
10°

Lhasa
Chongqing
Changsha Fuzhou

Yangtze (Chang)
Ryukyu Islands

UTAN
hu
Xiamen
Taipei

LADESH
Kunming
Guangzhou
Hong Kong
TAIWAN

haka
Nanning
Macao
Philippine
Sea

Mandalay
Hanoi
Gulf
of
Tonkin
LUZON

MYANMAR
(BURMA)
LAOS
Manila
PHILIPPINES

al
Vientiane
Da Nang
South
China
Sea

Yangon
(angoon)
THAILAND
VIETNAM
Cebu
MINDANAO

an
ds
ia)
Bangkok
CAMBODIA
Davao

Andaman
Sea
Phnom
Penh
Ho Chi Minh City
Sulu
Sea

Gulf of
Thailand
Kota Kinabalu
Celebes
Sea
Manado
NEW GUINEA

bar
nds
dia)
Bandar Seri Begawan
BRUNEI
Irian
Jaya

Medan
Kuching
BORNEO
Banda
Sea
Arafura
Sea

MALAYSIA

SUMATRA
Kuala
Lumpur
SINGAPORE
Singapore
INDONESIA

Padang
Banjarmasin
Makassar
Timor
Sea

Palembang
Java Sea
Dili
EAST
TIMOR

Jakarta
Surabaya
Kupang
AUSTRALIA

Bandung
JAVA
100°
110°
120°
130°
140°

PACIFIC
OCEAN

© GeoNova

INDIAN OCEAN

ATLANTIC OCEAN

Kismaayo

Nakuru
Nairobi ⊛
Kilimanjaro
5895 m (19,340 ft) ▲
Mwanza
SERENGETI
PLAIN
Arusha

RWANDA
Kgali ⊛
BURUNDI
Bujumbura ⊛
Bukavu
GREAT RIFT VALLEY

DEMOCRATIC
REPUBLIC OF
THE CONGO

L. Victoria

L. Tanganyika

Tabora
Dodoma ⊛
TANZANIA
Mbeya

COMOROS
Moroni ⊛

Mtwara
Nacala-
Porto
Nampula

Mtwara
Tanga
Zanzibar
Dar es Salaam
Mombasa

Antsiranana
Toamasina

MADAGASCAR

Antananarivo ⊛
Fianarantsoa

Toliara

Mozambique Channel

Quelimane

Tropic of Capricorn

MALAWI
Lilongwe ⊛
Chipata

Beira

Inhambane

L. Nyasa

L. Mweru

KATANGA
Lubumbashi
Likasi
Kitwe
Ndola
ZAMBIA
Lusaka ⊛
PLATEAU
Kolwezi
Kabwe

Kananga
Mbuji-Mayi
Kikwit
Tshikapa

Kinshasa ⊛
THE
CONGO
Brazzaville ⊛

GABON
Franceville
Pointe-Noire

Matadi

Cabinda
(Ang.)

Luanda ⊛

Lobito
Benguela

Namibe

Malanje

ANGOLA

Huambo

Menongue

Grootfontein

Windhoek ⊛
NAMIBIA

NAMIB DESERT

Walvis Bay

Lüderitz

Harare ⊛
ZIMBABWE
Bulawayo

L. Kariba

Livingstone

Francistown

BOTSWANA
KALAHARI
DESERT
Gaborone ⊛

Mutare

MOZAMBIQUE
Maputo ⊛
Mbabane ⊛
SWAZILAND
Newcastle
Pietermaritzburg
Durban

Pretoria ⊛
Johannesburg ⊛
Klerksdorp
Kimberley
Bloemfontein ⊛
LESOTHO
Maseru ⊛

SOUTH
AFRICA

East London
Port Elizabeth

Cape Town ⊛
Cape of Good Hope

*Cape
Agulhas*

ST. HELENA
(Brit.)

ASCENSION
(Brit.)

Port-
Gentil

Zambezi

Limpopo

Orange

© GeoNova

AFRICA

⊛ National Capital

• Other City

1:39,550,000

0   250   500   750 mi

0   250   500   750 km

Azimuthal Equal Area Projection

155

FACTS About NATIONS

Here are basic facts about each of the 194 independent nations in the world. The color of the heading for each country tells you what continent it belongs in. The population is an estimate for mid-2007. The currency entry shows how much one U.S. dollar was worth in each country's currency as of early 2007. The language entry gives official languages and other common languages.

COLOR KEY
- ● Africa
- ● Asia
- ● Australia
- ● Europe
- ● North America
- ● Pacific Islands
- ● South America

Afghanistan

- ► Capital: Kabul
- ► Population: 31,889,923
- ► Area: 250,001 sq. mi. (647,500 sq. km.)
- ► Currency: $1 = 49.14 afghanis
- ► Language: Afghan Persian (Dari), Pashto
- ► Did You Know? The national sport *buzkashi* is played on horseback and literally means "goat grabbing."

Albania
- ► Capital: Tirana
- ► Population: 3,600,523
- ► Area: 11,100 sq. mi. (28,748 sq. km.)
- ► Currency: $1 = 95.07 leke
- ► Language: Albanian, Greek
- ► Did You Know? In 2000, Tirana painted all the gray Communist-era buildings in the city in festive colors and patterns.

Algeria
- ► Capital: Algiers (El Djazair)
- ► Population: 33,333,216
- ► Area: 919,595 sq. mi. (2,381,740 sq. km.)
- ► Currency: $1 = 70.88 dinars
- ► Language: Arabic, French, Berber dialects
- ► Did You Know? Algeria's desert region contains large "sand seas" called *ergs* that have dunes up to 2,000 feet high.

Andorra

- ► Capital: Andorra la Vella
- ► Population: 71,822
- ► Area: 181 sq. mi. (468 sq. km.)
- ► Currency: $1 = .76 euros
- ► Language: Catalan, French, Castilian
- ► Did You Know? The average lifespan of people in Andorra is about 83 years, the highest of any country in the world.

Angola

- ► Capital: Luanda
- ► Population: 12,263,596
- ► Area: 481,354 sq. mi. (1,246,700 sq. km.)
- ► Currency: $1 = 79.80 kwanza
- ► Language: Portuguese, African languages
- ► Did You Know? Angola is the second largest oil-producer in sub-Saharan Africa after Nigeria.

Antigua & Barbuda

- ► Capital: St. John's
- ► Population: 69,481
- ► Area: 171 sq. mi. (443 sq. km.)
- ► Currency: $1 = 2.65 East Caribbean dollars
- ► Language: English
- ► Did You Know? Antigua was the first of the British Caribbean colonies to free its slaves, on August 1, 1834.

Bolivia

- **Capital:** La Paz (admin.); Sucre (judiciary)
- **Population:** 9,119,152
- **Area:** 424,164 sq. mi. (1,098,580 sq. km.)
- **Currency:** $1 = 7.99 bolivianos
- **Language:** Spanish, Quechua, Aymara
- **Did You Know?** Bolivia's administrative capital, La Paz, is the highest capital city in the world, at about 13,000 feet above sea level.

Bosnia and Herzegovina

- **Capital:** Sarajevo
- **Population:** 4,552,198
- **Area:** 19,741 sq. mi. (51,129 sq. km.)
- **Currency:** $1 = 1.49 convertible marka
- **Language:** Bosnian, Croatian, Serbian
- **Did You Know?** This country has three presidents, who serve consecutive eight-month terms.

Botswana

- **Capital:** Gaborone
- **Population:** 1,639,131
- **Area:** 231,804 sq. mi. (600,370 sq. km.)
- **Currency:** $1 = 6.17 pulas
- **Language:** Setswana, English
- **Did You Know?** The Kalahari Desert, an area of bush and grasslands, covers 84% of this country.

Brazil

- **Capital:** Brasília
- **Population:** 190,010,647
- **Area:** 3,286,488 sq. mi. (8,511,965 sq. km.)
- **Currency:** $1 = 2.09 reals
- **Language:** Portuguese, Spanish, English, French
- **Did You Know?** Brazil has won 5 men's soccer World Cups, the most of any country.

COLOR KEY
- ● Africa
- ● Asia
- ● Australia
- ● Europe
- ● North America
- ● Pacific Islands
- ● South America

Argentina

- **Capital:** Buenos Aires
- **Population:** 40,301,927
- **Area:** 1,068,302 sq. mi. (2,766,890 sq. km.)
- **Currency:** $1 = 3.10 pesos
- **Language:** Spanish, English, Italian, German, French
- **Did You Know?** About 90% of the population is urban; one-third lives in the capital.

Armenia

- **Capital:** Yerevan
- **Population:** 2,971,650
- **Area:** 11,506 sq. mi. (29,800 sq. km.)
- **Currency:** $1 = 446.48 drams
- **Language:** Armenian, Russian
- **Did You Know?** Armenia considers itself the first country to have formally adopted Christianity, in the year 301.

Australia

- **Capital:** Canberra
- **Population:** 20,434,176
- **Area:** 2,967,909 sq. mi. (7,686,850 sq. km.)
- **Currency:** $1 = 1.27 Australia dollars
- **Language:** English, Aboriginal languages
- **Did You Know?** Many animal species, including kangaroos, koalas, platypuses, dingos, and wombats, can be found in the wild only in Australia.

Austria

- **Capital:** Vienna
- **Population:** 8,199,783
- **Area:** 32,382 sq. mi. (83,870 sq. km.)
- **Currency:** $1 = .76 euros
- **Language:** German, Slovene, Croatian, Hungarian
- **Did You Know?** Austria's Hohe Tauern National Park is Central Europe's largest protected natural area.

Azerbaijan

- **Capital:** Baku
- **Population:** 8,120,247
- **Area:** 33,436 sq. mi. (86,600 sq. km.)
- **Currency:** $1 = .87 new manats
- **Language:** Azeri, Russian, Armenian
- **Did You Know?** In ancient times, Azerbaijan was a major hub of the Great Silk Road between China and Italy.

The Bahamas

- **Capital:** Nassau
- **Population:** 305,655
- **Area:** 5,382 sq. mi. (13,940 sq. km.)
- **Currency:** $1 = 1 Bahamian dollars
- **Language:** English, Creole
- **Did You Know?** About two-thirds of the population lives on New Providence, one of The Bahamas' nearly 700 islands.

WAforKids.com Go to *www.WAforKids.com* for more facts about nations.

157

Bahrain

- **Capital:** Manama
- **Population:** 708,573
- **Area:** 257 sq. mi. (665 sq. km.)
- **Currency:** $1 = .38 dinars
- **Language:** Arabic, English, Farsi, Urdu
- **Did You Know?** Bahrain appointed its first female judge in June 2006.

Bangladesh

- **Capital:** Dhaka
- **Population:** 150,448,339
- **Area:** 55,599 sq. mi. (144,000 sq. km.)
- **Currency:** $1 = 68.68 taka
- **Language:** Bangla, English
- **Did You Know?** About one-third of Bangladesh is flooded every year during monsoon season, between June and early October.

Barbados

- **Capital:** Bridgetown
- **Population:** 280,946
- **Area:** 166 sq. mi. (431 sq. km.)
- **Currency:** $1 = 1.99 Barbados dollars
- **Language:** English
- **Did You Know?** The grapefruit is considered one of the Seven Wonders of Barbados, as it is believed to have been developed in Barbados from other fruits.

Belarus

- **Capital:** Minsk
- **Population:** 9,724,723
- **Area:** 80,155 sq. mi. (207,600 sq. km.)
- **Currency:** $1 = 2,141.83 rubli
- **Language:** Belarusian, Russian
- **Did You Know?** Contamination from the 1986 Chernobyl nuclear power plant explosion, in neighboring Ukraine, continues to affect Belarus. High numbers of children have been diagnosed with cancer. Many people are unemployed because land that was contaminated could no longer be farmed.

Cameroon

- **Capital:** Yaoundé
- **Population:** 18,060,382
- **Area:** 183,568 sq. mi. (475,440 sq. km.)
- **Currency:** $1 = 499.34 CFA BEAC francs
- **Language:** English, French, African languages
- **Did You Know?** Cameroon has rain forests, sandy beaches, rolling savannas, volcanic mountain ranges, and over 200 ethnic groups, all in an area slightly larger than the state of California.

Canada

- **Capital:** Ottawa
- **Population:** 33,390,141
- **Area:** 3,855,103 sq. mi. (9,984,670 sq. km.)
- **Currency:** $1 = 1.16 Canada dollars
- **Language:** English, French
- **Did You Know?** The 2010 Olympic Winter Games will be held in Vancouver, British Columbia.

Cape Verde

- **Capital:** Praia
- **Population:** 423,613
- **Area:** 1,557 sq. mi. (4,033 sq. km.)
- **Currency:** $1 = 84.30 escudos
- **Language:** Portuguese, Crioulo
- **Did You Know?** More Cape Verdeans live abroad than live on the nation's islands. Severe droughts in the 20th century forced many to move.

Central African Republic

- **Capital:** Bangui
- **Population:** 4,369,038
- **Area:** 240,535 sq. mi. (622,984 sq. km.)
- **Currency:** $1 = 499.34 CFA BEAC francs
- **Language:** French, Sangho
- **Did You Know?** Former Prime Minister Barthélemy Boganda wrote the words to the national anthem, "La Renaissance" ("The Rebirth").

Chad

- **Capital:** N'Djamena
- **Population:** 10,238,807
- **Area:** 495,755 sq. mi. (1,284,000 sq. km.)
- **Currency:** $1 = 499.34 CFA BEAC francs
- **Language:** French, Arabic, Sara
- **Did You Know?** Scientists believe Lake Chad once was roughly the same size as the Caspian Sea, the largest lake in the world at 144,000 sq. mi. Lake Chad has shrunk to 550 sq. mi.

Chile

- **Capital:** Santiago
- **Population:** 16,284,741
- **Area:** 292,260 sq. mi. (756,950 sq. km.)
- **Currency:** $1 = 517.95 pesos
- **Language:** Spanish
- **Did You Know?** Chile is about 2,500 miles long but only 93.2 miles wide, from east to west.

China

- **Capital:** Beijing
- **Population:** 1,321,851,888
- **Area:** 3,705,407 sq. mi. (9,596,960 sq. km.)
- **Currency:** $1 = 7.75 yuan renminbi
- **Language:** Mandarin, and many dialects
- **Did You Know?** In the 17th century, China's Great Wall (actually a network of walls) extended some 3,700 miles.

Colombia

- **Capital:** Bogotá
- **Population:** 44,227,550
- **Area:** 439,736 sq. mi. (1,138,910 sq. km.)
- **Currency:** $1 = 2,219.98 pesos
- **Language:** Spanish
- **Did You Know?** Colombia is the only South American country that touches both the Caribbean Sea and the Pacific Ocean.

TAJ MAHAL AT AGRA, INDIA

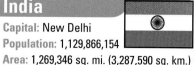

Haiti

- **Capital:** Port-au-Prince
- **Population:** 8,706,497
- **Area:** 10,714 sq. mi. (27,750 sq. km.)
- **Currency:** $1 = 37.60 gourdes
- **Language:** French, Creole
- **Did You Know?** Haiti gained independence from France in 1804 and, after the U.S., is the second oldest country in the Americas.

Honduras

- **Capital:** Tegucigalpa
- **Population:** 7,483,763
- **Area:** 43,278 sq. mi. (112,090 sq. km.)
- **Currency:** $1 = 18.84 lempiras
- **Language:** Spanish, Amerindian dialects
- **Did You Know?** Christopher Columbus was the first recorded European to reach Honduras, where he landed in 1502.

Hungary

- **Capital:** Budapest
- **Population:** 9,956,108
- **Area:** 35,919 sq. mi. (93,030 sq. km.)
- **Currency:** $1 = 191.58 forint
- **Language:** Hungarian (Magyar)
- **Did You Know?** Budapest was originally two separate cities, Buda and Pest. The two areas are separated by the Danube River.

Iceland

- **Capital:** Reykjavik
- **Population:** 301,931
- **Area:** 39,769 sq. mi. (103,000 sq. km.)
- **Currency:** $1 = 66.79 kronur
- **Language:** Icelandic, English
- **Did You Know?** The Althing, Iceland's assembly, established around the year 930, is the world's oldest surviving parliament.

India

- **Capital:** New Delhi
- **Population:** 1,129,866,154
- **Area:** 1,269,346 sq. mi. (3,287,590 sq. km.)
- **Currency:** $1 = 43.87 rupees
- **Language:** Hindi, English, Bengali, Urdu
- **Did You Know?** Jammu and Kashmir, part of a larger disputed region bordering India, Pakistan, and China, is India's only Muslim-majority state.

Indonesia

- **Capital:** Jakarta
- **Population:** 234,693,997
- **Area:** 741,100 sq. mi. (1,919,440 sq. km.)
- **Currency:** $1 = 9,043.95 rupiahs
- **Language:** Bahasa Indonesian, English, Dutch, Javanese
- **Did You Know?** Borobudur, located on the island of Java, is the largest Buddhist temple in the world.

Iran

- **Capital:** Tehran
- **Population:** 65,397,521
- **Area:** 636,296 sq. mi. (1,648,000 sq. km.)
- **Currency:** $1 = 9,231 rials
- **Language:** Farsi (Persian), Turkic, Kurdish
- **Did You Know?** Iran produces over a third of the world's pistachios—more than any other nation.

Iraq

- **Capital:** Baghdad
- **Population:** 27,499,638
- **Area:** 168,754 sq. mi. (437,072 sq. km.)
- **Currency:** $1 = 1,285.20 dinars
- **Language:** Arabic, Kurdish
- **Did You Know?** Iraq covers the Tigris-Euphrates Valley, site of one of the oldest known civilizations in the world. The Sumer existed there in the 4th millennium B.C.

COLOR KEY

- Africa
- Asia
- Australia
- Europe
- North America
- Pacific Islands
- South America

Ireland

- **Capital:** Dublin
- **Population:** 4,109,086
- **Area:** 27,135 sq. mi. (70,280 sq. km.)
- **Currency:** $1 = .76 euros
- **Language:** English, Irish
- **Did You Know?** The first known settlers at Dublin were Norsemen, or Vikings, who landed in the 9th century.

Israel

- **Capital:** Jerusalem
- **Population:** 6,426,679
- **Area:** 8,019 sq. mi. (20,770 sq. km.)
- **Currency:** $1 = 4.20 new shekels
- **Language:** Hebrew, Arabic, English
- **Did You Know?** Hebrew, Israel's official language, was revived as a spoken language in the 19th and 20th centuries; it was last spoken widely in ancient times.

Italy

- **Capital:** Rome
- **Population:** 58,147,733
- **Area:** 116,306 sq. mi. (301,230 sq. km.)
- **Currency:** $1 = .76 euros
- **Language:** Italian, German, French, Slovenian
- **Did You Know?** Italy has one of the highest cell phone use rates in the world, with about 124 cell phone subscriptions for every 100 people in the population.

Jamaica

- **Capital:** Kingston
- **Population:** 2,780,132
- **Area:** 4,244 sq. mi. (10,991 sq. km.)
- **Currency:** $1 = 67.26 Jamaica dollars
- **Language:** English, Jamaican Creole
- **Did You Know?** Jamaica's name comes from the Arawak Indian word *Xaymaca*, which means "isle of springs."

Japan

- **Capital:** Tokyo
- **Population:** 127,467,972
- **Area:** 145,883 sq. mi. (377,835 sq. km.)
- **Currency:** $1 = 119.33 yen
- **Language:** Japanese
- **Did You Know?** The 33.5-mile Seikan Tunnel, between Honshu and Hokkaido, is the longest railroad tunnel in the world.

Jordan

- **Capital:** Amman
- **Population:** 6,053,193
- **Area:** 35,637 sq. mi. (92,300 sq. km.)
- **Currency:** $1 = .71 dinars
- **Language:** Arabic, English
- **Did You Know?** The Dead Sea, on the Israel-Jordan border, is six times saltier than the ocean.

Kazakhstan

- **Capital:** Astana
- **Population:** 15,284,929
- **Area:** 1,049,155 sq. mi. (2,717,300 sq. km.)
- **Currency:** $1 = 124.11 tenge
- **Language:** Kazakh, Russian
- **Did You Know?** Baikonur Cosmodrome, the launching facility of the Russian Space Agency, is located in Kazakhstan.

Kenya

- **Capital:** Nairobi
- **Population:** 36,913,721
- **Area:** 224,962 sq. mi. (582,650 sq. km.)
- **Currency:** $1 = 69 shillings
- **Language:** Kiswahili, English
- **Did You Know?** Kenya's main port, Mombasa, was founded by Arab traders in the 11th century.

COLOR KEY

- ● Africa
- ● Asia
- ● Australia
- ● Europe
- ● North America
- ● Pacific Islands
- ● South America

Kiribati

- **Capital:** Tarawa
- **Population:** 107,817
- **Area:** 313 sq. mi. (811 sq. km.)
- **Currency:** $1 = 1.27 Australia dollars
- **Language:** English, I-Kiribati
- **Did You Know?** Kiribati is a grouping of islands spread across an area of the Pacific Ocean about the same size as the continental U.S.

Korea, North

- **Capital:** Pyongyang
- **Population:** 23,301,725
- **Area:** 46,541 sq. mi. (120,540 sq. km.)
- **Currency:** $1 = 170 won
- **Language:** Korean
- **Did You Know?** North and South Korea have officially been at war for over 50 years. A ceasefire has maintained the peace since 1953.

Korea, South

- **Capital:** Seoul
- **Population:** 49,044,790
- **Area:** 38,023 sq. mi. (98,480 sq. km.)
- **Currency:** $1 = 935.38 won
- **Language:** Korean
- **Did You Know?** The martial arts form Taekwondo is Korea's national sport. It means "way of the foot and fist."

Kuwait

- **Capital:** Kuwait City
- **Population:** 2,505,559
- **Area:** 6,880 sq. mi. (17,820 sq. km.)
- **Currency:** $1 = .29 dinars
- **Language:** Arabic, English
- **Did You Know?** Women were allowed to vote and run in parliamentary elections for the first time in 2007.

Kyrgyzstan

- **Capital:** Bishkek
- **Population:** 5,284,149
- **Area:** 76,641 sq. mi. (198,500 sq. km.)
- **Currency:** $1 = 38.65 soms
- **Language:** Kyrgyz, Russian
- **Did You Know?** The Manas, the Kyrgyz national epic, is thought to be the world's longest poem, at more than half a million lines long.

Laos

- **Capital:** Vientiane
- **Population:** 6,521,998
- **Area:** 91,429 sq. mi. (236,800 sq. km.)
- **Currency:** $1 = 10,048.20 kips
- **Language:** Lao, French, English
- **Did You Know?** Thousands of ancient stone jars—each large enough to fit a person—can be found in Laos' Plain of Jars. Archaeologists are not sure who made them or why.

Latvia

- **Capital:** Riga
- **Population:** 2,259,810
- **Area:** 24,938 sq. mi. (64,589 sq. km.)
- **Currency:** $1 = .54 lati
- **Language:** Latvian, Russian, Lithuanian
- **Did You Know?** Festival sing-alongs are immensely popular in Latvia. Riga usually holds the largest annual gathering with over 30,000 dancers, singers, and musicians.

Lebanon

- **Capital:** Beirut
- **Population:** 3,921,278
- **Area:** 4,015 sq. mi. (10,400 sq. km.)
- **Currency:** $1 = 1,511.50 pounds
- **Language:** Arabic, French, English, Armenian
- **Did You Know?** Lebanon has been famous for cedar trees for over 4,000 years. A cedar even appears on the country's flag.

SAVANNA IN KENYA

167

Lesotho

- **Capital:** Maseru
- **Population:** 2,012,649
- **Area:** 11,720 sq. mi. (30,355 sq. km.)
- **Currency:** $1 = 7.16 maloti
- **Language:** English, Sesotho, Zulu, Xhosa
- **Did You Know?** The Kingdom of Lesotho is completely surrounded by South Africa.

Liberia

- **Capital:** Monrovia
- **Population:** 3,193,942
- **Area:** 43,000 sq. mi. (111,370 sq. km.)
- **Currency:** $1 = 49 Liberia dollars
- **Language:** English, ethnic languages
- **Did You Know?** Liberia was founded in 1822 by freed African American slaves from the U.S. It became an independent republic in 1847.

Libya

- **Capital:** Tripoli
- **Population:** 6,036,914
- **Area:** 679,362 sq. mi. (1,759,540 sq. km.)
- **Currency:** $1 = 1.29 dinars
- **Language:** Arabic, Italian, English
- **Did You Know?** Libya had the world's highest temperature ever recorded, when it reached 136°F in 1922.

Liechtenstein

- **Capital:** Vaduz
- **Population:** 34,247
- **Area:** 62 sq. mi. (160 sq. km.)
- **Currency:** $1 = 1.23 Swiss francs
- **Language:** German, Alemannic dialect
- **Did You Know?** Liechtenstein is one of only two countries in the world (Uzbekistan is the other) that is "doubly landlocked." It has no coastline, and it is surrounded by countries without coastlines.

Lithuania

- **Capital:** Vilnius
- **Population:** 3,575,439
- **Area:** 25,174 sq. mi. (65,200 sq. km.)
- **Currency:** $1 = 2.63 litai
- **Language:** Lithuanian, Russian, Polish
- **Did You Know?** Lithuania is larger than the other Baltic states of Latvia and Estonia.

Luxembourg

- **Capital:** Luxembourg
- **Population:** 480,222
- **Area:** 998 sq. mi. (2,586 sq. km.)
- **Currency:** $1 = .76 euros
- **Language:** French, German, Luxembourgish
- **Did You Know?** Luxembourg's per capita gross national product (GDP) is nearly $66,000, the highest in the world.

Macedonia

- **Capital:** Skopje
- **Population:** 2,055,915
- **Area:** 9,781 sq. mi. (25,333 sq. km.)
- **Currency:** $1 = 46.87 denars
- **Language:** Macedonian, Albanian, Turkish
- **Did You Know?** Until 1913, Macedonia had been part of the Ottoman Empire for about 500 years.

Madagascar

- **Capital:** Antananarivo
- **Population:** 19,448,815
- **Area:** 226,657 sq. mi. (587,040 sq. km.)
- **Currency:** $1 = 2,005 ariary
- **Language:** Malagasy, French
- **Did You Know?** Located off Africa's coast, the island of Madagascar was settled 2,000 years ago by Malayan-Indonesian people.

COLOR KEY

- Africa
- Asia
- Australia
- Europe
- North America
- Pacific Islands
- South America

BRAZIL

Brazil is the largest country in South America. Most of the country has a warm tropical climate. Many different ethnic groups blend to make up the population in Brazil: descendants of Europeans, American Indians, and Africans. Children in Brazil are required to go to school until the age of 14, but some children in Brazil have to start working before then because they cannot afford to complete their schooling.

No matter a person's age, soccer is definitely Brazil's unofficial national sport. The Brazilian national team has won five World Cups. Some poorer kids play soccer in the street with as many feet as possible chasing the ball.

CHINA

China is located in Asia and is the second largest country in the world. Around 1.3 billion people live in China—more than in any other country.

Chinese life varies a lot depending on whether a person lives in a city or in a rural village. Because of government policies on family planning, most city children do not have brothers and sisters. Over half of the Chinese population makes a living by farming, and rural life tends to be harder than city life. From ages 6-14, children in the cities attend school six days a week, from 8 in the morning until 5 in the afternoon. Rural children have the same requirements, but the distance to and from schools can make attendance difficult.

Kids in China don't spend all their time working or in school, though. Favorite sports include basketball, table tennis, and swimming. China is eagerly getting ready to host the 2008 Summer Olympic Games in Beijing, when its national teams are expected to excel in swimming and diving, track and field, and gymnastics.

PAPUA NEW GUINEA

Most of **Papua New Guinea** is located on half of an island directly north of Australia (the other half of the island is part of Indonesia). It is dominated by mountainous rain forests. The country also includes more than 600 smaller islands.

The official language of Papua New Guinea is English, but most children live in rural settings where they speak one of over 800 other native languages. The geography, scattered population, and many languages of Papua New Guinea mean that most kids there do not have television.

NATIVE AMERICANS

Who spoke the unbreakable code during World War II? ➡ page 185

native Americans are thought to have arrived in the Americas 18,000 years ago, most likely from northeast Asia. Although their population decreased significantly through the 17th, 18th, and 19th centuries from disease and war, there are still hundreds of tribes or nations, each with its own unique language and traditions. From the names of states and towns to foods like corn and squash, the influence of Native American cultures can be found everywhere in America.

TIME LINE NORTH AMERICAN INDIANS

1492	Christopher Columbus made contact with Taino tribes on the island he named Hispaniola.
c.1600	Five tribes—Mohawk, Oneida, Onondaga, Cayuga, and Seneca—formed the Iroquois Confederacy in the Northeast.
1754-63	Many Native Americans fought with both French and British troops in the French and Indian War.
1821	Sequoyah completed an alphabet for the Cherokee language.
1827	Cherokee tribes in what is now Georgia formed the Cherokee Nation with a constitution and elected governing officials.
1830	Congress passed the Indian Removal Act, the first law that forced tribes to move so that U.S. citizens could settle certain areas of land.
1834	Congress created the Indian Territory for tribes removed from their lands. It covered the present-day states of Oklahoma, Kansas, and Nebraska.
1890	During the Wounded Knee Massacre, about 200 Sioux men, women, and children were killed in a battle with U.S. soldiers on a South Dakota reservation. It was the last major battle between Native Americans and U.S. forces.
1924	Congress granted all Native Americans U.S. citizenship.
1929	Charles Curtis, a member of the Kaw nation, became the first American of Indian ancestry elected vice president.
1985	Wilma Mankiller became the first female chief of the Cherokee Nation.

MAJOR CULTURAL AREAS OF NATIVE NORTH AMERICANS

Climate and geography influenced the culture of the people who lived in these regions. On the plains, for example, people depended on the great herds of buffalo for food. For Aleuts and Eskimos in the far north, seals and whales were an important food source. There are more than 560 tribes officially recognized by the U.S. government today and more than 56 million acres of tribal lands. Below are just a few well-known tribal groups that have lived in these areas.

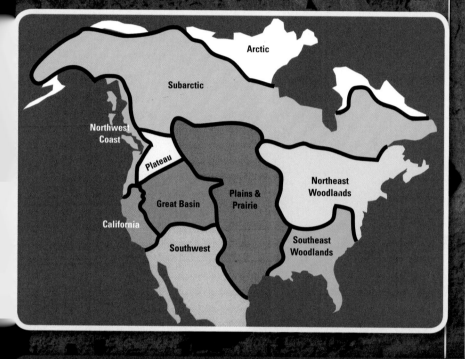

NORTHEAST WOODLANDS
The Illinois, Iroquois (Mohawk, Onondaga, Cayuga, Oneida, Seneca, and Tuscarora), Lenape, Menominee, Micmac, Narragansett, Potawatomi, Shawnee.

SOUTHEAST WOODLANDS
The Cherokee, Chickasaw, Choctaw, Creek, Seminole.

PLAINS & PRAIRIE The Arapaho, Blackfoot, Cheyenne, Comanche, Hidatsa, Kaw, Mandan, Sioux.

SOUTHWEST The Apache, Navajo, Havasupai, Mojave, Pima, Pueblo (Hopi, Isleta, Laguna, Zuñi).

GREAT BASIN The Paiute, Shoshoni, Ute.

CALIFORNIA The Klamath, Maidu, Miwok, Modoc, Patwin, Pomo, Wintun, Yurok.

PLATEAU The Cayuse, Nez Percé, Okanagon, Salish, Spokan, Umatilla, Walla Walla, Yakima.

NORTHWEST COAST The Chinook, Haida, Kwakiutl, Makah, Nootka, Salish, Tillamook, Tlingit, Tsimshian.

SUBARCTIC The Beaver, Chipewyan, Chippewa, Cree, Ingalik, Kaska, Kutchin, Montagnais, Naskapi, Tanana.

ARCTIC The Aleut, Eskimo (Inuit and Yinuk).

LARGEST U.S. TRIBAL GROUPINGS*

1. Cherokee, 309,459
2. Navajo, 293,802
3. Sioux, 120,066
4. Chippewa, 114,492
5. Choctaw, 87,541
6. Pueblo, 75,075
7. Apache, 62,921
8. Lumbee, 62,209
9. Eskimo, 51,577
10. Iroquois, 44,571

*2005 U.S. Census estimates. Figures are for people reporting only one tribal grouping.

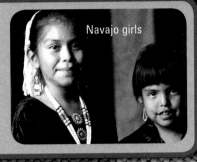
Navajo girls

Native American Populations by State*

State	Population	State	Population
Alabama	22,506	Nebraska	16,643
Alaska	106,147	Nevada	34,396
Arizona	300,224	New Hampshire	3,115
Arkansas	19,446	New Jersey	27,002
California	422,440	New Mexico	196,592
Colorado	52,204	New York	103,981
Connecticut	11,954	North Carolina	111,720
Delaware	3,384	North Dakota	33,754
Florida	76,405	Ohio	25,313
Georgia	27,373	Oklahoma	288,690
Hawaii	4,448	Oregon	49,919
Idaho	20,064	Pennsylvania	21,919
Illinois	38,945	Rhode Island	6,448
Indiana	16,928	South Carolina	15,590
Iowa	9,905	South Dakota	67,941
Kansas	25,786	Tennessee	16,494
Kentucky	8,518	Texas	155,356
Louisiana	26,806	Utah	32,942
Maine	7,293	Vermont	2,181
Maryland	17,857	Virginia	23,762
Massachusetts	18,340	Washington	104,131
Michigan	59,675	West Virginia	3,349
Minnesota	59,987	Wisconsin	51,971
Mississippi	13,115	Wyoming	12,114
Missouri	25,670	Wash., DC	1,856
Montana	60,402	U.S. total	2,863,001

*2005 U.S. Census estimates. Figures do not include people who reported belonging to other ethnic groups in addition to Native American.

TOTEM POLES

Northwest Coast Indians carve totem poles with painted images of animals and human faces. The carvings represent animals and spirits and may also tell stories about specific people or events. The poles are carved from tree trunks or smaller pieces of wood and may be used as memorials, gravemarkers, and as welcome signs in front of homes. The tallest totem pole, erected in 1994 and dismantled in 1997, was located in Victoria, British Columbia, Canada. It was 180 feet, 3 inches tall.

NATIVE AMERICAN GROUPS

TLINGIT

The Tlingit (pronounced CLINK-it) have lived on the islands and forested coasts of southeast Alaska for thousands of years. There are about 5,165 Tlingit today. The Tlingit used to be divided into clans and clan houses with complex family traditions. Today, most live in ordinary towns; they do not have reservations. They have a tribal company and have turned their traditional tasks like fishing (smoked salmon is a Tlingit specialty) and logging into jobs. Tlingit rarely speak their native language at home anymore. However, it is still taught in heritage schools with other traditional skills like weaving and carving totem poles. Every other year, the Tlingits meet with the nearby Haida and Tsimshian tribes for a weekend of traditional dances, songs, and stories at the Celebration festival in Juneau.

NAVAJO NATION (DINE)

The Navajo Nation spans 27,000 square miles across Arizona, New Mexico, and Utah and is America's most populated reservation with about 175,000 residents. Many Dine (dee-NAY), as they call themselves, still speak a highly descriptive and unique language called Athapaskan. It was used as a code in World War II and never cracked. Local radio still broadcasts sports in Athapaskan, including New Mexico State University's football games. High school sports, especially basketball and cross country, are important to the Navajo. The Dine belong to clans within their nation, which are passed down from a mother to her children.

SENECA

The Seneca are one of the nations that formed the Iroquois Confederacy (see time line). There are about 7,200 people who make up the Seneca Nation today. Most live on one of two reservations in western New York. People inherit their Seneca clan status through their mothers. Women have always been important in their society. When clan families used to share wooden longhouses, which could extend more than 100 feet, the oldest woman was always the leader. Corn, beans, and squash are traditional foods. Lacrosse is a traditional sport popular today. A lesser known sport is snowsnake, a game where a polished staff is thrown down an iced snow track.

NUMBERS

What do you call a 9-sided figure? ➡ page 189

From 0 to Infinity

*T*he set of numbers includes whole numbers like 8, negative numbers like –23, fractions like 2/27, decimals like 46.9 and even "irrational" numbers that cannot be expressed as a fraction, like π (see page 188). Zero and infinity are two particularly interesting numbers.

Zero

In Roman Numerals, I stands for 1 and X stands for 10. Do you know the Roman numeral for "0"? Probably not, because there isn't one. The Babylonians in Asia, Hindus in India, and Mayans in the Americas were among the first to use the idea of zero as a "placeholder." In our number system "10" means 1 "ten" and 0 "ones." The 0 in 10 is a "placeholder" in the ones column.

A "numeral" is a symbol that represents a number. The Babylonians used place value and the idea of zero. But at first they didn't have a numeral for zero, so they just left a blank space in where a zero should be, like if we wrote 10,301 as 1 3 1. That was confusing because there was no numeral "to hold the place." Later they used two wedges to stand for zero. The Mayans used a symbol that looks like an eye.

Zero has some cool properties. Any number multiplied by 0 equals zero. Any number added to 0 equals the original number.

Babylonian Zero   **Mayan Zero**

Infinity

∞ This symbol, which looks like an 8 lying on its side, represents infinity. Infinity can be very hard to picture, because it never ends. For example, infinity is just as far from the number 1 as it is from 1 million, or even from a 1 with 100 zeroes after it (known as a googol).

In math, numbers are thought of as infinite because you can always imagine a larger number. For example, what's the biggest number you know? Add 1 to that number; you have a bigger number. Negative numbers are infinite too.

Here's a puzzler: which is larger, the set of all counting numbers (1, 2, 3, 4…) or the set of all even numbers (2, 4, 6, 8…)? According to mathematicians' concept of infinity, they are the same size, infinite. For every counting number (for example, 1), there is a corresponding even number (for example, 2).

GAME THEORY

Game theory is a complicated area of math that uses numbers to try to predict how people might behave under certain circumstances. Mathematicians or economists might study how people decide to spend their money, how nations build up their armies, or how a soccer player decides where to aim a penalty kick.

One of the most famous situations in game theory is the Prisoner's Dilemma, which we'll call the Detention Dilemma. Two kids, Anthony and Becky, are in different rooms of the principal's office. They are accused of cheating on a test but their teacher isn't sure. The principal asks each student to confess. She tells them that there are three possible outcomes:

1. If both confess and agree to tell on the other, both have to stay after school for 5 days.

2. If neither agrees to confess and tell on the other student, both have to stay after school for just 1 day, because the principal cannot be sure if the students cheated.

3. If only one confesses and tells on the other, that confessor goes free for cooperating and the other has to stay after school for 20 days.

At first, you might think it would be best to confess, because there's the chance of not having to stay after school. But if both suspects choose this "selfish" strategy, the outcome is worse (5 days detention) than if they are "unselfish" and remain silent (1 day after school). People make similar decisions in business, politics, and even on TV shows like *Survivor,* where contestants often must decide whether to act selfishly or cooperate with the group in order to reach a goal.

PRIME TIME

A prime number is a number that can only be divided by itself and the number 1. So, prime numbers include: 2, 3, 5, 7, 11, 13, 17, and so on. All other positive numbers (other than 1) are called composite numbers, because they have at least two factors (numbers they can be divided by) other than 1. For example, 6 is a composite number: its factors are 1, 2, 3, and 6.

Mathematicians around the world participate in the Great Internet Mersenne Prime Search (GIMPS) project. These mathematicians use powerful computers to search for the biggest prime number.

In September 2006, two Missouri professors—Steven Boone and Curtis Cooper—found the biggest prime number yet discovered. It's expressed as a power. Powers work by multiplying the base number by as many times as the raised exponent number shows. So, $2^3 = 2 \times 2 \times 2 = 8$.

The prime number they found is $2^{32,582,657}$ minus 1. The number has 9,808,358 digits, enough to fill more than 10 *World Almanacs for Kids.*

Homework Help

Finding an area can be easy, if you know the not-so-secret formula.

AREA OF A SQUARE:

A plane figure with four sides is called a **quadrilateral**. A square is a quadrilateral with four right angles and four equal sides, like the figure you see here. To find the area for a square, use this formula: **SIDE X SIDE** (**SIDE X SIDE** can also be written as s^2, pronounced "side squared").

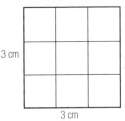

3 cm

3 cm

The sides of this square are each 3 centimeters long. So the area is 3 x 3, or 9. These are no longer centimeters but **square centimeters**.

AREA OF A RECTANGLE:

Rectangles are another type of quadrilateral. They have four right angles, but unlike a square, the sides are not all equal. To find the area of a rectangle, multiply **BASE x HEIGHT** (length x width).

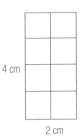

4 cm

2 cm

This rectangle has a base of 2 centimeters and a height of 4 centimeters. Its area is 8 square centimeters.

AREA OF A PARALLELOGRAM:

Parallelograms are quadrilaterals that have parallel opposite sides but no right angles. The formula for the area of a parallelogram is the same as for a rectangle—**BASE x HEIGHT**.

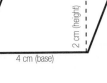

2 cm (height)

4 cm (base)

AREA OF A TRIANGLE:

A triangle is a three-sided plane figure. The prefix "tri" means three, which refers to the three points where the sides of a triangle meet.

To find the area for a triangle use **1/2 x (BASE x HEIGHT)** (first multiply the base by the height, then multiply that number by ½).

This triangle has a base of 2 centimeters and a height of 3 centimeters. So the area will be 3 square centimeters.

3 cm (height)

2 cm (base)

AREA OF A CIRCLE:

The distance around a circle is called its **circumference**. All the points on the circumference are an equal distance from the center. That distance is called the **radius**. A **diameter** is any straight line that has both ends on the circle and passes through its center. The diameter is twice the radius. To find a circle's area you need to use a number called **pi** (π) that equals about 3.14. The formula for a circle's area is **π x RADIUS x RADIUS (or π x RADIUS SQUARED)**.

3 cm
(radius)

For instance, this circle has a radius of 3 centimeters, so its area = π x 3 x 3, or π x 3^2; that is, about 3.14 x 9. This comes to 28.26 square centimeters.

What Is Pi? The Greek letter pi (π) stands for the number you get when you divide the circumference of a circle by its diameter. This number is always the same, no matter how big the circle is! The Babylonians discovered this in 2000 B.C. Actually, no one can say exactly what the value of π is. When you divide the circumference by the diameter it does not come out even, and you can keep going as many places as you want: 3.14159265 . . . it goes on to infinity.

How Many SIDES and FACES Do They Have?

When a figure is flat (two-dimensional), it is a **plane** figure. When a figure takes up space (three-dimensional), it is a **solid** figure. The flat surface of a solid figure is called a **face**. Plane and solid figures come in many different shapes.

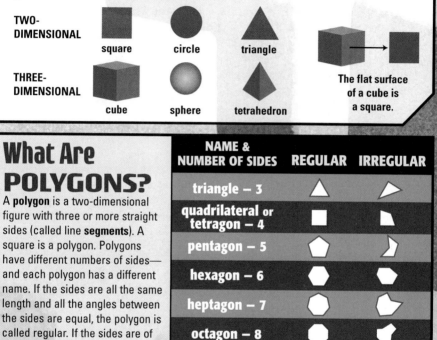

TWO-DIMENSIONAL

square   circle   triangle

THREE-DIMENSIONAL

cube   sphere   tetrahedron

The flat surface of a cube is a square.

What Are POLYGONS?

A **polygon** is a two-dimensional figure with three or more straight sides (called line **segments**). A square is a polygon. Polygons have different numbers of sides—and each polygon has a different name. If the sides are all the same length and all the angles between the sides are equal, the polygon is called regular. If the sides are of different lengths or the angles are not equal, the polygon is called irregular. At right are some regular and irregular polygons.

NAME & NUMBER OF SIDES	REGULAR	IRREGULAR
triangle – 3		
quadrilateral or tetragon – 4		
pentagon – 5		
hexagon – 6		
heptagon – 7		
octagon – 8		
nonagon – 9		
decagon – 10		

What Are Polyhedrons?

A polyhedron is a three-dimensional figure with four or more faces. Each face on a polyhedron is a polygon. Below are some polyhedrons with many faces.

tetrahedron   hexahedron   octahedron   dodecahedron   icosahedron
4 faces   6 faces   8 faces   12 faces   20 faces

◀ Great Pyramid of Khefren (a half-octahedron)

Homework Help

Have you ever wanted to be a human calculator? Here are some tricks to help you on your way.

Multiplying by 10, 100, or any other number that starts with a 1 and is followed by zeros is really easy. Just add the number of zeros to the number you are multiplying by. So, 6 x 1,000,000 = 6,000,000.

Multiplying by 5 can be easy. Start with 25, for example: 5 x 5 = 25. To multiply 5 by 6, count by fives six times until you get to 30. All multiplication is really a series of additions: 3 x 5 is the same as 5 + 5 + 5 = 15.

To multiply any single digit by 9, it's easiest to use your hands. Spread all ten fingers in front of you. For 9 x 3, put down your third finger from the left, your left middle finger. Then, count how many fingers are to the left of that finger (2) and how many fingers are to the right (7). So, 9 x 3 = 27. Try this trick with other factors.

Multiplying by 4 is a little harder. But think about this and it will make it easy: To multiply something by 4, just double the number twice. So, instead of thinking about 8 x 4, think of the operation as 8 + 8 = 16; 16 + 16 = 32. So, 8 x 4 = 32.

A Sudoku puzzle follows a few simple rules. Each square needs one number in it between 1 and 9. Each row must contain all numbers 1-9, each column must contain all numbers 1-9, and each of the nine-square units must have all numbers 1-9.

8				3		5		2
1	6	2		5	7		4	
3	4	5	8	1	2	7	9	6
	3	7	2	8				1
		6		7		4		8
4				6	9		5	
	1			9	8	3		
	2		1	4		6	8	
9				2	3		7	

ANSWERS ON PAGES 334-337.
FOR MORE PUZZLES GO TO
WWW.WAFORKIDS.COM

Alan Draper: Website Developer

What is a typical day like for you?

My company designs things for other companies, like logos, and packages, and web sites. That's where I come in. I'm a programmer, so I know lots of different computer languages. The languages HTML and CSS tell a web browser what goes on the page and how it should look. JavaScript tells the browser what it should do when a user does something, like changing the color of a button when you move your mouse over it. Then there are languages like SQL, Java, C#, ASP, and PHP, which can be used to take pictures or data from a database for display on a web page. I work with designers to figure out what is possible on a web site, and what is the most logical way to organize the site. That way it will be easy for visitors to use it.

What kind of special training did you need for your job?

I have learned a lot of what I do "on the job." Technology changes so fast that getting an advanced degree in one particular language or technology would be silly. So I am lucky that I got a Bachelor's degree in math and studied math in graduate school. Math helps me to pick up new ideas and technologies faster, and allows me to use those new technologies on different kinds of problems that I've never seen before.

How does math help you with your job?

The great thing about math is that it teaches you how to think about all kinds of problems. You can look at a new problem and say, "Aha! I've never solved this problem before,

but I've solved one pretty close to it, except for this or that detail." Then the details don't get in your way, because you understand how the general problem works.

I hate to steal a line from TV, but "We all use math every day," often without even knowing it. A web page is basically a grid, which is just like the coordinate system that you use in Algebra or Geometry. If you want to move things around on the page, you can use math to figure out how fast and how far to move them. Also, Algebra class is probably the first time that you learn to translate a problem in English into symbols in Math. And that's what you do all the time in computer programming. You decide what you want to do in English, and then translate it into whatever programming language you're using.

What's your favorite part of the job?

The best parts of my job are when I get a really hard problem, one that I have to think about, talk over with coworkers, and scribble diagrams to figure out. That's what keeps me excited about my job.

How did you get interested in math?

My mom used to fascinate me with math games while we were on car trips. I also had some great teachers who were always excited about math. They encouraged me to really think about problems instead of just churning through calculations, and they challenged me to find new ways to solve problems.

POPULATION

In what year did the U.S. population reach 200 million? ➡ page 195

WHERE DO PEOPLE LIVE?

In 1959, there were three billion people in the world. In 1999, there were six billion. According to United Nations (UN) estimates, the world population will have reached 6.6 billion by mid-2007 and will grow to 9.4 billion by 2050.

It's a big world out there! Our planet has about 196.9 million square miles of surface area, but about 70% of that is water. The total land area, 57.5 million square miles, is about 16 times the land area of the U.S.

Russia is the largest nation with over 6.5 million square miles of land. China is a distant second with 3.6 million square miles. The smallest countries are Vatican City and Monaco.

Populations

Largest (2007)

1. **China*** 1,321,851,888
2. **India** 1,129,866,154
3. **United States** 301,139,947
4. **Indonesia** 234,693,997
5. **Brazil** 190,010,647

Smallest (2007)

	COUNTRY	POPULATION
1.	Vatican City	932
2.	Tuvalu	11,992
3.	Nauru	13,528
4.	Palau	20,842
5.	San Marino	29,615

Source: U.S. Census Bureau, CIA *The World Factbook*

* Excluding Taiwan, pop. 23,174,294; Hong Kong, pop. 6,980,412; and Macau, pop. 456,989.

MOST SPARSELY POPULATED

	COUNTRY	PERSONS PER SQ MI
1.	Mongolia	4.8
2.	Namibia	6.5
3.	Australia	7.0
4.	Botswana	7.3
5.	Suriname	7.6

To get the population density, divide the population by the area. Density is calculated here according to land area, based on 2007 population.

MOST DENSELY POPULATED

	COUNTRY	PERSONS PER SQ MI*
1.	Monaco	43,394
2.	Singapore	17,273
3.	Vatican City	5,487
4.	Malta	3,294
5.	Maldives	3,186

* For comparison, New Jersey is the most densely populated state, with about 1,176 people per square mile in 2006.

FIVE LARGEST CITIES IN THE WORLD

Here are the five cities that had the most people, according to revised UN estimates for 2005. Numbers include people from the built-up area around each city (metropolitan area), not just the city. (See page 194 for the 10 biggest U.S. cities.)

CITY, COUNTRY	POPULATION	CITY, COUNTRY	POPULATION
1. Tokyo, Japan	35,197,000	4. Sao Paulo, Brazil	18,333,000
2. Mexico City, Mexico	19,411,000	5. Mumbai (Bombay), India	18,196,000
3. New York-Newark, U.S.	18,718,000		

All About
POPULATION GROWTH

There are more people in the world now than ever before. About four in every 10 people on Earth live in China or India. Historically, population growth rates were low but started to increase in the 17th and 18th centuries. Now, the UN estimates that approximately 76 million people are added to the planet each year. The world population is expected to reach 9.4 billion in 2050.

Most of the growth will be from population increases in poorer countries. In some developed countries like Japan and Russia, population is declining because families are having fewer children. Japan's population is projected to decline 22%, from 127.5 million in 2007 to 99.9 million in 2050. People aged 65 or older will make up 34% of the population.

India is expected to overtake China to become the world's most populous country by 2030. Its population is projected to climb an estimated 60% between 2007 and 2050, to 1.8 billion. Only about 17% of its population will be 65 or older. About 57% will be between 20 and 64.

What does all that mean? For Japan, there might be fewer workers and fewer people to take care of the elderly. Having more workers might help India develop its economy. But some people think high population growth puts a strain on the planet. More land has to be developed to provide people with housing and more food has to be grown.

POPULATION OF THE UNITED STATES, 2006

as of July 1, 2006

RANK & STATE NAME	POPULATION	RANK & STATE NAME	POPULATION
1. California (CA)	36,457,549	27. Oregon (OR)	3,700,758
2. Texas (TX)	23,507,783	28. Oklahoma (OK)	3,579,212
3. New York (NY)	19,306,183	29. Connecticut (CT)	3,504,809
4. Florida (FL)	18,089,888	30. Iowa (IA)	2,982,085
5. Illinois (IL)	12,831,970	31. Mississippi (MS)	2,910,540
6. Pennsylvania (PA)	12,440,621	32. Arkansas (AR)	2,810,872
7. Ohio (OH)	11,478,006	33. Kansas (KS)	2,764,075
8. Michigan (MI)	10,095,643	34. Utah (UT)	2,550,063
9. Georgia (GA)	9,363,941	35. Nevada (NV)	2,495,529
10. North Carolina (NC)	8,856,505	36. New Mexico (NM)	1,954,599
11. New Jersey (NJ)	8,724,560	37. West Virginia (WV)	1,818,470
12. Virginia (VA)	7,642,884	38. Nebraska (NE)	1,768,331
13. Massachusetts (MA)	6,437,193	39. Idaho (ID)	1,466,465
14. Washington (WA)	6,395,798	40. Maine (ME)	1,321,574
15. Indiana (IN)	6,313,520	41. New Hampshire (NH)	1,314,895
16. Arizona (AZ)	6,166,318	42. Hawaii (HI)	1,285,498
17. Tennessee (TN)	6,038,803	43. Rhode Island (RI)	1,067,610
18. Missouri (MO)	5,842,713	44. Montana (MT)	944,632
19. Maryland (MD)	5,615,727	45. Delaware (DE)	853,476
20. Wisconsin (WI)	5,556,506	46. South Dakota (SD)	781,919
21. Minnesota (MN)	5,167,101	47. Alaska (AK)	670,053
22. Colorado (CO)	4,753,377	48. North Dakota (ND)	635,867
23. Alabama (AL)	4,599,030	49. Vermont (VT)	623,908
24. South Carolina (SC)	4,321,249	50. District of Columbia (DC)	581,530
25. Louisiana (LA)	4,287,768	51. Wyoming (WY)	515,004
26. Kentucky (KY)	4,206,074	**TOTAL U.S. POPULATION**	**299,398,484**

Largest Cities in the United States

Cities grow and shrink in population. Below is a list of the largest cities in the United States in 2005 compared with their populations in 1950. Populations are for people living within the city limits only.

RANK & CITY	2005	1950
1. New York, NY	8,143,197	7,891,957
2. Los Angeles, CA	3,844,829	1,970,358
3. Chicago, IL	2,842,518	3,620,962
4. Houston, TX	2,016,582	596,163
5. Philadelphia, PA	1,463,281	2,071,605
6. Phoenix, AZ	1,461,575	106,818
7. San Antonio, TX	1,256,509	408,442
8. San Diego, CA	1,255,540	334,387
9. Dallas, TX	1,213,825	434,462
10. San Jose, CA	912,332	95,280

The Growing U.S. Population

1790: 3,929,214	1970: 203,211,926	
1850: 23,191,876	1990: 248,709,873	
1900: 76,212,168	2000: 281,421,906	
1930: 123,202,660	2007: 300,912,947	
1950: 151,325,798		

300,000,000
250,000,000
200,000,000
150,000,000
100,000,000
50,000,000

1790 1820 1850 1880 1910 1940 1970 2007

POPULATION TIME LINE

1790 Most populous state: Virginia, 692,000

1850 Most populous state: New York, 3.1 million

1900 Life expectancy at birth: 47.3 years
Population of Florida, 33rd most populous state: 529,000
Top country of birth of foreign-born population: Germany, 2.7 million
Percent of women participating in labor force: 20.6%
Number of cars registered in the U.S.: 8,000

1910 14.7% of U.S. population is foreign-born, highest percentage on record.
Population of Phoenix, Arizona: 11,134

1915 U.S. population reaches 100 million.

1930 Life expectancy at birth: 59.7 years
Top country of birth of foreign-born population: Italy, 1.8 million
Number of cars and trucks registered in the U.S.: 26.7 million

1950 Life expectancy at birth: 68.2 years
Population of Florida, 20th most populous state: 2.8 million
Percent of women participating in labor force: 29%
Number of cars and trucks registered in the U.S.: 48.9 million

1960 Population of Phoenix, Arizona, 29th most populous city: 439,170

1967 U.S. population reaches 200 million.

1970 4.7% of U.S. population is foreign-born, lowest percentage on record.

2000 Life expectancy at birth: 77 years
Population of Florida, 4th most populous state: 16 million
Top country of birth of foreign-born population: Mexico, 9.2 million
Percent of women participating in labor force: 59.9%
Number of cars and trucks registered in the U.S.: 220.7 million

2006 U.S. population reaches an estimated 300 million on October 17.
Population of Phoenix, Arizona, 6th most populous U.S. city: 1.5 million

The Many Faces of America:
IMMIGRATION

The number of people in the U.S. who were born in another country (foreign-born) reached 35.2 million in 2005, or about 11.7% of the population. This percentage has been rising since 1970, when it was at a low of 4.7%, and is at its highest since 1930. In the early 1900s, most immigrants came from Europe; in 2005, 45% of the foreign-born population were born in Latin America, and 26% were born in Asia.

Immigrants come for various reasons, such as to escape poverty or oppression and to make better lives for themselves and their children. The figures below, from the Department of Homeland Security, cover legal immigrants only. The U.S. government estimates that in the 1990s about 350,000 people each year came across the border illegally or overstayed a temporary visa. (Visas are official government documents that grant permission for a person to visit, work, or attend school in another country.) The Pew Hispanic Center estimated there were 11.5 to 12 million unauthorized immigrants in the U.S. in 2006, with the majority coming from Mexico.

What Countries Do Immigrants Come From?

Below are some of the birth countries of immigrants to the U.S. in 2005. Legal immigration from all countries to the U.S. totaled 1,122,373 in 2005.

COUNTRY	Number	Percent of total
Mexico	161,445	14.4
India	84,681	7.5
China	69,967	6.2
Philippines	60,748	5.4
Cuba	36,261	3.2
Vietnam	32,784	2.9
Dominican Republic	27,504	2.5
Korea	26,562	2.4
Colombia	25,571	2.3
Ukraine	22,761	2.0
Canada	21,878	1.9
El Salvador	21,359	1.9
United Kingdom	19,800	1.8
Russia	18,083	1.6

Where Do Immigrants Settle?

In 2005, about 62% of all immigrants to the U.S. moved to the states below. California received roughly one-third of all immigrants born in Vietnam, Mexico, and the Philippines and one-fourth of immigrants born in China and Korea. Florida received 85% of immigrants born in Cuba, over half of those born in Haiti, and about one-third of those born in Colombia. Nearly half of those born in the Dominican Republic chose to settle in New York.

California
232,023

New York
136,828

Florida
122,918

Texas
95,958

New Jersey
56,180

Illinois
52,419

This bar chart shows the states that received the highest number of immigrants in 2005.

◄ Immigrants entering the U.S. at Ellis Island in New York, early 1900s

196

All About ›› Hispanic AMERICANS

Hispanics are people who trace their heritage to Mexico, Puerto Rico, Cuba, or other Central or South American or Spanish cultures. They may be of any race. In 2005, there were approximately 41.9 million Hispanics in the U.S., making up about 14.5% of the population. Almost 60% were born in the U.S. The rest were born in another country.

Hispanic immigrants made up about 31.6% of the 1.1 million immigrants to the U.S. in 2005. Approximately 161,000 (14% of immigrants that year), were from Mexico. Large numbers of immigrants also came from Colombia, Cuba, El Salvador, and Guatemala.

In 2005, California had the most Hispanics of any state: 12,534,628, or nearly 30% of all Hispanics in the country. Texas ranked second with a Hispanic population of 7,882,254, or 18% of the nation's Hispanics. Florida followed with 8.2% of all Hispanics.

New Mexico had the highest percentage of Hispanics in its population. In 2005, close to 44% of New Mexico's population was Hispanic. California and Texas had the second- and third-highest percentage of Hispanics in their populations, with about 35% each.

U.S. Hispanic Population by Country of Origin, 2005

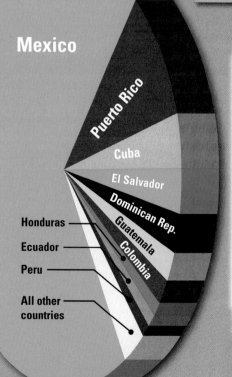

Country	Number	Percent of All Hispanics
Mexico	26,781,547	64.0
Puerto Rico	3,781,317	9.0
Cuba	1,461,574	3.5
El Salvador	1,239,640	3.0
Dominican Rep.	1,118,265	2.7
Guatemala	758,898	1.8
Colombia	730,510	1.7
Honduras	459,653	1.1
Ecuador	436,409	1.0
Peru	412,349	1.0
All other countries	1,285,957	3.1
Total U.S. Hispanic Population	**41,870,703**	100.0

Source: American Community Survey, U.S. Census Bureau

197

PRIZES & CONTESTS

What's the prize for winning the Rotten Sneaker Contest? ➡ page 201

NOBEL PRIZES

The Nobel Prizes are named after Alfred B. Nobel (1833–1896), a Swedish scientist who invented dynamite, and left money for these prizes. They are given every year for promoting peace, as well as for physics, chemistry, medicine, physiology, literature, and economics.

In 2006, Grameen Bank in Bangladesh and its founder Muhammad Yunis ◀ were awarded the Nobel Peace Prize "for their efforts to create economic and social development from below." Together they made available "micro-credit." It allowed poor individuals (mostly women) in Bangladesh to borrow small amounts of money to help them start a small business.

Past winners of the Nobel Peace Prize include:

2004 Wangari Maathai, activist, her Green Belt Movement in Kenya planted more than 30 million trees and promoted education, nutrition, and family planning.

2002 Jimmy Carter, former U.S. president and peace negotiator

1997 Jody Williams and the International Campaign to Ban Landmines

1993 Nelson Mandela, leader of South African blacks; **F.W. de Klerk** president of South Africa

1989 Dalai Lama, Tibetan Buddhist leader, forced into exile in 1959

1987 Oscar Arias Sánchez, president of Costa Rica, initiator of peace negotiations in Central America

1986 Elie Wiesel, Holocaust survivor and author

1979 Mother Teresa, leader of the order of the Missionaries of Charity, who care for the sick and dying in India

1964 Martin Luther King Jr., civil rights leader

1954 Albert Schweitzer, missionary, surgeon

1919 Woodrow Wilson, U.S. president who played a key role in founding the League of Nations

1905 Baroness Bertha von Suttner, early advocate of peace through international cooperation; first woman to win the prize.▼

ENTERTAINMENT *Awards*

2007 KIDS' CHOICE AWARDS

The 2007 Kids' Choice Awards were held Saturday, March 31, 2007, and hosted by ◀Justin Timberlake. For more information, go to:

WEB SITE www.nick.com

KIDS' CHOICE AWARDS

40 million kids voted in the 2007 Nickelodeon's Kids' Choice Awards. Winners included:

- Music Group: .... Black Eyed Peas
- Movie:............... *Pirates of the Caribbean: Dead Man's Chest*
- Book:................ The Harry Potter Series
- Video Game: .... *SpongeBob SquarePants: Creature from the Krusty Krab*
- Favorite TV Show: .... *American Idol*
- Cartoon: .... *SpongeBob SquarePants*
- TV Actor: .... Drake Bell
- TV Actress: .... Miley Cyrus
- Movie Actor: .... Adam Sandler
- Movie Actress: .... Dakota Fanning ▶
- Animated Movie: ..... *Happy Feet*
- Favorite Voice from an Animated Movie: .. Queen Latifah *(Ice Age: The Meltdown)*
- Male Singer: .... Justin Timberlake
- Female Singer: .... Beyoncé
- Song:................ Irreplaceable (Beyoncé)
- Athlete:.............. Shaquille O'Neal
- Wannabe Award:..... Ben Stiller

BEE INVOLVED

If you have a knack for spelling or an interest in world geography, then these two national contests may be for you.

National Spelling Bee

The **National Spelling Bee** was started in Louisville, Kentucky, by the *Courier-Journal* in 1925. Today, newspapers across the U.S. run spelling bees for kids 15 and under. Winners may qualify for the Scripps National Spelling Bee held in Washington, D.C., in late May or early June. If interested, ask your school principal to contact your local newspaper. (For a behind-the-scenes look at the National Spelling Bee, try the 2002 film *Spellbound*.)

Katharine Close, 13, from Asbury Park, New Jersey, won the 79th annual Scripps National Spelling Bee contest on June 1, 2006. After 20 rounds, she won the bee by correctly spelling the word "ursprache," which is defined as "a language that is the hypothetical ancestor to another language." This is the fifth time Katharine has competed in the National Spelling Bee. She finished tied for seventh in 2005.

WEB SITE www.spellingbee.com

Here are the words Katharine spelled on her way to the top. Some of them are just a little bit difficult!

gobemouche	clinamen
Galilean	recrementitious
chiragra	psittacism
bildungsroman	aubade
terrene	kanone
cucullate	izzat
synusia	tmesis
towhee	kundalini
shedu	ursprache
hukilau	

National Geographic Bee

After 9 rounds, the winner is . . .

Bonny Jain, a 12-year-old from Moline, Illinois. After 9 rounds of regular questions and a lightning elimination set, Bonny advanced to the championship round. He won by answering the question: Name the mountains that extend across much of Wales, from the Irish Sea to the Bristol Channel. (The answer: Cambrian Mountains)

Bonny won a $25,000 scholarship for college and a lifetime membership in the National Geographic Society. Bonny began competing in the Geographic Bee four years ago. In his first competition, he finished second in his school bee. Not a bad start, but Bonny wanted to go all the way. He worked at his geography and managed to take fourth place in 2005, before winning it all in 2006. "It feels pretty cool to have gotten up to the top of the nation from second in the school," Bonny said after his win. Geography isn't the only subject Bonny's good at. He made it to the seventh round of the 2006 National Spelling Bee.

This contest draws five million contestants from nearly 15,000 schools from the U.S., Puerto Rico, U.S. Virgin Islands, and the Pacific Territories. To enter, you must be in grade 4-8. School-level bees are followed by state-level bees and then the nationals. For more information: **WEB SITE** www.nationalgeographic.com/geobee

Odd Contests

I t just seems to be part of human nature to find out who is the best at something, no matter what it is! There are state, national, and international competitions in a wide variety of events. Most of them are normal ones such as foot races, trivia contests, and such. But then there are others that are just plain weird. Here are a few contests that are not very ordinary.

ROTTEN SNEAKER CONTEST

Held annually in Montpelier, Vermont, the Odor-Eaters Rotten Sneaker Contest was won in March 2007 by thirteen-year-old Katharine Tuck of Tooele, Utah. She made her shoes smelly by just wearing them during everyday work and play, but the sneakers almost made the panel of expert sniffers pass out. Tuck won $2,500, the Golden Sneaker Award trophy, a lifetime supply of Odor-Eaters®, and a trip to New York City. Her sneakers joined other winners' in the Odor-Eaters "Hall of Fumes." For more information, visit

WEB SITE www.odoreaters.com

POND SKIMMING

Big Mountain Resort in Whitefish, Montana, hosts a pond skimming contest in April, at the close of the skiing season. During the event, contestants ski or snowboard down a ski trail. At the bottom of the trail is a small pond built by the Big Mountain's grooming crew. Building up speed as they go down the hill, the contestants skim across the water of the pond and hopefully make it to the other side. Participants must wear regulation snow skis or snowboards. They are also encouraged to wear costumes or uniforms. Why? Because prizes are given for best costumes, and style counts.

WEB SITE http://www.bigmtn.com/

WORLD COW CHIP THROWING CONTEST Held every April in Beaver, Oklahoma. The object is to throw a chunk of dried cow dung (a "cow chip") as far as you can. The record is about 200.7 feet.

RECORDS

World Land Speed Record

British fighter pilot Andy Green holds this record. He averaged 763.035 miles per hour over two runs on October 15, 1997 at Black Rock Desert, NV. His driving speed broke the sound barrier in the process. The car, Thrust SSC, was powered by two airplane engines called turbofans.

Largest Flying Mammal

Malayan flying foxes weigh about 2 pounds. They can grow to have a wingspan of 5 feet. The bat lives in Southeast Asia and hunts for flowers, nectar, and fruit at night. It gets its name because its face looks like a fox's.

Youngest
to Top of Mount Everest

Mount Everest is the tallest mountain in the world at 29,035 feet tall. Ming Kipa Sherpa from Nepal was 15 when she reached the top of Mount Everest on May 24, 2003, along with her older brother and sister.

◄ *Ming Kipa Sherpa (right) with her sister, Lhakpa Sherpa*

Most **Poisonous** Snake

The inland taipan snake lives in the deserts of Australia. One bite can release venom strong enough to kill more than 100 people. Luckily, the 8-foot-long snake prefers eating rats.

Richest Person

Bill Gates has been named the richest person in the world for 13 years. In 2007, his net worth, or the cash value of everything he owns minus any debts, was $56 billion, according to *Forbes* magazine. The Microsoft chairman also heads the nation's largest charitable foundation with his wife, Melinda.

World's **Most** Visited **Mall**

The Mall of America in Bloomington, MN, draws about 40 million people each year to shop in about 520 stores. It also has an indoor NASCAR speedway, aquarium, wedding chapel, Lego Imagination Center, and the nation's largest indoor theme park.

Hot **Dog Eating** Record

In 2006, Takeru Kobayashi beat his own record by a quarter wiener. He scarfed down 53.75 hot dogs and buns in 12 minutes at the annual Nathan's Famous Fourth of July International Hot Dog contest at Coney Island in Brooklyn, New York.

RELIGION

Which religion has a goddess named Shakti? ➡ **page 205**

How did the universe begin? Why are we here on Earth? What happens to us after we die? For most people, religion provides answers to questions like these. Believing in a God or gods, or in a higher power, is one way people make sense of the world around them. Religion can also help guide people's lives.

Different religions have different beliefs. For example, Christians, Jews, and Muslims are monotheists, meaning they believe in only one God. Hindus are polytheists, meaning they believe in many gods. On this page and the next are some facts about the world's major religions.

Christianity

WHO STARTED CHRISTIANITY? Christianity is based on the teachings of Jesus Christ. He was born in Bethlehem between 8 B.C. and 4 B.C. and died about A.D. 29.

WHAT WRITINGS ARE THERE? The **Bible**, consisting of the Old Testament and New Testament, is the main spiritual text in Christianity.

WHAT DO CHRISTIANS BELIEVE? There is only one God. God sent his Son, Jesus Christ, to Earth. Jesus died to save humankind but later rose from the dead.

HOW MANY ARE THERE? Christianity is the world's biggest religion. In mid-2004, there were more than 2.1 billion Christians worldwide.

WHAT KINDS ARE THERE? More than one billion Christians are **Roman Catholics**, who follow the Pope's leadership. **Orthodox Christians** accept similar teachings but follow different leadership. **Protestants** disagree with many Catholic teachings. They believe in the Bible's authority.

Buddhism

WHO STARTED BUDDHISM? Siddhartha Gautama (the Buddha), around 525 B.C.

WHAT WRITINGS ARE THERE? The **Tripitaka**, or "Three Baskets," contains three collections of teachings, rules, and commentaries. There are also other texts, many of which are called **sutras**.

WHAT DO BUDDHISTS BELIEVE? Buddha taught that life is filled with suffering. Through meditation and deeds, one can end the cycle of endless birth and rebirth and achieve a state of perfect peace known as **nirvana**.

HOW MANY ARE THERE? In mid-2004, there were about 375 million Buddhists in the world, 98% of them in Asia.

WHAT KINDS ARE THERE? There are two main kinds: **Theravada** ("Way of the Elders") Buddhism, the older kind, is more common in countries such as Sri Lanka, Myanmar, and Thailand. **Mahayana** ("Great Vehicle") Buddhism is more common in China, Korea, Japan, and Tibet.

Hinduism

WHO STARTED HINDUISM? The beliefs of Aryans, who migrated to India around 1500 B.C., intermixed with the beliefs of the people who already lived there.

WHAT WRITINGS ARE THERE? The **Vedas** ("Knowledge") collect the most important writings in Hinduism, including the ancient hymns in the **Samhita** and the teachings in the **Upanishads**. Also important are the stories the **Bhagavad-Gita** and the **Ramayana**.

WHAT DO HINDUS BELIEVE? There is one divine principle, known as **brahman**; the various gods are only aspects of it. Life is an aspect of, yet separate from the divine. To escape a meaningless cycle of birth and rebirth (**samsara**), one must improve one's **karma** (the purity or impurity of one's past deeds).

HOW MANY ARE THERE? In mid-2004, there were about 851 million Hindus, mainly in India and places where people from India have immigrated to.

WHAT KINDS ARE THERE? Most Hindus are primarily devoted to a single deity, the most common being the gods **Vishnu** and **Shiva** and the goddess **Shakti**.

Islam

WHO STARTED ISLAM? Muhammad, the Prophet, about A.D. 622.

WHAT WRITINGS ARE THERE? The **Koran** (*al-Qur'an* in Arabic), regarded as the word of God. The **Sunna**, or example of the Prophet, is recorded in the **Hadith**.

WHAT DO MUSLIMS BELIEVE? People who practice Islam are known as Muslims. There is only one God. God revealed the Koran to Muhammad so he could teach humankind truth and justice. Those who "submit" (literal meaning of "Islam") to God will attain salvation.

HOW MANY ARE THERE? In mid-2004, there were approximately 1.3 billion Muslims, mostly in parts of Africa and Asia.

Judaism

WHO STARTED JUDAISM? Abraham is thought to be the founder of Judaism, one of the first monotheistic religions. He probably lived between 2000 B.C. and 1500 B.C.

WHAT WRITINGS ARE THERE? The most important is the **Torah** ("Law"), comprising the five books of Moses. The **Nevi'im** ("Prophets") and **Ketuvim** ("Writings") are also part of the Hebrew Bible.

WHAT DO JEWS BELIEVE? There is one God who created and rules the universe. One should be faithful to God and observe God's laws.

HOW MANY ARE THERE? In mid-2004, there were close to 15 million Jews around the world. Many live in Israel and the United States.

WHAT KINDS ARE THERE? In the U.S. there are three main forms: **Orthodox**, **Conservative**, and **Reform**. Orthodox Jews are the most traditional, following strict laws about dress and diet. Reform Jews are the least traditional. Conservative Jews are somewhere in-between.

Major Holy Days

FOR CHRISTIANS, JEWS, MUSLIMS, BUDDHISTS, AND HINDUS

CHRISTIAN HOLY DAYS

	2008	2009	2010
Ash Wednesday	February 6	February 25	February 17
Good Friday	March 21	April 10	April 2
Easter Sunday	March 23	April 12	April 4
Easter for Orthodox Churches	April 27	April 19	April 4
Christmas	December 25	December 25	December 25

*Russian and some other Orthodox churches celebrate Christmas in January.

JEWISH HOLY DAYS

The Jewish holy days begin at sundown the night before the first full day of the observance. The dates of first full days are listed below.

	2007-08 (5768)	2008-09 (5769)	2009-10 (5770)
Rosh Hashanah (New Year)	September 13, 2007	September 30, 2008	September 19, 2009
Yom Kippur (Day of Atonement)	September 22, 2007	October 9, 2008	September 28, 2009
Hanukkah (Festival of Lights)	December 5, 2007	December 22, 2008	December 12, 2009
Passover	April 20, 2008	April 9, 2009	March 30, 2010

ISLAMIC (MUSLIM) HOLY DAYS

The Islamic holy days begin at sundown the night before the first full day of the observance. The dates of first full days are listed below.

	2007 (1428)	2008 (1429)	2008-09 (1430)
Muharram 1 (New Year)	January 20	January 9	December 28, 2008
Mawlid (Birthday of Muhammad)	March 31	March 20	March 9, 2009
Ramadan (Month of Fasting)	September 12	September 1	August 21, 2009
Eid al-Fitr (End of Ramadan)	October 12	September 30	September 20, 2009
Eid al-Adha	December 20	December 8	November 27, 2009

BUDDHIST HOLY DAYS

Not all Buddhists use the same calendar to determine holidays and festivals. A few well-known Buddhist observances and the months in which they may fall are listed below.

NIRVANA DAY, **February:** Marks the death of Siddhartha Gautama (the Buddha).

VESAK OR VISAKAH PUJA (BUDDHA DAY), **April/May:** The most important holiday. Celebrates the birth, enlightenment, and death of the Buddha.

ASALHA PUJA (DHARMA DAY), **July:** Commemorates the Buddha's first teaching.

MAGHA PUJA OR SANGHA DAY, **February:** Commemorates the day when 1,250 of Buddha's followers (**sangha**) visited him without his calling them.

VASSA (RAINS RETREAT), **July-October:** A three-month period during Asia's rainy season when monks travel little and spend more time on meditation and study. Sometimes called Buddhist Lent.

HINDU HOLY DAYS

Different Hindu groups use different calendars. A few of the many Hindu festivals and the months in which they may fall are listed below.

MAHA SHIVARATRI, **February/March:** Festival dedicated to Shiva, creator and destroyer.

HOLI, **February/March:** Festival of spring.

RAMANAVAMI, **March/April:** Celebrates the birth of Rama, the seventh incarnation of Vishnu.

DIWALI, **October/November:** Festival of Lights.

All About ≫ Islam: Sunni and Shiite

There are two major groups of Muslims, the Sunnis and the Shiites. About 83% of the world's 1.3 billion Muslims are Sunni. They live all over the world but mostly in the Middle East, Africa, and Asia. Shiites make up the majority of Muslims in several countries, including Iran, Iraq, and Lebanon. The differences between these groups go back to the early years of Islam. The Sunnis accept an early follower of Muhammad, Abu Bakr, as Muhammad's successor. The Shiites believe that Ali ibn Abi Talib, the son-in-law and cousin of Muhammad, was Muhammad's rightful successor. Today, Sunnis and Shiites still follow different religious leaders and celebrate some different holidays. Historically, the Sunnis and Shiites have been opposed to each other, and even today, there is conflict in some areas between the two groups. The country of Iraq is an example of this. Minority Sunnis ruled and persecuted Shiites under the government of Saddam Hussein. Now Shiites represent the majority in government, and conflicts between the two groups have become violent.

Grand Ayatollah Ali al-Sistani, Iraqi Shiite religious leader ▶

SCIENCE

What common substance contains sodium fluoride? ➡ page 211

THE WORLD OF Science

The Latin root of the word "science" is *scire*, meaning "to know." There are many kinds of knowledge, but when people use the word *science* they usually mean a kind of knowledge that can be discovered and backed up by observation or experiments.

The branches of scientific study can be loosely grouped into the four main areas shown below. Each branch of science has more specific areas of study within it than can be listed here. For example, zoology includes entomology (study of insects), which in turn includes lepidopterology (the study of butterflies and moths)!

In answering questions about our lives, our world, and our universe, scientists must often draw from more than one discipline. Biochemists, for example, deal with the chemistry that happens inside living things. Paleontologists study fossil remains of ancient plants and animals. Astrophysicists study matter and energy in outer space. And mathematics, considered by many to be both an art and a science, is used by all scientists.

Physical Science

ASTRONOMY—stars, planets, outer space

CHEMISTRY—properties and behavior of substances

PHYSICS—matter and energy

Life Science (Biology)

ANATOMY—structure of the human body

BOTANY—plants

ECOLOGY—living things in relation to their environment

GENETICS—heredity

PATHOLOGY—diseases and their effects on the human body

PHYSIOLOGY—the body's biological processes

ZOOLOGY—animals

Earth Science

GEOGRAPHY—Earth's surface and its relationship to humans

GEOLOGY—Earth's structure

HYDROLOGY—water

METEOROLOGY—Earth's atmosphere and weather

MINERALOGY—minerals

OCEANOGRAPHY—the sea, including currents and tides

PETROLOGY—rocks

SEISMOLOGY—earthquakes

VOLCANOLOGY—volcanoes

Social Science

ANTHROPOLOGY—human cultures and physical characteristics

ECONOMICS—production and distribution of goods and services

POLITICAL SCIENCE—governments

PSYCHOLOGY—mental processes and behavior

SOCIOLOGY—human society and community life

SCIENCE

HOW DO
SCIENTISTS
MAKE DISCOVERIES? *THE SCIENTIFIC METHOD*

The scientific method was developed over many centuries. You can think of it as having five steps:

❶ Ask a question.

❷ Gather information through observation.

❸ Based on that information, make an educated guess (hypothesis) about the answer to your question.

❹ Design an experiment to test that hypothesis.

❺ Evaluate the results.

If the experiment shows that your hypothesis is wrong, make up a new hypothesis. If the experiment supports your hypothesis, then your hypothesis may be correct! However, it is usually necessary to test a hypothesis with many different experiments before it can be accepted as a scientific law—something that is generally accepted as true.

You can **apply the scientific method** to problems in everyday life. For example, suppose you plant some seeds and they fail to sprout. You would probably **ask** yourself, "Why didn't they sprout?"—and that would be step one of the scientific method. The next step would be to make **observations**; for example, you might take note of how deep the seeds were

planted, how often they were watered, and what kind of soil was used. Then, you would make an **educated guess** about what went wrong—for example, you might hypothesize that the seeds didn't sprout because you didn't water them enough. After that, you would **test** your hypothesis—perhaps by trying to grow the seeds again, under the exact same conditions as before, except that this time you would water them more frequently.

Finally, you would wait and **evaluate** the results of your experiment. If the seeds sprouted, then you could conclude that your hypothesis may be correct. If they don't sprout, you'd continue to use the method to find a scientific answer to your original question.

did you know?

More than 6,000 people die everyday because they don't have safe drinking water. A lot of those people are kids. In some countries, even water that looks clean can be full of bacteria. These bacteria cause serious illnesses like typhoid, dysentery, and cholera. That's why LifeStraw, a drinking straw that filters out harmful bacteria, was invented in 2005. The LifeStraw, which is about the size of a fat pencil, uses a combination of mesh filters, iodine beads, and active carbon to make water drinkable. The best part? When the company starts mass-producing the LifeStraw, it should only cost about $2 per person every year.

WHAT EVERYTHING *IS* MADE OF

Everything we see and use is made up of basic ingredients called elements. There are more than 100 elements. Most have been found in nature. Some are created by scientists in labs.

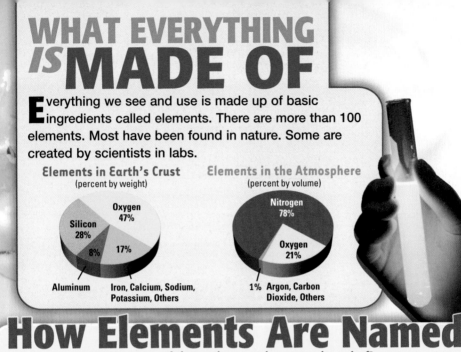

Elements in Earth's Crust
(percent by weight)

Oxygen 47%
Silicon 28%
8%
17%
Aluminum
Iron, Calcium, Sodium, Potassium, Others

Elements in the Atmosphere
(percent by volume)

Nitrogen 78%
Oxygen 21%
1% Argon, Carbon Dioxide, Others

How Elements Are Named
How many of these elements have you heard of?

Elements are named after places, scientists, figures in mythology, or properties of the element. But no element gets a name until the International Union of Pure and Applied Chemistry (IUPAC) accepts it. In November 2004, the 111th element was approved and named. Roentgenium, with symbol Rg, was discovered by German scientists in 1995.

NAME	SYMBOL	WHAT IT IS	WHEN FOUND	NAMED FOR
Aluminum	Al	metal	1825	*alumen*, Latin word for "alum"
Californium	Cf	radioactive metal	1950	state of California, and the University of California
Helium	He	gas	1868	the Greek word *helios*, meaning sun
Iodine	I	nonmetallic solid	1811	the Greek word *iodes*, meaning violet
Iridium	Ir	transitional metal	1804	the Latin word *iridis*, meaning rainbow
Krypton	Kr	gas	1898	the Greek word *kryptos*, meaning hidden
Nickel	Ni	transitional metal	1774	the German word *kupfernickel*, meaning devil's copper
Oxygen	O	gas	1500 B.C.	the Greek words *oxys genes*, meaning acid-forming
Tungsten	W	transitional metal	1783	the Swedish words *tung sten*, meaning heavy stone.
Uranium	U	radioactive metal	1789	the planet Uranus

ALL ABOUT...
Compounds

Carbon, hydrogen, nitrogen, and oxygen are the most common chemical elements in the human body. Many other elements may be found in small amounts. These include calcium, iron, phosphorus, potassium, and sodium.

When elements join together, they form compounds. Water is a compound made up of hydrogen and oxygen. Salt is a compound made up of sodium and chlorine.

Common Name	Contains the Compound	Contains the Elements
Bleach	hydrogen peroxide	hydrogen, oxygen
Fool's Gold	iron disulfide	iron, sulfur
Marble	calcium carbonate	calcium, carbon, oxygen
Rust	iron oxide	iron, oxygen
Sugar	sucrose	carbon, hydrogen, oxygen
Toothpaste	sodium fluoride	sodium, fluorine
Vinegar	acetic acid	carbon, hydrogen, oxygen

CHEMICAL SYMBOLS ARE SCIENTIFIC SHORTHAND

When scientists write the names of elements, they often use a symbol instead of spelling out the full name. The symbol for each element is one or two letters. Scientists write O for oxygen and He for helium. The symbols usually come from the English name for the element (C for carbon). The symbols for some of the elements come from the element's Latin name. For example, the symbol for gold is Au, which is short for *aurum*, the Latin word for gold.

CRIME SCENE INVESTIGATOR:

YOU DO IT

Crime scene investigation can be dirty work. How do investigators know how to clean things? They use trial and error. Collect four pennies that are too tarnished to read (ask your parents to help you find some). Then, experiment with the solutions below.

Which one is best for disolving tarnish off a copper penny? (Hint: Let the pennies soak for awhile. And make sure you have a clear space and clean towels for this experiment.)

> Ranch salad dressing
> Maple syrup

> Vinegar and baking soda
> Warm salt water

Physical Science

SOUND and LIGHT

What is Sound?

Sound is a form of energy that is made up of waves traveling through mass. When you "hear" a sound, it is actually your ear detecting the vibrations of molecules as the sound wave passes through. To understand sound, you first have to understand waves. Take a bowl full of water and drop a penny into the middle of it. You'll see little circular waves move away from the area where the penny hit, spread out toward the bowl's edges, and bounce back. Sound moves in the same way. The waves must travel through a gas, liquid, or a solid. In the vacuum of space, there is no sound because there are no molecules to vibrate. When you talk, your vocal chords vibrate to produce sound waves.

What is Light?

Light is a little tricky. It is a form of energy known as electromagnetic radiation that is emitted from a source. It travels as waves in straight lines and spreads out over a larger area the farther it goes. Scientists also think it goes along as particles known as photons. Light is produced in many ways, but mostly it comes from electrons that vibrate at high frequencies when heated to a high enough temperature.

Regular white light is made up of all the colors of the spectrum from red to violet. Each color has its own frequency. When you see a color on something, such as a red apple, that means that the apple absorbed all other colors of the spectrum and only reflected the red light. Things that are white reflect almost all the light that hits them. Things that are black, on the other hand, absorb all the light that hits them.

Light vs. Sound

Sound travels fast but light travels a whole lot faster. You've probably noticed that when you see lightning, you don't hear thunder until several seconds later. That's because the light reaches you before the sound. The speed of sound varies depending on temperature and air pressure (it also travels faster through liquids and solids). A jet traveling at about 761 miles per hour is considered to be flying at the "speed of sound." But this is nothing compared to light. It goes 186,000 miles per *second*! It goes the same speed no matter what. Scientists don't think anything in the universe can travel faster.

How Simple Machines Work

Simple machines are devices that make our lives easier. Cars could not run, skyscrapers couldn't be built, and elevators couldn't carry people up—if it weren't for simple machines.

Inclined Plane When trying to get a refrigerator onto the back of a truck, a worker will use a ramp, or inclined plane. Instead of lifting something heavy a short distance, we can more easily push it over a longer distance, but to the same height.
Examples: escalators, staircases, slides

Lever Any kind of arm, bar, or plank that can pivot on something (known as a fulcrum), is a lever. Depending on where the fulcrum is located on the lever, it can be used for different things.
Examples: shovel, bottle opener, "claw" part of a hammer used for prying out nails, seesaw

Wedge These machines are two inclined planes fastened onto each other to make a point. Wedges are used to pull things apart and even cut.
Examples: axes, knives

Wheel and Axle This is another kind of lever, but instead of going up and down, it goes around. The wheel is the lever and the axle on which it turns is the fulcrum.
Examples: cars, bicycles, wagons

Pulley A pulley is similar to a wheel and axle, except that there's no axle. It can be used to change both the direction and level force needed to move an object. The best example is a crane. An object is tied to a cable, which goes up and around the pulley, and down to the crane engine which is pulling it.
Examples: a block and tackle, a flag pole, tow trucks

Screw A screw is an inclined plane wrapped around a cylinder. In the case of a wood screw, as it is turned it travels deeper into the piece of wood. Another use of a screw is to hold things in place such as the lid on a jar.
Examples: drills, corkscrews

Biological Science

WHAT ARE LIVING THINGS MADE OF?

Plant cell

Cells are sometimes called the "building blocks" of all living things. Complex life forms have many cells. There are trillions of them in the human body.

There are two main kinds of cells: **eukaryotic** and **prokaryotic**. All the cells in your body—along with the cells of other animals, plants, and fungi—are eukaryotic. These contain several different structures, called **organelles**. Like tools in a toolbox, each kind of organelle has its own function. The **nucleus**, for example, contains most of the cell's DNA, while the **mitochondria** provide energy for the cell. The **ribosomes** are involved in making proteins.

Though both plant and animal cells are eukaryotic, they are different in a few ways. Animal cells rely only on mitochondria for energy, but plant cells also make use of another kind of organelle called a **chloroplast**. Chloroplasts contain chlorophyll, a green chemical plants use to make oxygen and energy from sunlight and water. This process is called **photosynthesis**. And unlike animal cells, plant cells are surrounded by a nonliving, rigid cell wall made of **cellulose**.

Prokaryotes (organisms with prokaryotic instead of eukaryotic cells) are all around you—and even inside of you. Most prokaryotes, such as bacteria, are single-celled. They don't have the variety of organelles that eukaryotic cells do.

WHAT IS DNA?

Every cell in every living thing (or organism) has **DNA**, a molecule that holds all the information about that organism. The structure of DNA was discovered in 1953 by the British scientist Francis Crick and the American scientist James Watson. James Watson was a *World Almanac* reader as a kid.

Lengths of connected DNA molecules, called **genes**, are tiny pieces of code. They determine what each organism is like. Almost all the DNA and genes come packaged in thread-like structures called **chromosomes**.

Humans have 46. There are 22 almost identical pairs, plus the X and Y chromosomes, which determine whether a human is male (one X chromosome and one Y chromosome) or female (two X chromosomes).

Genes are passed on from parents to children, and no two organisms (except clones or identical twins) have the same DNA.

Many things—the color of our eyes or hair, whether we're tall or short, our chances of getting certain diseases—depend on our genes.

What is the Human Genome?

The human genome contains 20,000 to 25,000 genes. That's fewer than the 50,000-plus genes of a rice plant! But unlike many other genes, human genes can produce more than one kind of protein. Proteins perform most life functions and make up a large part of cellular structures.

By studying human genes, scientists can learn more about hereditary diseases and get a better idea of how humans evolved.

Microbes Anton van Leeuwenhoek (pronounced Lay-wen-ook) made the first practical microscope in 1674. When he looked through it, he saw tiny bacteria, plant cells, and fungi, among other things. When he wrote about his findings, Leeuwenhoek called the creatures "wee beasties." We call them **microorganisms** ("micro" means *little*), or microbes. Before the microscope, people had no idea that there were millions of tiny living things crawling all over them.

Amoebas Amoebas (uh-ME-buhz) are eukaryotic jelly-like blobs of protoplasm that ooze through their microscopic world. They eat by engulfing their food and slowly digesting it. To move around, the cell extends a part of its goo to create something called a **pseudopod** (SOO-doh-pod), which means "false foot." The amoeba uses this to pull the rest of its "body" along. Amoebas normally live in water or on moist surfaces. In humans, most kinds of amoebas are harmless, but some cause diseases.

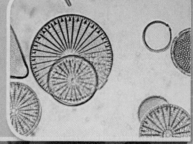

Diatoms Diatoms are one-celled algae that make glass shells to protect themselves. When they die, their shells collect at the bottom of the ocean in great numbers and form something called **diatomaceous earth**. It's gritty like sandpaper. Diatomaceous earth was once used in toothpaste to help scrape plaque off teeth. Nowadays, among other things, it is used as a pesticide—when sprayed in the air, it gets caught in the lungs of insects and slowly suffocates them.

CRIME SCENE INVESTIGATOR:

YOU DO IT

Crime scene investigation can involve dealing with blood. How do you know what you're looking at is blood, though, and not some other substance? Ask a parent to help you find Hemastix at a drug store. Then, ask a parent to prepare the solutions below for you. They should put a few drops on a plate for you.

> ketchup and water, mixed

> red watercolor paint

> blood (you can get this from a meat container)

Test each solution with a Hemastix. You can tell which one is blood because the Hemastix changes color.

SCIENCE Q&A

HOW DOES AN AIR CONDITIONER COOL A ROOM? Air conditioners work by cooling a small amount of air, and then blowing it across a room. They use a liquid called a **refrigerant**, which evaporates (turns into a gas) at low temperatures. When the refrigerant is exposed to air, the heat in the air evaporates the liquid, which cools the air (like when evaporating sweat cools your skin). A fan then blows it out to the room. Meanwhile, the refrigerant gas is forced through a tube, where pressure turns it back into a liquid, and it can be used again. A second tube brings in some more, warmer air, and the cycle begins again.

WHY DO PLANTS NEED SUNLIGHT? Sunlight—along with water and carbon dioxide, a gas found in the air—is necessary for photosynthesis. That's the process by which plants make their food. In fact, the word *photosynthesis* means *putting together* (synthesis) with *light* (photo). Leaves are the food factories in plants, where photosynthesis takes place. **Chlorophyll**, a chemical that gives leaves their green color, plays a key role in the process. Photosynthesis also releases oxygen into the atmosphere—a good thing, since that's what people breathe! In winter when there is less sunlight, photosynthesis slows down and then stops, and plants live off the food they have stored. When the green chlorophyll goes out of the leaves, they take on the color of other chemicals in them—that's how trees get their beautiful autumn leaves.

IS QUICKSAND FOR REAL? Yes, but it's not as deadly as it is in the movies. Quicksand forms when sand gets mixed with too much water and becomes loosened and soupy. It may look like normal sand, but if you were to step on it, the pressure from your foot would cause the sand to act more like a liquid, and you'd sink right in. In quicksand, the more you struggle, the more you'll sink. But if you remain still, you'll start to float. So if you ever do fall into quicksand, remember to stay calm, and don't move until you've stopped sinking. Then very slowly try to get flat on your stomach and crawl out. Quicksand isn't very common, but if you were to step in some, you're not likely to sink deeper than up to your waist.

WHY DO MY EARS POP WHEN I GO UP IN A PLANE? Ear popping is the sound made when the air pressure in your ears needs to even out with the air outside. In the middle part of each ear, there is a sac of air behind the eardrum. The air there usually has the same air pressure as the air outside. When you take off in an airplane, the air pressure outside the ear goes down, but the pressure inside the ear is still the same as it was on the ground. The inside air starts to push against the eardrum, causing pain. From the sac of air in each ear leads a tube called the Eustachian tube, which connects to the nasal passages and outside into the environment. When we swallow or yawn, the tubes open up allowing the pressure in the ear to become more like the pressure outside the ear. This causes the popping sound. The same thing happens when your plane goes to land.

YOU BE THE SCIENTIST QUI

Use the World Almanac for Kids 2008 to decide whether the statements below are true or false.

1. White light is a mixture of many different colors.
2. Petrology is the study of house pets.
3. The bigger the plant or animal, the more genes it has.
4. In a race between the two, light will always beat sound.
5. When using the scientific method, the first step is to design an experiment.
6. Some chemical symbols are shorthand for Latin words.
7. Water pressure deep in the ocean could actually crush a person.
8. Plants produce carbon dioxide when they breathe, like humans.
9. If you fall in quicksand, you should remain still to keep from sinking.
10. A shovel is a type of simple machine.

ANSWERS ON PAGES 334–337.
FOR MORE PUZZLES GO TO
WWW.WAFORKIDS.COM

⌂ ●WAforKids.c

Go to **WAforKids.com** to check out other awesome science a homework help, including:

- Information about famous scientists
- Interviews with people who turned their love of science int
- You Be the Scientist! Turn your kitchen into a laboratory by to get loads of bonus experiments and other cool science a

WHY DON'T BIRDS GET SHOCKED WHEN THEY PERCH ON POWER LINES? People (or animals) get electric shocks when a charge flows *through* them, from one place to another, using them as wires. For electricity to flow through anything, it has to have a way in and a way out. That's why most electrical cords you see are made of two insulated wires running side-by-side. If a bird were touching two different power lines, or a power line and something connected to the ground, electricity would flow through the bird, and the bird would get a nasty shock. Electricity doesn't flow through a bird when it stands only on one line.

HOW STRONG IS GRAVITY? Compared to other forces, gravity is weak. It may feel powerful on Earth, where it takes lots of energy for airplanes and rockets to leave the ground. But this is only because the planet is so massive that it pulls everything toward its center. Magnets use a force stronger than gravity when they stick on metal. And static electricity defies gravity when it makes your hair stand on end.

CAN YOU HEAR THE OCEAN IN A CONCH SHELL? No. What you really hear are sounds from the air around you. The shell acts as a mini-echo chamber, increasing and distorting the sounds so that they resemble the roar of ocean waves.

WHY CAN'T SCUBA DIVERS GO TO THE BOTTOM OF THE OCEAN? Pressure, that's why. On dry land at sea level, there is about 14.7 pounds per square inch (psi) of atmospheric pressure pressing down on you. That's like having a 14.7 pound weight placed on top of you. We don't feel it because we've adapted to it. In water, the pressure increases the deeper you go. For every 33 feet a person dives, it goes up by 14.7 psi. The pressure can get to be so great that it literally crushes people. Scuba divers don't normally go deeper than 100 feet without specialized equipment. Even then, it's hard to go lower than 300 feet because of the effects of pressure on the human body. Instead, people use specially-built submarines to reach the deepest parts of the oceans.

WHY DON'T OIL AND WATER MIX? Water and oil don't mix because they are made up of different kinds of molecules. Water molecules are **polar**, meaning that their negatively charged particles (electrons) are bunched up on one side, and their positively charged particles (protons in the atoms' nuclei) are bunched on the other. In oil molecules, on the other hand, positive and negative particles are spread out evenly, with no bunching. These molecules are **nonpolar**. Opposite charges attract each other, so water molecules cling to each other and not to oil molecules. Scientists actually call nonpolar molecules "hydrophobic," which means "fearful of water."

ARCHIMEDES (287 B.C.-212 B.C.), Greek mathematician and inventor who discovered that heavy objects could be moved using pulleys and levers. He was one of the first to test his ideas with experiments. He also is said to have shouted, "Eureka!" ("I have found it").

SIR ISAAC NEWTON (1642-1727), British scientist who worked out the basic laws of motion and gravity. He also showed that sunlight is made up of all the colors of the rainbow. He invented the branch of mathematics called **calculus** about the same time as the German scientist Gottfried von Leibniz (1646-1716), who was the first to make it widely known.

BENJAMIN BANNEKER (1731-1806), African American astronomer, mathematician, and writer. Banneker taught himself astronomy at the age of 58 and began publishing daily star and planet positions in his own almanac in 1792. He correctly predicted a 1789 solar eclipse that more famous astronomers missed. Banneker used his renown to argue against slavery, and exchanged letters with Thomas Jefferson on the topic.

CHARLES DARWIN (1809-1882), British scientist who is best known for his theory of **evolution by natural selection**. According to this theory, living creatures, by gradually changing so as to have the best chances of survival, slowly developed over millions of years into the forms they have today.

MARIE CURIE (1867-1934), a Polish-French physical chemist known for discovering **radium**, which is used to treat some diseases. She won the Nobel Prize for chemistry in 1911. She and her husband, Pierre Curie, also won the Nobel Prize for physics in 1903 for their work in radiation.

ALBERT E American revolution relationshi and energy influential won a Nob

LEAKEY, a Louis (1903- Richard (19 studied foss remains of e human ance in Africa. M discovery in 1959 of a sku 1.7 million ye old brought t worldwide fa after her hus son Richard

RACHEL CAR and leading e book *Silent S* used to kill pe wildlife. Event pesticides we

JANE GOODA who is a leadi behavior. Good chimpanzees u to "fish" for an chimpanzees h structures and written widely preservation of

STEPHEN HAW physicist and le **holes**—dense o gravity is so str escape them. H best-selling boo *of Time* (1988) a *Nutshell* (2001).

SPACE

Which planet could float in water? ➡ p. 222

The Solar System

Mercury Venus Earth Mars Jupiter Saturn Uranus Neptune

Planets

Dwarf Planets

Ceres Pluto Eris

The SUN is a STAR

Did you know that the Sun is a star, like the other stars you see at night? It is a typical, medium-size star. But because the Sun is much closer to our planet than any other star, we can study it in great detail. The diameter of the Sun is 865,000 miles—more than 100 times Earth's diameter. The gravity of the Sun is nearly 28 times the gravity of Earth.

How Hot Is the Sun? The surface temperature of the sun is close to 10,000° F, and it is believed that the Sun's inner core may reach temperatures around 28 million degrees! The Sun provides enough light and heat energy to support all forms of life on our planet.

Homework Help

Here's a useful way to remember the names of planets in order of their distance from the Sun. Think of this sentence: My Very Excellent Mother Just Sent Us Nachos.

M = Mercury, **V** = Venus, **E** = Earth, **M** = Mars, **J** = Jupiter, **S** = Saturn, **U** = Uranus,

N = Neptune

Can you think of a better way to remember the names of the planets now that Pluto is out (see page 223)? Let us know on our website www.waforkids.com

The Planets Are in Motion

The planets move around the Sun along elliptical paths called **orbits**. One complete path around the Sun is called a **revolution**. Earth takes one year, or 365¼ days, to make one revolution around the Sun. Planets that are farther away from the Sun take longer. Most planets have one or more moons. A moon orbits a planet in much the same way that the planets orbit the Sun. Each planet also spins or rotates on its axis. An axis is an imaginary line running through the center of a planet. The time it takes Earth to rotate on its axis equals one day.

Pluto

Planet Champions

Largest planet:
  Jupiter (88,732 miles diameter)

Smallest planet:
  Mercury (3,032 miles diameter)

Shortest orbit:
  Mercury (88 days)

Longest orbit:
  Neptune (164.8 years)

Tallest mountain:
  Mars (Olympus Mons, 15 miles high)

Hottest planet:
  Venus (867° F)

Coldest planet:
  Neptune (−330° F)

Shortest day:
  Jupiter (9 hours, 55 minutes, 30 seconds)

Longest day:
  Mercury (175.94 days)

No moons:
  Mercury, Venus

Most moons:
  Jupiter (63 known satellites)

WHAT IS AN ECLIPSE?

During a solar eclipse, the Moon casts a shadow on Earth. A total solar eclipse is when the Sun is completely blocked out. When this happens, the halo of gas around the Sun, called the **corona**, can be seen.

The next total solar eclipse will occur on August 1, 2008, but will only be seen in northern Canada, Greenland, and Asia.

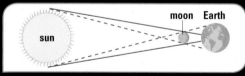

sun   moon   Earth

Sometimes Earth casts a shadow on the Moon. During a total lunar eclipse, the Moon remains visible, but it looks dark, often with a reddish tinge (from sunlight bent through Earth's atmosphere).

The next total lunar eclipse will take place on August 28, 2007, and will be seen in eastern Asia, Australia, the Pacific Ocean, and the Americas. The only total lunar eclipse in 2008 will happen on February 21, and will be seen in the Americas, Europe, Africa, and the Pacific.

sun   Earth   moon

THE PLANETS

❶ MERCURY

Average distance from the Sun: 36 million miles
Diameter: 3,032 miles
Average temp.: 333° F
Surface: silicate rock
Time to revolve around the Sun: 88 days
Day (synodic—midday to midday): 175.94 days
Number of moons: 0

 Mercury is the closest planet to the Sun, but it gets very cold there. Since Mercury has almost no atmosphere, most of its heat escapes at night, and temperatures can fall to –300° F.

❷ VENUS

Average distance from the Sun: 67 million miles
Diameter: 7,521 miles
Average temp.: 867° F
Surface: silicate rock
Time to revolve around the Sun: 224.7 days
Day (synodic): 116.75 days
Number of moons: 0

 Venus rotates in the opposite direction from all the other planets. Unlike on Earth, on Venus the Sun rises in the west and sets in the east.

❸ EARTH

Average distance from the Sun: 93 million miles
Diameter: 7,926 miles
Average temp.: 59° F
Surface: water, basalt, and granite rock
Time to revolve around the Sun: 365 ¼ days
Day (synodic): 24 hours
Number of moons: 1

 The diameter of Earth is 7,926 miles at the equator, but only 7,900 miles between the North and South Poles.

❹ MARS

Average distance from the Sun: 142 million miles
Diameter: 4,213 miles
Average temp.: –81° F
Surface: iron-rich basaltic rock
Time to revolve around the Sun: 687 days
Day (synodic): 24h 39m 35s
Number of moons: 2

 Mars is home to the largest mountain in the solar system, the massive Olympus Mons. It measures more than 340 miles across its base and is about 15 ½ miles high. That makes it about 10 miles taller than Mount Everest, which is the tallest mountain on the face of the Earth.

❺ JUPITER

Average distance from the Sun: 484 million miles
Diameter: 88,732 miles
Average temp.: –162° F
Surface: liquid hydrogen
Time to revolve around the Sun: 11.9 years
Day (synodic): 9h 55m 30s
Number of moons: 63

 Jupiter is a huge planet, but it rotates very quickly on its axis. A Jupiter day is only a dizzying 9 hours, 55 minutes long.

❻ SATURN

Average distance from the Sun: 887 million miles
Diameter: 74,975 miles
Average temp.: –218° F
Surface: liquid hydrogen
Time to revolve around the Sun: 29.5 years
Day (synodic): 10h 39m 23s
Number of moons: 56

 Saturn is the least dense planet in the solar system. If you could find a body of water big enough for it, Saturn would float!

7 URANUS

Average distance from the Sun: 1.8 billion miles
Diameter: 31,763 miles
Average temp.: −323° F
Surface: liquid hydrogen and helium
Time to revolve around the Sun: 84 years
Day (synodic): 17h 14m 23s
Number of moons: 27

Because Uranus is tipped 98 degrees on its axis, its north pole is dark for 42 years at a time.

8 NEPTUNE

Average distance from the Sun: 2.8 billion miles
Diameter: 30,603 miles
Average temp.: −330° F
Surface: liquid hydrogen and helium
Time to revolve around the Sun: 164.8 years
Day (synodic): 16d 6h 37m
Number of moons: 13

Triton, the largest of Neptune's moons, is considered the coldest object yet measured in the solar system, with an average temperature of −391° F.

Dwarf Planets

As of August 24, 2006, Pluto was no longer a planet. Pluto was reclassified a "dwarf planet" by the International Astronomical Union (IAU) when the organization changed the definition of 'planet.' The definition now says that a planet must "clear the neighborhood" around its orbit, which Pluto does not do. But Pluto is in good company. Two other bodies meet the new dwarf planet standards.

PLUTO

Average distance from the Sun: 3.6 billion miles
Diameter: 1,485 miles
Average temp.: −369° F
Surface: rock and frozen gases
Time to revolve around the Sun: 247.7 years
Day (synodic): 6d 9h 17m
Number of moons: 3

Pluto was discovered in 1930. It was named by an eleven-year-old girl, who happened to be really interested in mythology. Venetia Burney suggested the name Pluto, after the Roman god of the underworld, to her grandfather, who knew the astronomers who were trying to name it. Pluto has three natural satellites (moons), two of which were just discovered in 2005.

CERES, which orbits the sun in the asteroid belt between Mars and Jupiter, was also considered a planet for a short time after its discovery in the 1800s. It was then called an asteroid until it was named a dwarf planet in August 2006.

ERIS is the third (and largest) dwarf planet. Eris was only discovered in 2003, so scientists are still learning a lot about its features. It is the most distant object ever found to orbit the sun.

PLANET EARTH
SEASONS

The Earth spins on its axis of rotation. That's how we get day and night. But the Earth's axis isn't straight up and down. It is tilted about 23½ degrees. Because of this tilt, different parts of the globe get different amounts of sunlight during the year as the Earth orbits the Sun. This is how we have seasons.

AX

23.5°

WINTER Winter begins at the winter solstice (around December 21) in the Northern Hemisphere (north of the equator, where we live). Our hemisphere is tilted away from the Sun, so the Sun's rays reach us less directly. While days get longer during winter, they are still shorter than in spring and summer, so it's cold. Everything is reversed in the Southern Hemisphere, where it's summer!

SPRING At the vernal equinox (around March 21), daylight is 12 hours long throughout the world because the Earth is not tilted toward or away from the Sun. Days continue to get longer and the sunlight gets more direct in the Northern Hemisphere during spring.

Vernal Equinox

Summer Solstice

Winter Solstice

Autumnal Equinox

SUMMER The summer solstice (around June 21) marks the longest day of year in the Northern Hemisphere and the beginning of summer. The build-up of heat caused by more-direct sunlight during the long late spring and early

FALL After the autumnal equinox (around September 21) the Northern Hemisphere tilts away from the sun; sunlight is less direct and lasts less than 12 hours. The hemisphere cools off approaching winter.

THE MOON

The Moon is about 238,900 miles from Earth. It is 2,160 miles in diameter and has no atmosphere. The dusty surface is covered with deep craters. It takes the same time for the Moon to rotate on its axis as it does to orbit Earth (27 days, 7 hours, 43 minutes). This is why one side of the Moon is always facing Earth. The Moon has no light of its own but reflects light from the Sun. The lighted part of the Moon that we see changes in a regular cycle, waxing (growing) and waning (shrinking). It takes the Moon about 29½ days to go through all the "phases" in this cycle. This is called a lunar month.

PHASES OF THE MOON

| New Moon | Waxing Crescent | First Quarter | Waxing Gibbous | Full Moon | Waning Gibbous | Last Quarter | Waning Crescent | New Moon |

MOON Q&A

Why are there dark spots on the face of the Moon?

The dark spots you see on the face of the Moon are called *maria*. Maria are low plains made out of basalt, a fine, dark volcanic rock. The paler areas are mountains on the Moon's surface.

Does the Moon really cause the ocean tides?

Yes. Because the Moon is so big, its gravity causes the water in our seas and oceans to rise and fall as the Moon revolves around Earth. The Sun's gravitational pull also has an effect on ocean tides, but it is much weaker than the Moon's. That's because the Moon is so much closer to Earth than the Sun.

Are there any plans to go back to the Moon?

Right now, NASA is planning for another manned mission on the Moon no later than 2020. Other future Moon plans include a permanent lunar space station on the surface, probably on one of the Moon's poles.

EXPLORING SPACE

SOME UNMANNED MISSIONS
in the Solar System

LAUNCH DATE		
1962		**Mariner 2** First successful flyby of Venus.
1964		**Mariner 4** First probe to reach Mars, 1965.
1972		**Pioneer 10** First probe to reach Jupiter, 1973.
1973		**Mariner 10** Only U.S. probe to reach Mercury, 1974.
1975		**Viking 1 and 2** Landed on Mars in 1976.
1977		**Voyager 1** Reached Jupiter in 1979 and Saturn in 1980.
1977		**Voyager 2** Reached Jupiter in 1979, Saturn in 1981, Uranus in 1986, Neptune in 1989.
1989		**Magellan** Orbited Venus and mapped its surface.
1989		**Galileo** Reached Jupiter, 1995.
1996		**Mars Global Surveyor** Began mapping surface in 1999.
1996		**Mars Pathfinder** Landed on Mars. Carried a roving vehicle (Sojourner).
1997		**Cassini** Reached Saturn in June 2004.
2001		**Mars Odyssey** Began mapping and studying Mars in early 2002.
2003		**Mars rovers Spirit and Opportunity** Landed on Mars in early 2004.
2005		**Deep Impact** Reached comet Tempel 1 July 4, 2005 .
2006		**New Horizons** Launched January 19. Due to reach Pluto in 2015.

Artist's concept of the New Horizons spacecraft as it approaches Pluto and its three moons

Milestones
in Human Spaceflight

The U.S. formed NASA in 1958. It was in response to the Soviet Union's launching of the first artificial satellite *Sputnik I* on October 4, 1957. Since then, more than 400 astronauts have made trips into space to conduct research, visit orbiting space stations, and explore the Moon. Below are some of the biggest moments in human space flight.

1961 — On April 12, Soviet cosmonaut Yuri Gagarin, in *Vostok 1*, became the first person to orbit Earth. On May 5, U.S. astronaut Alan B. Shepard Jr. during the *Mercury 3* mission became the first American in space.

1962 — On February 20, U.S. astronaut John H. Glenn Jr. during the *Mercury 6* mission became the first American to orbit Earth.

1963 — From June 16 to 19, the Soviet spacecraft *Vostok 6* carried the first woman into space, Valentina V. Tereshkova.

1965 — On March 18, Soviet cosmonaut Aleksei A. Leonov became the first person to "walk" in space.

1966 — On March 16, U.S. *Gemini 8* became the first craft to dock with (become attached to) another vehicle (an unmanned Agena rocket).

1969 — On July 20, U.S. *Apollo 11's* lunar module *Eagle* landed on the Moon's surface in the area known as the Sea of Tranquility. Neil Armstrong was the first person ever to walk on the Moon.

1970 — In April, *Apollo 13* astronauts returned safely to Earth after an explosion damaged their spacecraft and prevented them from landing on the Moon.

1973 — On May 14, the U.S. put its first space station, *Skylab*, into orbit. The last *Skylab* crew left in January 1974.

1975 — On July 15, the U.S. launched an *Apollo* spacecraft and the Soviet Union launched a *Soyuz* spacecraft. Two days later, the American and Soviet crafts docked, and for several days their crews worked and spent time together in space.

1981 — *Columbia* was launched and became the first space shuttle to reach space.

1986 — On January 28, space shuttle *Challenger* exploded 73 seconds after takeoff. All seven astronauts, including teacher Christa McAuliffe, died. In February, the Soviet space station *Mir* was launched into orbit.

1995 — In June, *Atlantis* docked with *Mir* for the first time.

1998 — In December, *Endeavour* was launched with *Unity*, a U.S.-built part of the International Space Station (ISS). The crew attached it to the Russian-built *Zarya* control module. The first ISS crew arrived in November 2000.

2001 — The 15-year Russian *Mir* program ended.

2003 — On February 1, space shuttle *Columbia* disintegrated during its reentry into the Earth's atmosphere, killing the seven-member crew. China launched its first manned spacecraft on October 15.

2004 — On June 21, Mike Melvill piloted *SpaceShipOne,* the first privately funded spacecraft, into space.

2005 — Space shuttle *Discovery* was launched July 26. Its 13-day mission was to test new safety upgrades to the shuttle.

Same Stars, Different Pictures

When we look up in the sky, we see constellations in the shapes of ordinary things like animals, people, and tools. But the stories they tell—and the cultures that created their legends—are anything but ordinary.

ORION

Orion is one of the brightest and easiest to find constellations. Orion can only be seen in the night sky from November to April in the Northern Hemisphere. Also known as 'The Hunter,' Orion is accompanied in the night sky by his hunting dogs, the constellations Canis Major and Canis Minor.

Many legends about Orion come from Greek mythology, but there are a lot of differences between the stories. In one version, Orion is fighting the bull Taurus (another constellation). In another, Artemis (goddess of the hunt) falls in love with Orion and is tricked into killing him by her twin brother, Apollo. Artemis places him in the night sky to mourn him.

Ancient Egyptians associated the stars that make up Orion with Osiris, the Egyptian god of death and the underworld. Some people even say that three of the pyramids of Giza are meant to be a skymap of what we know as Orion's belt.

THE LITTLE DIPPER

The Little Dipper is so named because its seven brightest stars form the smaller of two constellations that resemble ladles, or dippers. Its more formal name is Ursa Minor, which means 'little bear.' The end of the handle on the Little Dipper is the star Polaris, also known as the North Star.

In the past, many travelers—especially the Vikings—steered by the North Star because it stays in the same part of the sky (roughly lined up with Earth's North Pole) all year. According to legend, Vikings across Scandinavia thought the Little Dipper represented the hammer of Thor, one of their gods.

Astrologers in ancient China carefully watched the movement of stars and planets. The Emperor was compared to the North Star and the stars that circled Polaris were his subjects. Some astrologers believed that the future could be read in the movements of the stars around Polaris. But the information was kept secret from everyone except the Emperor. It was feared that sharing the knowledge with outsiders would put the ruling family in danger.

Betelgeuse

Bellatrix

Alnilam   Mintaka

Alnitak

Orion Nebula

Saiph   Rigel

Polaris
(North Star)

Ursa Minor
(Little Dipper)

NGC 4414 Galaxy, as seen by Hubble Space Telescope

WHAT'S OUT THERE

What else is in space besides planets?

A **GALAXY** is a group of billions of stars held close together by gravity. The universe may have as many as 100 billion galaxies! The one we live in is called the Milky Way. Our Sun and planets are only a small part of it. Scientists think there are as many as 200 billion stars in the Milky Way!

NEBULA is the name astronomers give to any fuzzy patch in the sky, even galaxies and star clusters. Planetary nebulas come from the late stages of some stars, while star clusters and galaxies are groups of stars. Emission nebulas, reflection nebulas, and dark dust clouds are regions of gas and dust that may be hundreds of light-years wide and are often birthplaces of stars. Emission nebulas often give off a reddish glow, caused when their hydrogen gas is heated by hot, newly formed stars nearby. Dust particles in some areas reflect hot blue starlight and appear as reflection nebulas. Dark dust clouds, though still mainly gas, contain enough dust to absorb starlight and appear as dark nebulas.

BLACK HOLE is the name given to a region in space with gravity so strong that nothing can get out—not even light. Many black holes are probably formed when giant stars at least 20 times as massive as our Sun burn up their fuel and collapse, creating very dense cores. Scientists think bigger, "supermassive" black holes may form from the collapse of many stars in the centers of galaxies. Astronomers can't see black holes, because they do not give off light. They watch for signs, such as effects on the orbits of nearby stars, or X-ray bursts from matter being sucked into the black hole.

SATELLITES are objects that move in an orbit around a planet. Moons are natural satellites. Artificial satellites, launched into orbit by humans, are used as space stations and observatories. They are also used to take pictures of Earth's surface and to transmit communications signals.

ASTEROIDS are solid chunks of rock or metal that range in size from small boulders to hundreds of miles across. Some asteroids orbit other asteroids. Hundreds of thousands of asteroids orbit the Sun in the main asteroid belt between Mars and Jupiter.

COMETS are moving chunks of ice, dust, and rock that form huge gaseous heads and tails as they move nearer to the Sun. One of the most well-known is Halley's Comet. It can be seen about every 76 years and will appear again in the year 2061.

METEOROIDS are small pieces of stone or metal traveling in space. Most meteoroids are fragments from comets or asteroids that broke off from crashes in space with other objects. A few are actually chunks that blew off the Moon or Mars after an asteroid hit.

Comet Hale-Bopp, discovered in 1995

When a meteoroid enters the Earth's atmosphere, it usually burns up completely. This streak of light is called a **meteor**, or **shooting star**. If a piece of a meteoroid survives its trip through our atmosphere and lands on Earth, it is called a **meteorite**.

SPORTS

When was the first indoor pro football game? ➤ page 241

Can you "bend it like Beckham"? Drive through the paint all the way to the hoop? Nail a 360°? Whether you play in a league or with friends in the neighborhood, prefer a solo bike trip or a hike through a nearby park, there are lots of awesome ways to stay fit, have fun, and get your game on.

FAVORITE SPORTS

Here are some favorite sports or activities, and the number of U.S. kids who enjoy each .

	Boys (ages 6-17)			Girls (ages 6-17)	
1.	Bicycling	11.3 million	1.	Bicycling	10.1 million
2.	Basketball	9.8 million	2.	Walking/Hiking	9.0 million
3.	Bowling	8.2 million	3.	Bowling	8.9 million
4.	Football	8.1 million	4.	Volleyball	7.6 million
5.	Soccer	6.8 million	5.	Basketball	6.2 million
6.	Skateboarding	6.6 million	6.	Soccer	6.2 million
7.	Walking/Hiking	5.3 million	7.	In-Line Skating	5.5 million
8.	In-Line Skating	4.9 million	8.	Softball	5.0 million
9.	Baseball	4.8 million	9.	Scooter Riding	4.5 million
10.	Scooter Riding	4.5 million	10.	Ice Skating	4.3 million

Source: Sporting Goods Manufacturers Association, 2005

LITTLE LEAGUE

Little League Baseball is the largest youth sports program in the world. It began in 1939 in Williamsport, Pennsylvania, with 45 boys playing on three teams. Now about 2.7 million boys and girls ages 5 to 18 play on more than 200,000 Little League teams in more than 80 countries.

WEB SITE www.littleleague.org

STRANGE SPORTS

Most American kids are familiar with sports like soccer, basketball, baseball, and football, because they see them (and play them) all the time. But some sports are seldom played on American fields, courts, or gridirons. Imagine yourself playing one of these somewhat unfamiliar sports.

FOOTVOLLEY

Footvolley is a game that combines soccer and beach volleyball. People started playing it on Brazilian beaches in the 1960s, but it has become popular in other countries, too. The net is the same as the one used in beach volleyball, but players use a soccer ball instead of a volleyball. Unlike volleyball, players cannot use their hands. They may use only their feet, heads, and chests to get the ball over the net. Otherwise, the rules are the same as those in beach volleyball. Tournaments are held all over the world.

BICYCLE POLO

Bicycle polo is a combination of polo (a hockey-like game that is played on horseback) and bicycle riding. There are two teams in bicycle polo. Each player has a mallet which is slightly shorter than the ones used in traditional polo. They use these mallets to hit the ball. The object of the game is to maneuver the ball down the field and hit it into the opponent's goal. Players are not allowed to hit each other with their mallets, and their feet must stay on the bike's pedals at all times. If a player's feet touch the ground, he or she has to ride out of bounds and back in before hitting the ball again.

WEB SITE *bicyclepolo.org*

UNDERWATER HOCKEY

Underwater hockey, also known as "octopush," was invented by four English scuba divers in 1954. The game is played at the bottom of a swimming pool between two teams of six. Players wear fins, a diving mask, and a snorkel to play. They use a short stick 10-12 inches long to slide a 3-pound puck into the opposing team's goal underwater. Everyone on a team has to work together to score, since no one can go too long without coming up for air! World championships are held every two years. The 2006 tournament took place in Sheffield, England. The next tournament will be held in Durban, South Africa, in Sept. 2008.

WHO AM I ?

I was born June 23, 1979, in Rosebud, TX. I played college football at Texas Christian University. I was drafted in the first round of the 2001 NFL draft by the San Diego Chargers, and I still play for them. In 2006, I scored 186 points, breaking a 46-year-old NFL record for points scored in a single season. That year, I also set a new record for total touchdowns scored in a season, with 31. I ran for 28 of those, and set an NFL record for rushing touchdowns in a season. Many people compare me to great NFL running backs like Walter Payton and my childhood idol, Emmitt Smith.

Answer: LaDainian Tomlinson

THE OLYMPIC GAMES

The first Olympics were held in Greece more than 2,500 years ago. In 776 B.C. they featured just one event—a footrace. Boxing, wrestling, chariot racing, and the pentathlon (which consisted of five different events) came later. The Olympic Games were held every four years for more than 1,000 years, until A.D. 393, when the Roman emperor Theodosius stopped them. The first modern games were held in Athens in 1896. Winter Olympics were added in 1924.

2008 SUMMER OLYMPICS: BEIJING, CHINA

Beijing, China, will play host to 10,500 athletes from around the world during the 29th Olympiad. They will compete in more than 300 events in 28 sports.

Since being awarded the 2008 games, China has gone to great lengths to improve conditions in its cities. The government began several projects to clean up streets and to promote public health. This includes an anti-spitting campaign. In addition, Beijing authorities embarked on a campaign to teach its citizens to be more open toward foreign cultures.

Originally, the winter and summer games were both held every four years. But starting in 1994, the schedule changed. Now the winter and summer games alternate every two years. The next Winter Games will be held in Vancouver, Canada, in 2010. In 2012, the Summer Games will be held in London, England.

2008 SUMMER OLYMPIC SPORTS

Aquatics (diving, swimming, synchronized swimming, water polo)
Archery
Athletics (track & field)
Badminton
Baseball
Basketball
Boxing
Canoe/Kayak
Cycling (road, mountain, bike, track)

Equestrian (dressage, jumping, 3-day event)
Fencing
Field Hockey
Football (soccer)
Gymnastics (artistic, rhythmic, trampoline)
Handball
Judo
Modern Pentathlon (show jumping, running, fencing, pistol shooting, swimming)

Rowing
Sailing
Shooting
Softball
Table Tennis (ping-pong)
Taekwondo
Tennis
Triathlon
Volleyball (beach, indoor)
Weightlifting
Wrestling

SOME MAJOR LEAGUE RECORDS*

BATTERS

Most Home Runs

Career: 755, Hank Aaron (1954-76)
Season: 73, **Barry Bonds** (2001)
Game: 4, by 15 different players

Most Hits

Career: 4,256, Pete Rose (1963-86)
Season: 262, **Ichiro Suzuki** (2004)
Game: 7, Rennie Stennett (1975)

Most Stolen Bases

Career: 1,406, Rickey Henderson (1979-2003)
Season: 130, Rickey Henderson (1982)
Game: 6, Eddie Collins (1912)

PITCHERS

Most Strikeouts

Career: 5,714, Nolan Ryan (1966-93)
Season: 383, Nolan Ryan (1973)
Game: 20, **Roger Clemens** (1986, 1996); **Kerry Wood** (1998)

Most Wins

Career: 511, Cy Young (1890-1911)
Season: 41, Jack Chesbro (1904)

Most Saves

Career: 482, **Trevor Hoffman** (1993-2006)
Season: 57, Bobby Thigpen (1990)

*Through the 2006 season. Players in bold played in 2006. Game stats are for nine-inning games only.

JACKIE AND PEE WEE

Jackie Robinson made history in 1947 when he began playing for the Brooklyn Dodgers. He was the first African American to play in the major leagues. Robinson had to put up with a lot of racism and taunting. But he had the support of his friend and teammate Harold Henry "Pee Wee" Reese who was a white southerner from Ekron, Kentucky.

Pee Wee Reese was the Dodgers' captain and their starting shortstop. When Robinson joined the team, several Dodgers players were angry because they didn't want to play with a black man. But Reese didn't care about Robinson's race. He just wanted to play. At spring training in March 1947, Reese was the first player to welcome Robinson, and the two became friends.

Pee Wee Reese (throwing) with Jackie Robinson (background)

On May 14, 1947, the Dodgers were playing a game against the Cincinnati Reds in Cincinnati, OH. During the game, hecklers in the stands were yelling racial insults at Robinson, who was playing second base. Seeing that the insults were getting worse, Reese walked from his shortsop position over to Robinson and put his arm around his teammate. When the hecklers saw Reese, a white man, putting his arm around Robinson, they quieted down and the game continued. The teammates went on to become one of the best double play combinations in baseball. And Robinson never forgot Reese's gesture of support in the face of the unruly crowd.

BASEBALL Hall of Fame

The National Baseball Hall of Fame and Museum opened in 1939, in Cooperstown, New York. To be eligible for membership, players must be retired from baseball for five years. In 2007, Tony Gwynn and Cal Ripken Jr. were elected to "The Hall" by the traditional vote. Gwynn, who played his whole career for the San Diego Padres, is considered one of the best contact hitters in baseball history. Ripken, who played his whole career with the Baltimore Orioles, holds the record for the most consecutive games played with 2,632.

WEB SITE *www.baseballhalloffame.org*

BASKETBALL

Basketball began in 1891 in Springfield, Massachusetts, when Dr. James Naismith invented it, using peach baskets as hoops. At first, each team had nine players instead of five. Big-time pro basketball started in 1949, when the National Basketball Association (NBA) was formed. The Women's National Basketball Association (WNBA) began play in 1997.

LeBron James

GOT BALL?

Have you ever heard the saying, "if it ain't broke, don't fix it"? It means that if something works, you shouldn't try to change it. Well, that's exactly what the NBA tried to do during the 2006-2007 season. Instead of using leather balls, which the league had been using since its beginnings, the NBA tried switching to a new type of ball. The new ball was made from a synthetic composite microfiber. It was supposed to be easier to grip and did not require any "breaking in." Leather balls need to be practiced with before they can be used in games or else they're too slippery to handle. The synthetic balls were sticky to begin with. But when they got wet with sweat they became slippery. Leather balls are the opposite. They are tougher to handle when hands are dry. But once players' hands get sweaty, the leather ball becomes easy to handle and almost sticky. This made the leather ball a better choice.

Official leather NBA ball

From the beginning of the season, which started in November 2006, many players including LeBron James, Steve Nash, and Shaquille O'Neal complained about the synthetic balls. Besides the balls being slippery, players insisted that the new balls didn't bounce as well. Some even said that they were getting cuts on their hands from the new balls. After many complaints, the NBA decided to go back to using leather balls beginning Jan. 1, 2007.

Hall of Fame

The Naismith Memorial Hall of Fame in Springfield, Massachusetts, was founded to honor great basketball players, coaches, referees, and others important to the history of the game. The class, inducted in September 2007, included: NBA coach Phil Jackson; referee Marvin "Mendy" Rudolph; NCAA coach Roy Williams; WNBA coach Van Chancellor; international coaches Pedro Ferrandiz and Mirko Novosel; and the entire 1966 Texas Western College basketball team, which was the first team in NCAA history to win an NCAA National Championship with five starting African-American players. **WEB SITE** www.hoophall.com

Some **All-Time** NBA Records*

POINTS

Career: 38,387, Kareem Abdul-Jabbar (1969-89)

Season: 4,029, Wilt Chamberlain (1961-62)

Game: 100, Wilt Chamberlain (1962)

ASSISTS

Career: 15,806, John Stockton (1984-2003)

Season: 1,164 John Stockton (1990-91)

Game: 30, Scott Skiles (1990)

REBOUNDS

Career: 23,924, Wilt Chamberlain (1959-73)

Season: 2,149, Wilt Chamberlain (1960-61)

Game: 55, Wilt Chamberlain (1960)

3-POINTERS

Career: 2,560, Reggie Miller (1987-2005)

Season: 267, Dennis Scott (1996-97)

Game: 12, **Kobe Bryant** (2003); **Donnyell Marshall** (2005)

*Through the 2005-2006 season. Players in bold were active in the 2006-2007 season.

Highlights of the
2006 WNBA Season

The Detroit Shock beat the Sacramento Monarchs, 3 games to 2, on September 9, 2006, to win the WNBA Championship. Detroit guard Deanna Nolan was named the series MVP. Nolan averaged 17.8 points and shot 44.6% from the field over the course of the series. It was the Shock's second championship in four years.

Scoring Leader:
- Diana Taurasi, Phoenix Mercury
  Points: 860
  Average: 25.3

Rebounding Leader:
- Cheryl Ford, Detroit Shock
  Rebounds: 363
  Average: 11.3

Assists Leader:
- Nikki Teasley, Washington Mystics
  Assists: 183
  Average: 5.38

Cheryl Ford of Detroit (L) and DeMya Walker of Sacramento (R).

COLLEGE BASKETBALL

The men's National Collegiate Athletic Association (NCAA) Tournament began in 1939. Today, it is a spectacular 65-team extravaganza. The Final Four weekend, when the semi-finals and finals are played, is one of the most-watched sports competitions in the U.S. The Women's NCAA Tournament began in 1982 and has soared in popularity.

THE 2006 NCAA TOURNAMENT RESULTS

MEN'S FINAL FOUR
Semi-Finals:
Florida 76, UCLA 66
Ohio State 67, Georgetown 60

Final:
Florida 84, Ohio State 75

Most Outstanding Player:
Corey Brewer, Florida

WOMEN'S FINAL FOUR
Semi-Finals:
Tennessee 56, North Carolina 50
Rutgers 59, LSU 35

Final:
Tennessee 59, Rutgers 46

Most Outstanding Player:
Candace Parker, Tennessee

FOOTBALL

Football began as a college sport. The first game that was like today's football took place between Yale and Harvard in New Haven, Connecticut, on November 13, 1875. The modern National Football League started in 1922. The rival American Football League began in 1960. The two leagues played the first Super Bowl in 1967. In 1970, the leagues merged to become the NFL as we know it today, with an American Football Conference (AFC) and a National Football Conference (AFC).

Super Bowl XLI, Colts Beat the Bears in the Rain

The Indianapolis Colts beat the Chicago Bears, 29 to 17, at Dolphin Stadium in Miami, Florida, to win Super Bowl XLI. Coaches Tony Dungy of the Colts and Lovie Smith of the Bears were the first African Americans to coach in the Super Bowl. Colts quarterback Peyton Manning was named Super Bowl MVP. He completed 25 passes out of 38 thrown, and threw for one touchdown. It was the Colts' first championship in 36 years. Their last one came in 1971.

Tony Dungy (L) and Peyton Manning (R)

RUSHING YARDS: LaDainian Tomlinson, San Diego Chargers, 1,815
RUSHING TDS: LaDainian Tomlinson, San Diego Chargers, 28
RECEPTIONS: Andre Johnson, Houston Texans, 103
RECEIVING YARDS: Chad Johnson, Cincinnati Bengals, 1,369
RECEIVING TDS: Terrell Owens, Dallas Cowboys, 13
PASSING YARDS: Drew Brees, New Orleans Saints, 4,418
PASSER RATING: Peyton Manning, Indianapolis Colts, 101.0
PASSING TDS: Peyton Manning, Indianapolis Colts, 31
SCORING: LaDainian Tomlinson, San Diego Chargers, 186
INTERCEPTIONS: Asante Samuel, New England Patriots, 10; Champ Bailey, Denver Broncos, 10
SACKS: Shawne Merriman, San Diego Chargers, 17

2006 NFL LEADERS

Pro Football Hall of Fame

Football's Hall of Fame in Canton, Ohio, was founded in 1963 by the National Football League to honor outstanding players, coaches, and contributors.

Guard Gene Hickerson, wide receiver Michael Irvin, guard/tackle/center Bruce Matthews, tight end Charlie Sanders, running back Thurman Thomas, and cornerback Roger Wehrli were to be inducted in August 2007.

WEB SITE www.profootballhof.com

Famous Pro Football Firsts

Old Madison Square Garden

1925 to 1931 called the Steam Roller. Their home stadium was called the Cyclodrome. In 1925, the Steam Roller played host to the visiting Chicago Cardinals (today's Arizona Cardinals). The teams were to play a four-game series over six days. Just before the second game, heavy rains made the Cyclodrome unplayable. So the game was moved to nearby Kinsley Park Stadium where floodlights had recently been installed. The night game was played in front of a crowd of 6,000. Chicago won, 16 to 0.

FIRST INDOOR GAME December 28, 1902, World Series of Pro Football Tournament, Madison Square Garden, New York City, New York. New York vs. Syracuse Athletic Club

Today, nine NFL teams have indoor stadiums. Many people think that indoor football is a relatively new development, but the first indoor pro football game was actually played in 1902. The team called "New York" was actually made up of players from two NFL teams in Philadelphia. They lost to Syracuse Athletic Club, 5-0, in front of a crowd of 3,500. Syracuse went on to win the tournament.

FIRST GAME PLAYED UNDER THE LIGHTS November 6, 1929, Kinsley Park Stadium, Providence, Rhode Island. Providence Steam Roller vs. Chicago Cardinals

Providence used to have an NFL team from

THE FIRST FORWARD PASS October 27, 1906, Massillon, Ohio. Massillon Tigers vs. Benwood-Moundsville

In the old days of football, the forward pass was not allowed. Teams would only run the ball. This was fine in the beginning, but after a while running the ball became too difficult. To open up the game, National Collegiate Athletic Association in 1906 voted to allow the forward pass. The same rule was adopted by the pros. The first forward pass in a college game took place in a game between St. Louis University and Carroll College on Sept. 5, 1906, when SLU's Bradbury Robinson threw a pass to Jack Schneider. The first known forward pass in a pro game took place in a game between the Massillon Tigers and Benwood-Moundsville. George Parratt of Massillon threw a pass to Dan "Bullet" Riley. Massillon won 61-0.

NFL All-Time Record Holders*

RUSHING YARDS
Career: 18,355, Emmitt Smith (1990-2004)
Season: 2,105, Eric Dickerson (1984)
Game: 295, Jamal Lewis (2003)

RECEIVING YARDS
Career: 22,895, Jerry Rice (1985-2004)
Season: 1,848, Jerry Rice (1995)
Game: 336, Willie Anderson (1989)

PASSING YARDS
Career: 61,361, Dan Marino (1983-99)
Season: 5,084, Dan Marino (1984)
Game: 554, Norm Van Brocklin (1951)

POINTS SCORED
Career: 2,434, Gary Anderson (1982-2004)
Season: 186, LaDainian Tomlinson (2006)
Game: 40, Ernie Nevers (1929)

*Through the 2006 season.

COLLEGE FOOTBALL

College football is one of America's most colorful and exciting sports. The National Collegiate Athletic Association (NCAA), founded in 1906, oversees the sport today.

The second-ranked Florida Gators beat the heavily favored first-ranked Ohio State Buckeyes, 41-14, in Glendale, Arizona, on January 8, 2007, in the BCS Championship game. The game began with a 93-yard touchdown kickoff return by Ohio State's Ted Ginn, Jr. But Florida came back and got touchdowns on each of their next three drives. Florida went ahead and never looked back. Chris Hetland, quarterback for Florida, was named the game MVP.

The win earned Florida a first place standing in the college football polls, while Ohio State dropped to second.

TOP 5 COLLEGE TEAMS

Chosen by the Associated Press Poll and the Coaches Poll. As of the end of the 2006-07 season.

Rank	AP	Coaches Poll
1	Florida	Florida
2	Ohio State	Ohio State
3	LSU	LSU
4	USC	USC
5	Boise State	Wisconsin

HEISMAN TROPHY

Ohio State Buckeyes' quarterback Troy Smith was the 2006 recipient of the Heisman Trophy. Smith received 801 first-place votes and won the Heisman by 1,662 points. Both were the second-best marks in the 71-year history of the award. The 22-year-old Smith, a senior, led the Buckeyes to a perfect 12-0 record during the 2006 season. Smith threw for 2,507 yards and 30 touchdowns through the air. He finished with a passer rating of 167.9, fourth in the nation. Over his college career, Smith was 25-2 as a starter. Smith was the sixth player from Ohio State to win the award, and the first since 1995.

ALL-TIME DIVISION I NCAA LEADERS

RUSHING YARDS

1. 6,397, Ron Dayne, Wisconsin
2. 6,297, Ricky Williams, Texas
3. 6,082, Tony Dorsett, Pittsburgh
4. 6,026, DeAngelo Williams, Memphis
5. 5,598, Charles White, USC

PASSING YARDS

1. 17,072, Timmy Chang, Hawaii
2. 15,031, Ty Detmer, Brigham Young
3. 12,746, Tim Rattay, Louisiana Tech
4. 12,541, Chris Redman, Louisville
5. 12,429, Kliff Kingsbury, Texas Tech

Great Moment in *College Football*

JANUARY 2, 1984, ORANGE BOWL: MIAMI 31, NEBRASKA 30.
The underdog Miami Hurricanes led the top-ranked, undefeated Nebraska Cornhuskers, 17-0. But the 'Huskers didn't give up—they even scored a TD on a trick play known as the "fumblerooski." The quarterback put the ball on the ground, where it was picked up by a lineman who ran it into the end zone. Miami still led, 31-17, in the fourth quarter, but Nebraska scored two more TDs to pull within a point of the 'Canes. After their final score, Nebraska tried a two-point conversion that would have given them the win. But quarterback Turner Gill's pass was blocked, and Miami earned the victory and a national championship.

GOLF

Golf began in Scotland as early as the 1400s. The first golf course in the U.S. opened in 1888 in Yonkers, NY. The sport has grown to include both men's and women's professional tours. And millions play just for fun.

The men's tour in the U.S. is run by the Professional Golf Association (PGA). The four major championships (with the year first played) are:
- British Open (1860)
- United States Open (1895)
- PGA Championship (1916)
- Masters Tournament (1934)

The women's tour in the U.S. is guided by the Ladies Professional Golf Association (LPGA). The four major championships are:
- United States Women's Open (1946)
- McDonald's LPGA Championship (1955)
- Nabisco Championship (1972)
- Women's British Open (1976)

The All-Time "Major" Players

These pro golfers have won the most major championships as of March 2007. Tiger Woods and Annika Sorenstam won majors in 2006.

MEN
1. Jack Nicklaus, 18
2. Tiger Woods, 12
3. Walter Hagan, 11
4. Ben Hogan, 9
   Gary Player, 9

WOMEN
1. Patty Berg, 15
2. Mickey Wright, 13
3. Louise Suggs, 11
4. Babe Didrikson Zaharias, 10
   Annika Sorenstam, 10

Jack Nicklaus

GYMNASTICS

Although the sport dates back to ancient Egypt, modern-day gymnastics began in Europe in the early 1800s. It has been part of the Olympics since 1896. The first World Gymnastic Championships were held in Antwerp, Belgium, in 1903.

Men today compete in the All-Around, High Bar, Parallel Bars, Rings, Vault, Pommel Horse, Floor Exercises, and Team Combined. The women's events are the All-Around, Uneven Parallel Bars, Balance Beam, Floor Exercises, and Team Combined. In rhythmic gymnastics, women compete in All-Around, Rope, Hoop, Ball, Clubs, and Ribbon.

U.S. gymnast Nastia Liukin (born October 30, 1989) hopes to bring her past success to the Beijing Olympics in 2008. On an injured ankle, the Russian-born daughter of an Olympic gymnast helped the U.S. team win the silver medal at the 2006 World Championships. Liukin also finished second in the uneven bars.

Nastia Liukin

ICE HOCKEY

Ice hockey began in Canada in the mid-1800s. The National Hockey League (NHL) was formed in 1916. In 2006, the NHL had 30 teams—24 in the U.S. and 6 in Canada.

HIGHLIGHTS

In 2006, the Carolina Hurricanes defeated the Edmonton Oilers in seven games to win their first Stanley Cup title in the franchise's 27-year history. Hurricanes' rookie goalie Cam Ward won the Conn Smythe Trophy as MVP of the NHL post-season.

San Jose Sharks center Joe Thornton won the Hart Trophy as NHL MVP. He was the regular-season points leader with 125.

On November 26, 2005, the N.Y. Rangers and Washington Capitals played the longest shootout in NHL history. The game ended with a shot from Rangers defenseman Marek Malik in the 15th round.

SEASON	WINNER	RUNNER-UP
1990-91	Pittsburgh Penguins	Minnesota North Stars
1991-92	Pittsburgh Penguins	Chicago Black Hawks
1992-93	Montreal Canadiens	Los Angeles Kings
1993-94	New York Rangers	Vancouver Canucks
1994-95	New Jersey Devils	Detroit Red Wings
1995-96	Colorado Avalanche	Florida Panthers
1996-97	Detroit Red Wings	Philadelphia Flyers
1997-98	Detroit Red Wings	Washington Capitals
1998-99	Dallas Stars	Buffalo Sabres
1999-2000	New Jersey Devils	Dallas Stars
2000-01	Colorado Avalanche	New Jersey Devils
2001-02	Detroit Red Wings	Carolina Hurricanes
2002-03	New Jersey Devils	Anaheim Mighty Ducks
2003-04	Tampa Bay Lightning	Calgary Flames
2004-05	Season cancelled	
2005-2006	Carolina Hurricanes	Edmonton Oilers

Some All-Time NHL Records*

GOALS SCORED
Career: 894, Wayne Gretzky (1979-99)
Season: 92, Wayne Gretzky (1981-82)
Game: 7, Joe Malone (1920)

GOALIE WINS
Career: 551, Patrick Roy (1984-2003)
Season: 47, Bernie Parent (1973-74)

*Through 2005-06 season

POINTS
Career: 2,857, Wayne Gretzky (1979-99)
Season: 215, Wayne Gretzky (1985-86)
Game: 10, Darryl Sittler (1976)

GOALIE SHUTOUTS
Career: 103, Terry Sawchuk (1949-70)
Season: 22, George Hainsworth (1928-29)

WHO AM I?

I was born in Dartmouth, Nova Scotia, Canada, on August 7, 1987. I grew up in nearby Cole Harbour. My father played hockey for the Montreal Canadiens. I was the number one draft pick in 2005, taken by the Pittsburgh Penguins. The position I play is center. I'm the youngest player in the history of the NHL to score 100 points in a season.

Answer: Sydney Crosby

SOCCER
THE MLS CUP

The Houston Dynamo beat the New England Revolution, 4-3, on November 12, 2006, at Pizza Hut Park in Frisco, Texas. The game was tied 1-1 after a scoreless regulation, and two overtime periods. After four rounds of PKs, the score stood at 3-3. Then in the fifth round, Houston Dynamo forward Brian Ching scored to put the Dynamo ahead and give them the win. Ching was named the MLS Cup's most valuable player.

The Beckham Rule

The Los Angeles Galaxy announced on January 11, 2007, that they had signed superstar English midfielder David Beckham. His five-year deal with the Galaxy was worth $250 million. In terms of yearly salary, it was the richest sports contract ever signed in the U.S. Beckham, who had been playing for the Spanish club team Real Madrid, was once among the best in the world. But in recent years, many say that Beckham had lost a step. Others think he will be a star player in the MLS.

The deal to bring Beckham to the U.S. was made possible on November 11, 2006, by the so-called "Beckham rule." The rule allows each MLS club to go over the league's salary limit for one specially designated player. The new rule is called the Beckham rule because it was made to lure a player of his caliber to the MLS.

Brian Ching

Clint Mathis, left, shoots for goal against Chris Albright

MLS ALL TIME LEADERS

Most Goals, Game: 5, Clint Mathis, August 26, 2000
Most Goals, Season: 27, Roy Lassiter, 1996
Most Assists, Season: 26, Carlos Valderrama, 2000
Most Goals, Career: 108, Jason Kreis
Most Shutouts, Season: 16, Tony Meola, 2000
Lowest Goals Against Average, Season: 0.91, Kevin Hartman, 1999

FIFA WOMEN'S WORLD CUP: CHINA 2007

The 5th FIFA Women's Soccer World Cup will begin in September 2007. Matches will be held in five cities across China. They are Chengdu, Hangzhou, Shanghai, Tianjin, and Wuhan.

Coached by Greg Ryan, the U.S. women's team went undefeated in winning the CONCACAF (Confederation of North, Central American and Caribbean Association of Football) championship. In fact, the U.S. women's side has never lost a CONCACAF match; the first was in 1991. Going into China, the U.S. will be the favorite. They will be led by veteran forward Kristine Lilly, who recorded 13 goals and 7 assists in 2006. Another player to watch is forward Abby Wambach. She recorded 17 goals and 8 assists in 2006. In goal should be

TENNIS

Modern tennis began in 1873. It was based on court tennis. In 1877 the first championships were held in Wimbledon, near London. In 1881 the first official U.S. men's championships were held at Newport, Rhode Island. Six years later, the first U.S. women's championships took place, in Philadelphia. The four most important ("grand slam") tournaments today are the Australian Open, the French Open, the All-England (Wimbledon) Championships, and the U.S. Open.

Grand Slam Tournaments

ALL-TIME GRAND SLAM SINGLES WIN

MEN	Australian	French	Wimbledon	U.S.	Total
Pete Sampras (b. 1971)	2	0	7	5	14
Roy Emerson (b. 1936)	6	2	2	2	12
Bjorn Borg (b. 1956)	0	6	5	0	11
Rod Laver (b. 1938)	3	2	4	2	11
Roger Federer (b. 1981)**	3	0	4	3	10
Bill Tilden (1893-1953)	*	0	3	7	10
WOMEN					
Margaret Smith-Court (b. 1942)	11	5	3	5	24
Steffi Graf (b. 1969)	4	6	7	5	22
Helen Wills Moody (1905-1998)	*	4	8	7	19
Chris Evert (b. 1954)	2	7	3	6	18
Martina Navratilova (b. 1956)	3	2	9	4	18

*Never played in tournament. **Player active in 2007. Wins as of February 2007.

SPORTS SCRAMBLE

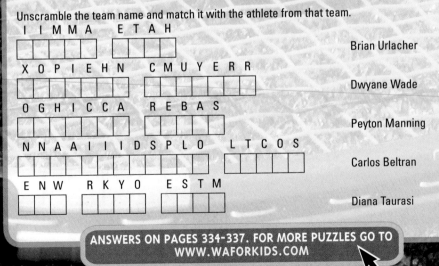

Unscramble the team name and match it with the athlete from that team.

I I M M A   E T A H

Brian Urlacher

X O P I E H N   C M U Y E R R

Dwyane Wade

O G H I C C A   R E B A S

Peyton Manning

N N A A I I I D S P L O   L T C O S

Carlos Beltran

E N W   R K Y O   E S T M

Diana Taurasi

ANSWERS ON PAGES 334-337. FOR MORE PUZZLES GO TO WWW.WAFORKIDS.COM

X Games

The X Games were first held in June 1995 in Newport, Rhode Island. Considered the Olympics of action sports, star X Games athletes include skateboarders Paul Rodriguez Jr. and Danny Way Jr., super motocross champion Jeremy McGrath, BMX freestyler Dave Mirra, and snowboarder Shaun White.

2007 Winter X Games
About 230 athletes from all over the world competed in the 11th annual Winter X Games, held January 24-28 at Buttermilk Mountain in Aspen/Snowmass, Colorado. Events included Snowboarding, Skiing, SnoCross (snowmobiling), and Moto X (off-road motorcycling). Jamie Anderson made history when she won the gold medal in women's snowboard slopestyle. The 16-year-old was the youngest Winter X competitor to win a gold medal. Jamie's big sister, Joanie, won first place in the snowboardcross. Together, the Anderson sisters were named Winter X Games Female Athletes of the Year. The 2008 Winter X Games will be held in January 2008.

Jamie Anderson ▶

Summer X Games
The Summer X Games, held every year since 1995, feature competitions in such events as In-Line Skating, Bike Stunt, Downhill BMX, Moto X, Skateboarding, Surfing, and Wakeboarding. The 13th X Games were set to be held in August 2007 in Los Angeles, CA.

WEB SITE http://expn.go.com

did you know?
Speedboarder Gary Hardwick holds the record for the fastest speed reached on a skateboard, standing up without the aid of other vehicles or engines. Hardwick was clocked at 62.55 mph during a competition in Fountain Hills, Arizona, on September 26, 1998.

◀ Travis Pastrana

X-FACT-ORS

X During the 2006 X Games, Travis Pastrana performed the first double back flip on a motorcycle in competition in the Men's Freestyle Motorcross. Pastrana won gold in the event.

X Snowmobiler Chris Burandt, in 2007, became the first person ever to perform a snowmobile backflip in X Games competition.

X Shaun White became the first athlete to medal in both Summer and Winter X Games competitions when he nabbed the Skateboard Vert silver medal at the 2005 X Games.

TECHNOLOGY & COMPUTERS

How does the Nintendo Wii remote work? ➡ page 251

COMPUTER HIGHLIGHTS TIME LINE

1623	Wilhelm Schickard built the first machine that could automatically add, subtract, multiply, and divide. He called it a "calculating clock."
1946	The first electronic, programmable, general-purpose computer was invented. It was called ENIAC, for "Electronic Numerical Integrator and Computer."
1967	The Advanced Research Projects Agency (ARPA) allotted money toward creating a computer network. It became ARPAnet, which evolved into the Internet.
1968	The first hypertext system was built by Douglas Engelbart of Stanford Research Institute. Called NLS (oN Line System), the system's design allowed users to move text and data with a mouse (which Engelbart invented in 1963).
1971	The "floppy disk" was introduced by IBM as a means of affordable portable storage.
1975	The Altair 8800 entered the market. It was the first widely sold personal microcomputer.
1975	Microsoft was founded by 20-year-old Bill Gates and 22-year-old Paul Allen. Ten years later, they released the first version of Windows.
1977	The Apple II, Apple's first fully packaged system with a keyboard, was introduced.
1990	The World Wide Web was first launched with one server by British physicist Tim Berners-Lee. He also created Uniform Resource Locators (URLs), the Hypertext Transfer Protocol (HTTP), and Hypertext Markup Language (HTML).
2002	The 1 billionth personal computer was shipped to stores in April, according to research firm Gartner.
2007	One Laptop Per Child ships their first XO computers to schoolchildren in developing nations like Rwanda and Uruguay.

🏠 ●WAforKids.com ↱

Go to www.WAforKids.com and type 248 into the code box for more facts and fun:

- Test your technological savvy with a chapter quiz
- Learn about mind-boggling inventions and famous scientists
- Get more homework help on how computers work, computer languages, and the Internet

COMPUTER TALK

BIT The smallest unit of data.

BROWSER A program to help get around the Internet.

BUG OR GLITCH An error in a program or in the computer.

BYTE An amount of data equal to 8 bits.

CHIP A small piece of silicon holding the circuits used to store and process information.

COOKIE Some websites store information like your password on your computer's hard drive. When you go back to that site later, your browser sends the information (the "cookie") to the website.

DOWNLOAD To transfer information from a host computer to a personal computer through a network connection or modem.

ENCRYPTION The process of changing information into a code to keep others from reading it.

FLASH MEMORY Rewriteable ROM memory that saves information without power. Popular in handheld devices like memory cards or MP3 players.

GIG OR GIGABYTE (GB) An amount of information equal to 1,024 megabytes, or (in some situations) 1,000 megabytes.

HTTP Hypertext Transfer Protocol is the method of file exchange used on the World Wide Web.

K Stands for *kilo*, or "thousand," in Greek. For example, "6K" stands for 6,000 bytes.

LURKER A person who visits message boards or social websites but never contributes.

MEGABYTE (MB) An amount of information equal to 1,048,516 bytes, or (in some situations) 1 million bytes.

NETWORK A group of computers linked together so that they can share information.

RAM OR RANDOM ACCESS MEMORY Memory your computer uses to open programs and store your work until you save it to a hard drive or disk. Information in RAM disappears when the computer is turned off.

ROM OR READ ONLY MEMORY Memory that contains permanent instructions for the computer and cannot be changed. The information in ROM stays after the computer is turned off.

RSS OR REALLY SIMPLE SYNDICATION Code that allows Web users to automatically receive updates from blogs or other news sites.

SPYWARE Software that observes computer activity without the user's knowledge. May record key strokes or fill the screen with ads.

URL OR UNIFORM RESOURCE LOCATOR The technical name for a website address.

VIRUS A program that damages other programs and data. It gets into a computer through the Internet or shared disks.

WI-FI OR WIRELESS FIDELITY Technology that allows people to link to other computers and the Internet from their computers without wires.

249

IM (INSTANT MESSAGE) DICTIONARY

ATM At the moment

BRB Be right back

BTW By the way

GTG Got to go

IDK I don't know

IMHO In my humble opinion

JK Just kidding

K or KK OK

LOL Laughing out loud

NM Nothing much or Nevermind

NP No problem

OMG Oh my God

OTP On the phone

PPL People

PWN To "own" (or beat someone in a game)

ROFL Rolling on the floor laughing

SRY Sorry

THX Thanks

TLDR Too long, didn't read

TTFN Ta ta for now

TTYL Talk to you later

W00t (expression of joy)

WTG Way to go

WU? What's up?

IM chat — File Edit Insert People — Warning Level: 0%

WAforKidsFan: Hey, whatz up?!
AlmanacGurl08: I'm @ the computer lab.
WAforKidsFan: fun fun fun. So, do you wanna do something tonite?
AlmanacGurl08: Sure, Let's get some pizza
WAforKidsFan: Okay
AlmanacGurl08: GTG - I'll IM you when I leave.

Warn Block Expressions Games Video Talk Send

CAN YOU FIND THESE WORDS?

They go across, up, down, backward, and diagonally. Some letters are used for more than one word, and some are not used at all.

BLOG
BOOKMARK
BROWSER
BYTE
COOKIE
DOWNLOAD
EMAIL
ENCRYPTION
GIG
INTERNET
LINK
NETWORK
PRINT
RSS
SPYWARE
STREAMING
URL
VIRUS
WIFI
WIKI
WORLDWIDEWEB

E	N	C	R	Y	P	T	I	O	N	D	N	K	B	O	O	J	C
B	P	R	C	E	R	R	E	D	O	C	Y	E	Y	J	B	N	D
S	S	I	M	S	I	F	I	W	A	I	W	V	K	P	P	T	M
S	T	A	R	E	N	N	N	A	Y	E	E	I	I	N	G	M	G
B	I	R	H	W	T	L	A	M	D	G	U	B	Z	R	I	P	U
L	F	C	E	N	O	U	L	I	F	E	Y	O	P	Z	U	L	R
W	I	K	I	A	G	E	W	G	W	Q	T	O	L	Z	N	S	L
U	X	J	D	I	M	D	R	R	I	N	X	K	K	V	H	M	G
Q	E	Y	X	X	L	I	T	A	T	G	R	M	R	K	A	O	E
O	T	E	N	R	E	T	N	I	W	E	V	A	O	G	L	B	R
K	Y	Y	O	C	J	L	X	G	S	Y	F	R	W	B	A	R	R
P	B	W	C	A	N	X	Z	W	C	C	P	K	T	Q	N	R	H
W	S	P	A	F	A	S	O	T	C	Q	N	S	E	T	B	D	H
C	O	K	I	M	X	R	C	O	O	K	I	E	N	V	S	R	O
O	Y	X	H	G	B	E	Q	H	Y	I	Q	U	C	A	G	L	F

ANSWERS ON PAGES 334-337.
FOR MORE PUZZLES GO TO
WWW.WAFORKIDS.COM

NINTENDO'S Wii REMOTE

The Nintendo Wii video game console uses a wireless controller (the Wii remote) that you wave through the air or point at the screen to control the action in games. It looks simple, but there is a lot of complicated technology involved.

Q: How does the Wii know that you're waving the remote?

A: Inside the remote is a computer chip called an **accelerometer**. When you move or tilt the remote, thin pieces of silicon move inside a magnetic field on the chip. This information is sent by radio waves to the console, which calculates how you are moving the remote and with how much force.

Q: How can the Wii tell when you're pointing at the screen?

A: The remote can't "see" what you're pointing at on the TV screen. Instead, a sensor bar placed above or below the TV helps to locate the remote in space. The bar emits **infrared** beams (invisible light with a very short wavelength). These are sensed by the remote. Once the remote "sees" the sensor bar's beams, it can tell the Wii where it is and which way it is pointing.

Q: How does the remote send all this information to the Wii?

A: When you push buttons on the remote or wave it around, those commands are sent to the console with **Bluetooth** signals. Bluetooth is a type of radio signal that works over short ranges. Some other gadgets like cell phones and personal organizers also transmit information with Bluetooth. Bluetooth also carries signals from the console to the remote that tell it when to vibrate or make sounds.

THE XO LAPTOP

One Laptop Per Child (OLPC), a non-profit organization started by Massachusetts Institute of Technology professor Nicholas Negroponte, wants every school-aged kid around the world to have a laptop to help them learn and connect with each other. OLPC created the XO, a durable and easy to use laptop that costs about $150. Millions are being sent to developing countries in 2007.

Q: How will kids be able to connect computers in such far away places?

A: Each laptop can communicate with other XOs within a third of a mile. Those users appear in an onscreen "neighborhood" as stick people that you can interact with. Any internet connection is automatically shared between computers in the neighborhood.

Q: What does the laptop do?

A: It can surf the web and receive email. It has a video camera, speakers, and microphone for talking with other users. There is an extra large touchpad for drawing or writing. Kids can team up over the network using software for writing, drawing, making music, and playing games.

Q: How is the XO different from regular laptops?

A: The case can withstand wind, rainstorms, and rough use. The screen can be adjusted for easy reading in bright sunlight. It can produce its own electricity by cranking a handle, pulling a cord, or pushing a pedal. One minute of pulling a cord provides ten minutes of power. It uses less than a tenth of the energy needed by most laptops.

WEB SITE *www.laptop.org*

TRANSPORTATION

Which city's subway is called "the tube"? ➡ page 254

Getting from There to Here:
A SHORT HISTORY OF TRANSPORTATION

5000 B.C.
People harness animal-muscle power. Oxen and donkeys carry heavy loads.

3500 B.C.
Egyptians create the first sailboat. Before this, people made rafts or canoes and paddled them with poles or their hands.

983
First locks to raise water level are built on China's Grand Canal. By 1400, a 1,500-mile water highway system was developed.

1450s
Portuguese build fast ships with three masts. These plus the compass usher in an age of exploration.

1681
France's 150-mile Canal du Midi connects the Atlantic Ocean with the Mediterranean Sea.

5000 B.C.

3500 B.C.
In Mesopotamia (modern-day Iraq), vehicles with wheels are invented. But the first wheels are made of heavy wood, and the roads are terrible.

800
Fast, shallow-draft longships make Vikings a powerful force in Europe from 800 to 1100.

Around 1000
Using magnetic compasses, Chinese are able to sail long distances in flat-bottomed ships called junks.

1660s
Horse-drawn stagecoaches begin running in France. They stop at "stages" to switch horses and passengers—the first mass transit system.

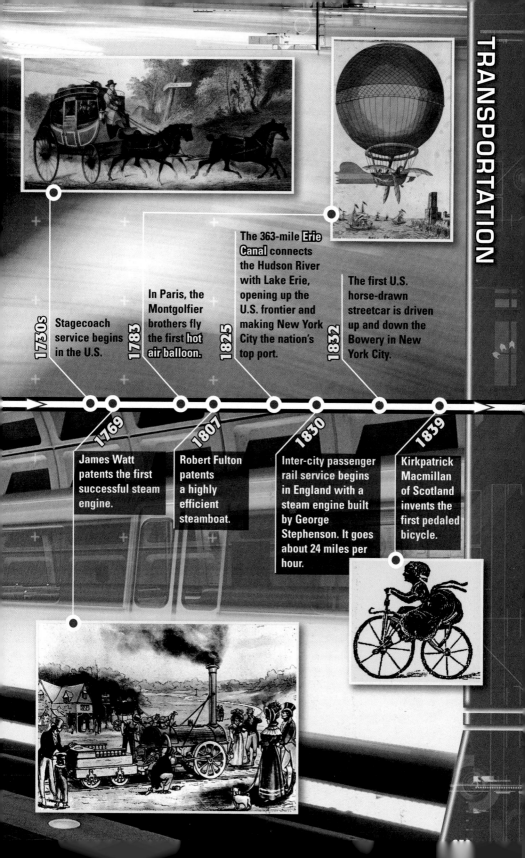

1730s Stagecoach service begins in the U.S.

1783 In Paris, the Montgolfier brothers fly the first hot air balloon.

1825 The 363-mile Erie Canal connects the Hudson River with Lake Erie, opening up the U.S. frontier and making New York City the nation's top port.

1832 The first U.S. horse-drawn streetcar is driven up and down the Bowery in New York City.

1769 James Watt patents the first successful steam engine.

1807 Robert Fulton patents a highly efficient steamboat.

1830 Inter-city passenger rail service begins in England with a steam engine built by George Stephenson. It goes about 24 miles per hour.

1839 Kirkpatrick Macmillan of Scotland invents the first pedaled bicycle.

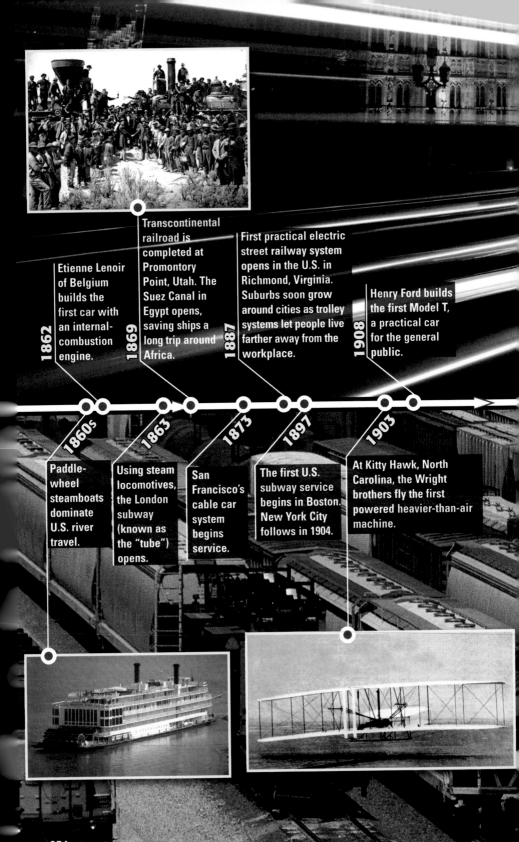

Etienne Lenoir of Belgium builds the first car with an internal-combustion engine.

1862

Transcontinental railroad is completed at Promontory Point, Utah. The Suez Canal in Egypt opens, saving ships a long trip around Africa.

1869

First practical electric street railway system opens in the U.S. in Richmond, Virginia. Suburbs soon grow around cities as trolley systems let people live farther away from the workplace.

1887

Henry Ford builds the first Model T, a practical car for the general public.

1908

1860s

1863

1873

1897

1903

Paddle-wheel steamboats dominate U.S. river travel.

Using steam locomotives, the London subway (known as the "tube") opens.

San Francisco's cable car system begins service.

The first U.S. subway service begins in Boston. New York City follows in 1904.

At Kitty Hawk, North Carolina, the Wright brothers fly the first powered heavier-than-air machine.

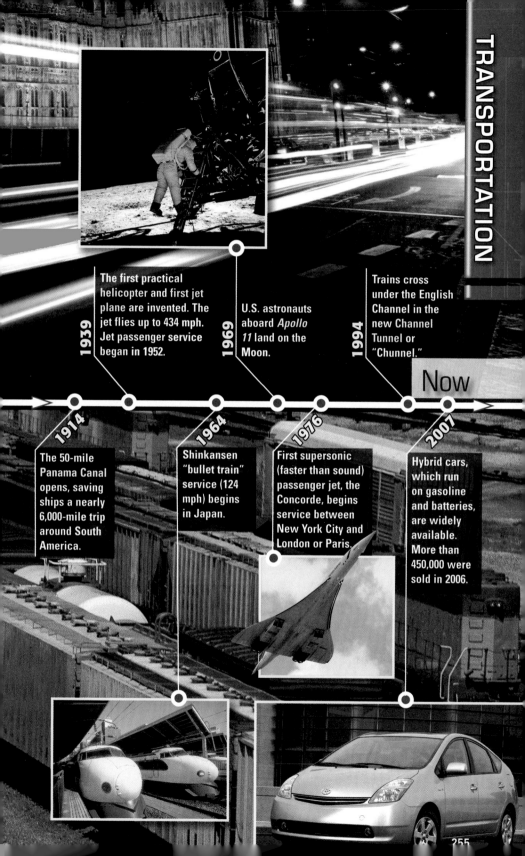

1939 The first practical helicopter and first jet plane are invented. The jet flies up to 434 mph. Jet passenger service began in 1952.

1969 U.S. astronauts aboard *Apollo 11* land on the Moon.

1994 Trains cross under the English Channel in the new Channel Tunnel or "Chunnel."

Now

1914 The 50-mile Panama Canal opens, saving ships a nearly 6,000-mile trip around South America.

1964 Shinkansen "bullet train" service (124 mph) begins in Japan.

1976 First supersonic (faster than sound) passenger jet, the Concorde, begins service between New York City and London or Paris.

2007 Hybrid cars, which run on gasoline and batteries, are widely available. More than 450,000 were sold in 2006.

TRAVEL

Where can you find the world's largest tire? ➡ page 258

In the late 13th century, famed Italian adventurer Marco Polo took a winding 5,600-mile journey overland from Venice, Italy, to Beijing, China. When he returned to Venice, Polo published a chronicle of his travels. The stories were so fantastic that many people didn't believe his tales.

You may not be taking a journey of thousands of miles on your next trip, but the excitement of traveling is the same. People travel for all kinds of reasons—business, fun, or to see distant friends and relatives. But whatever the reason, people have always had the desire to stretch their legs, explore new places, and have adventures that others may—or may not—believe.

▶ The World's 10 Most-Visited Countries*	▶ The 10 Most-Visited U.S. States*
1. France	1. California
2. Spain	2. Florida
3. U.S.	3. Texas
4. China	4. New York
5. Italy	5. Pennsylvania
6. United Kingdom	6. Illinois
7. Hong Kong	7. Ohio
8. Mexico	8. North Carolina
9. Germany	9. Georgia
10. Austria	10. Virginia
*2005	*2004

World's Five Most-Visited Amusement Parks*

1. Magic Kingdom (Lake Buena Vista, Florida), 16.2 million
2. Disneyland (Anaheim, California), 14.6 million
3. Tokyo Disneyland (Japan), 13 million
4. Tokyo Disney Sea (Japan), 12 million
5. Disneyland Paris (Marne-La-Vallee, France), 10.2 million

*2005

AMUSEMENT PARKS

The first amusement parks appeared in Europe more than 400 years ago. Attractions included flower gardens, bowling, music, and a few simple rides.

Today's amusement parks are much more impressive. With super-fast roller coasters, parades, shows, and other attractions, amusement parks now have something to amuse just about anyone. Here's a look at some of the most popular amusement parks in the U.S.

FABULOUS FACTS

Biggest Park: Walt Disney World, Lake Buena Vista, Florida, 28,000 acres

Most Rides: 68, Cedar Point, Sandusky, Ohio

Most Roller Coasters: 17, Cedar Point, Sandusky, Ohio

Fastest Roller Coaster: 128 mph, Kingda Ka, Six Flags Great Adventure, Jackson, New Jersey

Tallest Roller Coaster: 456 feet, Kingda Ka, Six Flags Great Adventure, Jackson, New Jersey

Maverick, new roller coaster at Cedar Point.

▶ **Cedar Point (Sandusky, OH)** One of the oldest amusement parks in the U.S., Cedar Point (on Lake Erie) opened in 1870. Its first roller coaster, the Switchback Railway, opened in 1892. It had a then-dizzying 25-foot-high hill, on which riders traveled at about 10 mph. Today at Cedar Point, the Top Thrill Dragster roller coaster reaches a height of 420 feet, and the cars zip along at a top speed of 120 mph! There are also plenty of other attractions, including Soak City, which features water rides and a wave pool.

▶ **Walt Disney World (Lake Buena Vista, Florida)** Four different theme parks make up Walt Disney World. The Magic Kingdom is a Disneyland-style amusement park. It opened in 1971 and is the most-visited amusement park in the world. EPCOT opened in 1982. It consists of two parts. Future World showcases technology with attractions like Mission: Space. The World Showcase features food and attractions distinct to 11 different countries. The other two Disney World theme parks are zoo-themed Animal Kingdom (opened in 1998), and Disney-MGM Studios (1989).

▶ **Universal Studios Florida/Islands of Adventure (Orlando, Florida)** Universal Studios opened in 1990 and visitors have been "riding the movies" there ever since. Rides, shows, and other attractions feature favorite movie and TV characters, like Shrek, and take visitors behind the scenes. Islands of Adventure has been open since 1999. The rides and attractions there pay tribute to favorite characters from books and comic books, like Spiderman, the Incredible Hulk, and Dr. Doom.

ROAD TRIP

Wherever you are, there is likely to be a festival, amusement park, historic site, or national park just a short drive away. A road trip—short or long—can be lots of fun, with plenty of interesting sights along the way.

The first cross-country drive was made in 1903. H. Nelson Jackson and Sewall K. Crocker (and a bulldog named Bud) drove from San Francisco to New York City in an early car known as a Winton. There were few roads or bridges in the West, and lots of mud everywhere. The whole trip took 63 days and cost $8,000, including the price of the car. In 1909, Alice Huyler Ramsey became the first woman to drive across the U.S. Her trip from New York to San Francisco took 59 days.

By 1930, there were 23 million cars on the road. More than half of American families owned one. (Today in the U.S. there are more vehicles than licensed drivers.) People wanted to see things and go places—especially west. The first coast-to-coast highway was the Lincoln Highway, which was finished by 1930. The most famous highway was Route 66, completed in 1926, connecting Chicago to Los Angeles. Now called "Historic Route 66," it still has billboards and giant statues advertising its famous hotels, attractions, and restaurants.

H. Nelson Jackson

A ROADSIDE SAMPLER:

Lunch Box Museum Located in Columbus, Georgia, the Lunch Box Museum has more than 3,500 lunchboxes on display. Even though the boxes are old, you may recognize some of the cartoon and TV heroes on them. ▶

Winchester Mystery House This spooky, sprawling mansion in San Jose, California, has 160 rooms, 950 doors, and 10,000 windows. Staircases lead into ceilings, windows cut into floors, and one door opens onto an 8-foot drop into a kitchen sink.

World's Largest Tire Located in Allen Park, Michigan, the Uniroyal Tire stands 80 feet tall. It was built for the 1964-65 World's Fair in New York. After the fair, it was moved to where it is now. In 1998, Uniroyal stabbed the tire with an 11-foot-long, 250 lb nail (the largest nail in the world) to show the toughness of Uniroyal tires. The nail was removed and sold. But the tire is as sturdy as ever.

World's Largest Solar System Scale Model This solar system model follows about 40 miles of highway U.S. 1 in northern Maine—from the sun, 50 feet in diameter, at the University of Maine at Presque Isle to tiny Pluto, 1 inch in diameter, mounted on a visitor center wall in Houlton. Area volunteers are planning to add the new dwarf planets, Ceres and Eris.

TRAVEL WORD SEARCH

```
X S U I T C A S E F S D G E C V B O G X
B D G F K J M H B O V S C F A O L L V J
E P R S H R A I N F O R E S T L G D S Z
W U N C G E D P L A N E V M X R I F B C
H E Q E D G S V B U A D G K N V A A F A
K R V N H N E H L T X V J E H B N I E R
D T D I U B M C R O A D T R I P T T N I
E O Z C G Y G V B M Q E U U E L E H C B
G R L T R X L M N O F M Y T J L S F D B
G I U R T Z C E Q B V B X N E S S U A E
R C W A C S B E R I K K G E D S B L B A
I O D I I T R Y M L N L E V A R T B T N
C W F L E H C R O E G N V D C M F H R N
V R E S Y E G E U M R R K A R T Y K E E
E G A G G U L V N N A V S D F G Y I S F
L E T U J G B I T V N S E R O H S A E S
C S B D F I K R M M I W J E T W B S D Q
A L A S K A H O C N T B B I L A N E D R
P Q W I M R E D K C E G T J D F C X E H
I C J Y N R U A I O D N F M L K U R T S
T S D G O A F R N U O I Q H G S F E N D
A B C L Y F G O L N M M E R G N I K I H
N D P S B H I L E T E O T R Y J J J A S
Z X V B L K I O Y R G Y X G F W U I P F
E W G T J J F C C Y A W H G I H H R D X
```

Can you find these words?

They go across, up, down, backward, and diagonally. Some letters are used for more than one word, and some are not used at all.

ADVENTURE
ALASKA
AUTOMOBILE
CARIBBEAN
COLORADO RIVER
COUNTRY
DENALI
EL CAPITAN

EL YUNQUE
EXPLORE
GEYSER
GIANTESS
GRANITE DOME
HIGHWAY
HIKING
JET

LUGGAGE
MOUNT MCKINLEY
OLD FAITHFUL
PAINTED DESERT
PLANE
PUERTO RICO
RAIN FOREST
ROAD TRIP

SCENIC TRAIL
SEASHORE
SHIP
SUITCASE
TRAIN
TRAVEL
WYOMING

ANSWERS ON PAGES 334-337. FOR MORE PUZZLES GO TO
WWW.WAFORKIDS.COM

259

NATIONAL PARKS

The world's first national park was Yellowstone, established in 1872. Today in the U.S., there are 57 national parks, including one in the Virgin Islands and one in American Samoa. The National Park Service oversees 390 areas in all, also including national monuments, battlefields, military parks, historic parks, historic sites, lakeshores, seashores, recreation areas, scenic rivers and trails, and the White House—84.4 million acres in all! For more information, you can write the National Park Service, Department of the Interior, 1849 C Street NW, Washington, D.C. 20240. **WEB SITE** *www.nps.gov/parks.html*

YOSEMITE NATIONAL PARK This park, established in 1890, covers 761,266 acres in east-central California. It has the world's largest concentration of granite domes—mountain-like rocks that were created by glaciers millions of years ago. You can see many of them rising thousands of feet above the valley floor. Two of the most famous are Half Dome, which looks smooth and rounded, and El Capitan, which is the biggest single granite rock on Earth. Skilled climbers come from all over the world to scale this 3,000-foot-high wall of rock. Yosemite Falls, which drops 2,425 feet, is the highest waterfall in North America. It is actually two waterfalls, called the upper and lower falls, connected by a series of smaller waterfalls. Yosemite also features lakes, meadows, and giant sequoia trees, and is home to bighorn sheep and bears.

GRAND CANYON NATIONAL PARK
This national park, established in 1919, has one of the world's most spectacular landscapes, covering more than a million acres in northwestern Arizona. The canyon is 6,000 feet deep at its deepest point and 15 miles wide at its widest. Most of the 40 identified rock layers that form the canyon's 277-mile-long wall are exposed, offering a detailed look at the Earth's geologic history. The walls display a cross section of the Earth's crust from as far back as two billion years ago. The Colorado River—which carved out the giant canyon—still runs through the park, which is a valuable wildlife preserve with many rare, endangered animals. The pine and fir forests, painted deserts, plateaus, caves, and sandstone canyons offer a wide range of habitats.

1607

Jamestown, Virginia, the first permanent English settlement in North America, is founded by Captain John Smith.

1609

Henry Hudson sails into **New York Harbor,** explores the Hudson River. Spaniards settle Santa Fe, New Mexico.

1619

The first African **slaves** are brought to Jamestown. (Slavery is made legal in 1650.)

1620

Pilgrims from England arrive at Plymouth, Massachusetts, on the *Mayflower.*

1626

Peter Minuit buys **Manhattan** island for the Dutch from Manahata Indians for goods worth $24. The island is renamed New Amsterdam.

1630

Boston is founded by Massachusetts colonists led by John Winthrop.

FAMOUS WORDS FROM THE DECLARATION OF INDEPENDENCE, JULY 4, 1776

"We hold these truths to be self-evident, that all men are created equal, that they are endowed by their Creator with certain unalienable rights, that among these are life, liberty, and the pursuit of happiness."

1770

Boston Massacre: During a demonstration against English taxes, protestors began throwing rocks at English troops. The troops opened fire, killing 7 .

1773

Boston Tea Party: English tea is thrown into the harbor to protest a tax on tea.

1775

Fighting at **Lexington and Concord,** Massachusetts, marks the beginning of the American Revolution.

1776

The Declaration of Independence is approved July 4 by the Continental Congress (made up of representatives from the American colonies).

1781

British General **Charles Cornwallis** surrenders to the Americans at Yorktown, Virginia, ending the fighting in the Revolutionary War.

The New Nation
1784-1900

1784

The first successful daily **newspaper** in the U.S., the *Pennsylvania Packet & General Advertiser*, is published.

1787

The **Constitutional Convention** meets to write a Constitution for the U.S.

1789

The new **Constitution** is approved by the states. George Washington is chosen as the first president.

1800

The federal government moves from Philadelphia to a new capital, **Washington, D.C.**

1803

The U.S. makes the **Louisiana Purchase** from France. The Purchase doubles the area of the U.S.

WHO ATTENDED THE CONVENTION?

The **Constitutional Convention** met in Philadelphia in the hot summer of 1787. Most of the great founders of America attended. Among those present were George Washington, James Madison, and John Adams. They met to form a new government that would be strong and, at the same time, protect the liberties that were fought for in the American Revolution. The Constitution they created is still the law of the United States.

1836

Texans fighting for independence from Mexico are defeated at the **Alamo**.

1838

Cherokee Indians are forced to move to Oklahoma, along "The **Trail of Tears**." On the long march, thousands died because of disease and the cold weather.

1844

The **first telegraph** line connects Washington, D.C., and Baltimore.

1846-1848

U.S. war with Mexico: Mexico is defeated, and the United States takes control of the Republic of Texas and of Mexican territories in the West.

1848

The discovery of **gold** in California leads to a "rush" of 80,000 people to the West in search of gold.

1852

Uncle Tom's Cabin is published.

UNCLE TOM'S CABIN

Harriet Beecher Stowe's novel about the **suffering of slaves** was an instant bestseller in the North and banned in most of the South. When President Abraham Lincoln met Stowe, he called her "the little lady who started this war" (the Civil War).

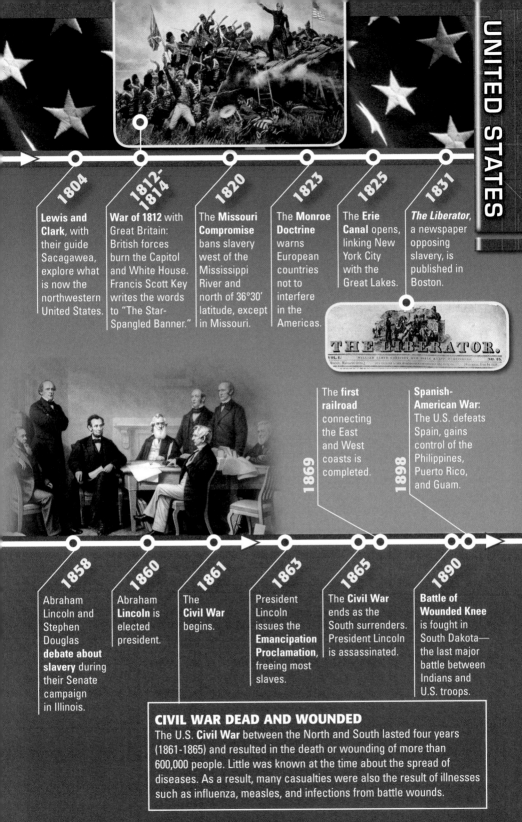

1804

Lewis and Clark, with their guide Sacagawea, explore what is now the northwestern United States.

1812-1814

War of 1812 with Great Britain: British forces burn the Capitol and White House. Francis Scott Key writes the words to "The Star-Spangled Banner."

1820

The **Missouri Compromise** bans slavery west of the Mississippi River and north of 36°30' latitude, except in Missouri.

1823

The **Monroe Doctrine** warns European countries not to interfere in the Americas.

1825

The **Erie Canal** opens, linking New York City with the Great Lakes.

1831

The Liberator, a newspaper opposing slavery, is published in Boston.

THE LIBERATOR.

1869

The **first railroad** connecting the East and West coasts is completed.

1898

Spanish-American War: The U.S. defeats Spain, gains control of the Philippines, Puerto Rico, and Guam.

1858

Abraham Lincoln and Stephen Douglas **debate about slavery** during their Senate campaign in Illinois.

1860

Abraham **Lincoln** is elected president.

1861

The **Civil War** begins.

1863

President Lincoln issues the **Emancipation Proclamation**, freeing most slaves.

1865

The **Civil War** ends as the South surrenders. President Lincoln is assassinated.

1890

Battle of Wounded Knee is fought in South Dakota—the last major battle between Indians and U.S. troops.

CIVIL WAR DEAD AND WOUNDED

The U.S. **Civil War** between the North and South lasted four years (1861-1865) and resulted in the death or wounding of more than 600,000 people. Little was known at the time about the spread of diseases. As a result, many casualties were also the result of illnesses such as influenza, measles, and infections from battle wounds.

United States Since 1900

WORLD WAR I
In **World War I** the United States fought with Great Britain, France, and Russia (the Allies) against Germany and Austria-Hungary. The Allies won the war in 1918.

1903
The United States begins digging the **Panama Canal**. The canal opens in 1914, connecting the Atlantic and Pacific oceans.

1908
Henry Ford introduces the **Model T** car, priced at $850.

1916
Jeannette Rankin of Montana becomes the first woman elected to Congress.

1917-1918
The United States joins **World War I** on the side of the Allies against Germany.

1927
Charles A. **Lindbergh** becomes the first person to fly alone nonstop across the Atlantic Ocean.

1929
A stock market crash marks the beginning of the **Great Depression**.

1954
The U.S. Supreme Court **forbids racial segregation** in public schools.

SCHOOL SEGREGATION
The U.S. Supreme Court ruled that **separate schools** for black students and white students were **not equal**. The Court said such schools were against the U.S. Constitution. The ruling also applied to other forms of segregation (separation of the races supported by some states.)

WE PROTEST SCHOOL SEGREGATION

1963
President John **Kennedy** is assassinated.

1964
Congress passes the **Civil Rights Act**, which outlaws discrimination in voting and jobs.

1965
The United States sends first soldiers to fight in the **Vietnam War**.

1968
Civil rights leader **Martin Luther King Jr.** is assassinated in Memphis. Senator **Robert F. Kennedy** is assassinated in Los Angeles.

1969
U.S. Astronaut Neil Armstrong becomes the **first person** to walk **on the moon**.

1973
U.S. participation in the **Vietnam War ends**.

THE GREAT DEPRESSION

The stock market crash of October 1929 led to a period of severe hardship for the American people—the **Great Depression**. As many as 25 percent of all workers could not find jobs. The Depression lasted until the early 1940s. The Depression also led to a great change in politics. In 1932, Franklin D. Roosevelt, a Democrat, was elected president. He served as president for 12 years, longer than any other president.

1933
President Franklin D. Roosevelt's **New Deal** increases government help to people hurt by the Depression.

1941
Japan attacks **Pearl Harbor**, Hawaii. The United States enters World War II.

1945
Germany and Japan surrender, **ending World War II**. Japan surrenders after the U.S. drops atomic bombs on Hiroshima and Nagasaki.

1947
Jackie Robinson becomes the **first black baseball player** in the major leagues when he joins the Brooklyn Dodgers.

1950-1953
U.S. armed forces fight in the **Korean War**.

WATERGATE

In June 1972, five men were arrested in the **Watergate** building in Washington, D.C., for trying to bug telephones in the offices of the Democratic National Committee. Some of those arrested worked for the committee to re-elect President Richard Nixon. Later it was discovered that Nixon was helping to hide information about the break-in.

1991
The Persian Gulf War: The United States and its allies defeat Iraq.

2000
George W. Bush narrowly defeats Al Gore in a closely fought presidential race.

2004-2006
Bush defeats John Kerry to win a new term. Democrats retake Congress in 2006 elections.

1974
President Richard **Nixon resigns** because of the Watergate scandal.

1979
U.S. **hostages** are taken **in Iran**, beginning a 444-day crisis that ends with their release in 1981.

1981
Sandra Day O'Connor becomes the **first woman** on the U.S. Supreme Court.

1985
U.S. President Ronald Reagan and Soviet leader Mikhail Gorbachev begin working together to **improve relations** between their countries.

1999
After an **impeachment** trial, the Senate finds President Bill Clinton not guilty.

2001
Hijacked jets crashed into the World Trade Center and the **Pentagon**, September 11, killing about 3,000 people.

2003
U.S.-led forces invade Iraq and remove dictator **Saddam Hussein**.

285

African Americans:
A Time Line

Would you like to learn more about the history of African Americans from the era of slavery to the present? These events and personalities can be a starting point. Can you add some more?

Rev. Dr. Martin Luther King Jr. ▶

1619	○	First Africans are brought to Virginia as slaves.
1831	●	Nat Turner starts a **slave revolt** in Virginia that is unsuccessful.
1856-57	○	**Dred Scott**, a slave, sues to be freed because he had left slave territory, but the Supreme Court denies his claim.
1861-65	●	The North defeats the South in the brutal Civil War; the **13th Amendment** ends nearly 250 years of slavery. The Ku Klux Klan is founded.
1865-77	○	Southern blacks play leadership roles in government under **Reconstruction**; the 15th Amendment (1870) gives black men the right to vote.
1896	●	Supreme Court rules in a case called *Plessy versus Ferguson* that segregation is legal when facilities are "**separate but equal.**" Discrimination and violence against blacks increase.
1910	○	W. E. B. Du Bois (1868–1963) founds National Association for the Advancement of Colored People (NAACP), fighting for equality for blacks.
1920s	●	African American culture (jazz music, dance, literature) flourishes during the **Harlem Renaissance**.
1954	○	Supreme Court rules in a case called ***Brown versus Board of Education*** *of Topeka* that school segregation is unconstitutional.
1957	●	Black students, backed by federal troops, enter recently desegregated Central High School in **Little Rock**, Arkansas.
1955-65	○	**Malcolm X** (1925–65) emerges as key spokesman for black nationalism.
1963	●	**Rev. Dr. Martin Luther King Jr.** (1929–68) gives his "I Have a Dream" speech at a march that inspired more than 200,000 people in Washington, D.C.—and many others throughout the nation.
1964	○	Sweeping **civil rights bill** banning racial discrimination is signed by President Lyndon Johnson.
1965	●	King leads protest march in **Selma**, Alabama; blacks riot in **Watts** section of Los Angeles.
1967	○	Gary, Indiana, and Cleveland, Ohio, are first major U.S. cities to elect **black mayors**; Thurgood Marshall (1908–93) becomes first African American on the **Supreme Court**.
1995	●	Hundreds of thousands of black men take part in "**Million Man March**" rally in Washington, D.C., urging responsibility for families and communities.
2001	○	**Colin Powell** becomes first African American secretary of state.
2005	●	**Condoleezza Rice** becomes first African American woman secretary of state.

These people of color made big contributions to the growth of the United States as a free country.

HARRIET TUBMAN (1821-1913) escaped slavery when she was in her twenties. Before the Civil War, she repeatedly risked her life to lead hundreds of slaves to freedom by way of a network of homes and churches called the "Underground Railroad."

LEWIS LATIMER (1848-1928), American inventor and son of runaway slaves who patented a more durable version of Thomas Edison's light bulb by using a carbon filament instead of paper. He worked on the patent for the telephone and oversaw the installation of public lights throughout New York, Philadelphia, London, and Montreal. He also invented the first railroad-car toilet.

ROSA PARKS (1913–2005) is called the mother of America's civil rights movement. When she refused to give up her bus seat to a white man in 1955, blacks in Montgomery, Alabama, started a boycott of the bus system, which led to desegregation of the city's buses. After her death she became the first woman (and 31st person) in history to lie in honor in the Capitol Rotunda in Washington, D.C.

MALCOLM X (1925–1965) was a forceful Muslim leader who spoke against injustices toward blacks and promoted the idea of black pride and independence. He was assassinated by rivals in 1965. His life story, *The Autobiography of Malcolm X*, helped make him a hero to many African Americans.

CESAR CHAVEZ (1927-1993), a Mexican American who was raised in migrant worker camps, started a national farm workers union, the United Farm Workers of America, in 1966. He organized boycotts that eventually made growers agree to better conditions for field workers.

REV. DR. MARTIN LUTHER KING JR. (1929–1968) was the most influential leader of the U.S. civil rights movement from the mid-1950s to his assassination in 1968. In 1964 he received the Nobel Peace Prize. His wife, **CORETTA SCOTT KING** (1927-2006), helped carry on his work.

ERIC SHINSEKI (born 1942) was the first Asian-American to achieve the rank of four-star general in the U.S. Army. He was also, from 1999-2003, the first Asian-American to serve as the Chief of Staff of the U.S. Army. He retired in 2003.

ANTONIO VILLARAIGOSA (born 1953), a Mexican American, in 2005 became the first Latino mayor of Los Angeles since the 1870s. He is a former labor leader and speaker of the California State Assembly.

OPRAH WINFREY (born 1954) has won many awards as a talk show host, actress, writer, publisher, and film producer. Through Oprah's Angel Network, she has collected millions of dollars to help people in need.

ELAINE CHAO (born 1954) moved with her family to the U.S. from Taiwan when she was eight years old and did not speak any English. After years of public service, including a term as director of the Peace Corps, Chao in 2001 became the 24th secretary of labor and the first Asian American woman in U.S. history to be appointed to a president's cabinet.

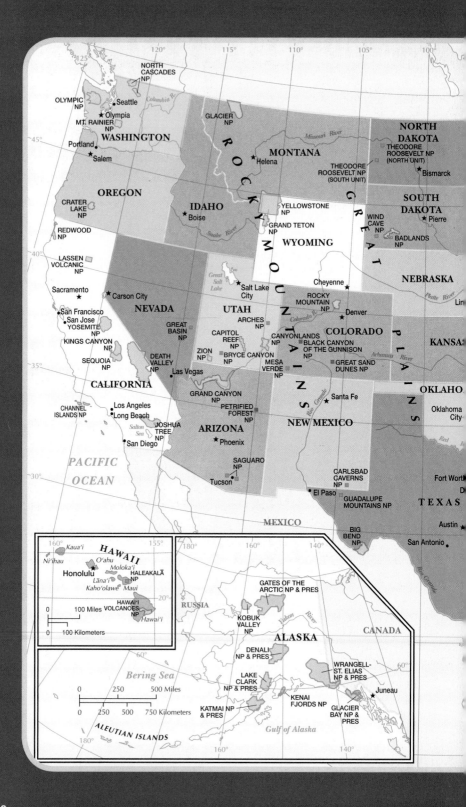

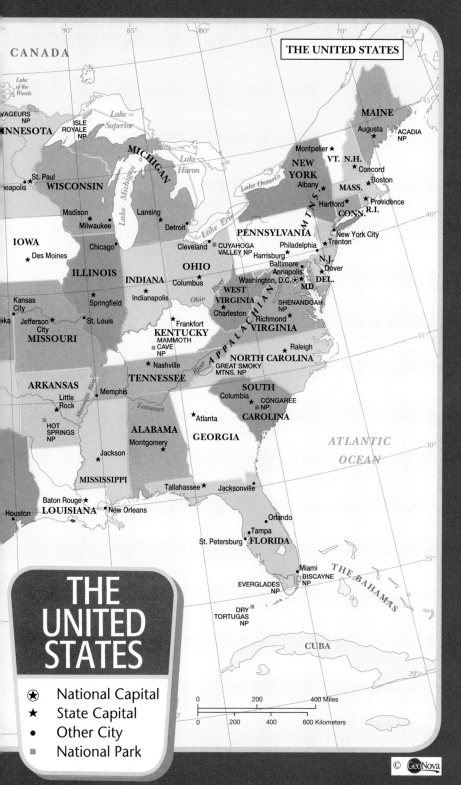

THE UNITED STATES

CANADA

90° · 85° · 80° · 75° · 70° · 65°

Lake of the Woods

VAGEURS NP

NNESOTA

ISLE ROYALE NP

Lake Superior

MAINE

Augusta ★

ACADIA NP

45°

MICHIGAN

Lake Huron

Montpelier ★

NEW YORK

VT. N.H.

Concord ★

Boston ★

St. Paul ★

neapolis

WISCONSIN

Lake Michigan

Lake Ontario

Albany ★

MASS.

Hartford ★

Providence ★

Madison ★

Milwaukee

Lansing ★

Detroit

Lake Erie

PENNSYLVANIA

CONN.

R.I.

40°

IOWA

Chicago

Cleveland

CUYAHOGA VALLEY NP

Philadelphia ★

New York City

Des Moines ★

ILLINOIS

OHIO

Columbus ★

Harrisburg ★

Baltimore

Trenton ★

N.J.

INDIANA

Indianapolis ★

Annapolis

Washington, D.C. ⊛

Dover ★

DEL.

Kansas City

Springfield ★

St. Louis

Ohio River

WEST VIRGINIA

MD.

eka

Jefferson City ★

Frankfort ★

Charleston ★

SHENANDOAH NP

MISSOURI

KENTUCKY

MAMMOTH CAVE NP

Richmond ★

VIRGINIA

35°

Nashville ★

GREAT SMOKY MTNS. NP

Raleigh ★

ARKANSAS

TENNESSEE

NORTH CAROLINA

Little Rock ★

Memphis

Mississippi River

Tennessee River

SOUTH

Columbia ★

CONGAREE NP

HOT SPRINGS NP

Atlanta ★

CAROLINA

ALABAMA

GEORGIA

ATLANTIC OCEAN

30°

Montgomery ★

Jackson ★

MISSISSIPPI

Tallahassee ★

Jacksonville

Baton Rouge ★

LOUISIANA

New Orleans

Houston

Orlando

Tampa

St. Petersburg

FLORIDA

THE BAHAMAS

25°

Miami

BISCAYNE NP

EVERGLADES NP

DRY TORTUGAS NP

CUBA

20°

THE UNITED STATES

⊛ National Capital
★ State Capital
• Other City
■ National Park

0   200   400 Miles

0 200 400 600 Kilometers

© GeoNova

How the states

ALABAMA comes from an Indian word for "tribal town."

Alaska

ALASKA comes from *alakshak*, the Aleutian (Eskimo) word meaning "peninsula" or "land that is not an island."

ARIZONA comes from a Pima Indian word meaning "little spring place" or the Aztec word *arizuma*, meaning "silver-bearing."

ARKANSAS is a variation of Quapaw, the name of an Indian tribe. Quapaw means "south wind."

CALIFORNIA is the name of an imaginary island in a Spanish story. It was named by Spanish explorers of Baja California, a part of Mexico.

COLORADO comes from a Spanish word meaning "red." It was first given to the Colorado River because of its reddish color.

CONNECTICUT comes from an Algonquin Indian word meaning "long river place."

DELAWARE is named after Lord De La Warr, the English governor of Virginia in colonial times.

FLORIDA, which means "flowery" in Spanish, was named by the explorer Ponce de León, who landed there during Easter.

GEORGIA was named after King George II of England, who granted the right to create a colony there in 1732.

HAWAII probably comes from *Hawaiki,* or *Owhyhee,* the native Polynesian word for "homeland."

IDAHO's name is of uncertain origin, but it may come from a Kiowa Apache name for the Comanche Indians.

Hawaii

ILLINOIS is the French version of *Illini,* an Algonquin Indian word meaning "men" or "warriors."

INDIANA means "land of the Indians."

IOWA comes from the name of an American Indian tribe that lived on the land that is now the state.

KANSAS comes from a Sioux Indian word that possibly meant "people of the south wind."

KENTUCKY comes from an Iroquois Indian word, possibly meaning "meadowland."

LOUISIANA, which was first settled by French explorers, was named after King Louis XIV of France.

MAINE means "the mainland." English explorers called it that to distinguish it from islands nearby.

Maine

MARYLAND was named after Queen Henrietta Maria, wife of King Charles I of England, who granted the right to establish an English colony there.

MASSACHUSETTS comes from an Indian word meaning "large hill place."

MICHIGAN comes from the Chippewa Indian words *mici gama*, meaning "great water" (referring to Lake Michigan).

MINNESOTA got its name from a Dakota Sioux Indian word meaning "cloudy water" or "sky-tinted water."

MISSISSIPPI is probably from Chippewa Indian words meaning "great river" or "gathering of all the waters," or from an Algonquin word, *messipi.*

MISSOURI comes from an Algonquin Indian term meaning "river of the big canoes."

MONTANA comes from a Latin or Spanish word meaning "mountainous."

NEBRASKA comes from "flat river" or "broad water," an Omaha or Otos Indian name for the Platte River.

NEVADA means "snow-clad" in Spanish. Spanish explorers gave the name to the Sierra Nevada Mountains.

NEW HAMPSHIRE was named by an early settler after his home county of Hampshire, in England.

NEW JERSEY was named for the English Channel island of Jersey.

NEW MEXICO was given its name by 16th-century Spaniards in Mexico.

New Mexico

NEW YORK, first called New Netherland, was renamed for the Duke of York and Albany after the English took it from Dutch settlers.

NORTH CAROLINA, the northern part of the English colony of Carolana, was named for King Charles I.

NORTH DAKOTA comes from a Sioux Indian word meaning "friend" or "ally."

OHIO is the Iroquois Indian word for "good river."

OKLAHOMA comes from a Choctaw Indian word meaning "red man."

OREGON may have come from *Ouaricon-sint,* a name on an old French map that was once given to what is now called the Columbia River. That river runs between Oregon and Washington.

PENNSYLVANIA meaning "Penn's woods," was the name given to the colony founded by William Penn.

RHODE ISLAND may have come from the Dutch "Roode Eylandt" (red island) or may have been named after the Greek island of Rhodes.

SOUTH CAROLINA, the southern part of the English colony of Carolana, was named for King Charles I.

SOUTH DAKOTA comes from a Sioux Indian word meaning "friend" or "ally."

TENNESSEE comes from "Tanasi," the name of Cherokee Indian villages on what is now the Little Tennessee River.

TEXAS comes from a word meaning "friends" or "allies," used by the Spanish to describe some of the American Indians living there.

Texas

UTAH comes from a Navajo word meaning "upper" or "higher up."

VERMONT comes from two French words, *vert* meaning "green" and *mont* meaning "mountain."

VIRGINIA was named in honor of Queen Elizabeth I of England, who was known as the Virgin Queen because she was never married.

WASHINGTON was named after George Washington, the first president of the United States. It is the only state named after a president.

WEST VIRGINIA got its name from the people of western Virginia, who formed their own government during the Civil War.

WISCONSIN comes from a Chippewa name that is believed to mean "grassy place." It was once spelled *Ouisconsin* and *Mesconsing.*

WYOMING comes from Algonquin Indian words that are said to mean "at the big plains," "large prairie place," or "on the great plain."

Pennsylvania

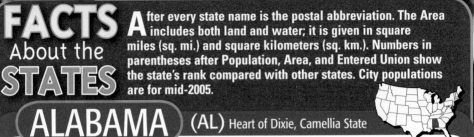

FACTS About the STATES

After every state name is the postal abbreviation. The Area includes both land and water; it is given in square miles (sq. mi.) and square kilometers (sq. km.). Numbers in parentheses after Population, Area, and Entered Union show the state's rank compared with other states. City populations are for mid-2005.

ALABAMA (AL) Heart of Dixie, Camellia State

Birmingham

Montgomery

POPULATION (2006): 4,599,030 (23rd) **AREA:** 52,419 sq. mi. (30th) (135,765 sq. km.) 🌼 Camellia 🐦 Yellowhammer 🌲 Southern longleaf pine 🎵 "Alabama" **ENTERED UNION:** December 14, 1819 (22nd) ⭐ Montgomery **LARGEST CITIES (WITH POP.):** Birmingham, 231,483; Montgomery, 200,127; Mobile, 191,544; Huntsville, 166,313

⚙ clothing and textiles, metal products, transportation equipment, paper, industrial machinery, food products, lumber, coal, oil, natural gas, livestock, peanuts, cotton

 Montgomery was the capital of the Confederacy during the early months of the Civil War between February 18 and May 21, 1861. The Confederate capital then moved to Richmond, Virginia.

ALASKA (AK) The Last Frontier

Anchorage

Juneau ⭐

POPULATION (2006): 670,053 (47th) **AREA:** 663,267 sq. mi. (1st) (1,717,854 sq. km.) 🌼 Forget-me-not 🐦 Willow ptarmigan 🌲 Sitka spruce 🎵 "Alaska's Flag" **ENTERED UNION:** January 3, 1959 (49th) ⭐ Juneau **LARGEST CITIES (WITH POP.):** Anchorage, 275,043; Fairbanks, 31,324; Juneau, 30,987; Sitka, 8,986

⚙ oil, natural gas, fish, food products, lumber and wood products, fur

 In 1867, the U.S. purchased Alaska from Russia for $7.2 million, or about 2 cents per acre. When Alaska was admitted to the Union as the 49th state in 1959, it increased the area of the U.S. by 20%.

ARIZONA (AZ) Grand Canyon State

Phoenix
⭐
Tucson

POPULATION (2006): 6,166,318 (16th) **AREA:** 113,998 sq. mi. (6th) (295,253 sq. km.) 🌼 Blossom of the Saguaro cactus 🐦 Cactus wren 🌲 Paloverde 🎵 "Arizona" **ENTERED UNION:** February 14, 1912 (48th) ⭐ Phoenix **LARGEST CITIES (WITH POP.):** Phoenix, 1,461,575; Tucson, 515,526; Mesa, 442,780; Glendale, 239,435; Chandler, 234,939; Scottsdale, 226,013

⚙ electronic equipment, transportation and industrial equipment, instruments, printing and publishing, copper and other metals

 You can find London Bridge in Lake Havasu City, AZ. Built in London, England, in the 1830s, the bridge was taken down and sold to Robert P. McCulloch in 1968. He re-assembled it on Lake Havasu in 1971.

⦿WAforKids.com Go to *www.WAforKids.com* for even more U.S. facts.

292

ARKANSAS (AR) Natural State, Razorback State

POPULATION (2006): 2,810,872 (32nd) **AREA:** 53,179 sq. mi. (29th) (137,733 sq. km.) 🌸Apple blossom 🐦Mockingbird 🌲Pine 🎵"Arkansas" **ENTERED UNION:** June 15, 1836 (25th) ⭐Little Rock **LARGEST CITIES (WITH POP.):** Little Rock, 184,564; Fort Smith, 82,481; Fayetteville, 66,655; Springdale, 60,096

⚙️ food products, paper, electronic equipment, industrial machinery, metal products, lumber and wood products, livestock, soybeans, rice, cotton, natural gas

Little Rock ⭐

did you know? *The only working diamond mine in the U.S. is located in Murfreesboro, AR, at Crater of Diamonds State Park. It is also the only diamond-producing site in the world that is open to the public. Visitors can keep whatever diamonds they find.*

CALIFORNIA (CA) Golden State

POPULATION (2006): 36,457,549 (1st) **AREA:** 163,696 sq. mi. (3rd) (423,971 sq. km.) 🌸Golden poppy 🐦California valley quail 🌲California redwood 🎵"I Love You, California" **ENTERED UNION:** September 9, 1850 (31st) ⭐Sacramento **LARGEST CITIES (WITH POP.):** Los Angeles, 3,844,829; San Diego, 1,255,540; San Jose, 912,332; San Francisco, 739,426; Long Beach, 474,014; Fresno, 461,116; Sacramento, 456,441; Oakland, 395,274

⚙️ transportation and industrial equipment, electronic equipment, oil, natural gas, motion pictures, milk, cattle, fruit, vegetables

Sacramento ⭐
San Francisco
Los Angeles
San Diego

did you know? *In Death Valley, the hottest and driest place in the U.S., the summer temperatures soar above 115° F. It also has the lowest elevation in the U.S. at 282 feet below sea level.*

COLORADO (CO) Centennial State

POPULATION (2006): 4,753,377 (22nd) **AREA:** 104,094 sq. mi. (8th) (269,602 sq. km.) 🌸Rocky Mountain columbine 🐦Lark bunting 🌲Colorado blue spruce 🎵"Where the Columbines Grow" **ENTERED UNION:** August 1, 1876 (38th) ⭐Denver **LARGEST CITIES (WITH POP.):** Denver, 557,917; Colorado Springs, 369,815; Aurora, 297,235; Lakewood, 140,671; Fort Collins, 128,026

Denver ⭐
Colorado Springs

⚙️ instruments and industrial machinery, food products, printing and publishing, metal products, electronic equipment, oil, coal, cattle

did you know? *The Anasazi Indians built entire cities into cliffsides across the American southwest. The settlements built between 1100 and 1300 at Mesa Verde in southwestern Colorado are the largest and best preserved.*

Key: 🌸Flower 🐦Bird 🌲Tree 🎵Song ⭐Capital ⚙️Important Products

CONNECTICUT (CT) Constitution State, Nutmeg State

Hartford

POPULATION (2006): 3,504,809 (29th) **AREA:** 5,543 sq. mi. (48th) (14,356 sq. km.) ❁Mountain laurel 🐦American robin 🌳White oak 🎵"Yankee Doodle" **ENTERED UNION:** January 9, 1788 (5th) ⭐ Hartford **LARGEST CITIES (WITH POP.):** Bridgeport, 139,008; New Haven, 124,791; Hartford, 124,397; Stamford, 120,045; Waterbury, 107,902

⚙ aircraft parts, helicopters, industrial machinery, metals and metal products, electronic equipment, printing and publishing, medical instruments, chemicals, dairy products, stone

did you know? The Hartford Courant *is the country's oldest newspaper in continuous publication. It started as a weekly in 1764. George Washington once placed an ad in the paper to rent out some of his land in Mount Vernon, VA.*

DELAWARE (DE) First State, Diamond State

Dover
⭐

POPULATION (2006): 853,476 (45th) **AREA:** 2,489 sq. mi. (49th) (6,446 sq. km.) ❁Peach blossom 🐦Blue hen chicken 🌳American holly 🎵"Our Delaware" **ENTERED UNION:** December 7, 1787 (1st) ⭐Dover **LARGEST CITIES (WITH POP.):** Wilmington, 72,786; Dover, 34,288; Newark, 30,060

⚙ chemicals, transportation equipment, food products, chickens

did you know? *The Mason-Dixon line is an L-shaped border that separates Delaware, Pennsylvania, and Maryland. Charles Mason and Jeremiah Dixon drew it in the 1760s to settle a dispute between the colonies. The border is marked to this day with stones about every 1,000 feet.*

FLORIDA (FL) Sunshine State

Tallahassee
⭐
Jacksonville

Miami ●

POPULATION (2006): 18,089,888 (4th) **AREA:** 65,755 sq. mi. (22nd) (170,305 sq. km.) ❁Orange blossom 🐦Mockingbird 🌳Sabal palmetto palm 🎵"Old Folks at Home" **ENTERED UNION:** March 3, 1845 (27th) ⭐Tallahassee (population, 155,171) **LARGEST CITIES (WITH POP.):** Jacksonville, 782,623; Miami, 386,417; Tampa, 325,989; St. Petersburg, 249,079; Hialeah, 220,485; Orlando, 213,223; Ft. Lauderdale, 167,380

⚙ electronic and transportation equipment, industrial machinery, printing and publishing, food products, citrus fruits, vegetables, livestock, phosphates, fish

NASA's main launch site, the Kennedy Space Center, is located on Cape Canaveral on the state's eastern coast. Since 1962, many famous spaceflights have launched there, including the Apollo missions to the Moon and more than 117 space shuttle flights.

 WAforKids.com | Go to *www.WAforKids.com* for even more U.S. facts.

294

GEORGIA (GA) Empire State of the South, Peach State

POPULATION (2006): 9,363,941 (9th) **AREA:** 59,425 sq. mi. (24th) (153,910 sq. km.) 🌸Cherokee rose 🐦Brown thrasher 🌲Live oak 🎵"Georgia on My Mind" **ENTERED UNION:** January 2, 1788 (4th) ⭐Atlanta **LARGEST CITIES (WITH POP.):** Atlanta, 470,688; Augusta, 190,782; Columbus, 185,271; Savannah, 128,453; Athens, 103,238

⚙ clothing and textiles, transportation equipment, food products, paper, chickens, peanuts, peaches, clay

⭐ **Atlanta**

 Blackbeard Island Wildlife Refuge, just off the coast of Georgia, is named for Blackbeard the pirate (real name Edward Teach). Blackbeard used the island as a hideout sometime around 1716. No buried treasure has been found there.

HAWAII (HI) Aloha State

POPULATION (2006): 1,285,498 (42nd) **AREA:** 10,931 sq. mi. (43rd) (28,311 sq. km.) 🌸Yellow hibiscus 🐦Hawaiian goose 🌲Kukui 🎵"Hawaii Ponoi" **ENTERED UNION:** August 21, 1959 (50th) ⭐Honolulu **LARGEST CITIES (WITH POP.):** Honolulu, 377,379; Hilo, 40,759; Kailua, 36,513; Kaneohe, 34,970

⚙ food products, pineapples, sugar, printing and publishing, fish, flowers

⭐ **Honolulu**

The most massive volcano in the world, Mauna Loa ("Long Mountain"), is located on the island of Hawaii, the "Big" island. About four-fifths of the volcano lies underwater, but its peak reaches 13,681 feet above sea level.

IDAHO (ID) Gem State

POPULATION (2006): 1,466,465 (39th) **AREA:** 83,570 sq. mi. (14th) (216,445 sq. km.) 🌸Syringa 🐦Mountain bluebird 🌲White pine 🎵"Here We Have Idaho" **ENTERED UNION:** July 3, 1890 (43rd) ⭐Boise **LARGEST CITIES (WITH POP.):** Boise, 193,161; Nampa, 71,713; Pocatello, 53,372; Idaho Falls, 52,338

⚙ potatoes, hay, wheat, cattle, milk, lumber and wood products, food products

⭐ **Boise**

In 1951, an experimental nuclear reactor built near Arco, ID became the first to produce electricity that was usable in homes and buildings. In 1955, Arco became the world's first town to have all of its power generated by a nuclear reactor.

Key: 🌸Flower 🐦Bird 🌲Tree 🎵Song ⭐Capital ⚙Important Products

ILLINOIS (IL) Prairie State

POPULATION (2006): 12,831,970 (5th) **AREA:** 57,914 sq. mi. (25th) (149,997 sq. km.) ⚘Native violet 🐦Cardinal 🌳White oak 🎵"Illinois" **ENTERED UNION:** December 3, 1818 (21st) ⭐Springfield **LARGEST CITIES (WITH POP.):** Chicago, 2,842,518; Aurora, 168,181; Rockford, 152,916; Naperville, 141,579; Joliet, 136,208; Springfield, 115,668; Peoria, 112,685

⚙ industrial machinery, metals and metal products, printing and publishing, electronic equipment, food products, corn, soybeans, hogs

Chicago • Springfield ⭐

The Chicago River, which today flows away from Lake Michigan, used to flow in the opposite direction. Between 1898 and 1900, engineers dug what became known as the Sanitary and Ship Canal, or Main Canal, connecting the Chicago River to the Mississippi River. This caused the water to reverse its flow.

INDIANA (IN) Hoosier State

POPULATION (2006): 6,313,520 (15th) **AREA:** 36,418 sq. mi. (38th) (94,322 sq. km.) ⚘Peony 🐦Cardinal 🌳Tulip poplar 🎵"On the Banks of the Wabash, Far Away" **ENTERED UNION:** December 11, 1816 (19th) ⭐Indianapolis **LARGEST CITIES (WITH POP.):** Indianapolis, 784,118; Fort Wayne, 223,341; Evansville, 115,918; South Bend, 105,262; Gary, 98,715

⚙ transportation equipment, electronic equipment, industrial machinery, iron and steel, metal products, corn, soybeans, livestock, coal

Indianapolis ⭐

True to its motto, "Crossroads of America," Indiana has more miles of interstate highway per square mile than any other state.

IOWA (IA) Hawkeye State

POPULATION (2006): 2,982,085 (30th) **AREA:** 56,272 sq. mi. (26th) (145,744 sq. km.) ⚘Wild rose 🐦Eastern goldfinch 🌳Oak 🎵"The Song of Iowa" **ENTERED UNION:** December 28, 1846 (29th) ⭐Des Moines **LARGEST CITIES (WITH POP.):** Des Moines, 194,163; Cedar Rapids, 123,119; Davenport, 98,845; Sioux City, 83,148

⚙ corn, soybeans, hogs, cattle, industrial machinery, food products

Des Moines ⭐

The only member of the Lewis and Clark expedition to die was Sgt. Charles Floyd. He died from peritonitis near present-day Sioux City, IA. A monument stands where he was buried.

⬛WAforKids.com Go to *www.WAforKids.com* for even more U.S. facts.

296

KANSAS (KS) Sunflower State

POPULATION (2006): 2,764,075 (33rd) **AREA:** 82,277 sq. mi. (15th) (213,096 sq. km.) ✿Native sunflower ♪Western meadowlark ♣Cottonwood ♪"Home on the Range" **ENTERED UNION:** January 29, 1861 (34th) ★Topeka **LARGEST CITIES (WITH POP.):** Wichita, 354,865; Overland Park, 164,811; Kansas City, 144,210; Topeka, 121,946

Topeka ★

Wichita ●

✿ cattle, aircraft and other transportation equipment, industrial machinery, food products, wheat, corn, hay, oil, natural gas

did you know? *The Chisholm Trail, used by cowboys to drive cattle from Texas through Indian Territory (now Oklahoma), ended in Abilene, KS. Wyatt Earp, marshall of Dodge City, was among the legendary lawmen who kept peace in the rowdy frontier towns along the way.*

KENTUCKY (KY) Bluegrass State

POPULATION (2006): 4,206,074 (26th) **AREA:** 40,409 sq. mi. (37th) (104,659 sq. km.) ✿Goldenrod ♪Cardinal ♣Tulip poplar ♪"My Old Kentucky Home" **ENTERED UNION:** June 1, 1792 (15th) ★Frankfort (population, 27,660) **LARGEST CITIES (WITH POP.):** Louisville, 556,429; Lexington, 268,080; Owensboro, 55,459; Bowling Green, 52,272

Louisville ● Frankfort ★

✿ coal, industrial machinery, electronic equipment, transportation equipment, metals, tobacco, cattle

did you know? *More than 360 miles of natural caves and underground passageways have been mapped under Mammoth Cave National Park. It's the largest network of natural tunnels in the world and extends up to 1,000 miles.*

LOUISIANA (LA) Pelican State

POPULATION (2006): 4,287,768 (25th) **AREA:** 51,840 sq. mi. (31st) (134,265 sq. km.) ✿Magnolia ♪Eastern brown pelican ♣Cypress ♪"Give Me Louisiana" **ENTERED UNION:** April 30, 1812 (18th) ★Baton Rouge **LARGEST CITIES (WITH POP.):** New Orleans, 454,863; Baton Rouge, 222,064; Shreveport, 198,874; Lafayette, 112,030

Baton Rouge ★

New ● Orleans

✿ natural gas, oil, chemicals, transportation equipment, paper, food products, cotton, fish

did you know? *Louisiana is the only state whose legal system comes from Napoleonic Code, the system put into place in France by Napoleon Bonaparte. This is because Louisiana used to belong to France. The law codes of the other 49 states are based on English common law, which was practiced in England. The differences are minor.*

Key: ✿Flower ♪Bird ♣Tree ♪Song ★Capital ✿Important Products

MAINE (ME) Pine Tree State

POPULATION (2006): 1,321,574 (40th) **AREA:** 35,385 sq. mi. (39th) (91,647 sq. km.) ❀ White pine cone and tassel ✦ Chickadee ✿ Eastern white pine ♪ "State of Maine Song" **ENTERED UNION:** March 15, 1820 (23rd) ★ Augusta (population, 18,551) **LARGEST CITIES (WITH POP.):** Portland, 63,889; Lewiston, 36,050; Bangor, 31,074

✿ paper, transportation equipment, wood and wood products, electronic equipment, footwear, clothing, potatoes, milk, eggs, fish, seafood

Augusta ★

did you know?
Maine is nearly as big as the five other New England states (Connecticut, Massachusetts, New Hampshire, Rhose Island, Vermont) combined. About 90% of all U.S. lobsters and 30% of all U.S. blueberries are harvested there.

MARYLAND (MD) Old Line State, Free State

Baltimore ●
Annapolis ★
Washington, D.C. ★

POPULATION (2006): 5,615,727 (19th) **AREA:** 12,407 sq. mi. (42nd) (32,134 sq. km.) ❀ Black-eyed susan ✦ Baltimore oriole ✿ White oak ♪ "Maryland, My Maryland" **ENTERED UNION:** April 28, 1788 (7th) ★ Annapolis (population, 36,196) **LARGEST CITIES (WITH POP.):** Baltimore, 635,815; Frederick, 57,907; Gaithersburg, 57,698; Rockville, 57,402; Bowie, 53,878

✿ printing and publishing, food products, transportation equipment, electronic equipment, chickens, soybeans, corn, stone

did you know?
Maryland's official state sport is jousting. Competitors on horseback ride through a course and use their lances to collect rings. Competitors are called either "knights" or "maids."

MASSACHUSETTS (MA) Bay State, Old Colony

Boston ★

POPULATION (2006): 6,437,193 (13th) **AREA:** 10,555 sq. mi. (44th) (27,337 sq. km.) ❀ Mayflower ✦ Chickadee ✿ American elm ♪ "All Hail to Massachusetts" **ENTERED UNION:** February 6, 1788 (6th) ★ Boston **LARGEST CITIES (WITH POP.):** Boston, 559,034; Worcester, 175,898; Springfield, 151,732; Lowell, 103,111; Cambridge, 100,135

✿ industrial machinery, electronic equipment, instruments, printing and publishing, metal products, fish, flowers and shrubs, cranberries

did you know?
The chocolate chip cookie was invented in Whitman, MA, in the 1930s by Ruth Wakefield.

●WAforKids.com Go to *www.WAforKids.com* for even more U.S. facts.

MICHIGAN (MI) Great Lakes State, Wolverine State

POPULATION (2006): 10,095,643 (8th) **AREA:** 96,716 sq. mi. (11th) (250,493 sq. km.) ❁ Apple blossom 🐦 Robin 🌲 White pine 🎵 "Michigan, My Michigan" **ENTERED UNION:** January 26, 1837 (26th) ⭐ Lansing **LARGEST CITIES (WITH POP.):** Detroit, 886,671; Grand Rapids, 193,780; Warren, 135,311; Sterling Heights, 128,034; Flint, 118,551; Lansing, 115,518; Ann Arbor, 113,271

⚙ automobiles, industrial machinery, metal products, office furniture, plastic products, chemicals, food products, milk, corn, natural gas, iron ore, blueberries

did you know? Battle Creek, the headquarters for Kellogg's, Ralston Foods, and the Post Cereal division of Kraft Foods, is known as the Cereal Capital of the World.

Lansing
Detroit

MINNESOTA (MN) North Star State, Gopher State

POPULATION (2006): 5,167,101 (21st) **AREA:** 86,939 sq. mi. (12th) (225,171 sq. km.) ❁ Pink and white lady slipper 🐦 Common loon 🌲 Red pine 🎵 "Hail! Minnesota" **ENTERED UNION:** May 11, 1858 (32nd) ⭐ St. Paul **LARGEST CITIES (WITH POP.):** Minneapolis, 372,811; St. Paul, 275,150; Rochester, 94,950; Duluth, 84,896; Bloomington, 81,164

⚙ industrial machinery, printing and publishing, computers, food products, scientific and medical instruments, milk, hogs, cattle, corn, soybeans, iron ore

did you know? The "Land of 10,000 Lakes" has 11,842 lakes bigger than 10 acres within its borders. One out of every six Minnesotans owns a boat, the highest rate of any state.

Minneapolis
St. Paul

MISSISSIPPI (MS) Magnolia State

POPULATION (2006): 2,910,540 (31st) **AREA:** 48,430 sq. mi. (32nd) (125,433 sq. km.) ❁ Magnolia 🐦 Mockingbird 🌲 Magnolia 🎵 "Go, Mississippi!" **ENTERED UNION:** December 10, 1817 (20th) ⭐ Jackson **LARGEST CITIES (WITH POP.):** Jackson, 177,977; Gulfport, 72,464; Biloxi, 50,209

⚙ transportation equipment, furniture, electrical machinery, lumber and wood products, cotton, rice, chickens, cattle

Jackson

did you know? In 1902, President Theodore "Teddy" Roosevelt went bear hunting in Mississippi. He refused to shoot a bear that had been tied to a tree by his companions. The story inspired some toy makers to create a stuffed toy bear, which they called "Teddy's Bear." That's how the teddy bear was born.

Key: ❁ Flower 🐦 Bird 🌲 Tree 🎵 Song ⭐ Capital ⚙ Important Products

MISSOURI (MO) Show Me State

POPULATION (2006): 5,842,713 (18th) **AREA:** 69,704 sq. mi. (21st) (180,533 sq. km.) Hawthorn Bluebird Dogwood "Missouri Waltz" **ENTERED UNION:** August 10, 1821 (24th) Jefferson City (population, 39,079) **LARGEST CITIES (WITH POP.):** Kansas City, 444,965; St. Louis, 344,362; Springfield, 150,298; Independence, 110,208

transportation equipment, electrical and electronic equipment, printing and publishing, food products, cattle, hogs, milk, soybeans, corn, hay, lead

did you know? *The Gateway Arch in St. Louis, which honors the spirit of the western pioneers, is the tallest monument (630 feet high) in the U.S.*

MONTANA (MT) Treasure State

POPULATION (2006): 944,632 (44th) **AREA:** 147,042 sq. mi. (4th) (380,837 sq. km.) Bitterroot Western meadowlark Ponderosa pine "Montana" **ENTERED UNION:** November 8, 1889 (41st) Helena (population, 26,353) **LARGEST CITIES (WITH POP.):** Billings, 98,721; Missoula, 62,923; Great Falls, 56,338; Bozeman, 33,535

cattle, copper, gold, wheat, barley, wood and paper products

did you know? *Montanan Jeanette Rankin in 1917 became the first woman to serve in the U.S. House of Representatives. She was the only member of Congress to vote against the U.S. taking part in both World War I and World War II.*

NEBRASKA (NE) Cornhusker State

POPULATION (2006): 1,768,331 (38th) **AREA:** 77,354 sq. mi. (16th) (200,346 sq. km.) Goldenrod Western meadowlark Cottonwood "Beautiful Nebraska" **ENTERED UNION:** March 1, 1867 (37th) Lincoln **LARGEST CITIES (WITH POP.):** Omaha, 414,521; Lincoln, 239,213; Bellevue, 47,334; Grand Island, 44,546

cattle, hogs, milk, corn, soybeans, hay, wheat, sorghum, food products, industrial machinery

did you know? *Nebraska has the only unicameral (one house) state legislature in the U.S. Called the Nebraska Unicameral, its members are called Senators and they serve four-year terms. The head of their legislature is called the Speaker.*

NEVADA (NV) Sagebrush State, Battle Born State, Silver State

POPULATION (2006): 2,495,529 (35th) **AREA:** 110,561 sq. mi. (7th) (286,352 sq. km.) 🌸Sagebrush 🐦Mountain bluebird 🌲Single-leaf piñon, bristlecone pine 🎵"Home Means Nevada" **ENTERED UNION:** October 31, 1864 (36th) ⭐Carson City (population, 54,311) **LARGEST CITIES (WITH POP.):** Las Vegas, 545,147; Henderson, 232,146; Reno, 203,550; North Las Vegas, 176,635

⚙ gold, silver, cattle, hay, food products, plastics, chemicals

⭐ Carson City

Las Vegas

did you know? Extending for about 110 miles, Lake Mead is the largest artificial lake in the U.S. It provides water for Nevada, Arizona, California, and northern Mexico. It was formed on the Colorado River when the Hoover Dam was built in 1936.

NEW HAMPSHIRE (NH) Granite State

POPULATION (2006): 1,314,895 (41st) **AREA:** 9,350 sq. mi. (46th) (24,216 sq. km.) 🌸Purple lilac 🐦Purple finch 🌲White birch 🎵"Old New Hampshire" **ENTERED UNION:** June 21, 1788 (9th) ⭐Concord **LARGEST CITIES (WITH POP.):** Manchester, 109,691; Nashua, 87,321; Concord, 42,336

⚙ industrial machinery, electric and electronic equipment, metal products, plastic products, dairy products, maple syrup and maple sugar

did you know? New Hampshire was the first colony to declare its independence from England and start its own government in 1776—six months before the Declaration of Independence was signed.

Concord ⭐

NEW JERSEY (NJ) Garden State

POPULATION (2006): 8,724,560 (11th) **AREA:** 8,721 sq. mi. (47th) (22,587 sq. km.) 🌸Purple violet 🐦Eastern goldfinch 🌲Red oak 🎵none **ENTERED UNION:** December 18, 1787 (3rd) ⭐Trenton **LARGEST CITIES (WITH POP.):** Newark, 280,666; Jersey City, 239,614; Paterson, 149,843; Elizabeth, 125,809; Trenton, 84,639

⚙ chemicals, pharmaceuticals/drugs, electronic equipment, nursery and greenhouse products, food products, tomatoes, blueberries, and peaches

Newark •

⭐ Trenton

did you know? The city of Paterson is one of the birthplaces of the Industrial Revolution in America. In the 1790s, the Society for Establishing Useful Manufacturers built a factory on the Passaic River. Until the early 20th century, Paterson produced many types of goods, including large amounts of silk fabric, inspiring the nickname "Silk City."

Key: 🌸Flower 🐦Bird 🌲Tree 🎵Song ⭐Capital ⚙Important Products

NEW MEXICO (NM) Land of Enchantment

Santa Fe ★

Albuquerque •

POPULATION (2006): 1,954,599 (36th) **AREA:** 121,589 sq. mi. (5th) (314,914 sq. km.) ❁ Yucca ♫ Roadrunner ❁ Piñon ♪ "O, Fair New Mexico" **ENTERED UNION:** January 6, 1912 (47th) ★ Santa Fe **LARGEST CITIES (WITH POP.):** Albuquerque, 494,236; Las Cruces, 82,671; Santa Fe, 70,631; Rio Rancho, 66,599

⚙ electronic equipment, foods, machinery, clothing, lumber, transportation equipment, hay, onions, chiles

did you know? *Carlsbad Caverns National Park contains Lechuguilla Cave, the deepest cave in the U.S. It is more than 1,570 feet deep. Hundreds of thousands of bats swarm out of the caverns every night to feed on insects.*

NEW YORK (NY) Empire State

Albany ★

• Buffalo

New York City •

POPULATION (2006): 19,306,183 (3rd) **AREA:** 54,556 sq. mi. (27th) (141,299 sq. km.) ❁ Rose ♫ Bluebird ❁ Sugar maple ♪ "I Love New York" **ENTERED UNION:** July 26, 1788 (11th) ★ Albany (population, 93,779) **LARGEST CITIES (WITH POP.):** New York, 8,143,197; Buffalo, 279,745; Rochester, 211,091; Yonkers, 196,425; Syracuse, 141,683

⚙ books and magazines, automobile and aircraft parts, toys and sporting goods, electronic equipment, machinery, clothing and textiles, metal products, milk, cattle, hay, apples

did you know? *New York City is the largest city in the U.S. and was the nation's first capital. It was also the home of another major first in American history— the first pizza restaurant in the U.S. opened there in 1895.*

NORTH CAROLINA (NC) Tar Heel State, Old North State

Raleigh ★

• Charlotte

POPULATION (2006): 8,856,505 (10th) **AREA:** 53,819 sq. mi. (28th) (139,391 sq. km.) ❁ Dogwood ♫ Cardinal ❁ Pine ♪ "The Old North State" **ENTERED UNION:** November 21, 1789 (12th) ★ Raleigh **LARGEST CITIES (WITH POP.):** Charlotte, 610,949; Raleigh, 341,530; Greensboro, 231,962; Durham, 204,845; Winston-Salem, 193,755; Fayetteville 129,928

⚙ clothing and textiles, tobacco and tobacco products, industrial machinery, electronic equipment, furniture, cotton, soybeans, peanuts

did you know? *English settlers established a colony on North Carolina's Roanoke Island in 1585, but abandoned it a year later. A second colony was founded in 1587, but had mysteriously disappeared by 1590.*

WAfor**Kids**.com Go to *www.WAforKids.com* for even more U.S. facts.

NORTH DAKOTA (ND) Peace Garden State

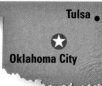

Bismarck

POPULATION (2006): 635,867 (48th) **AREA:** 70,700 sq. mi. (19th) (183,112 sq. km.) 🌸 Wild prairie rose 🐦 Western meadowlark 🌳 American elm 🎵 "North Dakota Hymn" **ENTERED UNION:** November 2, 1889 (39th) ⭐ Bismarck **LARGEST CITIES (WITH POP.):** Fargo, 90,672; Bismarck, 57,377; Grand Forks, 49,792; Minot, 34,984

⚙ wheat, barley, hay, sunflowers, sugar beets, cattle, sand and gravel, food products, farm equipment, high-tech electronics

The state's nickname is taken from the International Peace Garden, which straddles the boundary between North Dakota and Manitoba in Canada.

OHIO (OH) Buckeye State

Cleveland

Columbus ⭐

Cincinnati

POPULATION (2006): 11,478,006 (7th) **AREA:** 44,825 sq. mi. (34th) (116,096 sq. km.) 🌸 Scarlet carnation 🐦 Cardinal 🌳 Buckeye 🎵 "Beautiful Ohio" **ENTERED UNION:** March 1, 1803 (17th) ⭐ Columbus **LARGEST CITIES (WITH POP.):** Columbus, 730,657; Cleveland, 452,208; Cincinnati, 308,728; Toledo, 301,285; Akron, 210,795; Dayton, 158,873

⚙ metal and metal products, transportation equipment, industrial machinery, rubber and plastic products, electronic equipment, printing and publishing, chemicals, food products, corn, soybeans, livestock, milk

Though it was admitted to the Union in 1803, Ohio didn't technically become a state until 1953. Because of an oversight, Congress didn't formally vote on the resolution to admit Ohio as a state until August 7, 1953, when it made Ohio's statehood official, retroactive to 1803.

OKLAHOMA (OK) Sooner State

Tulsa

⭐ **Oklahoma City**

POPULATION (2006): 3,579,212 (28th) **AREA:** 69,898 sq. mi. (20th) (181,035 sq. km.) 🌸 Mistletoe 🐦 Scissor-tailed flycatcher 🌳 Redbud 🎵 "Oklahoma!" **ENTERED UNION:** November 16, 1907 (46th) ⭐ Oklahoma City **LARGEST CITIES (WITH POP.):** Oklahoma City, 531,324; Tulsa, 382,457; Norman, 101,719; Lawton, 90,234; Broken Arrow, 86,228

⚙ natural gas, oil, cattle, nonelectrical machinery, transportation equipment, metal products, wheat, hay

The American Indian nations called the Five Civilized Tribes (Cherokee, Chickasaw, Choctaw, Creek, and Seminole) were resettled in eastern Oklahoma by the federal government between 1817 and 1842.

Key: 🌸 Flower   🐦 Bird   🌳 Tree   🎵 Song   ⭐ Capital   ⚙ Important Products

OREGON (OR) Beaver State

POPULATION (2006): 3,700,758 (27th) **AREA:** 98,381 sq. mi. (9th) (254,806 sq. km.) 🌼Oregon grape 🐦Western meadowlark 🌲Douglas fir 🎵"Oregon, My Oregon" **ENTERED UNION:** February 14, 1859 (33rd) ⭐Salem **LARGEST CITIES (WITH POP.):** Portland, 533,427; Salem, 148,751; Eugene, 144,515; Gresham, 96,072

⚙ lumber and wood products, electronics and semiconductors, food products, paper, cattle, hay, vegetables, Christmas trees

Oregon's natural features have some real depth to them. Hells Canyon, 7,900 feet deep at its maximum, is one of the deepest canyons in the world. Crater Lake, which gets as deep as 1,932 feet, is the deepest lake in the U.S.

PENNSYLVANIA (PA) Keystone State

POPULATION (2006): 12,440,621 (6th) **AREA:** 46,055 sq. mi. (33rd) (119,282 sq. km.) 🌼Mountain laurel 🐦Ruffed grouse 🌲Hemlock 🎵"Pennsylvania" **ENTERED UNION:** December 12, 1787 (2nd) ⭐Harrisburg (population, 48,540) **LARGEST CITIES (WITH POP.):** Philadelphia, 1,463,281; Pittsburgh, 316,718; Allentown, 106,992; Erie, 102,612

⚙ iron and steel, coal, industrial machinery, printing and publishing, food products, electronic equipment, transportation equipment, stone, clay and glass products

An enormous fire has been burning since 1962 in the coal mines below the town of Centralia. Fewer than 20 people remain in the town. Surface temperatures have been measured at over 700°F.

RHODE ISLAND (RI) Little Rhody, Ocean State

POPULATION (2006): 1,067,610 (43rd) **AREA:** 1,545 sq. mi. (50th) (4,002 sq. km.) 🌼Violet 🐦Rhode Island red 🌲Red maple 🎵"Rhode Island" **ENTERED UNION:** May 29, 1790 (13th) ⭐ Providence **LARGEST CITIES (WITH POP.):** Providence, 176,862; Warwick, 87,233; Cranston, 81,614; Pawtucket, 73,742

⚙ costume jewelry, toys, textiles, machinery, electronic equipment, fish

Rhode Island is the smallest state in the U.S. It was the last of the original 13 colonies to ratify the Constitution (in 1790).

●WAfor**Kids**.com Go to *www.WAforKids.com* for even more U.S. facts.

SOUTH CAROLINA (SC) Palmetto State

POPULATION (2006): 4,321,249 (24th) **AREA:** 32,020 sq. mi. (40th) (82,931 sq. km.) 🌸Yellow jessamine 🐦Carolina wren 🌳Palmetto 🎵"Carolina" **ENTERED UNION:** May 23, 1788 (8th) ⭐Columbia **LARGEST CITIES (WITH POP.):** Columbia, 117,088; Charleston, 106,712; North Charleston, 86,313; Rock Hill, 59,554

Columbia ⭐

⚙ clothing and textiles, chemicals, industrial machinery, metal products, livestock, tobacco, Portland cement

did you know? More battles of the American Revolution were fought in South Carolina than in any other colony. The first shots of the Civil War were fired on Fort Sumter in Charleston harbor, in April, 1861.

SOUTH DAKOTA (SD) Mt. Rushmore State, Coyote State

POPULATION (2006): 781,919 (46th) **AREA:** 77,116 sq. mi. (17th) (199,730 sq. km.) 🌸Pasqueflower 🐦Chinese ring-necked pheasant 🌳Black Hills spruce 🎵"Hail, South Dakota" **ENTERED UNION:** November 2, 1889 (40th) ⭐Pierre (population, 14,012) **LARGEST CITIES (WITH POP.):** Sioux Falls, 139,517; Rapid City, 62,167; Aberdeen, 24,098

⭐ **Pierre**

⚙ food and food products, machinery, electric and electronic equipment, corn, soybeans

did you know? The Corn Palace in Mitchell is redecorated every year with themed murals made from corn, grains, and grasses by local artisans. When winter comes, birds and squirrels munch away the exterior.

TENNESSEE (TN) Volunteer State

POPULATION (2006): 6,038,803 (17th) **AREA:** 42,143 sq. mi. (36th) (109,150 sq. km.) 🌸Iris 🐦Mockingbird 🌳Tulip poplar 🎵"My Homeland, Tennessee"; "When It's Iris Time in Tennessee"; "My Tennessee"; "Tennessee Waltz"; "Rocky Top" **ENTERED UNION:** June 1, 1796 (16th) ⭐Nashville **LARGEST CITIES (WITH POP.):** Memphis, 672,277; Nashville, 549,110; Knoxville, 180,130; Chattanooga, 154,762

⭐ **Nashville**

Memphis ●

⚙ chemicals, machinery, vehicles, food products, metal products, publishing, electronic equipment, paper products, rubber and plastic products, tobacco

did you know? The Grand Ole Opry, the world's longest-running live radio program, was first broadcast from Nashville in 1925. It was originally called the WSM Barn Dance, but the name changed to the Grand Ole Opry in 1927.

Key: 🌸Flower 🐦Bird 🌳Tree 🎵Song ⭐Capital ⚙Important Products

TEXAS (TX) Lone Star State

POPULATION (2006): 23,507,783 (2nd) **AREA:** 268,581 sq. mi. (2nd) (695,622 sq. km.) ✿ Bluebonnet 🐦 Mockingbird 🌰 Pecan 🎵 "Texas, Our Texas" **ENTERED UNION:** December 29, 1845 (28th) ⭐ Austin **LARGEST CITIES (WITH POP.):** Houston, 2,016,582; San Antonio, 1,256,509; Dallas, 1,213,825; Austin, 690,252; Fort Worth, 624,067; El Paso, 598,590; Arlington, 362,805; Corpus Christi, 283,474; Plano, 250,096

⚙ oil, natural gas, cattle, milk, eggs, transportation equipment, chemicals, clothing, industrial machinery, electrical and electronic equipment, cotton, grains

Before it became a state in 1845, Texas had been an independent republic for about nine years. It had declared its independence after Texans defeated Mexican General Antonio López de Santa Anna on April 21, 1836. Sam Houston was its first president.

UTAH (UT) Beehive State

POPULATION (2006): 2,550,063 (34th) **AREA:** 84,899 sq. mi. (13th) (219,887 sq. km.) ✿ Sego lily 🐦 Seagull 🌲 Blue spruce 🎵 "Utah, This is the Place" **ENTERED UNION:** January 4, 1896 (45th) ⭐ Salt Lake City **LARGEST CITIES (WITH POP.):** Salt Lake City, 178,097; Provo, 113,459; West Valley City, 113,300; West Jordan, 91,444

⚙ transportation equipment, medical instruments, electronic parts, food products, steel, copper, cattle, corn, hay, wheat, barley

Early white settlers in Utah were saved from starvation by seagulls, the state bird. In 1848, hordes of locusts came into the Salt Lake Valley and began devouring the settlers' crops. All seemed lost before a flock of seagulls flew in and ate the locusts, saving the crops.

VERMONT (VT) Green Mountain State

POPULATION (2006): 623,908 (49th) **AREA:** 9,614 sq. mi. (45th) (24,900 sq. km.) ✿ Red clover 🐦 Hermit thrush 🌲 Sugar maple 🎵 "These Green Mountains" **ENTERED UNION:** March 4, 1791 (14th) ⭐ Montpelier (population, 8,026) **LARGEST CITIES (WITH POP.):** Burlington, 38,531; Essex Junction, 19,146; Colchester, 17,165; Rutland, 17,046

⚙ machine tools, furniture, scales, books, computer parts, foods, dairy products, apples, maple syrup

The Green Mountain Boys who famously fought against the British during the American Revolution were originally formed in 1770 to fight off New York settlers. When the revolution broke out, the Vermonters and New Yorkers set aside their differences and united against the British.

WAforKids.com Go to *www.WAforKids.com* for even more U.S. facts.

VIRGINIA (VA) Old Dominion

POPULATION (2006): 7,642,884 (12th) **AREA:** 42,774 sq. mi. (35th) (110,784 sq. km.) 🌸 Dogwood 🐦 Cardinal 🌲 Dogwood 🎵 "Carry Me Back to Old Virginia" **ENTERED UNION:** June 25, 1788 (10th) ⭐ Richmond **LARGEST CITIES (WITH POP.):** Virginia Beach, 438,415; Norfolk, 231,954; Chesapeake, 218,968; Arlington, 195,965; Richmond, 193,777; Newport News, 179,899

⚙️ transportation equipment, textiles, chemicals, printing, machinery, electronic equipment, food products, coal, livestock, tobacco, wood products, furniture

Nancy Langhorne Astor in 1919 became the first woman to serve in the British House of Commons. She was born and raised in Virginia.

WASHINGTON (WA) Evergreen State

POPULATION (2006): 6,395,798 (14th) **AREA:** 71,300 sq. mi. (18th) (184,666 sq. km.) 🌸 Western rhododendron 🐦 Willow goldfinch 🌲 Western hemlock 🎵 "Washington, My Home" **ENTERED UNION:** November 11, 1889 (42nd) ⭐ Olympia (population, 43,519) **LARGEST CITIES (WITH POP.):** Seattle, 573,911; Spokane, 196,818; Tacoma, 195,898; Vancouver, 157,493; Bellevue, 117,137

⚙️ aircraft, lumber, pulp and paper, machinery, electronics, computer software, aluminum, processed fruits and vegetables

Mount Rainier is the tallest volcano in the lower 48 states. It hasn't erupted in centuries. However, another volcano in Washington, Mount St. Helens, had a huge eruption on May 18, 1980. It lasted 9 hours and destroyed 230 square miles of woods. It is still active today.

WEST VIRGINIA (WV) Mountain State

POPULATION (2006): 1,818,470 (37th) **AREA:** 24,230 sq. mi. (41st) (62,755 sq. km.) 🌸 Big rhododendron 🐦 Cardinal 🌲 Sugar maple 🎵 "The West Virginia Hills"; "This Is My West Virginia"; "West Virginia, My Home Sweet Home" **ENTERED UNION:** June 20, 1863 (35th) ⭐ Charleston **LARGEST CITIES (WITH POP.):** Charleston, 51,176; Huntington, 49,198; Parkersburg, 32,020; Wheeling, 29,639

⚙️ coal, natural gas, fabricated metal products, chemicals, automobile parts, aluminum, steel, machinery, cattle, hay, apples, peaches, tobacco

On October 16, 1859, abolitionist leader John Brown and 18 others seized the federal arsenal in Harpers Ferry in an attempt to end slavery by force. Federal troops captured him and he was put to death in Charlestown later that year.

Key: 🌸 Flower 🐦 Bird 🌲 Tree 🎵 Song ⭐ Capital ⚙️ Important Products

WISCONSIN (WI) Badger State

POPULATION (2006): 5,556,506 (20th) **AREA:** 65,498 sq. mi. (23rd) (169,639 sq. km.) 🌸Wood violet 🐦Robin 🍁Sugar maple 🎵"On, Wisconsin!" **ENTERED UNION:** May 29, 1848 (30th) ⭐Madison **LARGEST CITIES (WITH POP.):** Milwaukee, 578,887; Madison, 221,551; Green Bay, 101,203; Kenosha, 95,240; Racine, 79,392

⚙️ paper products, printing, milk, butter, cheese, foods, food products, motor vehicles and equipment, medical instruments and supplies, plastics, corn, hay, vegetables

The first ever ice cream sundaes were served in the towns of Manitowoe and Two Rivers in 1851.

Madison ⭐ • Milwaukee

WYOMING (WY) Cowboy State

POPULATION (2006): 515,004 (50th) **AREA:** 97,814 sq. mi. (10th) (253,337 sq. km.) 🌸Indian paintbrush 🐦Western meadowlark 🌳Plains cottonwood 🎵"Wyoming" **ENTERED UNION:** July 10, 1890 (44th) ⭐Cheyenne **LARGEST CITIES (WITH POP.):** Cheyenne, 55,731; Casper, 51,738; Laramie, 26,050

⚙️ oil, natural gas, petroleum (oil) products, cattle, wheat, beans

Cheyenne ⭐

Wyoming is also known as the Equality State and has many firsts for women in America: Women were first given the right to vote while it was still a territory in 1869. Eliza Stewart was the first woman to be part of a grand jury in 1870. Nellie Tayloe Ross became the first female governor in 1925.

COMMONWEALTH OF PUERTO RICO (PR)

⭐ San Juan

HISTORY: Christopher Columbus landed in Puerto Rico in 1493. Puerto Rico was a Spanish colony for centuries, then was ceded (given) to the United States in 1898 after the Spanish-American War. In 1952, still associated with the United States, Puerto Rico became a commonwealth with its own constitution. **POPULATION (2006):** 3,927,776 **AREA:** 5,324 sq. mi. (13,789 sq. km.) 🌸Maga 🐦Reinita 🌳Ceiba **NATIONAL ANTHEM:** "La Borinqueña" ⭐San Juan **LARGEST CITIES (WITH POP.):** San Juan, 428,591; Bayamón, 222,195; Carolina, 187,472; Ponce, 182,387; Caguas, 142,378

⚙️ chemicals, food products, electronic equipment, clothing and textiles, industrial machinery, coffee, sugarcane, fruit, hogs

Puerto Ricans have most of the same rights as other Americans, but they cannot vote in U.S. presidential elections and they have no voting representatives in the federal government. They don't have to pay federal taxes.

●WAforKids.com Go to *www.WAforKids.com* for even more U.S. facts.

308

WASHINGTON, D.C.
The Capital of the
UNITED STATES

LAND AREA: 61 square miles **POPULATION (2006):** 581,530
FLOWER: American beauty rose **BIRD:** Wood thrush

WEB SITE www.dc.gov • www.washington.org

HISTORY Washington, D.C., became the capital of the United States in 1800, when the federal government moved there from Philadelphia. The city of Washington was designed and built to be the capital. It was named after George Washington. Many of its major sights are on the Mall, an open grassy area that runs from the Capitol to the Potomac River.

CAPITOL, which houses the U.S. Congress, is at the east end of the Mall on Capitol Hill. Its dome can be seen from far away.

JEFFERSON MEMORIAL, a circular marble building located near the Potomac River, is partly based on a design by Thomas Jefferson for the University of Virginia.

LIBRARY OF CONGRESS, research library for Congress and the largest library in the world, is on Independence Avenue across the street from the Capitol.

LINCOLN MEMORIAL, at the west end of the Mall, is built of white marble and styled like a Greek temple. Inside is a large, seated statue of Abraham Lincoln. His Gettysburg Address is carved on a nearby wall.

NATIONAL ARCHIVES, on Constitution Avenue, holds the Declaration of Independence, Constitution, and Bill of Rights.

NATIONAL WORLD WAR II MEMORIAL, located between the Lincoln Memorial and the Washington Monument at the Mall, honors the 16 million Americans who served during the war.

SMITHSONIAN INSTITUTION has 18 museums (2 of them are in New York City), including the new National Museum of the American Indian, the National Air and Space Museum and the Museum of Natural History. The National Zoo is part of the Smithsonian.

U.S. HOLOCAUST MEMORIAL MUSEUM presents the history of the Nazis' murder of more than six million Jews and millions of other people from 1933 to 1945. The exhibit *Daniel's Story* tells the story of the Holocaust from a child's point of view.

WASHINGTON MONUMENT is a white marble pillar, or obelisk, standing on the Mall and rising to more than 555 feet. From the top there are wonderful views of the city.

WHITE HOUSE, at 1600 Pennsylvania Avenue, has been the home of every U.S. president except George Washington.

WOMEN IN MILITARY SERVICE FOR AMERICA MEMORIAL, near the entrance to Arlington National Cemetery in Virginia. It honors the 2 million women who have served in the U.S. armed forces.

VIETNAM VETERANS MEMORIAL, located near the Lincoln Memorial, includes a wall with all the names of those killed or missing in action during the conflict.

◀ Jefferson Memorial

VOLUNTEERING

What is a TayBear, and who is it for? ➡ page 311

AMERICANS HELP OUT

Does spending your Saturday working in a soup kitchen sound like fun? Well, it is fun! You get to meet new people and help your community. It's true that volunteers don't get paid money, but sometimes feeling like you did a good thing is worth a lot more than a paycheck.

GET INVOLVED

Religious Groups

Many people volunteer through their religious community. Churches often organize soup kitchens, even homeless shelters. After Hurricane Katrina and Hurricane Rita, United Catholic Charities sent volunteers to the Gulf Coast to help provide food and shelter—as well as hugs and encouragement. They helped over 300,000 people.

↑ HURRICANE EVACUATION ROUTE

School Groups

Most schools in the United States offer opportunities for their students to volunteer. Some schools sponsor bake sales to raise money for a cause, while others may ask their students to volunteer at a nursing home, where they read or play games with elderly people. In Washington State, some high school students join the Washington Reading Corps and help elementary school students improve their reading. Does your school have any volunteering opportunities? If not, maybe you could start one! Try organizing a food drive or ask your fellow students to donate old winter coats to charities.

Neighborhood Groups

Many kids' groups and clubs like Boy and Girl Scouts and Campfire participate in neighborhood volunteering projects such as cleaning up a local park or organizing a car wash to raise money for a cause. Maybe you and your friends could spend a Saturday picking up trash around your neighborhood or mowing lawns for elderly people in your community. There are also neighborhood associations that hold monthly meetings. Attend the next one and donate your time and muscle power to an upcoming project.

VOLUNTEERING SUPERSTARS

Bear Therapy

When she was 7 years old, Taylor Crabtree started her own company, called TayBear. With the help of some friends, she painted and sold hair clips. Then she used the profits to buy teddy bears for kids with cancer and chronic blood diseases. Her original goal was to buy only 50 bears, but in 10 years she has given away more than 20,000 bears to hospitals across the country. More than 1,600 other kids have helped out by painting hair clips and putting TayBear tags on the toys. In 2006, Taylor was honored by *People* magazine as one of its top five heroes of the year. She has said that starting her company at a young age made her less self-centered, and she thinks "it would be great if everyone was a little more that way."

Smart Sacks

High-school students from Tennessee and Georgia volunteer their time to the Chattanooga Area Food Bank's Sack Pack program. The students fill sacks with granola bars, fruit, canned soup, and other foods. Every Friday, the sacks are delivered to needy elementary school children in 17 nearby schools. The children receive enough food to last the entire weekend. They may also do better in class: a scientific study from Tufts University found that undernourished children performed less well in school.

Understanding Autism

In 2006, four 16-year-old students in Singapore started a project to help children with autism, a disability that affects communication and social skills. They helped children with the disorder to create and illustrate short stories about "acceptance." The volunteers then turned those stories into a book called *Colourful Minds*. They also bought a cart that will allow autistic children to sell the book and other artwork in a nearby mall. Volunteer Lee Li Long says that this will help youths with autism to interact with the community, and also make the public "more aware of their talents."

WEATHER

What is a sundog? ➡ see below

WEIRD WEATHER FACTS

The tradition of **Groundhog Day** can be traced back to the Christian festival of Candlemas, which also occurs on February 2. In the Middle Ages, people believed that certain animals (like bears or badgers) came out of hibernation on that day to check the weather. If the sun was shining and the animal saw its shadow, the animal would return to hibernation, and there would be six more weeks of winter. If the animal did not see its shadow, then spring was on its way.

Since 1887, people in Punxsutawney, PA, have relied on a groundhog (actually, a series of groundhogs) named Punxsutawney Phil to make a forecast on February 2. The forecast is just for fun, though, because the weather on one particular day cannot be used to predict a whole season.

Winds are known by specific names in certain parts of the world. Here is a sample:

Föhn, or foehn—Warm, dry wind that travels down a mountain's leeward side, or the side of the mountain facing away from the wind. This occurs after a cool, moist wind travels up and over the side of the mountain facing the wind. Originally used to refer to a wind in the Alps.
Chinook—A föhn wind common in the Rocky Mountains. Named after a Native American tribe.
Mistral—Strong, cold, dry wind that blows from the northwest across the southern coast of France. It can reach speeds of up to about 85 miles per hour.
Sirocco—Warm, humid wind that originates as a hot, dry wind in North Africa. It picks up moisture as it crosses the Mediterranean and brings rain to Europe.

A **sundog**, or parhelia, is a phenomenon caused by light passing through or reflecting off of ice crystals in the atmosphere. Sundogs appear as bright spots of light on either side of the Sun. If you drew a line through sundogs and the Sun, the line would be parallel to the horizon.

WEATHER WORDS

 climate The typical weather in a particular area.

 front A boundary between two air masses.

 heat index A measure of how hot it feels when high humidity is combined with high temperatures. If it is very humid, 90°F can feel like 100°F.

 precipitation Water that falls from clouds as rain, snow, hail, or sleet.

 ultraviolet index A measure of how intense the ultraviolet (UV) radiation reaching Earth's surface in the middle of the day will be. The higher the number, the more likely you are to get sunburn. If the UV index is 6, people are urged to wear sunscreen and a hat. The UV index depends on cloud cover and the time of year. It's likely to be higher in the spring and summer.

 wind chill A measure of how cold it feels when there is wind. When it is 35°F and the wind is 15 miles an hour, it will feel like 25°F.

RECORD TEMPERATURES BY STATE
(Through 2006)

Coldest Temperature

Hottest Temperature

STATE	Lowest °F	Lowest Latest date	Highest °F	Highest Latest date
Alabama	−27	Jan. 30, 1966	112	Sept. 5, 1925
Alaska	−80	Jan. 23, 1971	100	June 27, 1915
Arizona	−40	Jan. 7, 1971	128	June 29, 1994
Arkansas	−29	Feb. 13, 1905	120	Aug. 10, 1936
California	−45	Jan. 20, 1937	134	July 10, 1913
Colorado	−61	Feb. 1, 1985	118	July 11, 1888
Connecticut	−32	Jan. 22, 1961	106	July 15, 1995
Delaware	−17	Jan. 17, 1893	110	July 21, 1930
Florida	−2	Feb. 13, 1899	109	June 29, 1931
Georgia	−17	Jan. 27, 1940	112	Aug. 20, 1983
Hawaii	12	May 17, 1979	100	Apr. 27, 1931
Idaho	−60	Jan. 18, 1943	118	July 28, 1934
Illinois	−36	Jan. 5, 1999	117	July 14, 1954
Indiana	−36	Jan. 19, 1994	116	July 14, 1936
Iowa	−47	Feb. 3, 1996	118	July 20, 1934
Kansas	−40	Feb. 13, 1905	121	July 24, 1936
Kentucky	−37	Jan. 19, 1994	114	July 28, 1930
Louisiana	−16	Feb. 13, 1899	114	Aug. 10, 1936
Maine	−48	Jan. 19, 1925	105	July 10, 1911
Maryland	−40	Jan. 13, 1912	109	July 10, 1936
Massachusetts	−35	Jan. 12, 1981	107	Aug. 2, 1975
Michigan	−51	Feb. 9, 1934	112	July 13, 1936
Minnesota	−60	Feb. 2, 1996	114	July 6, 1936
Mississippi	−19	Jan. 30, 1966	115	July 29, 1930
Missouri	−40	Feb. 13, 1905	118	July 14, 1954
Montana	−70	Jan. 20, 1954	117	July 5, 1937
Nebraska	−47	Dec. 22, 1989	118	July 24, 1936
Nevada	−50	Jan. 8, 1937	125	June 29, 1994
New Hampshire	−47	Jan. 29, 1934	106	July 4, 1911
New Jersey	−34	Jan. 5, 1904	110	July 10, 1936
New Mexico	−50	Feb. 1, 1951	122	June 27, 1994
New York	−52	Feb. 18, 1979	108	July 22, 1926
North Carolina	−34	Jan. 21, 1985	110	Aug. 21, 1983
North Dakota	−60	Feb. 15, 1936	121	July 6, 1936
Ohio	−39	Feb. 10, 1899	113	July 21, 1934
Oklahoma	−27	Jan. 18, 1930	120	June 27, 1994
Oregon	−54	Feb. 10, 1933	119	Aug. 10, 1898
Pennsylvania	−42	Jan. 5, 1904	111	July 10, 1936
Rhode Island	−25	Feb. 5, 1996	104	Aug. 2, 1975
South Carolina	−19	Jan. 21, 1985	111	June 28, 1954
South Dakota	−58	Feb. 17, 1936	120	July 15, 2006
Tennessee	−32	Dec. 30, 1917	113	Aug. 9, 1930
Texas	−23	Feb. 8, 1933	120	June 28, 1994
Utah	−69	Feb. 1, 1985	117	July 5, 1985
Vermont	−50	Dec. 30, 1933	105	July 4, 1911
Virginia	−30	Jan. 22, 1985	110	July 15, 1954
Washington	−48	Dec. 30, 1968	118	Aug. 5, 1961
West Virginia	−37	Dec. 30, 1917	112	July 10, 1936
Wisconsin	−55	Feb. 4, 1996	114	July 13, 1936
Wyoming	−66	Feb. 9, 1933	115	Aug. 8, 1983

Record temperatures may have occurred on earlier dates. Dates listed here are for most recent occurrence of a record temperature.

WEIGHTS & MEASURES

How many quarts are in a gallon? ➡ page 316

Metrology isn't the study of weather. (That's meteorology.) It is the science of measurement. Almost everything you use every day is measured—either when it is made or when it's sold. Materials for buildings and parts for machines must be measured carefully so they will fit together. Clothes have sizes so you'll know which to choose. Many items sold in a supermarket are priced by weight or by volume.

EARLIEST MEASUREMENTS

The human body was the first "ruler." An "inch" was the width of a thumb; a "hand" was five fingers wide; a "foot" was—you guessed it—the length of a foot! A "cubit" ran from the elbow to the tip of the middle finger (about 20 inches), and a "yard" was the length of a whole arm.

Later, measurements came from daily activities, like plowing. A "furlong" was the distance an ox team could plow before stopping to rest (now we say it is about 220 yards). The trouble with these units was that they were different from person to person, place to place, and ox to ox.

MEASUREMENTS WE USE TODAY

The official system in the U.S. is the customary system (sometimes called the imperial or English system). Scientists and most other countries use the International System of Units (metric system). The Weights and Measures Division of the U.S. National Institute of Standards and Technology (NIST) makes sure that a gallon of milk in California is the same as one in New York. When the NIST was founded in 1901, there were as many as eight different "standard" gallons in the U.S. and four different legal measures of a "foot" in Brooklyn, New York, alone.

ANCIENT MEASURE

1 foot =
length of a person's foot

1 yard =
from nose to fingertip

1 acre =
land an ox could plow in a day

12 inches

3 feet or 36 inches

4,840 square yards

MODERN MEASURE

TAKING TEMPERATURES

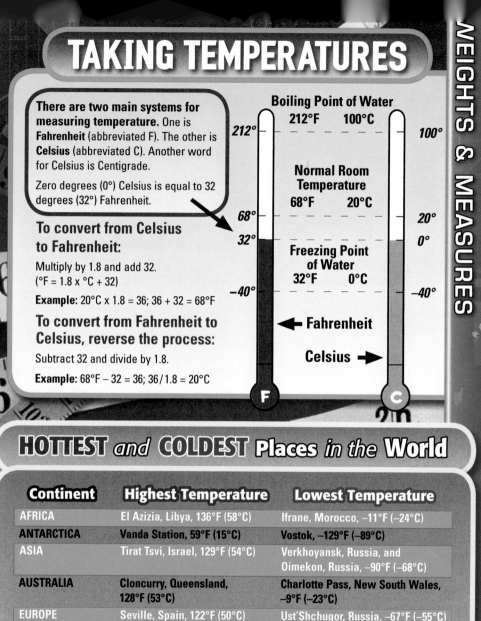

There are two main systems for measuring temperature. One is **Fahrenheit** (abbreviated F). The other is **Celsius** (abbreviated C). Another word for Celsius is Centigrade.

Zero degrees (0°) Celsius is equal to 32 degrees (32°) Fahrenheit.

To convert from Celsius to Fahrenheit:

Multiply by 1.8 and add 32.
($°F = 1.8 \times °C + 32$)

Example: 20°C x 1.8 = 36; 36 + 32 = 68°F

To convert from Fahrenheit to Celsius, reverse the process:

Subtract 32 and divide by 1.8.

Example: 68°F – 32 = 36; 36 / 1.8 = 20°C

Boiling Point of Water
212°F   100°C

Normal Room Temperature
68°F   20°C

Freezing Point of Water
32°F   0°C

← **Fahrenheit**

Celsius →

212°
68°
32°
–40°

100°
20°
0°
–40°

F   **C**

HOTTEST and COLDEST Places in the World

Continent	Highest Temperature	Lowest Temperature
AFRICA	El Azizia, Libya, 136°F (58°C)	Ifrane, Morocco, –11°F (–24°C)
ANTARCTICA	Vanda Station, 59°F (15°C)	Vostok, –129°F (–89°C)
ASIA	Tirat Tsvi, Israel, 129°F (54°C)	Verkhoyansk, Russia, and Oimekon, Russia, –90°F (–68°C)
AUSTRALIA	Cloncurry, Queensland, 128°F (53°C)	Charlotte Pass, New South Wales, –9°F (–23°C)
EUROPE	Seville, Spain, 122°F (50°C)	Ust'Shchugor, Russia, –67°F (–55°C)
NORTH AMERICA	Death Valley, California, 134°F (57°C)	Snag, Yukon Territory, Canada, –81°F (–63°C)
SOUTH AMERICA	Rivadavia, Argentina, 120°F (49°C)	Sarmiento, Argentina, –27°F (–33°C)

did you know? The 2006 average annual temperature for the contiguous U.S. (55°F) was the warmest on record, according to scientists at the NOAA National Climatic Data Center in Asheville, NC. Annual temperature records date back to 1895.

The basic unit of **length** in the U.S. system is the **inch**. Length, width, and thickness all use the inch or larger related units.

1 foot (ft.) = 12 inches (in.)

1 yard (yd.) = 3 feet = 36 inches

1 rod (rd.) = 5½ yards

1 furlong (fur.) = 40 rods = 220 yards
= 660 feet

1 mile (mi.) (also called statute mile) =
8 furlongs = 1,760 yards = 5,280 feet

1 nautical mile = 6,076.1 feet = 1.15 statute miles

1 league = 3 miles

Area is used to measure a section of a two-dimensional surface like the floor or a piece of paper. Most area measurements are given in **square units**. Land is measured in **acres**.

1 square foot (sq. ft.) = 144 square inches
(sq. in.)

1 square yard (sq. yd.) = 9 square feet =
1,296 square inches

1 square rod (sq. rd.) = 30¼ square yards

1 acre = 160 square rods = 4,840 square yards
= 43,560 square feet

1 square mile (sq. mi.) = 640 acres

CAPACITY

Units of **capacity** are used to measure how much of something will fit into a container. **Liquid measure** is used to measure liquids, such as water or gasoline. **Dry measure** is used with large amounts of solid materials, like grain or fruit. Although both liquid and dry measures use the terms "pint" and "quart," they mean different amounts and should not be confused.

Dry Measure

1 quart (qt.) = 2 pints (pt.)
1 peck (pk.) = 8 quarts
1 bushel (bu.) = 4 pecks

Liquid Measure

1 gill = 4 fluid ounces (fl. oz.)
1 pint (pt.) = 4 gills = 16 ounces (oz.)
1 quart (qt.) = 2 pints = 32 ounces
1 gallon (gal.) = 4 quarts = 128 ounces

For measuring most U.S. liquids,
1 barrel (bbl.) = 31½ gallons

For measuring oil, 1 barrel = 42 gallons

Cooking Measurements

The measurements used in cooking are based on the **fluid ounce**.
1 teaspoon (tsp.) = ⅙ fluid ounce (fl. oz.)
1 tablespoon (tbsp.) = 3 teaspoons
= ½ fluid ounce
1 cup = 16 tablespoons = 8 fluid ounces
1 pint = 2 cups
1 quart (qt.) = 2 pints (pt.)
1 gallon (gal.)= 4 quarts

VOLUME

The amount of space taken up by a three-dimensional object (or the amount of space available within an object) is measured in **volume**. Volume is usually expressed in **cubic units**. If you wanted to buy a room air conditioner and needed to know how much space there was to be cooled, you could measure the room in cubic feet.

1 cubic foot (cu. ft.) = 12 inches x 12 inches
x 12 inches = 1,728
cubic inches (cu. in.)

1 cubic yard (cu. yd.) = 27 cubic feet

DEPTH

Some measurements of length are used to measure ocean depth and distance.

1 fathom = 6 feet (ft.)
1 cable = 120 fathoms = 720 feet

WEIGHT

Although 1 cubic foot of popcorn and 1 cubic foot of rock take up the same amount of space, it wouldn't feel the same if you tried to lift them. We measure heaviness as **weight**. Most objects are measured in **avoirdupois weight** (pronounced a-ver-de-POIZ):

1 dram (dr.) = 27.344 grains (gr.)
1 ounce (oz.) = 16 drams = 437.5 grains
1 pound (lb.) = 16 ounces
1 hundredweight (cwt.) = 100 pounds
1 ton = 2,000 pounds (also called short ton)

THE **METRIC** SYSTEM

The metric system was created in France in 1795. Standardized in 1960 and given the name International System of Units, it is now used in most countries and in scientific works. The system is based on 10, like the decimal counting system. The basic unit for length is the **meter**. The **liter** is a basic unit of volume or capacity, and the **gram** is a basic unit of mass. Related units are made by adding a prefix to the basic unit. The prefixes and their meanings are:

milli- = $\dfrac{1}{1,000}$

centi- = $\dfrac{1}{100}$

deci- = $\dfrac{1}{10}$

deka- = 10

hecto- = 100

kilo- = 1,000

For Example

millimeter (mm) = $\dfrac{1}{1,000}$ of a meter

kilometer (km) = 1,000 meters

milligram (mg) = $\dfrac{1}{1,000}$ of a gram

kilogram (kg) = 1,000 grams

To get a rough idea of measurements in the metric system, it helps to know that a **liter** is a little more than a quart. A **meter** is a little over a yard. A **kilogram** is a little over 2 pounds. And a **kilometer** is just over half a mile.

Homework Help Converting Measurements

From:	Multiply by:	To get:	From:	Multiply by:	To get:
inches	2.5400	centimeters	centimeters	.3937	inches
inches	.0254	meters	centimeters	.0328	feet
feet	30.4800	centimeters	meters	39.3701	inches
feet	.3048	meters	meters	3.2808	feet
yards	.9144	meters	meters	1.0936	yards
miles	1.6093	kilometers	kilometers	.621	miles
square inches	6.4516	square centimeters	square centimeters	.1550	square inches
square feet	.0929	square meters	square meters	10.7639	square feet
square yards	.8361	square meters	square meters	1.1960	square yards
acres	.4047	hectares	hectares	2.4710	acres
cubic inches	16.3871	cubic centimeters	cubic centimeters	.0610	cubic inches
cubic feet	.0283	cubic meters	cubic meters	35.3147	cubic feet
cubic yards	.7646	cubic meters	cubic meters	1.3080	cubic yards
quarts (liquid)	.9464	liters	liters	1.0567	quarts (liquid)
ounces	28.3495	grams	grams	.0353	ounces
pounds	.4536	kilograms	kilograms	2.2046	pounds

WORLD HISTORY

Which country was founded in part by convicted criminals? ➡ page 327

Each of the five sections in this chapter tells the history of a major region of the world: the Middle East, Africa, Asia, Europe, or the Americas. Major events from ancient times to the present are described under the headings for each region.

THE ANCIENT MIDDLE EAST

▲ *hieroglyphics*

4000–3000 B.C. The world's first cities are built by the Sumerian peoples in Mesopotamia, now southern Iraq. Sumerians develop a kind of writing called **cuneiform**. Egyptians develop a kind of writing called **hieroglyphics**.

2700 B.C. Egyptians begin building the great pyramids in the desert.

1792 B.C. Some of the first written laws are created in Babylonia. They are called the Code of Hammurabi.

1200 B.C. Hebrew people settle in Canaan in Palestine after escaping from slavery in Egypt. They are led by the prophet Moses.

1000 B.C. King David unites the Hebrews in one strong kingdom. ▶

ANCIENT PALESTINE

Palestine was invaded by many different peoples after 1000 B.C., including the Babylonians, Egyptians, Persians, and Romans.

336 B.C. Alexander the Great, King of Macedonia, builds an empire from Egypt to India.

ISLAM: A RELIGION GROWS IN THE MIDDLE EAST A.D. 610–632
Around 610, the prophet Muhammad starts to proclaim and teach Islam. This religion spreads from Arabia to all the neighboring regions in the Middle East and North Africa. Its followers are called Muslims.

THE KORAN
The holy book of Islam is the Koran. It was related by Muhammad beginning in 611.

▲ *The Koran*

THE SPREAD OF ISLAM
The Arab armies that went across North Africa brought great change:
• The people who lived there were converted to Islam.
• The Arabic language replaced many local languages as an official language. North Africa is still an Arabic-speaking region today, and Islam is the major faith.

63 B.C. Romans conquer Palestine and make it part of their empire.

Around 4 B.C. Jesus Christ, the founder of the Christian religion, is born in Bethlehem. He is crucified about A.D. 29.

A.D. 632 Muhammad dies. By now, Islam is accepted in Arabia as a religion.

641 Arab Muslims conquer the Persians.

Late 600s Islam begins to spread to the west into Africa and Spain.

▼ *The pyramids at Giza*

THE MIDDLE EAST

THE UMAYYAD AND ABBASID DYNASTIES The Umayyads (661-750) and the Abbasids (750-1256) are the first two Muslim-led dynasties. Both empires stretched across northern Africa and the Middle East into Asia.

711–732 Umayyads invade Europe but are defeated by Frankish leader Charles Martel in France. This defeat halts the spread of Islam into Western Europe.

1071 Muslim Turks conquer Jerusalem.

1095–1291 Europeans try to take back Jerusalem and other parts of the Middle East for Christians during the Crusades.

1300-1900s The Ottoman Turks, who are Muslims, create a huge empire, covering the Middle East, North Africa, and part of Eastern Europe. European countries take over portions of it beginning in the 1800s.

1914-1918 World War I begins in 1914. Most of the Middle East falls under British or French control.

1921 Two new Arab kingdoms are created: Transjordan and Iraq. The French take control of Syria and Lebanon.

1922 Egypt becomes independent from Britain.

JEWS MIGRATE TO PALESTINE Jews began migrating to Palestine in the 1880s. In 1945, after World War II, many Jews who survived the Holocaust migrated to Palestine.

1948 The state of Israel is created.

THE ARAB-ISRAELI WARS Arab countries near Israel (Egypt, Iraq, Jordan, Lebanon, and Syria) attack the new country in 1948 but fail to destroy it. Israel and its neighbors fight wars again in 1956, 1967, and 1973. Israel wins each war. In the 1967 war, Israel captures the Sinai Desert from Egypt, the Golan Heights from Syria, and the West Bank from Jordan.

1979 Egypt and Israel sign a peace treaty. Israel returns the Sinai to Egypt.

◀ *Anwar al-Sadat, Jimmy Carter, Menachem Begin celebrate signing of peace treaty.*

THE MIDDLE EAST AND OIL About 20% of the oil we use to drive cars, heat homes, and run machines comes from the Middle East. Many countries rely on oil imports from the region, which has more than half the world's crude oil reserves.

The 1990s and 2000s

• In 1991, the U.S. and its allies go to war with Iraq after Iraq invades Kuwait. Iraq is defeated and signs a peace agreement but is accused of violating it. In 2003, the U.S., Britain, and other allies invade Iraq and remove the regime of Saddam Hussein. Free elections are held and a democratic government is formed, but violence there continues.

• Tensions between Israel and the Palestinians increase. In 2005, Israel pulls out from Gaza. In 2006, Palestinian elections in the West Bank and Gaza bring Hamas, an organization that has historically been dedicated to eliminating the state of Israel, to power.

Dome of the Rock and the Western Wall, Jerusalem ▼

ANCIENT AFRICA

ANCIENT AFRICA In ancient times, northern Africa was dominated by the Egyptians, Greeks, and Romans. However, we know very little about the lives of ancient Africans south of the Sahara Desert. They did not have written languages. What we learn about them comes from weapons, tools, and other items from their civilization.

2000 B.C. The Nubian Kingdom of Kush, rich with gold, ivory, and jewels, arises south of Egypt. It is a major center of art, learning, and trade until around A.D. 350.

1000 B.C. Bantu-speaking people around Cameroon begin an 1,800-year expansion into much of eastern and southern Africa.

500 B.C. Carthage, an empire centered in Tunisia, becomes rich and powerful through trading. Its ports span the African coast of the Mediterranean Sea. Rome defeats Carthage and its most famous leader, ◄Hannibal, during the second Punic War (218-201 B.C.).

• The Nok in Nigeria are the earliest users of iron for tools and weapons south of the Sahara Desert. They are also known for their terracotta sculptures.

• The Christian Kingdom of Aksum in northern Ethiopia becomes a wealthy trading center on the Red Sea for treasures like ivory. It makes its own coins and monuments, many of which survive today.

By A.D. 700 Ghana, the first known empire south of the Sahara Desert, takes power through trade around the upper Senegal and Niger Rivers. Its Mande people control the trade in gold from nearby mines to Arabs in the north.

By 900 Arab Muslim merchants bring Islam to the Bantu speakers along the east coast of Africa, creating the Swahili language and culture. Traders in Kenya and Tanzania export ivory, slaves, perfumes, and gold to Asia.

1054-1145 Islamic Berbers unite into the Almoravid Kingdom centered at Marrakech, Morocco. They spread into Ghana and southern Spain.

1230-1400s A Mande prince named Sundiata (the "Lion King") forms the Mali Kingdom where Ghana once stood. Timbuktu becomes its main city.

1250-1400s Great Zimbabwe becomes the largest settlement (12,000-20,000 Bantu-speaking people) in southern Africa.

1464-1591 As Mali loses power, Songhai rises to become the third and final great empire of western Africa.

1481 Portugal sets up the first permanent European trading post south of the Sahara Desert at Elmina, Ghana. Slaves, in addition to gold and ivory, are soon exported.

1483-1665 Kongo, the most powerful kingdom on central Africa's west coast, provides thousands of slaves each year for Portugal. Portugal's colony Angola overtakes the Kongo in 1665.

Camel train moving across the Sahara ▶

AFRICA

1650-1810 Slave trading peaks across the "Slave Coast" from eastern Ghana to western Nigeria as competing African states sell tens of thousands of captured foes each year to competing European traders.

THE AFRICAN SLAVE TRADE

African slaves were taken to the Caribbean to harvest sugar on European plantations. Later, slaves were taken to South America and the United States. The ships from Africa were overcrowded and diseased. About 20% of the slaves died during the long journey.

1652 The Dutch East India Company sets up a supply camp in southern Africa at the Cape of Good Hope (later Cape Town). Dutch settlers and French Protestants called Huguenots establish Cape Colony. Their descendants are known as the Boers or Afrikaners and develop a distinct language and culture.

1792 Freed slaves, mostly from Britain and the Americas, found Freetown in Sierra Leone.

1803 Denmark is the first European country to ban slave trading. Britain follows in 1807, the U.S. in 1808. Most European nations ban the trade by 1820, but illegal trading continues for decades.

1814 Britain purchases the Dutch South African colony at Cape Town. British colonists arrive after 1820.

1816-28 The Zulus, ruled by the chieftain Shaka, dominate eastern South Africa.

1835-43 The "Great Trek" (march) of the Boers away from British Cape Town.

1884-85 European nations meet in Berlin and agree to divide control of Africa. No African states are invited to the agreements. The "Scramble for Africa" lasts until World War I. Only Ethiopia and Liberia remain independent.

1899-1902 Great Britain and the Boers fight in South Africa in the Boer War. The Boers accept British rule but are allowed a role in government.

1948 The white Afrikaner-dominated South African government creates the policy of apartheid ("apartness"), the total separation of races. Blacks are banned from many restaurants, theaters, schools, and jobs. Apartheid sparks protests, many of which ended in bloodshed.

1957 Ghana gains independence from Britain, becoming the first territory in Africa below the Sahara to regain freedom from European rule. Over the next 20 years, the rest of Africa would gain independence.

1990-94 South Africa abolishes its policy of apartheid. In 1994, Nelson Mandela becomes South Africa's first black president. ▶

1994 Fighting between Hutu and Tutsi ethnic groups in Rwanda leads to the massacre of more than 800,000 civilians.

1998-2004 Fighting in the Democratic Republic of the Congo involves 9 nations. About 4 million die, mostly from starvation and disease. While the war is officially over by 2003, fighting continues.

◀ **2006** Ellen Johnson-Sirleaf becomes president of Liberia, and Africa's first elected female leader.

A savanna in Kenya

ANCIENT ASIA

3500 B.C. People settle in the Indus River Valley of India and Pakistan and the Yellow River Valley of China.

2500 B.C. Cities of Mohenjo-Daro and Harappa in Pakistan become centers of trade and farming.

Around 1523 B.C. Shang peoples in China build walled towns and use a kind of writing based on pictures. This writing develops into the writing Chinese people use today.

Around 1050 B.C. Chou peoples in China overthrow the Shang and control large territories.

 563 B.C. Siddhartha Gautama is born in India. He becomes known as the Buddha—the "Enlightened One"—and is the founder of the Buddhist religion (Buddhism).

551 B.C. The Chinese philosopher Confucius is born. His teachings—especially rules about how people should treat each other— spread throughout China and are still followed today.

320–232 B.C.
- Northern India is united under the emperor Chandragupta Maurya.
- Asoka, emperor of India, sends Buddhist missionaries throughout southern Asia to spread the Buddhist religion.

221 B.C. The Chinese begin building the Great Wall. Its main section is more than 2,000 miles long and is meant to keep invading peoples out.

202 B.C. The Han people of China win control of all of China.

A.D. 320 The Gupta Empire controls northern India. The Guptas, who are Hindus, drive the Buddhist religion out of India. They are well known for their many advances in mathematics and medicine.

618 The Tang dynasty begins in China. The Tang dynasty is well known for music, poetry, and painting. They export silk and porcelains as far away as Africa.

THE SILK ROAD Around 100 B.C., only the Chinese knew how to make silk. To get this light, comfortable material, Europeans sent fortunes in glass, gold, jade, and other items to China. The exchanges between Europeans and Chinese created one of the greatest trading routes in history—the Silk Road. Chinese inventions such as paper and gunpowder were also spread via the Silk Road. Europeans found out how to make silk around A.D. 500, but trade continued until about 1400.

960 The Northern Sung dynasty in China makes advances in banking and paper money. China's population of 50 million doubles over 200 years, thanks to improved ways of farming that lead to greater food production.

The Forbidden City

ASIA

1000 The Samurai, a warrior people, become powerful in Japan. They live by a code of honor known as *Bushido*. ▶

1180 The Khmer Empire in Cambodia becomes widely known for its beautiful temples.

1206 The Mongol leader Genghis Khan creates an empire that stretches from China to India, Russia, and Eastern Europe.

1264 Kublai Khan, grandson of Genghis Khan, rules China as emperor from his new capital at Beijing.

1368 The Ming dynasty comes to power in China. The Ming drive the Mongols out of the country.

1526 The Mughal Empire in India begins under Babur. The Mughals are Muslims who invade and conquer India.

1644 The Ming dynasty in China is overthrown by the Manchu peoples.

1839 The Opium War takes place in China between the Chinese and the British. The British and other Western powers want to control trade in Asia. The Chinese want the British to stop selling opium to the Chinese. Britain wins the war in 1842.

1858 The French begin to take control of Indochina (Southeast Asia).

1868 In Japan, Emperor Meiji comes to power. Western ideas begin to influence the Japanese.

▼ *Statues from Angkor Wat temple, Cambodia*

THE JAPANESE IN ASIA Japan became a powerful country during the early 20th century. In the 1930s, Japan began to invade some of its neighbors. In 1941, the United States and Japan went to war after Japan attacked the U.S. Navy at Pearl Harbor, Hawaii.

1945 Japan is defeated in World War II after the U.S. drops atomic bombs on the Japanese cities of Hiroshima and Nagasaki.

1947 India and Pakistan become independent from Great Britain.

1949 China comes under the rule of the Communists led by Mao Zedong. The Communist government abolishes private property and takes over all businesses. ▶

1950–1953 **THE KOREAN WAR** North Korea, a Communist country, invades South Korea. The U.S. and other nations join to fight the invasion. China joins North Korea. The fighting ends in 1953. Neither side wins.

1954–1975 **THE VIETNAM WAR** The French are defeated in Indochina in 1954 by Vietnamese nationalists. The U.S. sends troops in 1965 to fight on the side of South Vietnam against the Communists in the North. The U.S. withdraws in 1973. In 1975, South Vietnam is taken over by North Vietnam.

1989 Chinese students protest for democracy, but the protests are crushed by the army in Beijing's Tiananmen Square.

The 1990s Britain returns Hong Kong to China (1997). China builds its economy, but does not allow democracy.

The 2000s U.S.-led military action overthrows the Taliban regime in Afghanistan (2001) and seeks to root out terrorists there. North Korea admits it has been developing nuclear weapons, and Iran is believed to be developing them.

A powerful earthquake in the Indian Ocean in December 2004 sets off huge waves (tsunamis) that kill more than 226,000 people in Indonesia, Sri Lanka, and other countries.

4000 B.C. People in Europe start building monuments out of large stones called megaliths, such as Stonehenge in England.

2500 B.C.–1200 B.C.
The Minoans and the Mycenaeans
- People on the island of Crete (Minoans) in the Mediterranean Sea built great palaces and became sailors and traders.
- People from Mycenae invaded Crete and destroyed the power of the Minoans.

THE TROJAN WAR The Trojan War was a conflict between invading Greeks and the people of Troas (Troy) in Southwestern Turkey around 1200 B.C. Although little is known today about the real war, it has become a part of Greek mythology (pages 140-141). According to legend, a group of Greek soldiers hid inside a huge wooden horse. The horse was pulled into the city of Troy. Then the soldiers jumped out of the horse and conquered Troy.

900-600 B.C. Celtic peoples in Northern Europe settle on farms and in villages and learn to mine for iron ore.

600 B.C. Etruscan peoples take over most of Italy. They build many cities and become traders.

SOME ACHIEVEMENTS OF THE GREEKS
The early Greeks were responsible for:
- The first governments that were elected by people.
- Great poets such as Homer, who composed the *Iliad* and the *Odyssey*.
- Great thinkers such as Socrates, Plato, and Aristotle.
- Great architecture, like the Parthenon and the Temple of Athena Nike on the Acropolis in Athens.

▲ *Socrates*

431 B.C. The Peloponnesian Wars begin between the Greek cities of Athens and Sparta. The wars end in 404 B.C. when Sparta wins.

338 B.C. King Philip II of Macedonia in northern Greece conquers all of Greece.

336 B.C. Philip's son Alexander the Great becomes king. He makes an empire from the Mediterranean Sea to India. For the next 300 years, Greek culture dominates this vast area.

264 B.C.–A.D. 476
THE ROMAN EMPIRE
The city of Rome in Italy begins to expand and capture surrounding lands. The Romans gradually build a great empire and control all of the Mediterranean region. At its height, the Roman Empire includes Western Europe, Greece, Egypt, and much of the Middle East. It lasts until A.D. 476.

Stonehenge

ROMAN ACHIEVEMENTS

- Roman law. Many of our laws are based on Roman law.
- Great roads to connect their huge empire. The Appian Way, south of Rome, is a Roman road that is still in use today.
- Aqueducts to bring water to the people in large cities.
- Great sculpture. Roman statues can still be seen in Europe.
- Great architecture. The Colosseum, which still stands in Rome today, is an example.
- Great writers, such as the poet Virgil, who wrote the *Aeneid*.

49 B.C. A civil war breaks out that destroys Rome's republican form of government.

45 B.C. Julius Caesar becomes the sole ruler of Rome but is murdered one year later by rivals.

27 B.C. Octavian becomes the first emperor of Rome. He takes the name Augustus. A peaceful period of almost 200 years begins.

THE CHRISTIAN FAITH
Christians believe that Jesus Christ is the Son of God. The history and beliefs of Christianity are found in the New Testament of the Bible. Christianity spread slowly throughout the Roman Empire. The Romans tried to stop the new religion and persecuted the Christians. They were forced to hold their services in hiding, and some were crucified. Eventually, more and more Romans became Christian.

A painting of Jesus Christ

THE BYZANTINE EMPIRE, centered in modern-day Turkey, was the eastern half of the old Roman Empire. Byzantine rulers extended their power into western Europe; the Byzantine Emperor Justinian ruled parts of Spain, North Africa, and Italy. Constantinople (now Istanbul, Turkey) became the capital of the Byzantine Empire in A.D. 330.

A.D. 313 The Roman Emperor Constantine gives full rights to Christians. He eventually becomes a Christian himself.

▲ *Constantine*

410 The Visigoths and other barbarian tribes from northern Europe invade the Roman Empire and begin to take over its lands.

476 The last Roman emperor, Romulus Augustus, is overthrown.

768 Charlemagne becomes king of the Franks in northern Europe. He rules a kingdom that includes parts of France, Germany, and northern Italy.

800 Feudalism becomes important in Europe. Feudalism means that poor farmers are allowed to farm a lord's land in return for certain services to the lord.

896 Magyar peoples found Hungary.

800s–900s Viking warriors and traders from Scandinavia begin to move into the British Isles, France, and parts of the Mediterranean.

989 The Russian state of Kiev becomes Christian.

▼ *The Colosseum, Rome*

1066 William of Normandy, a Frenchman, successfully invades England and makes himself king. He is known as William the Conqueror.

1096–1291 THE CRUSADES In 1096, Christian leaders sent a series of armies to try to capture Jerusalem from the Muslims. In the end, the Christians did not succeed. However, trade increased greatly between the Middle East and Europe.

1215 The Magna Carta was a document agreed to by King John of England and the English nobility. The English king agreed that he did not have absolute power and had to obey the laws of the land. The Magna Carta was an important step toward democracy.

▲ *King John*

1290 The Ottoman Empire begins. It is controlled by Turkish Muslims who conquer lands in the eastern Mediterranean and the Middle East.

1337 The Hundred Years' War begins in Europe between France and England. The war lasts until 1453 when France wins.

1348 The bubonic plague (Black Death) begins in Europe. As much as one-third of the whole population of Europe dies from this disease, caused by the bite of infected fleas.

1453 The Ottoman Turks capture the city of Constantinople and rename it Istanbul.

1517 THE REFORMATION
The Protestant Reformation split European Christians apart. It started when German priest Martin Luther broke away from the Roman Catholic pope.

▲ *Martin Luther*

1534 King Henry VIII of England breaks away from the Roman Catholic church. He names himself head of the English (Anglican) church.

1558 The reign of King Henry's daughter Elizabeth I begins in England.

1588 The Spanish Armada (fleet of warships) is defeated by the English navy as Spain tries to invade England.

1600s The Ottoman Turks expand their empire through most of eastern and central Europe.

1618 Much of Europe is destroyed in the Thirty Years' War, which ends in 1648.

1642 The English civil war begins. King Charles I fights against the forces of the Parliament. The king is defeated, and executed in 1649. His son, Charles II, returns as king in 1660.

1789 THE FRENCH REVOLUTION The French Revolution ended the rule of kings in France and led to democracy there. At first, however, there were wars and times when dictators took control. Many people were executed. King Louis XVI and Queen Marie Antoinette were overthrown in the Revolution, and both were executed in 1793.

◄ *Arc de Triomphe, Paris*

1762 Catherine the Great becomes Empress of Russia. She extends the Russian Empire.

1799 Napoleon Bonaparte, an army officer, becomes dictator of France. Under his rule, France conquers most of Europe by 1812.

1815 Napoleon's forces are defeated by the British and German armies at Waterloo (in Belgium). Napoleon is exiled to a remote island and dies there in 1821.

1848 Revolutions break out in countries of Europe. People force their rulers to make more democratic changes.

1914–1918 WORLD WAR I IN EUROPE
At the start of World War I in Europe, Germany, Austria-Hungary, and the Ottoman Empire opposed England, France, Russia, and, later, the U.S. (the Allies). The Allies win in 1918.

▼ *Tsar Nicholas II*

1917 The czar is overthrown in the Russian Revolution. The Bolsheviks (Communists) under Vladimir Lenin take control. Millions are starved, sent to labor camps, or executed under Joseph Stalin (1929-1953).

THE RISE OF HITLER Adolf Hitler became dictator of Germany in 1933. He joined forces with rulers in Italy and Japan to form the Axis powers. In World

▲ *Italy's Benito Mussolini and Adolf Hitler*

War II (1939-1945), the Axis powers were defeated by the Allies—Great Britain, the Soviet Union, and the U.S. During his rule, Hitler's Nazis killed millions of Jews and other people in the Holocaust.

The 1990s Communist governments in Eastern Europe are replaced by democratic ones. Divided Germany becomes one nation, and the Soviet Union breaks up. The European Union (EU) forms. The North Atlantic Treaty Organization (NATO) bombs Yugoslavia in an effort to protect Albanians driven out of the Kosovo region.

2005 Riots in Paris suburbs express the discontent of France's large minority Muslim population, which numbers 5-6 million.

2007 Bulgaria and Romania join the EU, bringing the number of EU nations to 27.

All About »» AUSTRALIA

Australian aborigines (native peoples) have lived there for more than 60,000 years. In the 17th century, Portuguese, Dutch, and Spanish expeditions explored Australian coasts. In the 1770s, Capt. James Cook of Britain made three voyages to the continent, cementing Britain's claims of ownership. On May 13, 1787, Capt. Arthur Phillip brought 11 ships from Britain, carrying convicts and guards. Although the first communities were prison colonies, regular immigrants settled around the continent over the 19th century. Wool and mining were major industries. Australia was established as a commonwealth of Great Britain on January 1, 1901. Today, Australia is a country of more than 20 million people. It is famous for exotic animals like kangaroos and koalas. It is also the home of actors Heath Ledger and Nicole Kidman. The Sydney Opera House is a world-famous landmark.

Sydney Opera House ▶

THE AMERICAS

10,000-8000 B.C. People in North and South America gather plants for food and hunt animals using stone-pointed spears.

Around 3000 B.C. People in Central America begin farming, growing corn and beans for food.

1500 B.C. Mayan people in Central America begin to live in small villages.

500 B.C. People in North America begin to hunt buffalo to use for meat and for clothing.

100 B.C. The city of Teotihuacán is founded in Mexico. It becomes the center of a huge empire extending from central Mexico to Guatemala. Teotihuacán contains many large pyramids and temples.

A.D. 150 Mayan people in Guatemala build many centers for religious ceremonies. They create a calendar and learn mathematics and astronomy.

900 Toltec warriors in Mexico begin to invade lands of Mayan people. Mayans leave their old cities and move to the Yucatan Peninsula of Mexico.

1000 Native Americans in the southwestern United States begin to live in settlements called pueblos. They learn to farm.

1325 Mexican Indians known as Aztecs create the huge city of Tenochtitlán and rule a large empire in Mexico. They are warriors who practice human sacrifice.

1492 Christopher Columbus sails from Europe across the Atlantic Ocean and lands in the Bahamas, in the Caribbean Sea. This marked the first step toward the founding of European settlements in the Americas.

Christopher ▲
Columbus

1500 Portuguese explorers reach Brazil and claim it for Portugal.

1519 Spanish conqueror Hernán Cortés travels into the Aztec Empire in search of gold. The Aztecs are defeated in 1521 by Cortés. The Spanish take control of Mexico. ▶

WHY DID THE SPANISH WIN? How did the Spanish defeat the powerful Aztec Empire in such a short time? One reason is that the Spanish had better weapons. Another is that many Aztecs died from diseases brought to the New World by the Spanish. The Aztecs had never had these illnesses before, and so did not have immunity to them. Also, many neighboring Indians hated the Aztecs as conquerors and helped the Spanish to defeat them.

1534 Jacques Cartier of France explores Canada.

1583 The first English colony in Canada is set up in Newfoundland.

1607 English colonists led by Captain John Smith settle in Jamestown, Virginia. Virginia was the oldest of the Thirteen Colonies that turned into the United States.

1619 First African slaves arrive in English-controlled America.

1682 The French explorer René Robert Cavelier, sieur de La Salle, sails down the Mississippi River. The area is named Louisiana after the French King Louis XIV.

Chac Mool, Mayan Figure ▶

THE AMERICAS

EUROPEAN COLONIES By 1700, most of the Americas are under the control of Europeans:

Spain: Florida, southwestern United States, Mexico, Central America, western South America.

Portugal: eastern South America.

France: central United States, parts of Canada.

England: eastern U.S., parts of Canada.

Holland: eastern U.S., West Indies, eastern South America.

1700s European colonies in North and South America grow in population and wealth.

1775-1783 AMERICAN REVOLUTION The American Revolution begins in 1775 when the first shot is fired in Lexington, Massachusetts. The thirteen original British colonies in North America become independent under the Treaty of Paris, signed in 1783.

SIMÓN BOLÍVAR: LIBERATOR OF SOUTH AMERICA In 1810, Simón Bolívar began a revolt against Spain. He fought against the Spanish and in 1924 became president of the independent country of Greater Colombia. As a result of his leadership, ten South American countries became independent from Spain by 1830.

1810-1910 MEXICO'S REVOLUTION In 1846, Mexico and the United States go to war. Mexico loses parts of the Southwest and California to the U.S. A revolution in 1910 overthrows Porfirio Díaz.

Porfirio Diaz ▶

Becoming Independent

Most countries of Latin America gained independence from Spain in the early 1800s. Others weren't liberated until much later.

COUNTRY	YEAR OF INDEPENDENCE
Argentina	1816
Bolivia	1825
Brazil	1822[1]
Chile	1818
Colombia	1819
Ecuador	1822
Guyana	1966[2]
Mexico	1821
Paraguay	1811
Peru	1824
Suriname	1975[3]
Uruguay	1825
Venezuela	1821

[1] From Portugal. [2] From Britain. [3] From the Netherlands.

1867 The Canadian provinces are united as the Dominion of Canada.

1898 THE SPANISH-AMERICAN WAR Spain and the U.S. fight a brief war in 1898. Spain loses its colonies Cuba, Puerto Rico, and the Philippines.

U.S. POWER IN THE 1900s During the 1900s, the U.S. sent troops to various countries, including Mexico (1914; 1916–1917), Nicaragua (1912–1933), Haiti (1915–1934; 1994–1995), and Panama (1989). In 1962, the U.S. went on alert when the Soviet Union put missiles on Cuba.

1994 The North American Free Trade Agreement (NAFTA) increases trade between the U.S., Canada, and Mexico.

2001 Radical Muslim terrorists crash planes into U.S. targets, killing about 3,000 people; the U.S. launches a "war on terrorism."

2003 U.S.-led forces invade Iraq and overthrow the regime of Saddam Hussein.

2007 With a population of about 12 million unauthorized migrants, the U.S. debates immigration reform.

THEN & NOW

10 Years Ago–1997

Then: Diana, the Princess of Wales and former wife of Britain's Prince Charles, died in a car crash in Paris. She was survived by their two young sons, Prince William (then 15 years old) and Prince Harry (then 12).

Now: Prince Charles is married to Camilla Parker-Bowles. As of early 2007, Prince Harry was a military officer and was planning to be deployed to Iraq in 2007. Prince William completed his military training in 2006 and is also hoping to serve active duty.

Then: Madeleine Albright was sworn in as the first-ever woman secretary of state and the highest ranking woman in the U.S. government. ▶

Now: As of April 2007, Condoleezza Rice is secretary of state, the second woman and second African American ever to hold that post.

50 Years Ago–1957

Then: A year after British, French, and Israeli forces took over the Suez Canal in Egypt, Israel returned the Sinai Peninsula to Egypt and handed over the Gaza Strip to United Nations forces.

Now: Israel re-occupied the Gaza Strip after the 1967 war, then withdrew in 2005 and left it under control of the Palestinian Authority government. The Israeli-Palestinian dispute continues to be a major world issue 59 years after the founding of Israel.

◀**Then:** President Dwight Eisenhower sent federal troops to enforce a court order and escort nine black students into a former all-white high school in Little Rock, Arkansas. The governor had used state National Guardsmen to block them, and there were fears for the students' safety because of angry mobs.

Now: The high school is a National Historic Site and known as one of the state's best schools.

100 Years Ago–1907

Then: President Theodore Roosevelt sent a fleet of 16 battleships (the "Great White Fleet") to tour the world and show off American power combined with a desire for peace. This project reflected one of Roosevelt's favorite mottos: "Speak softly and carry a big stick."

Now: The United States is the world's only superpower, but is engaged in an ongoing "war on terrorism."

400 Years Ago–1607

In May 1607 a group of about 100 colonists on three ships landed in a marshy area on the coast of Virginia. They started "Jamestown," the first permanent English settlement in America. The colonists had to deal with food shortages, disease, fires, and Indian raids, but the settlement lasted for about 100 years. Jamestown has been restored and is now part of the Colonial National Historic Park in Virginia.

Sailing ships at Jamestown settlement

THEN & NOW FROM 2008

10 Years Ago–1998

Then: The House impeached President Bill Clinton for lying under oath and concealing information. He was acquitted by the Senate in 1999.

Now: Since leaving office in 2001, President Clinton has written a best-selling book and worked hard to promote aid for humanitarian issues around the world. His wife, Hillary Rodham Clinton, is a U.S. senator and is running for president in 2008.

Then: For the first time ever, scientists in Britain and the U.S. mapped the genome of a polycellular organism, a worm.

Now: Scientists have mapped the entire human genome. Now, they can study genes for information about disease.

50 Years Ago–1958

Then: The first successful American satellite, *Explorer 1*, was launched. Congress approved creation of the National Aeronautics and Space Administration (NASA) in October.

Now: Americans landed on the moon in 1969 and sent many different satellites and rockets into space to explore our solar system. Today, new ships are being built to take more people to the moon, and more probes will be sent to the surface of Mars.

Then: National Airlines operates the first domestic jet passenger service in the U.S., between New York and Miami.

Now: U.S. airlines carry more than 600 million passengers on domestic flights each year.

500 Years Ago–1508

In 1508, Roman Catholic Pope Julius II asked Michelangelo to paint the ceiling of the Sistine Chapel in Rome. It took Michelangelo four years to finish it, but today the ceiling is still a masterpiece. In 1989, a 10-year restoration of the painting was completed.

100 Years Ago–1908

▲Then: Wilbur and Orville Wright fulfilled a contract with the U.S. Army Signal Corps to produce a plane that could fly for 10 minutes at a speed of 40 miles per hour.

Now: NASA's X-43A scramjet is the fastest unmanned, jet-powered aircraft, flying at about Mach 9.6, or nearly 7,000 mph.

Then: Henry Ford produced the first Model T, a low-cost car that would later be made on a factory assembly line. Ford would sell 15 million Model Ts.

Now: More than 136 million cars are registered in America. In 2007, Ford had two models of hybrid (gasoline-electric) cars on the market and three more in development.

Then: U.S. President Theodore Roosevelt created the U.S. Army Reserve.

Now: The U.S. Army Reserve is made up of more than 189,000 troops and is playing a major role in the war in Iraq.

WOMEN IN HISTORY

The following women played important roles in shaping some of history's biggest events.

CLEOPATRA (69-30 B.C.), queen of Egypt famous for her association with Roman leaders Julius Caesar and Mark Antony. After her father's death, Cleopatra, at the age of about 17, and her 12-year-old brother Ptolemy jointly ruled. By custom, they were forced to marry each other. A few years later, she was sent away, but came back to rule when Caesar defeated her enemies. For a time, she lived with Caesar in Rome until his assassination in 44 B.C. She later went back to Egypt, where she met and married Antony.

JOAN OF ARC (1412-1431), heroine and patron saint of France, known as the Maid of Orléans. She led French troops to a big victory over the English in the Battle of Orléans (1429), a turning point in the Hundred Years' War. Joan believed she was guided by voices from God, and she dressed like a male soldier. In 1431, she was burned at the stake as a heretic. The Catholic Church later declared her innocent, and she was made a saint in 1920. She is the subject of many monuments, paintings, and works of literature.

CATHERINE THE GREAT (1729-1796), empress of Russia (1762-1796). Catherine made Russia a European power and greatly expanded the territory of the Russian Empire. She raised the status of the nobles by granting them privileges such as freedom from military service and legal control over their serfs. She promoted culture as well as the education of women and religious tolerance.

SOJOURNER TRUTH (c. 1797-1883), abolitionist and women's rights activist (born Isabella Baumfree). She was raised as a slave on an estate in upstate New York. She escaped in 1826. In 1843, she became a traveling preacher and took the name Sojourner Truth. She traveled widely, speaking out against slavery and for women's rights. Her famous speech, "Ain't I a Woman?" was about how women were as smart and strong as men.

SUSAN B. ANTHONY (1820-1906), social reformer who, with Elizabeth Cady Stanton, led the struggle for women's rights. She was a lifelong campaigner for women's suffrage, but died 14 years before the adoption of the 19th Amendment, which allowed women to vote. She opposed the use of liquor and worked to free slaves. In 1979, the U.S. Mint issued the Susan B. Anthony dollar coin in her honor.

FLORENCE NIGHTINGALE (1820-1910), British nurse and founder of modern nursing. She was a superintendent of female nurses during the Crimean War in Turkey, where she trained nurses and helped set up field hospitals, saving many lives. In 1860 she founded the first professional nursing school, at Saint Thomas's Hospital in London. In 1907, she became the first woman to receive the British Order of Merit.

MARIE CURIE (1867-1934),

Polish-French physical chemist known for discovering the radioactive element radium, which is used to treat some diseases. She also discovered the rare element polonium (named after Poland, her country of birth). She won the Nobel Prize for chemistry in 1911. She and her husband, Pierre Curie, also won the Nobel Prize for physics in 1903 for their work on radiation. Sadly, her work led to her death—she died from radiation poisoning.

BILLIE JEAN KING (born 1943),

American tennis player who became a symbol for women's equality. King won 12 Grand Slam singles titles. But her most famous victory may have been in the 1973 "Battle of the Sexes" match, when she beat male player Bobby Riggs in 3 straight sets. King helped start the first successful women's pro tennis tour in 1970. In 1971, she became the first woman athlete to win more than $100,000 in one season.

JODY WILLIAMS (born 1950) is an

activist who helped found the International Campaign to Ban Landmines. A landmine is a weapon which is placed in the ground and explodes when triggered by a vehicle or person. More than 15,000 people are injured or killed by landmines each year. Williams travels the world, speaking about how landmines kill and injure innocent civilians and working with governments to effect a worldwide ban. Williams and her organization won the 1997 Nobel Peace Prize for their work.

▲BETTY FRIEDAN (1921-2006),

American feminist leader whose book *The Feminine Mystique* (1963) challenged the idea that women could be happy only as wives and mothers. She was a co-founder (1966) and the first president (1966-1970) of the National Organization for Women (NOW), which seeks equal rights for women.

VALENTINA TERESHKOVA

(born 1937), Russian cosmonaut and the first woman in space. During her 3-day spaceflight in June 1963 aboard the *Vostok 6,* she orbited Earth 48 times. Five months later, she married cosmonaut Andrian Nikolayev. In 1964, she gave birth to a daughter, the first child born to parents who had both flown in space.

▲ DR. MAE JEMISON (born 1956)

was the first African American woman to go into space. She flew on the 1992 space shuttle *Endeavour* as a science mission specialist. She was born in Decatur, Alabama, and grew up in Chicago, Illinois. Dr. Jemison is a medical doctor who also has degrees in chemical engineering and African and African American studies.

ANSWERS

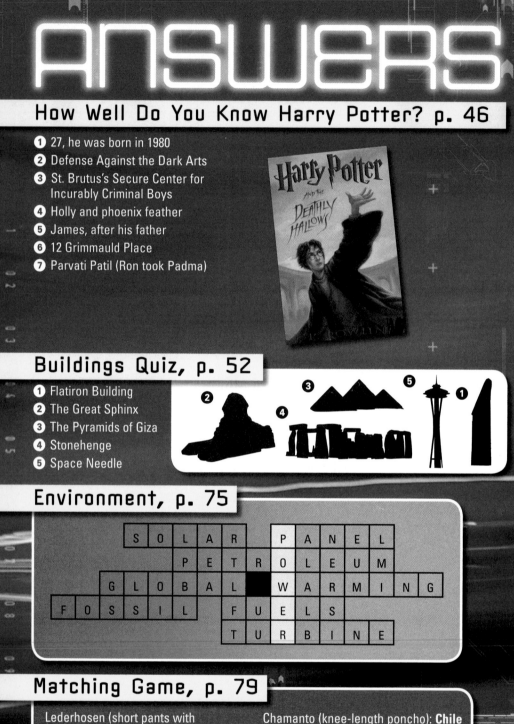

How Well Do You Know Harry Potter? p. 46

1. 27, he was born in 1980
2. Defense Against the Dark Arts
3. St. Brutus's Secure Center for Incurably Criminal Boys
4. Holly and phoenix feather
5. James, after his father
6. 12 Grimmauld Place
7. Parvati Patil (Ron took Padma)

Buildings Quiz, p. 52

1. Flatiron Building
2. The Great Sphinx
3. The Pyramids of Giza
4. Stonehenge
5. Space Needle

Environment, p. 75

SOLAR PANEL
PETROLEUM
GLOBAL WARMING
FOSSIL FUELS
TURBINE

Matching Game, p. 79

Lederhosen (short pants with suspenders): **Germany**

Pien-fu (2-piece robe): **China**

Kikoi (sarong-type skirt): **Uganda**

Chamanto (knee-length poncho): **Chile**

Kamiks (watertight boots): **Arctic Inuit people**

Kaftan (belted shirt-dress): **Morocco**

Jokes and Riddles, p. 118–119

1 The President **2** One combined bale **3** Your eardrum **4** He's dead. **5** Your lap **6** You take your feet off the floor. **7** For beating the eggs **8** They're both the capital of England. **9** It gets wet. **10** It's too far to walk. **11** Language **12** They're both in the middle of water. **13** The shoppers are a woman, her daughter, and her granddaughter. **14** Grow older **15** A hole **16** Halfway. After that, the deer is running out of the woods. **17** Your word **18** A newspaper **19** A garbage truck **20** If his horse is named Friday! **21** The letter M **22** E, N, T; they stand for one, two, three, four, five, etc. **23** Your breath **24** A chalkboard **25** T-h-a-t **26** One **27** All of them **28** Yesterday, today and tomorrow **29** Nine **30** Because he's living. **31** No. He'd be dead. **32** Umbrellas **33** Hisssss- tory **34** Take away his credit card. **35** Time to get a new fence. **36** When it turns into a driveway **37** A chair **38** You're the bus driver, how old are you? **39** There are no stairs, it's a one-story house. **40** You don't bury survivors.

Word Connect, p. 119

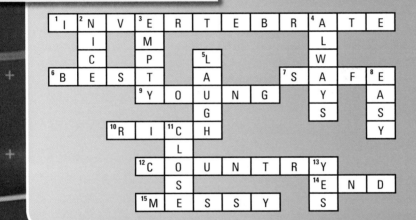

Movies & TV Match-Up, p. 133

Mac & Blooregard: *Foster's Home for Imaginary Friends*
Katara & Sokka: *Avatar: The Last Airbender*
Will & Elizabeth: *Pirates of the Caribbean*
Peter & Mary Jane: *Spider-Man*

Susan & Reed: *Fantastic Four*
Sophie & Calcifer: *Howl's Moving Castle*
Addie & Geena: *Unfabulous*
Quinn & Lola: *Zoey 101*

Sudoku, p. 190

8	7	9	4	3	6	5	1	2
1	6	2	9	5	7	8	4	3
3	4	5	8	1	2	7	9	6
5	3	7	2	8	4	9	6	1
2	9	6	5	7	1	4	3	8
4	8	1	3	6	9	2	5	7
6	1	4	7	9	8	3	2	5
7	2	3	1	4	5	6	8	9
9	5	8	6	2	3	1	7	4

Science, p. 219

① **True**. White light is a mixture of all the colors of the rainbow, or visible spectrum.

② **False**. Petrology is the study of rocks.

③ **False**. The number of genes does not determine size. A rice plant has more than 50,000 genes. Humans are much larger, but their genome contains only 20,000-25,000 genes.

④ **True**. Light travels much faster than sound.

⑤ **False**. When using the scientific method the first step is to ask a question.

⑥ **True**. Other chemical symbols are based on elements' English names.

⑦ **True**. The pressure increases as you travel below the surface of the water. Even scuba divers don't normally go deeper than 100 feet without special equipment.

⑧ **False**. Plants absorb carbon dioxide and release oxygen, and technically don't breathe.

⑨ **True**. The more you struggle, the more you'll sink. If you remain still, you'll start to float.

⑩ **True**. A shovel is an example of a lever, a simple machine used for many different tasks.

Sports Scramble, p. 246

Miami Heat: **Dwyane Wade**
Phoenix Mercury: **Diana Taurasi**
Chicago Bears: **Brian Urlacher**

Indianapolis Colts: **Peyton Manning**
New York Mets: **Carlos Beltran**

Technology, p.250

```
E N C R Y P T I O N D N K B O O J C
B P R C E R R E D O C Y E Y J B N D
S S I M S I F I W A I W V K P P T M
S T A R E N N A Y E E I I N G M G
B I R H W T L A M D G U B Z R I P U
L F C E N O U L I F E Y O P Z U L R
W I K I A G E W G W Q T O L Z N S L
U X J D I M D R R I N X K K V H M G
Q E Y X X L I T A T G R M R K A O E
O T E N R E T N I W E V A O G L B J
K Y Y O C J L X G S Y F R W B A R R
P B W C A N X Z W C C P K T Q N R H
W S P A F A S O T C Q N S E T B D H
C O K I M X R C O O K I E N V S R O
O Y X H G B E Q H Y I Q U C A G L F
```

INDEX

Photo Credits

This product/publication includes images from Artville, Comstock, Corbis Royalty-Free, Corel Stock Photo Library, Digital Stock, Digital Vision, EyeWire Images, IndexOpen.com, Ingram Publishing, One Mile Up Inc., PhotoDisc, Rubberball Productions, which are protected by the copyright laws of the U.S., Canada, and elsewhere. Used under license.

FRONT COVER: Mayan statue, © iStockphoto.com/Franziska Richter; iPhone, Newscom. **INSIDE BACK COVER**: Smith, AP Images; **BACK COVER**: *Harry Potter and the Goblet of Fire*, Warner Brothers/Photofest; *Shrek*, Dreamworks/Photofest; Manning, AP Images. **3:** Ciara, AP Images; Houdini, Library of Congress (LOC) LC-USZNC4-81. **4:** Underwood; Supersonic car, AP Images. **6:** *Ugly Betty* and *Dancing With the Stars*, ABC/Photofest, *The Dog Whisperer*, Mark Theissan/National Geographic. **7:** *American Idol*, Fox Broadcasting Company/Photofest; *Zoey 101*, © Apollo Media All Rights Reserved. Nickelodeon, Zoey 101, and all related titles, logos , and characters are trademarks of Viacom International, Inc. **8-9:** *Shrek the Third*, Paramount Pictures/Photofest; *The Simpsons Movie*, Fox/Photofest; *Bridge to Terabithia*, Buena Vista/Photofest. **10-11:** *Pirates of the Caribbean: At World's End*, Buena Vista Pictures/Photofest; *Harry Potter and the Order of the Phoenix*, Warner Brothers/Photofest; *Nancy Drew*, Melissa Sue Gordon. **12-13:** *Dreamgirls*, Dream Works SKG/Photofest; Cyrus, Ciara, The All American Rejects, AP Images. **14:** Manning, AP Images; Smith & Dungy, Getty Images. **15:** Federer, Woods, AP Images. **16:** Beckham, Howard, AP Images. **17:** Cena, Lilly, AP Images. **18:** Bush & Soldier, Pelosi, Ford, AP Images; Ford service, U.S. Dept. of Defense (DoD) photo by William D. Moss. **19:** U.S. population, Getty Images; Subway Hero, AP Images. **20:** Jellyfish & Pigeon, Photos.com. **24:** Ostrich, Pronghorn Antelope, Giraffe, Hummingbird, Photos.com. **25:** Chimpanzee, Cicada, Tortoise, Photos.com. **27:** Polar Bear, Photos.com. **28:** Penguins, Photos.com. **29:** Moth, Photos.com; Squid, AP Photo/Tsunemi Kubodera of the National Science Museum of Japan, HO. **30:** Ant colony, John Kurtz. **31:** On the Job, Katherine Miller. **35:** Art Project, © Evan Schwartz. **36:** Mozart, LOC LC-USZ62-87246; Fanning, AP Images; Chavez, U.S. Dept. of Labor. **37:** Washington, LOC LC-USZ62-49568, "The Rock", Delgado, AP Images. **38:** Missy Elliot, UPI Photo/Phil McCarten/Landov; Key, LOC LC-USZ62-53017; Sandler, AP Images. **39:** Mayer, AP Images; Rice, U.S. Dept. of State; Barton, LOC LC-USZ62-108565. **41:** Maria Dal Molin & Arcangelo Bez, courtesy of Edward A. Thomas. **42:** *The Higher Power of Lucky, Copper Sun*, ATHENEUM BOOKS FOR YOUNG READERS; *Septimus Heap, Book 3: Physik*, © 2007, HarperCollins Publishers. **43:** J.K. Rowling, Richard Young; Cleary, © 2002, Alan McEwan; Dahl, LOC LC-USZ62-116610. **44:** *Something Upstairs*, © 1997, HarperCollins Publishers; *Walk Two Moons*, © 2005 HarperCollins Publishers; *Little House in the Big Woods*, © 2007, HarperCollins Publishers. **45:** *Queen Bee*, Graphix/Scholastic; *At Her Majesty's Request: An African Princess in Victorian England*, © 1999, HarperCollins Publishers. **46-47:** Hogwarts School, *Harry Potter and the Prisoner of Azkaban, Harry Potter and the Goblet of Fire*, Warner Brothers/Photofest. **47:** *Harry Potter* Book Covers 1-7, Arthur A. Levine Books/Scholastic. **48:** Empire State Building, Photos.com. **49:** Skyscraper, LOC LC-USZ62-69629. **50:** La Sagrada, Arche de la Defense, Photos.com; Glass House, Ron Blunt; Disney Hall, Tom Bonner. **51:** Notre Dame, Photos.com. **52:** Bridges, Photos.com. **53:** Bridge diagram, John Kurtz. **54:** Disabled boy at camp, American Camp Assoc. **55:** Boy at Hip-Hop Camp, Photo by Janet Century; Boys at Future Inventors Camp, Courtesy of Camp Invention, a program of the National Inventors Hall of Fame ® Foundation. **56:** Booth, LOC LC-USZ62-25166; Capone, AP Images. **58:** Hurricane diagram, Steve Toole. **59:** Tornado, © iStockphoto.com/Sean Martin. **63:** Lusitania, LOC LC-USZC4-10986; Blizzard of 1888, NOAA. **65:** Red Rock Canyon, © iStockphoto.com/Chee-Onn Leong; Prairie, © iStockphoto.com/Kimberly Deprey; Great Barrier Reef, © iStockphoto.com; **67:** Everglades, © iStockphoto.com/Tomasz Szymanski. **70:** Atmosphere, Global Warming, Steve Toole. **71:** Polar ice, NASA/GSFC; Polar ice cap, NASA/NRDC; Penguins, Photos.com. **74:** Solar panel, © iStockphoto.com/Tom Tomczyk. **76:** 1900s fashion, LOC; 1960s fashion, © iStockphoto.com/Jaimie Duplass. **77:** *Saturday Night Fever*, Paramount Pictures/Photofest; Hip Hop kids, Photos.com. **78:** David Reynolds in kilt, © Thomas Flynn; Wigs, © iStockphoto.com/Amanda Rohde. **79:** Kimono, © iStockphoto.com/David Davis; Veil, © iStockphoto.com/Anneke Schram. **80-81:** Play-Doh, PLAY-DOH and the PLAY-DOH logo are trademarks identifying quality modeling compound products produced exclusively by Hasbro. © 2007 Hasbro. All Rights Reserved; Samorost Video Game, © Jakub Kvorsky. **83:** Girl blowing gum, © iStockphoto.com/Eileen Hart. **87:** Ann Bancroft & Liv Arnesen, Courtesy of yourexploration.com. **92:** Carly Roman, © Edward A. Thomas. **97:** Brain diagram, John Kurtz. **101**: Pirate, squirrel, Photos.com. **103:** Diwali, Ramadan, Christmas, AP Images. **106:** Kid reading, salamander, Photos.com. **107:** Thanksgiving dinner, kid on school bus, Photos.com. **110:** Carver, LOC LC-J601-302; Bell, LOC LC-USZ62-104276; Edison, LOC LC-DIG-CWPBH-04044; Tesla coil, © Peter Terren. **111:** Benz, LOC LC-USZ62-48300; Parachute, LOC LC-DIG-ppmsca-02504; Segway, © 2001-2006 Segway, Inc. **120:** Houdini, LOC LC-USZNC4-81; Angel, AP Images. **121:** Magic tricks, © Aram A. Schvey. **122:** Continental Army, LOC LC-USZC4-2135; *USS Constitution*, U.S. Navy/Photographer's Mate Chief John E. Gay; Federal Soldier, LOC LC-B8184-10086; Charge of San Juan Hill, LOC LC-USZ62-26060. **123:** Recruiting poster, LOC LC-USZC4-3859; Yalta, Army Signal Corps Collection in the U.S. National Archives; *USS Missouri*, National Archives; Thunderbolt II, U.S. Air Force. **124:** Afghanistan, DoD/Spc. Michael Zuk, U.S. Army; Iraq, DoD/Photographer's Mate 1st Class Bart A. Bauer. **125:** Medal of Honor, DoD; Purple Heart, armed-guard.com; Michael Novosel, The United States Army Medical Department Regiment; Audie Murphy, AP Images. **127:** John Adams Dollar, U.S. Mint; **130:** *The Simpsons*, Fox/Photofest. **131:** *Survivor: Panama*, BILL INOSHITA/CBS/Landov; *Madagascar*, Dreamworks/Photofest. **132:** *The Wizard of Oz*, MGM/Photofest; *Charlie and the Chocolate Factory*, Warner Brothers/Photofest. **133:** *The Princess Diaries*, Disney/Photofest; *The Princess Diaries* (book), © 1997, HarperCollins Publishers; *The Chronicles of Narnia*, Walt Disney Pictures/Photofest; *The Chronicles of Narnia* (book), © 2001, HarperCollins Publishers. **134:** Rose Center, © D. Finnin/AMNH; Smithsonian Castle, Keith Stanley www.kestan.com. **135:** *Night at the Museum*, 20th Century Fox/Photofest; Interpreter with half pike, Jamestown-Yorktown Foundation. **136:** Underwood, AP Images; *Breakin' 2: Electric Boogaloo*, TriStar/Photofest. **137:** Blige, AP Images; Rascal Flatts, 2007 Getty Images. **139:** Maya Park, © Zoë Kashner; Break dancing, ©Devin Wagner; *Mad Hot Ballroom*, Just One Productions/Photofest. **142:** Ban Ki-Moon, UN Photo. **180:** Egyptian children, AP Images. **181:** New Guinea children, © UNESCO/Rocky Roe; Brazilian children, © Jacques Jangoux/Alamy. **182**: Teepee, Photos.com. **184:** Totem, © Edward A. Thomas. **185:** Tlingit, Seneca Indians, AP Images; Navajo Indian Code Talkers, DoD/U.S. Dept. of the Navy/U.S. Marine Corps. **196:** Ellis Island, LOC LC-B2-5202-12. **198:** Muhammad Yunis, UN Photo/Devra Berkowitz. **199:** Timberlake, Fanning, AP Images. **201:** Big Mountain Pond Skimming, Brian Schott. **202:** Ming Kipa, KAZUHIRO NOGI/AFP/Getty Images; Supersonic car, AP Images; Malayan Flying Fox, Dave King. **203:** Kobayashi, AP Images; Mall of America, courtesy of Bob Cole; Taipan, Nichole Duplaix; Gates, Microsoft Corporation. **204-205:** Buddha, Temple, Dome, Torah, Photos.com. **206:** Service, © iStockphoto.com/Franky De Meyer; Shofar, © iStockphoto.com/Howard Sandler; Afternoon prayer, © iStockphoto.com/Teion Van damm. **207:** Monks, Diwali, © iStockphoto.com/Bryan Busovicki; al-Sistani, REUTERS/HO/Landov. **209:** LifeStraw ®, Vestergaard Frandsen. **212:** Oscilloscope, © Loren Winters/Visuals Unlimited; Light, Michael Meyerhofer. **213:** Axe, Pulley, See Saw, Photos.com. **215:** Amoeba, © Wim van Egmond/Visuals Unlimited; Van Leeuwenhoek, © History of Science Collections, University of Oklahoma Libraries. **216:** Ear, Photos.com. **218:** Newton, LOC LC-USZ62-10191; Darwin, LOC LC-USZ61-104; Mary & Louis Leakey, Source unknown. **220:** Eight planets, International Astronomical Union. **223:** Ceres, NASA, ESA, J Parker (Southwest Research Institute), P. Thomas (Cornell University), L. McFadden (University of Maryland, College Park), and M. Mutchler and Z. Levay (STScI); Pluto, NASA, ESA, H. Weaver (JHU/APL), A Stern (SwRI), and the HST Pluto Companion Search Team. **226:** New Horizons, Johns Hopkins University Applied Physics Laboratory/Southwest Research Institute (JHU APL/SwRI); Mars Rover, NASA/JPL-Caltech. **231:** Bicycle Polo Bill Matheson & Scott Jordan, © Norm Carr; Tomlinson, AP Images. **232:** Gymnast, © iStockphoto.com/Galina Barskaya. **233:** Paralympics, Special Olympics, AP Images. **234:** Hornish, AP Images; Indy 500, LOC LC-DIG-ggbain-13113. **236:** St. Louis Cardinals, AP Images. **237:** Reese & Robinson, AP Images. **238:** Basketball Hall of Fame, Naismith Memorial Basketball Hall of Fame; basketball, James, AP Images. **239:** Ford, AP Images. **240:** Dungy & Manning, Joe Robbins/Getty Images. **242-247:** Smith, Nicklaus, Liukin, Crosby, Ching, Mathis, Anderson, Pastrana, AP Images. **251:** XO computer, Fuse Project. **252:** Viking ship, *Historic Tales*, Vol. 1 by Charles Morris. **253:** Coach, LOC LC-USZC4-3266; Hot air balloon, LOC LC-DIG-ppmsca-03478. **254:** Gold Spike, Courtesy of the Oakland Museum of California; Wright Flyer, LOC LC-DIG-pprs-00626. **255:** Apollo 11, NASA; Hybrid car, AP Images. **256-257:** Las Vegas, Getty Images; Maverick, Cedar Point amusement park/resort. **258:** Lunch boxes, Lunch Box Museum; Jackson, Special Collections, University of Vermont. **260-261:** National Parks, Photos.com. **269:** Pelosi, U.S. Congress. **270:** Supreme Court, LARRY DOWNING/Reuters/Landov. **271-276:** U.S. Presidents, LOC except p. 276 – Johnson, Lyndon B. Johnson Library; George W. Bush, Eric Draper – The White House. **278:** Madison, LOC LC-USZC4-6776; Lane, LOC LC-DIG-cwpbh-00692; Lincoln, LOC LC-DIG-01028; Hoover, LOC LC-USZ62-25811; Kennedy, LOC LC-USZ62-21796; Ford, LOC LC-USZC4-2019 DLC; Bush, Eric Draper-The White House. **280:** de Leon, LOC LC-USZ62-3106; **281:** Pilgrims, LOC LC-USZ62-3461, Cornwallis, LOC LC-USZC2-3052. **282:** Constitutional Convention, NARA. **283:** Battle of New Orleans LOC LC-USZC2-3796; Emancipation Proclamation, LOC LC-DIG-pga-02502. **284:** Rankin, LOC LC-DIG-ggbain-23838; School segregation, NARA. **285:** Reagan & Gorbachev, Ronald Reagan Presidential Library; Desert Storm, U.S. Air Force; 9/11 Pentagon, DoD. **287:** Choa, U.S. Dept. of Labor. **290-291:** Alaska, © Edward A. Thomas; Hawaii, Maine, New Mexico, Pennsylvania, Texas, National Park Service. **311:** Smart Sacks, Chattanooga Area Food Bank. **312:** Punxsutawney Phil, AP Images. **314:** One Yard, © Timothy N. Bryk. **318:** Hieroglyphics, © Edward A. Thomas; Koran, © iStockphoto.com/Wael Hamdan. **319:** Carter, Jimmy Carter Library & Museum. **320:** Camel train, © iStockphoto.com/Graeme Purdy. **321:** Sirleaf-Johnson, UN Photo/Mark Garten. **322:** Buddha, Photos.com. **323:** Samurai, LOC. **324:** Stonehenge, Socrates, Trojan Horse, Photos.com. **325:** Jesus Christ, LOC LC-USZC2-2971. **326:** John, *Cassell's History of England*, Century Edition; Luther, LOC LC-USZC4-6895. **327:** Sydney Opera House, Photos.com; Hitler & Mussolini, NARA. **328:** Columbus, LOC LC-USZC4-1717, Cortes, LOC LC-USZ62-47764. **329:** Diaz, LOC LC-USZ62-100275. **330:** Desegregation, Time & Life Pictures/Getty Images; Albright, U.S. Dept. of State. **331**: 3-D Protein, U.S. Dept. of Energy, Human Genome Program; Wright flyer, LOC LC-USZ62-91463. **332-333:** Joan of Arc, © iStockphoto.com/Alex Chaney; Nightingale, LOC LC-USZ62-5877; Truth, LOC LC-USZ62-119343; Friedan, LOC, LC-USZ62-115844; Curie, LOC LC-USZ62-91224; King, AP Images; Jemison, NASA; **334:** *Harry Potter and the Deathly Hallows*, Arthur A. Levine/Scholastic.

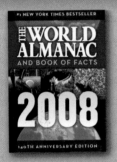